Praise for *How to Think Logically*

"I don't think there should be any doubt that this is an excellent book; it presents the essential topics for an introductory course on critical thinking with clarity and attention to detail. I look forward to using this textbook in my course!"

—Stephen C. Ferguson II, North Carolina A & T State University

"I am convinced this textbook will make an important and unique contribution to the currently available materials. The authors do an excellent job of presenting the basic principles of argument reconstruction, and I think that students using this book will be in a better position to apply their critical thinking skills to arguments and issues."

—Lisa H. Schwartzman, Michigan State University

"This book fills an important gap in the current market by presenting informal logic in a way that makes clear its relationship to philosophical reasoning. This is welcome, and will be appreciated by instructors."

—Lee McIntyre, Simmons College

"An outstanding approach to the teaching of critical reasoning. Seay and Nuccetelli convey the principles of logic and rigorous analysis by means of understandable explanations and exercises."

—Gregory P. Fields, Southern Illinois University

"The text is challenging in a way that actually fosters interest, but is still accessible to any student... The abundant detail included is enough to keep my students happily occupied on those rainy Oregon afternoons."

—Will Cowling, Oregon State University

"Focusing on "knowing how" rather than "knowing that" is the right move to make. There is a logical thread that connects each chapter, and the necessary topics are introduced at just the right time and place... The writing is precise, intellectually challenging, and theoretically sound."

—Kevin Zanelotti, Radford University

D0082210

PENGUIN ACADEMICS

HOW TO THINK LOGICALLY

GARY SEAY

Medgar Evers College, City University of New York

SUSANA NUCCETELLI

St. Cloud State University

PEARSON
Longman

New York San Francisco Boston
London Toronto Sydney Tokyo Singapore Madrid
Mexico City Munich Paris Cape Town Hong Kong Montreal

In memory of our fathers,
Victorio Nuccetelli and Joe Seay

Editor-in-Chief: *Eric Stano*
Executive Marketing Manager: *Ann Stypuloski*
Supplements Editor: *Brian Belardi*
Production Manager: *Stacey Kulig*
Project Coordination, Text Design, and Electronic Page Makeup:
    Pre-PressPMG
Senior Cover Designer/Manager: *Nancy Danahy*
Cover Image: © *Photographer's Choice/Getty Images, Inc.*
Senior Manufacturing Buyer: *Alfred C. Dorsey*
Printer and Binder: *R.R. Donnelley and Sons/Harrisonburg*
Cover Printer: *Phoenix Color Corporation/Hagerstown*

Library of Congress Cataloging-in-Publication Data
Seay, Gary.
    How to think logically / Gary Seay, Susana Nuccetelli.
        p. cm.
    Includes bibliographical references and index.
    ISBN-13: 978-0-321-33777-1 (alk. paper)
    ISBN-10: 0-321-33777-8 (alk. paper)
    1. Reasoning 2. Logic. 3. Critical thinking. I. Nuccetelli, Susana.
II. Title.
    BC177.S384 2007
    160--dc22

                                        2007017724

Please visit us at www. ablongman. com

ISBN 13: 978-0-321-33777-1
ISBN 10: 0-321-33777-8

1 2 3 4 5 6 7 8 9 10—DOH—10 09 08 07

brief contents

detailed contents

preface

This book is intended for introductory courses in logic and critical thinking, but its scope is well beyond that of the usual textbooks. Our aim in writing it was to produce a text that truly preserves rigor on basic principles of logic and at the same time raises questions that bear on some substantive issues in other areas of philosophy, such as epistemology, ethics, philosophy of language, and philosophy of science. *How to Think Logically* offers a clear and straightforward approach to the techniques of reasoning that most instructors will wish to cover in an introductory course in logic or critical reasoning, but it also incorporates discussions of issues such as what it means for a belief or statement to be true, how we determine whether we should trust our beliefs, and how we distinguish between reliable and unreliable hypotheses and between rationality and irrationality in assessing our systems of beliefs. This is a book, then, that is meant to appeal to students who are intellectually curious and who might go on to take other courses in philosophy. Our experience in using it in our classes suggests that it is an effective tool in encouraging undergraduates to pursue further study in the subject.

At the same time, *How to Think Logically* is a user-friendly text designed for students who have never encountered philosophy before and for whom a systematic approach to analytical thinking might be an unfamiliar exercise. Where issues of philosophical import are raised, care has been taken to use language appropriate for beginners. In each chapter, the writing style is simple and direct, with jargon kept to a minimum. Symbolism is also kept simple. Scattered through the text are special-emphasis boxes in which important points are summarized to help students focus on crucial distinctions and fundamental ideas. In spite of the complexity of the topics in the book, its fourteen chapters unfold in a way that undergraduates will find understandable and easy to follow. Even so, the book maintains a punctilious regard for the principles of logic. At no point does it compromise rigor.

How to Think Logically provides a guide to the analysis, reconstruction, and evaluation of arguments. In this way, it is meant to help students learn to distinguish good reasoning from bad. It is grounded in our conviction that informal logic courses must aim at developing a philosophical competence that is more a "knowing how" than a "knowing that." Thus it includes material designed to help students develop techniques for supporting what they say—putting various pieces of information together in a way that is consistent while avoiding common mistakes in inference—and for questioning claims that may be mistaken, make no sense, or lack adequate evidential support. On the other hand, neither natural deduction nor the predicate calculus is included here, since we think that they really belong in an introductory course in symbolic logic. We have, however, retained the rudiments of symbolic notation and an introduction to propositional arguments, including the use of both truth tables and informal proofs to check for validity.

The book is divided into four parts. In Part I, students are introduced to the concept of an argument and to methods of assessing the quality of the beliefs on which our inferences are drawn. Chapter 1 offers step-by-step explanations of the basic techniques involved in argument analysis, focusing on its descriptive and normative aspects. Chapters 2 and 3 discuss how the building blocks of reasoning—beliefs and the statements that are their linguistic expressions—may be assessed in terms of their good-making and bad-making features, which we call their "virtues" and "vices." Attention to this is essential to critical thinking, since it is presupposed in any attempt to understand logical relations such as consistency, entailment, and "being a reason for," which are analyzed throughout the book. Also, as part of our discussion in Chapter 2, we offer a new approach incorporating the interface between belief and statement. Part II is devoted entirely to argument, showing different ways in which conclusions can be drawn. In Chapter 4, we first present a method for the accurate reconstruction of arguments and then draw a distinction between conclusive and nonconclusive reasons that is shown to be the basis for the distinction between deductive and inductive arguments. Chapter 5 presents an account of deduction and validity and shows students how to recognize entailment. Chapter 6 offers an extended treatment of induction, and this provides a springboard into a discussion of informal fallacies in Chapter 7, where students learn about several ways in which the abuse of induction can lead to fallacious arguments. In connection with Chapters 4, 5, and 6, students are also introduced to some fundamental issues in moral philosophy, philosophical logic, and the philosophy of science. In Part III, which comprises Chapters 7 through 10, twenty of the most common informal fallacies are examined, beginning in each case with an example of how the fallacy may arise in the context of everyday discourse and concluding with tips on how to avoid the mistake in question. Here students are shown how some very basic confusions may lead to defective reasoning, and they learn to spot these subversions of reason so as not to be misled. They also learn ways of checking their own arguments to be sure that they commit no fallacies themselves. Part IV, which comprises Chapters 11 through 14, offers a feature that we hope many instructors will appreciate: a detailed treatment of some common elementary procedures for determining validity in propositional logic and traditional syllogistic logic. Here students will be able to go well beyond the intuitive procedures introduced in Chapter 5.

How to Think Logically is presented in a format that will be accessible to freshman-level students. It assumes no previous acquaintance with logic, informal reasoning, or any other area of philosophy. It uses short sentences in its explanations and easy examples from a variety of everyday contexts, and it takes care to explain to its readers the cash value of what they learn for real-life applications. The chapters themselves are also kept short, so students can concentrate on manageable units of new information as they make their way through an unfamiliar landscape. Moreover, each chapter is designed as a self-contained unit, so that instructors can decide for themselves the combination of chapters to use and the order in which to cover the various topics according to the needs of different types of courses. In each chapter, a feature called the "Philosopher's Corner" offers a short discussion of a philosophical topic related to the material presented there. These discussions focus on a wide variety of different subjects from different areas of the discipline. Instructors will find this feature of the book especially useful for introducing beginning students to the connections between logic and other branches of philosophy.

To help students learn by testing their analytical skills in solving problems, chapters include exercises as well as study questions and lists of key words. Where appropriate, exercises include sample answers; in the back of the book, there is a key with answers to selected exercises. (An instructor's comprehensive answer manual and a test bank for use with this book are available online at Longman's Instructor Resource Center at *www.ablongman.com*.) Within each chapter there are also section summaries emphasizing crucial points to be remembered as critical thinking competence is sharpened. Among the exercises is also a feature we have called, "Your Own Thinking Lab," where students are encouraged to take an active part in constructing arguments, counterexamples, sentences of relevant kinds, and thought experiments. At the end of every chapter there is a comprehensive summary and a feature called the "Writing Project," where students are assigned to write a short composition on a topic related to one of the subjects discussed in the chapter. At the end of the book, there is a glossary of important terms, so students can easily review the meanings of words as they read.

We have also been concerned to produce a concise textbook that students can actually afford. Unlike many other textbooks on logic and critical thinking now available, *How to Think Logically* does not attempt an exhaustive treatment of fundamentals but contains only as much material as an instructor can realistically cover in a 15-week semester. To an ever more cost-conscious student population now facing dramatic tuition hikes at many institutions, it thus offers the advantage of economy.

Acknowledgments

Several people deserve special thanks for their help in putting this book together. We are especially grateful to Priscilla McGeehon and Eric Stano, our editors at Longman, for their patience and insightful criticisms as we revised the manuscript. The book is much better as result of their suggestions. We are also indebted to our student assistants, Ronnie Garza at the University of Texas Pan American and Chad Kainz, Teresa Handberg, and David Coss at St. Cloud State University, for their skills in computer graphics and unflagging energy in the assembly of the typescript. Finally, we thank those insightful individuals who commented on various portions of the manuscript while we were developing it:

Marshell Bradley, Sam Houston State University; Kyle Broom, University of Illinois; Keith Brown, California State University; Will Cowling, University of Oregon; Steven Crain, University of St. Francis; Stephen Ferguson, North Carolina A & T; Gregory Fields, Southern Illinois University; Nada Gligorov, Hunter College; Jeffrey Koperski, Saginaw Valley State University; Keith Korez, University of Lousiana at Lafayette; Michael LaBossiere, Florida A & M University; Leo McIntyre, Simmons College; Matthew Olsen, University of Illinois; Michael Patton, University of Montevallo; Andrew Pavelich, Illinois Wesleyan University; Lisa Schwartzman, Michigan State University; W. Christopher Stewart, Houghton College; Eddie Thomas, Mercer University; Mike VanQuickenbourne, Everett Community College; Augustine Yaw Frimpong-Mansoh, California State University Bakersfield; and Kevin Zanelotti, Radford University.

GARY SEAY has taught formal and informal logic since 1979 at the City University of New York, where he is presently associate professor of philosophy at Medgar Evers College. He is the author of journal articles on moral philosophy and bioethics. With Susana Nuccetelli, he is editor of *Themes from G. E. Moore: New Essays in Epistemology and Ethics* (Oxford University Press, 2007), *Philosophy of Language: The Central Topics* (Rowman & Littlefield, 2007), and *Latin American Philosophy: An Introduction With Readings* (Prentice Hall, 2004).

SUSANA NUCCETELLI is associate professor of philosophy at St. Cloud State University in Minnesota. Her essays in epistemology and philosophy of language have appeared in *Analysis, Metaphilosophy, The Philosophical Forum, Inquiry,* and *The Southern Journal of Philosophy,* among other journals. She is editor of *New Essays in Semantic Externalism and Self-Knowledge* (MIT Press, 2003) and author of *Latin American Thought: Philosophical Problems and Arguments* (Westview Press, 2002). She is co-editor of *The Blackwell Companion to Latin American Philosophy* (Blackwell, forthcoming, 2008).

The Building Blocks of Reasoning

What Is Logical Thinking? And Why Should We Care?

After reading this chapter, you'll be able to answer questions about logical thinking such as

- What is its subject matter?
- How does its approach to reasoning differ from that of neuroscience and psychology?
- What is an inference or argument?
- Which are the main dimensions of logical thinking?
- How does logical thinking differ from formal logic?
- How do we distinguish arguments from nonarguments?
- What are the steps in argument analysis?
- What does logical thinking have to do with philosophy?

1.1 The Study of Reasoning

Logical thinking or informal logic is a branch of philosophy devoted entirely to the study of reasoning. Although it shares this interest with other philosophical and scientific disciplines, it differs from them in a number of ways. Compare, for example, cognitive psychology and neuroscience. These also study the faculty of reasoning but are chiefly concerned with the mental and physiological processes underlying it. By contrast, logical thinking focuses on the *outcomes* of such processes: certain logical relations among beliefs that obtain when reasoning is at work. It also focuses on logical relations among statements; provided that speakers are sincere, these express logical relations among beliefs, as we shall see.

Inference or Argument

As far as logical thinking is concerned, reasoning consists in such logical relations. Prominent among them is a relation whereby one or more beliefs are taken to offer support for another. Known as *inference* or *argument*, this relation obtains whenever a thinker entertains one or more beliefs as being *reasons* for another. Here is an inference where a belief does succeed in supporting another belief:

1 All whales are mammals; *therefore* some mammals are whales.

In (1), the logical relation of inference between these two beliefs is conclusive in this sense: if the reason ("All whales are mammals") is true, then the supported belief ("Some mammals are whales") must also be. But compare this:

2 No oranges from Florida are small; *therefore* no oranges from the United States are small.

In (2), the logical relation of inference between the beliefs is *non*conclusive, since the reason offered ("No oranges from Florida are small") could be true and the belief it attempts to support ("No oranges from the United States are small") false. But (2) by no means illustrates the worst-case scenario. In other inferences, a belief or beliefs thought to support another belief might altogether fail to do so. See, for example, the following:

3 No oranges are apples; *therefore* all mushrooms are plants.

Since in (3) "therefore" occurs between the two beliefs, it is clear that "No oranges are apples" is taken to be a reason for "All mushrooms are plants." Yet it is not. Although these two beliefs both happen to be true, neither actually supports the other. Here is another such case, this time one involving false beliefs:

4 All lawyers are thin; *therefore* the current pope is Chinese.

Since in (4) the component beliefs have little to do with each other, neither of them actually supports the other. As in the case of (3), here too the inference fails, whether the beliefs that make it up are actually true or false.

Success and failure in inference are logical thinking's central topic. We shall now look more closely at how it approaches this subject.

1.2 Logic and Reasoning

Dimensions of the Subject

Inference is the most fundamental relation arising between beliefs or thoughts when reasoning is at work. Logical thinking studies this and other logical relations with an eye toward:

1. Describing patterns of reasoning
2. Evaluating good- and bad-making features of reasoning
3. Sanctioning rules for maximizing reasoning's good-making features

Each of these may be thought of as a dimension of logical thinking. The first describes logical relations, which initially requires identifying common patterns of inference. The second distinguishes good and bad traits in those relations. And the third sanctions rules for adequate reasoning—that is, *norms* that could help us maximize the good (and minimize the bad) traits of our reasoning. The picture that emerges is as in Box 1.

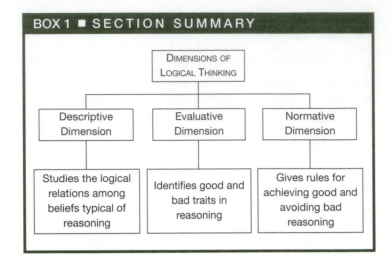

Understanding these dimensions is crucial to successful reasoning. Since the third dimension especially bears on how well we perform at reasoning, it may be said to have *normative worth* or *cash value*. Its cash value consists in the prescriptions it issues for materially improving our reasoning. But this dimension depends on the other two, for useful prescriptions for adequate reasoning require accurate descriptions of the common logical relations established by reasoning (such as inference). And they require adequate criteria to distinguish good and bad features in those relations.

Formal Logic

What we're calling "logical thinking" is often known as *informal logic*. This discipline shares with another branch of philosophy, *formal logic*, its interest in inference and other logical relations. Informal and formal logic differ, however, in their scope and methods. Formal logic is also known as *symbolic logic*. It develops its own formal languages for the purpose of constructing systems of proofs. Any such system consists of basic symbolic expressions, the initial vocabulary of the formal language, and rules for operations with them. The latter include, first, rules for forming new expressions and, second, rules of inference that enable us to determine which formulas are the logical consequence of other formulas. Formal logic, then, takes inference to be a relation among formulas—one that holds whenever a formula follows from one or more other formulas. Such a relation is expressed in a symbolic notation, which may be quite complex, and although it may sometimes be translated into a natural language (such as English, Arabic, or Chinese), it need not be. As far as formal logic is concerned, inference is a relation among formulas. It need be neither a relation among beliefs nor one among statements. Furthermore, it need not be identified with the outcome of ordinary reasoning.

Informal Logic

By contrast, logical thinking is *informal logic*. For one thing, it requires no such formal languages. Although it sometimes introduces symbols, it may in fact be conducted entirely in a natural language. Moreover, it is wholly devoted to the study of inference as a relation among beliefs—or among statements, the linguistic expressions of belief. Thus, by contrast with symbolic logic, logical thinking is completely focused on the study of *logical relations as they occur when ordinary reasoning is at work*. Its three dimensions can be shown relevant to reasoning in a variety of common contexts, as when we deliberate about issues involving

BOX 2 ■ SOME USES OF LOGICAL THINKING	
A criminal trial:	*Is the defendant guilty? What shall we make of the alibi?*
A domestic question:	*What's the source of that noise? A storm? A truck unloading in the street?*
A scientific puzzle:	*How to choose among equally supported yet opposite scientific theories?*
A philosophical issue:	*Are mind and body the same thing or different?*
An ethical problem:	*Is euthanasia morally right? What about abortion?*
A political decision:	*Who should be president of the United States?*
A financial decision:	*Shall I follow my broker's advice and invest in this new fund?*
A health matter:	*Given my medical records, is exercise good for me? Can I eat donuts?*

The study of the inferences we make in these and other contexts is approached by logical thinking from its three distinct dimensions: once it describes the logical relations underlying such cases of reasoning, it evaluates them, and it determines whether they conform to rules of good reasoning. Why, then, should we care about logical thinking? Because the situations where competent reasoning is required are exceedingly common. They arise whenever we wish to do well in intellectual tasks such as those listed above. Each of us has faced them at some point—for example, in attempting to convince someone of a view, in writing on a controversial issue, or simply in deciding between two seemingly well-supported yet incompatible claims. To succeed in meeting these ordinary challenges requires the ability to think logically. Let's now have a closer look at the requirements of this crucial competence.

Exercises

I. Review Questions

1. How does logical thinking differ from scientific disciplines that study reasoning?
2. Logical thinking is sometimes called "informal logic." What does this mean? And what is formal logic?
3. What is the main topic of logical thinking?
4. In what sense are beliefs and statements parallel?
5. What is the logical relation of inference?
6. Could an inference fail completely? If so, how? If not, why not?
7. What are the different dimensions of logical thinking?
8. Which dimension of logical thinking is relevant to determining *reasoning's good- and bad-making traits*?
9. What does it mean to say that logical thinking's normative dimension has "cash value"?
10. What is a natural language?

II. YOUR OWN THINKING LAB

1. Construct two inferences.

2. Construct a conclusive inference (one in which, if the reason or reasons given are true, the supported belief must be true).

3. Construct a nonconclusive inference (one in which the reason or reasons given could be true and the supported belief false).

4. Construct a failed inference.

5. Describe a scenario for which logical thinking could help a thinker in everyday life.

6. Describe a scenario for which logical thinking could help *with your own* studies.

7. Imagine someone saying that thinking logically has no normative worth. How would you respond?

8. "All cats are carnivorous animals. No carnivorous animals are vegetarian; therefore no cats are vegetarian" is a conclusive inference. Why? Not all inferences are conclusive. Explain.

9. Consider, "All geckos are nocturnal. Therefore there will be peace in the Middle East next year." What's the matter with this inference?

10. Consider, "Politicians are all crooks. Therefore it never snows in the Rio Grande Valley." What's the matter with this inference?

1.3 Arguments and Nonarguments

An inference is a certain relation among *beliefs* whereby one of them is taken to be supported by one or more others. When this is expressed in a language, we call it an "argument." Thus, there is an argument when a parallel relation obtains among *statements*, which—provided that we are sincere and competent—can be considered the expression of our beliefs. Statements, to which we turn in Chapter 2 (see also Box 3 here), are therefore the building blocks from which arguments are constructed.

BOX 3 ■ STATEMENT AND SENTENCE TYPES

✔ Every statement has a truth value: it is either *true* (e.g., "All elephants are mammals") or *false* (e.g., "Tokyo is the capital of Canada").

✔ Not all sentences are suitable for making statements. Only the so-called *declarative* ones are (e.g., "It is raining").

✔ Sentences of the following types aren't:
  1. *Expressive* sentences (e.g., "What a lovely day!");
  2. *Imperative* sentences (e.g., "Please close the door"); and
  3. *Interrogative* sentences ("What did you do last weekend?") (More on this in Chaper 2).

But not all relations between them constitute arguments. Suppose someone says:

5   Philadelphia is a large city, and Chicago is larger still, but New York is the largest of all.

Although (5) is made up of three simple statements grouped together, it does not amount to an argument, for there is no attempt at presenting a supported claim; that is, the statements are not arranged so that one of them makes a claim for which the others purport to give reasons. Rather, they are just three conjoined statements within a single sentence. Compare:

6   I think, therefore I am.

7   All lawyers are attorneys. Perry Mason is a lawyer. Thus Perry Mason is an attorney.

8   No sturgeons are surgeons. Only surgeons can legally perform a coronary bypass. Hence, no sturgeons can legally perform a coronary bypass.

9   A Volkswagen beetle (the old one) is faster than a bicycle. A Buick is faster than a Volkswagen beetle. A Maserati is faster than a Buick. It follows that a Maserati is faster than a bicycle.

In each of these, a claim is made and at least one other statement is offered in support of that claim. But not all arguments are arrangements of statements in which a claim is actually supported (since arguments, as we shall see later, may be defective in various ways). This, however, need not concern us just yet. Before we can turn to the question of when an argument succeeds in supporting the claim it makes, we must first look at a basic feature that all arguments share.

Every argument consists of at least two statements: one that makes a claim of some sort and one or more others that attempt to support it. The statement that makes the claim is the conclusion, and that which attempts to offer support for it is the premise (or premises, if there are more than one).

Now clearly we are introducing some special terminology here. For in everyday English, "argument" most often means "having words," in the sense of having a dispute. But that is very different from the more technical use of "argument" in logical thinking, where its meaning is similar to that common in a court of law. In a trial, each attorney is expected to present an argument. This amounts to making a claim (e.g., "My client is innocent") and then giving some reasons to support it ("He was visiting relatives on the night of the crime"). In doing this, the attorney is not having a dispute with someone in the courtroom; rather, she is making an assertion and offering reasons that supposedly back it up. This is very much like what we mean by "argument" in logical thinking. An argument is a group of statements that attempt to make a supported claim. On this definition, then, an argument is not a verbal confrontation between two hostile parties; it is something one person can do all by herself.

In addition, since we understand arguments as made up of statements, the sentences used to state premises and conclusions must be either true or false. As a consequence, no set of sentences put at the service of the expressive use of language—such as those of poetry and song lyrics—counts as an argument for our purposes. The reason for insisting on this is that one of our goals as logical thinkers is to be able to tell whether an argument is valid or not. As we shall see later, this requires that we consider whether the conclusion of an argument would be true if all its premises were true. But since sentences in expressive language are neither true nor false, even those that may seem to represent states of affairs actually lack truth value. (Ironically, the very thing poets prize as a strength in language, logical thinkers rule out; but poetry and logical thinking have different aims.)

Before we look more closely at argument, let's sum up what we already know about this relation among statements:

BOX 4 ■ SECTION SUMMARY

- In logical thinking, the meaning of the term "argument" is similar to that common in a court of law.
- For a set of statements to be an argument, one of them must be presented as supported by the other or others.
- An argument, then, consists of two or more statements: a conclusion that makes a claim of some sort and one or more premises that are the reasons offered to support that claim.

1.4 Argument Analysis

Reconstructing and Evaluating Arguments

One essential competence that all logical thinkers must have is the ability to analyze arguments. What, exactly, is required for this competence? It involves knowing

1. How to recognize arguments
2. How to identify the logical relation between their parts
3. How to evaluate arguments

Recognizing arguments and identifying the logical relations among their parts are essential to the process of reconstructing an argument. Reconstruction begins by paying close attention to the piece of spoken or written language we wish to analyze. One must read a passage carefully or listen attentively in order to determine whether or not a claim is being made, with reasons offered in support of it. If we have identified a conclusion and at least one premise, we can then be confident that the passage does contain an argument. The next step is to put the parts of the argument into an orderly arrangement, so that the relation between premise/s and conclusion becomes more evident.

Argument reconstruction is the first step in argument analysis; argument evaluation is the second. In the former, we identify

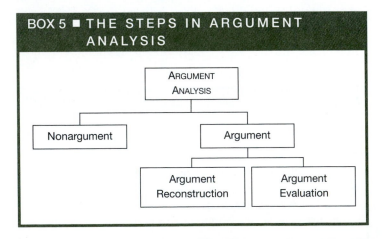

BOX 5 ■ THE STEPS IN ARGUMENT ANALYSIS

the parts of an argument; in the latter, we assess whether an argument's premises do actually succeed in supporting its conclusion, thereby giving reasons for it. But before we can move ahead to the evaluation of arguments, we must first make sure that we are indeed able to reconstruct them properly. There is, then, one more thing to which we must pay attention before we can go further, and that is the matter of how to distinguish correctly between premises and conclusion.

Identifying Premises and Conclusion

Let's now reconstruct some of the above arguments. We begin by identifying each argument's conclusion and premise/s. Once that's done, we can then rewrite the premise/s first and the conclusion last, listing each with a number, which makes it easy to refer to any given part of the argument. If there are two or more premises, the order does not matter (except when we employ a certain technique of evaluation that we'll discuss later). It is also customary to introduce, before the conclusion, either a line or the word "therefore" to indicate that what comes next is the conclusion. In this book, we'll adopt the convention of using a line to signal that a conclusion is being drawn; when you see it, you should think: "therefore." The first step in the reconstruction of (6) through (9) above gives us:

6   1. I think.
    2. I am.

7   1. All lawyers are attorneys.
    2. Perry Mason is a lawyer.
    3. Perry Mason is an attorney.

8   1. No sturgeons are surgeons.
    2. Only surgeons can legally perform a coronary bypass.
    3. No sturgeons can legally perform a coronary bypass.

9   1. A Volkswagen beetle is faster than a bicycle.
    2. A Buick is faster than a Volkswagen beetle.
    3. A Maserati is faster than a Buick.
    4. A Maserati is faster than a bicycle.

(6), (7), (8), and (9) all have a conclusion and at least one premise (though, as shown here, there may be more; in some arguments, there will be many premises). In all cases, the premise/s have been listed first and the conclusion last. But "premise" and "conclusion" do not mean "statement that comes first," and "statement that comes last," respectively. Rather, the premise of an argument is a reason given in an attempt to support a certain conclusion. And the conclusion is the claim that is to be supported. When an argument is offered in a natural language—such as English, Russian, Spanish, or Japanese—sometimes the conclusion does come last. But it does not have to: it can come at the beginning of the argument equally well, or in the middle of it. The same holds for the premises: although they sometimes come at the beginning, they don't have to. They can come after the conclusion; or there can be some premises at the beginning, then the conclusion, then more premises. What is essential to a premise is that it must be a statement offered in support of some other statement (the conclusion). As we shall see later, sometimes the attempted support succeeds and other times it fails. But let us now consider some more examples of arguments.

10 **Aunt Theresa won't vote in the Republican primary next week** because she is a Democrat, and Democrats can't vote in a Republican primary election.

11 **Simon's cellphone will cause an incident at the Metropolitan Museum,** since art museums don't allow cellphone use in the galleries, and Simon's is always ringing.

12 It gets lousy gas mileage, so **I ought to sell the SUV as soon as possible!** After all, it is just too expensive to maintain that vehicle, and besides, it pollutes the atmosphere worse than a regular car.

In each of these arguments, the conclusion is in boldface. As you can see, in both (10) and (11) it comes first, followed by two premises. But in (12), a premise comes first, followed by the conclusion, which is itself followed by two more premises.

Premise and Conclusion Indicators

We have seen that the premises of an argument are sentences offered in support of a certain claim or conclusion. But how can we tell, in any actual argument, which is which? As the examples considered so far demonstrate, when arguments are presented in everyday language, the order of premises and conclusion can be scrambled in various ways. So how do we know which is which? Fortunately, there are some words and phrases that are often helpful in determining this. These are of two kinds: premise indicators and conclusion indicators. Premise indicators include such expressions as

because	given that	as
for the reason that	follows from	since
assuming that	whereas	in as much as
is a consequence of	for	provided that
after all	in that	considering that

When we see one of these expressions, it very often means that a premise is coming next. In other words, one of these (or another synonymous expression) may precede the statements of an argument that are its premises. You can see this in some of the above arguments. Recall:

10 Aunt Theresa won't vote in the Republican primary next week, because she is a Democrat, and Democrats can't vote in a Republican primary election.

11 Simon's cell phone will cause an incident at the Metropolitan Museum, since art museums don't allow cell-phone use in the galleries, and Simon's is always ringing.

In (10), "because" is used as a premise indicator; in (11), the premise indicator is "since." In (12), "after all" functions as an indicator of two of its premises:

12 It gets lousy gas mileage, so I ought to sell the SUV as soon as possible! After all, it is just too expensive to maintain that vehicle, and besides, it pollutes the atmosphere worse than a regular car.

We must, however, be careful here. This method is more like a rule of thumb and is not 100 percent dependable; not all occurrences of these words and phrases actually do indicate that premises are coming next. But many do. How to recognize when they mean this and when they don't is a competence acquired with practice, and you'll be getting some of that when you do the exercises in this chapter. Conclusion indicators are a little more reliable. They include such expressions as

WHAT IS LOGICAL THINKING?
AND WHY SHOULD WE CARE?

16

therefore	suggests that
from this we can see that	thus
hence	accordingly
we may conclude that	recommends that
so	supports that
we may infer that	for this reason
entails that	consequently
it follows that	as a result

When we see one of these words or phrases, it usually means that a conclusion is coming after it. There are a few exceptions, but for the most part conclusion indicators are reliable. Arguments containing instances of them can be seen in some of the examples above. In (6), "therefore" functions as a conclusion indicator, as does "thus" in (7):

6   I think, *therefore* I am.

7   All lawyers are attorneys. Perry Mason is a lawyer. *Thus* Perry Mason is an attorney.

In (8), the conclusion indicator is "hence"; and in (9) it's "it follows that":

8   No sturgeons are surgeons. Only surgeons can legally perform a coronary bypass. *Hence*, no sturgeons can legally perform a coronary bypass.

9   A Volkswagen beetle is faster than a bicycle. A Buick is faster than a Volkswagen beetle. A Maserati is faster than a Buick. *It follows that* a Maserati is faster than a bicycle.

Again, you will get more practice in recognizing conclusion indicators when you do the exercises in this chapter. But as we just noted, the indicators are reliable only *for the most part* and not 100 percent of the time. What, then, are some cases where these expressions do *not* function as indicators of premises or conclusions? Consider the following:

13 Since he first came to New York in 1979, Max has read *El Diario* every day.

14 Alice took out a health insurance policy on her own because her employer did not provide a health plan as a part of her employment contract.

In (13), "since" is not functioning as a premise indicator. Although there are two statements in this sentence, they do not amount to an argument because neither statement attempts to offer support for the other. Here "since" serves merely to introduce a temporal reference: the sentence describes a sequence of actions taken over time, beginning in the past. In (14), there are two statements, but it would be a mistake to think that the first is a conclusion and the second a premise introduced by "because." Rather, the whole sentence is an explanation, not an argument. The last statement serves *to account for* the action described in the first, not to offer support for it. Here is another case in which words that often are premise indicators have some other function:

15 The best way to maintain the peace is to be prepared for war. As a means to peace, disarmament will surely fail.

This is not an argument, because neither statement really attempts to offer support for the other (in fact, they are both saying much the same thing). This should make us suspect that "for" in the first statement and "as" in the second are not serving here as premise indicators at all. This suspicion would be correct, for although both words sometimes serve as premise indicators, neither is doing so in (15).

Again, we must bear in mind that learning how to recognize when words of these kinds are functioning as indicators comes with practice. As with learning to ride a bicycle, one gets better at it by doing it. The more one works at trying to see the distinction and to draw it correctly, the easier it becomes. You'll get some practice on this later in the exercises.

Arguments with No Premise or Conclusion Indicator

A further problem, however, must be noted at this point: not all arguments have premise or conclusion indicators! Some have none at all. When this happens in a given set of statements that do constitute an argument, there is simply no other reliable way of identifying premises and conclusion than to ask yourself: "What claim is being made?" (That will be the conclusion.) And "Which statements are attempting to offer support for the claim that is being made?" (Those are the premises.) Consider this example:

16 Crocodiles aren't really dangerous at all. I've seen them on television many times, and they seem very peaceful. And I remember seeing Paul Hogan wrestle one in the movie *Crocodile Dundee.*

This is plainly an argument—a rather bad one—yet it has no indicators of any kind. Even so, we can easily see what its conclusion is: it's the first statement. This is because the first statement is making the claim for which the other three statements are obviously trying to offer support. (That the support here seems a bit dim-witted does not change the fact that the last three statements are functioning as premises; it only means that the argument does not really succeed—it gives no good reason to accept the conclusion.) Here we don't really need indicators to be able to recognize that the conclusion is at the beginning of the argument and that the premises come after it. Arguments do, however, often have some indicators of premises and/or the conclusion. And if they have even one of these, that is usually enough to tell you what's what. For arguments that lack such indicators altogether, asking the questions suggested above will be sufficient for this purpose.

Exercises

III. Review Questions

1. What are argument's premise and conclusion indicators?
2. What are the parts of an argument?

3. How should the parts of an argument be arranged if one wants to display them in logical order?
4. How many premises could an argument have?
5. How are the premises related to the conclusion of an argument? That is, what are premises *for*? What is their purpose with respect to the conclusion?
6. What sense of the word "argument" is irrelevant to logical thinking?
7. What are the steps in argument analysis?
8. What is involved in reconstructing an argument?
9. Can premises with no indicators be identified? Explain.
10. What should you ask yourself to identify the conclusion of an argument?

IV. Which of the following passages contain arguments, and which don't? *(For exercises marked with a star, there are answers in the back of the book.)*

1. According to a report in the *Daily Times-Gazette*, Senator Smith denied the accusation that he had misused public funds on a trip to Aruba with a French film star. However, he admitted that there was an appearance of wrongdoing, and he vowed not to do it again.

   SAMPLE ANSWER: No argument

2. Some muskrats are not nocturnal, for naturalists who have studied the habits of these animals have determined that there is evidence of muskrats feeding during the day and sleeping at night. _____

3. All architectural engineers have studied mathematics. It follows that Judith has studied mathematics, since Judith is an architectural engineer. _____

* 4. Since 1979, Pam has lived in Berlin. She has worked for Deutsche Bank, but now she is looking forward to retirement and has bought a villa in Corsica. _____

5. Heard melodies are sweet, but those unheard are sweeter; therefore ye soft pipes play on; not to the sensual ear, but, more endeared, pipe to the spirit ditties of no tone... (Keats—from "Ode on a Grecian Urn"). _____

6. I have bought several CDs at The Noble Book Barn, and all have proved defective. One was supposed to be Nina Simone and turned

out to be the Beastie Boys. Another was missing some tracks. Two others had static that distorted the sound. Therefore The Noble Book Barn is not a reliable store for CDs. _____

7. Elena should dump that creep Oscar and improve her life! After all, Oscar has been nothing but trouble for her. He sneaks around with other women behind her back, and he spends all his money at the racetrack. _____

8. John is not going to class today, because he is wearing a leather jacket, and he never goes to class wearing that jacket. _____

9. They all felt that Jane was the sort of woman who needed help. I,on the other hand, saw that she was capable of drawing on inner resources that made her impervious to all adversity. _____

*10. Although Ed's new BMW will outrun nearly every other car in town, it was not a good idea to buy it, for it costs him a lot to maintain it. And on his meager salary, he will never be able to keep up with the monthly payments on it. _____

11. August in Argentina is winter, but only in the gentle way that winter manifests itself in the sunny latitudes of South America. One can enjoy a meal at an outdoor table of a restaurant. _____

12. Since I am a fraternal (nonidentical) twin, I can report that in early childhood each brother learns exactly how to relate to the other but has no idea how to relate to other children. _____

*13. Let me not to the marriage of true minds admit impediments. Love is not love that alters when it alteration finds, or bends with the remover to remove. Oh no! It is an ever fixèd mark, that looks on tempests and is not shaken, a star to every wand'ring bark, whose worth's unknown although his height be taken... (Shakespeare—from "Sonnet 116").

_____

14. Companies should incorporate top Latino professionals. For one thing, Latino purchasing power is approaching $800 billion in the United States. _____

15. To dance beneath the diamond sky with one hand waving free, silhouetted by the sea, circled by the circus signs, with all memory and fate driven far beneath the waves, let me forget about today until tomorrow! Hey, Mr. Tambourine Man, play a song for me! In the jingle-jangle morning I'll come following you. (Bob Dylan—from "Mr. Tambourine Man"). _____

*16. If judges were strict with criminals, then all offenses would be punished. But some offenses are not punished. So judges are not strict with criminals. _____

17. It occurred to me that, because twins are genetically identical, their sons are actually half-brothers! _____

*18. Since I went on my first date in high school, more than 200 species of frogs have disappeared forever. _____

19. The Mississippi River rises in the lake country of northern Minnesota and flows southward all the way to the Gulf of Mexico. Over the course of this great distance, it divides the eastern watershed of the United States from the western, and drains all the rivers for hundreds of miles in both directions in the middle of the continent. _____

*20. *Superman* cost more than $200 million. Most movies that cost more than $200 million do well. It follows that *Superman* will do well. _____

21. Harry Potter is smart and escapes all the traps this movie sets for him. _____

22. Tracey will easily pass the MEDCAT exams. People who get straight A's in their science courses easily pass the MEDCAT exams, and she got straight A's in hers. _____

V. **In each passage above containing an argument, underline its conclusion.**

VI. **For each of the following arguments, put premises in parentheses and underline the conclusion. Use angles "< >" and square brackets "[ ]" to mark indicators of premises and conclusion, respectively.**

1. SAMPLE: <Since> (all the Dobermans I have known were dangerous) and (my neighbor's new dog Franz is a Doberman), [it follows that] Franz is dangerous.

2. Rev. Sharpton has no chance of being elected this time because his campaign is not well financed, and any politician who is not well financed has no real chance of being elected.

* 3. Badgers are native to southern Wisconsin. After all, they are always spotted there.

4. Since all theoretical physicists have studied quadratic equations, no theoretical physicists are dummies at math, for no one who has studied quadratic equations is a dummy at math.

5. Thousands of salamanders have been observed by naturalists and none has ever been found to be warm-blooded. We may conclude that no salamanders are warm-blooded animals.

* 6. In the past, every person who ever lived did eventually die. This suggests that all human beings are mortal.

7. Since architects regularly study engineering, Frank Gehry did, for he is an architect.

8. Britney Spears's new CD is her most innovative album so far. It's got the best music of any new pop music CD this year, and all the DJs are playing it on radio stations all across the country. Accordingly, Britney Spears's new CD is sure to win an award this year.

* 9. Online education is a great option for working adults in general, regardless of their ethnic background. For one thing, there is a large population of working adults who simply are not in a position to attend a traditional university.

10. Any airline that can successfully pass some of the increases in costs on to its passengers will be able to recover from higher fuel costs. South Airlink Airlines seems able to successfully pass some of the increases in costs on to its passengers. As a result, South Airlink Airlines will remain in business.

11. Jackrabbits can be found in Texas. Jackrabbits are speedy rodents. Hence, some speedy rodents can be found in Texas.

*12. There is evidence that galaxies are flying outward and apart from each other, so the cosmos will grow darker and colder.

VII. Your Own Thinking Lab

1. Construct two arguments, one in favor of legalized abortion, the other against it.

2. What's the matter with accepting the two arguments proposed for (1) at once?

3. Construct two arguments: one for the conclusion that God exists and one for the conclusion that He doesn't exist.

4. Some people argue that the death penalty is morally appropriate as a punishment for murder, but others argue for the opposite view.

For which of these two positions might it be appropriate to use as a premise "Murderers deserve to die"?

5. Construct an argument with the premise "Murderers deserve to die," listing its parts in logical order.

1.5 The Philosopher's Corner
What Is Philosophical About All This?

Before we go on, we should note that logical thinking is a part of philosophy. But how do the above concerns amount to *philosophy*? What is distinctively philosophical about them? The answer is that *logical thinking* takes a special approach to beliefs, and this is an approach characteristic of philosophy. When we're engaged in logical thinking, we're concerned not simply with *declaring* our beliefs, describing them, or being proud of them, etc. We're concerned with asking whether our beliefs can be supported by good reasons–and, where reasons are given, asking whether that attempted support succeeds. Philosophy is interested in the reasons for belief, so that it may be determined whether certain beliefs are *justified*, all things considered. And to that end, it is essential to analyze the relations among them, such as argument or inference, whereby some beliefs are entertained as justifications (in the sense of reasons) for others. Rules governing these argument analyses are increasingly complex the further philosophy goes into the subject, and from these complexities many significant philosophical issues and problems arise.

Now it will be noticed immediately that this reflective, analytical approach to beliefs is similar in some very basic ways to what happens in the sciences. But this should come as no surprise, since in fact all of the sciences developed out of philosophy. Physics, biology, astronomy, psychology, and all of the other natural and social sciences were once part of philosophy; but, over the past 500 years, they have gradually broken away to form separate disciplines as their own distinctive empirical (i.e., observationally based) methodologies have taken hold and become clearly articulated. So philosophers, when they look for good reasons to back up certain beliefs, are simply expressing a concern for careful, clear-headed thinking–*logical thinking*–which has been fundamental to the western tradition for a very long time, in the sciences as well as philosophy. But it is in philosophy that we find the origins of this approach: the notion that beliefs are justified only when they can be supported by good reasons in a persuasive, properly constructed argument.

Exercises

VIII. Some of the following passages exemplify attitudes toward belief compatible with logical thinking and others don't. Indicate which are compatible and which are incompatible.

1. I believe that I contracted malaria on my visit to the Amazon rain forest, because I have the symptoms of the disease, scientists have identified the *Anopheles* mosquito as a carrier of malaria, and such mosquitoes are known to be common in the Amazon rain forest.

   SAMPLE ANSWER: Compatible

2. I don't care what people actually do. I've always believed that people are basically good, because that's what I was raised to believe.
   _____

* 3. When I reflect on the justification of my beliefs, I always conclude that it cannot be other than that they are shared by many in my society.
   _____

4. I was always taught that it's ethical to eat meat, but now I have to examine some moral arguments before I can be sure that my belief is justified. _____

* 5. The reason I believe that Julius Caesar was assassinated is that all reputable historians agree that he was. I know this from my extensive research in Roman history. _____

6. I believe that there is life after death, and about this I refuse to entertain any doubt! _____

7. I believe that water is composed of two parts hydrogen and one part oxygen, because I've performed the hydrolysis of water in my chemistry class and discovered its composition by direct observation.
   _____

8. Lying is usually wrong. I believe this because, since I would not like others to lie to me, I should probably not lie to them; and after all, perhaps it's wrong to treat others differently from the way we'd want to be treated ourselves. _____

9. There must be a meaning to life. I'm sure we're all put here for a purpose! It would never occur to me to question such an obvious thing, and I never will question it. That's my belief. _____

*10. What goes around comes around! You knows it's true, man! I'll always believe that. _____

■ Writing Project

Select a claim you feel very strongly about and write a short essay (about two pages) explaining what you take to be the best reasons for that claim. Keep this essay on file, since you'll go back to it for a critical assessment at the end of this course. By the way, never forget to give full references for your sources if you use any!

■ Chapter Summary

In this book, "LOGIC" means mostly *informal logic.*

"formal logic" = *symbolic logic*

Logic studies *reasoning*, but in a way different from psychology and neuroscience, since logic is

- Not concerned with brain processes
- Not concerned with cause-effect explanations
- Concerned with **outcomes:** logical relations between beliefs and logical relations between statements

Why Be Logical Thinkers?

Situations where careful reasoning is required include

- Supporting our beliefs
- Acquiring new, supported beliefs
- Persuading others of our beliefs
- Putting various pieces of information together in a way that makes sense
- Deciding between opposite views
- Avoiding common mistakes in reasoning
- Questioning beliefs that may be mistaken, make no sense, or lack adequate evidence

Dimensions of Logical Thinking

1. Descriptive dimension – describes patterns of logical relation in inferences.
2. Evaluative dimension – distinguishes good and bad traits in those relations.
3. Normative dimension – formulates rules to guide further reasoning (so as to maximize good outcomes and minimize the bad).

The second dimension raises the question "What are the criteria for good and bad reasoning?"

Also to be kept in mind are the following:

1. Statements express beliefs.

   Beliefs are mental states.

   Statements are linguistic expressions with truth values.

2. INFERENCE or ARGUMENT: one of the most important relations among statements.

   Inference – one or more beliefs are thought to support another belief.

   Argument – one or more statements are offered to support some claim.

3. Argument analysis has two parts: argument reconstruction and argument evaluation.

4. How to reconstruct an argument

   A. **Begin by examining a passage carefully.** Distinguish arguments from nonarguments. Keep in mind that, to be an argument at all, a passage must make a claim and offer some reason/s for it. Identify the argument, if any. Once you've done this, move to B.

   B. **Identify premise/s and conclusion.** Premise and conclusion indicators, if available, can help you here, so you should look for them first; if there are any, they will usually reveal the premise/s and conclusion. But if there aren't any, ask yourself "What claim is being made?" (the answer will be the argument's conclusion). If there is a claim, then ask yourself "What are the reason/s offered for it?" (the answer will be the argument's premise/s). Once you have identified premise/s and conclusion, move to C.

C. **List the parts of the argument in order.** Premise/s first and conclusion last, separated by a line.

5. What's distinctively *philosophical* about all this is the emphasis on *support for beliefs*: beliefs (expressible as statements) need backing up by good reasons, and some putative reasons succeed in doing this while others don't.

■ Key Words

Informal logic	Premise indicator
Formal logic	Conclusion indicator
Dimensions of logical thinking	Normative worth
Argument	Inference
Premise	Truth value
Conclusion	Statement
Argument analysis	Natural language
Empirical method	Justification

Thinking Logically and Speaking One's Mind

Chapter Objectives

In this chapter you'll learn about some factors that make a difference in the acceptability of an inference and also some aspects of natural language that can affect the precision of the statements that make up the arguments in which one's inferences are expressed. These include

- The way in which the acceptability of an inference depends on logical connections among the parts that make it up and on their degree of evidential support
- The distinction between truth and evidence
- The logical irrelevance of linguistic merit and rhetorical power in weighing rational acceptability
- The role of propositions as the contents of beliefs and linguistic expressions such as statements

- The three basic uses of language
- Four types of sentence and their relation to uses of language
- How to distinguish between direct and indirect and between literal and nonliteral uses of language
- A philosophical distinction between "type" and "token" and "use" and "mention" in language

2.1 Rational Acceptability

Logical Connectedness

In our thinking about a great number of different subjects, some common features of acceptable reasoning are *logical connectedness* and *the support of evidence*. When a group of beliefs or statements has either of these (or both), that constitutes a good reason for having them. Here we shall look at logical connectedness, which obtains when there is an adequate relation of inference. In any such case, the beliefs are logically connected, so that at least one of them is supported by the others. The strength of their logical connectedness is proportional to the strength of the inference: the stronger the inference, the more logical connectedness obtains among the beliefs that make it up. Beliefs with a good share of logical connectedness are the kind of reasoning we *ought to* engage in—provided that they also meet other conditions, such as being based on solid evidence. But logical connectedness is a matter of degree: some combinations of beliefs might have it only in a qualified sense, others might have it absolutely. In addition, some groups of beliefs may lack it entirely. Consider these:

1 Florida is on the Gulf of Mexico. Any state on the Gulf of Mexico has mild winters. *Therefore* Florida has mild winters.

Inference (1) has a high degree of logical connectedness, since its premises support its conclusion strongly. By contrast,

2 Florida has mild winters, and so do Hawaii and Texas; *therefore* most U.S. states have mild winters.

has a low degree of logical connectedness, for although this inference's premises are true, its conclusion could be false (as it is in this case). Now consider,

3 Florida is a subtropical state on the Gulf of Mexico; *therefore* computers have replaced typewriters.

Here premise and conclusion have no logical connectedness at all. Thus, (1), (2), and (3) illustrate decreasing degrees of logical connectedness. Since (1) clearly has it, logical thinkers who recognize this—together with the fact that the offered reasons in (1) are based on sufficient evidence—cannot reject its conclusion without a serious failure of reasoning. At the same time, since logical connectedness partly determines whether an inference is rationally acceptable, neither (2) nor (3) qualifies for rational acceptability. After all, (2) lacks a sufficient degree of logical connectedness and (3) doesn't have it at all. Neither is a model of the sort of reasoning logical thinkers *ought to* engage in.

Now why should we care about rational acceptability at all? Because whether or not a given piece of reasoning can fulfil its goal depends on its being rationally acceptable. As we've seen, the sort of reasoning exemplified by adequate inferences is crucial to our ability to think logically. But no reasoning that lacks rational acceptability could succeed in achieving its goal— whether this be solving a problem, making a sound decision, or

---

BOX 1 ■ SECTION SUMMARY

Logical Connectedness's Cash Value

- Logical connectedness consists in an adequate relation between the premises and conclusion of an argument or inference.
- Recall that inference is a relation whereby one belief is supported by one or more other beliefs.
- Rational acceptability depends not only on logical connectedness but also on evidential support. When an inference is based on beliefs sufficiently supported by the evidence, its rational acceptability is proportional to its share of logical connectedness. That is, any deficiency in the latter would undermine the inference's rational acceptability.

learning about the environment, others, or oneself. On the other hand, when reasoning is used for persuading an audience or winning a debate, any deficiency in rational acceptability would make it vulnerable to objections.

Evidential Support

For a great number of beliefs, their rational acceptability also requires that they have *evidential support*: that is, that they be supported by data from observation. Beliefs have evidential support when the *total evidence* points to their being true. But what, exactly, is meant by "total evidence"? It's *all* relevant information about a belief (or beliefs) available to the thinker. It includes evidence for the belief and also evidence against it. Thus, the total evidence for a belief requires careful consideration of any information pointing to its being false as well as information pointing to its being true. The total evidence, then, is the result of "factoring in" partial evidence of both kinds. For any given belief, the upshot of considering the total evidence is one of the following:

	Scenario		Evidential Support Status
I	Most of the relevant evidence points to a belief's being true.	➡	It is *supported* by the evidence.
II	Most of the relevant evidence points to a belief's being false.	➡	It is *undermined* by the evidence.
III	The evidence is "split," equally pointing to a belief's being true and to its being false.	➡	It is *not supported* by the evidence.

Only beliefs that fall within category (1) may be said to be "supported by the evidence."

Note that although *logical connectedness* and *evidential support* are both needed for rational acceptability, they are independent of each other. After all, any piece of reasoning could have one without having the other. For example,

4 Anyone who breaks a mirror will have seven years' bad luck. Today I broke a mirror. Therefore, I'll have seven years' bad luck.

(4) plainly has logical connectedness: if the reasons offered for "I'll have seven years' bad luck" were true, then this conclusion would also be true. Yet the total evidence does not point to the truth of (4)'s first premise. Premises that fall short of being supported by the evidence available are of no help in making a conclusion rationally acceptable.

Consider, on the other hand,

5   In abortion, the fetus dies. Therefore abortion is murder.

Here the reason offered (that in abortion the fetus dies) has evidential support. Yet, as it stands, (5) lacks logical connectedness and thus rational acceptability. The upshot for logical thinkers is

When engaging in reasoning by inference, at all times
- Maximize the logical connectedness among beliefs.
- Favor beliefs supported by the evidence.

Truth and Evidence

What matters for the evidential support of a belief is not that it *is true*, but rather that the total evidence available to the thinker points to its being true. This allows for a range of combinations. To begin with, a false belief could be supported by the evidence. Consider

6   The earth does not revolve.

For people in the Middle Ages, this belief was supported by the evidence. As far as they could tell, the belief was true (all information then available pointed to its being true). Yet since (6) is false, those people were in error.

At the same time, a true belief could fail to be supported by the evidence. That would be the case of

7   There are atoms.

Before the twentieth century, there was not enough evidence pointing to (7)'s being true. *Truth* and *evidence*, then, are different concepts that must not be confused. *Truth* concerns how things are. A belief is true if and only if things *are* as represented by it.

BOX 2 ■ SECTION SUMMARY

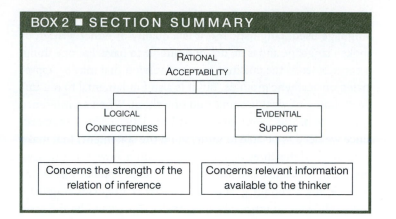

Evidence involves the information about how things are that is available to thinkers, which could turn out to be misleading or even false. Of the two, it is only evidence that bears on rational acceptability. This does not undermine the importance of truth, however, which is always desirable for its own sake.

2.2 Beyond Rational Acceptability

Linguistic Merit

The features so far identified as making up the rational acceptability of beliefs may also be present in statements. Since thought and language are parallel in many respects, as we saw, we can assume the following:

> When speakers are sincere and competent,
> ■ Their statements express what they believe.
> ■ Their arguments express relations of inference established among their beliefs.

Groups of statements, however, may have a number of other features that are irrelevant to their rational acceptability. Prominent among them is *linguistic merit,* which results from a combination of grammatical, syntactical, and stylistic factors such as concision, adequate vocabulary, and compliance with the rules of the language used. Linguistic merit is a quality of either written or spoken language and is no doubt desirable to have. For one thing, it contributes to the qualities of an expression that may be appreciated on aesthetic grounds. But it is also fundamental to our understanding of what is being said or written. When an inference is put into words, some degree of linguistic merit is required, since we need to be able to understand the statements that make it up. Beyond this threshold of understanding, however, linguistic merit can make *no difference to the rational acceptability* of an inference, for a certain group of statements may lack linguistic merit while being rationally acceptable. That would be the case, for example, of any group of poorly expressed statements that nonetheless constitute a strong inference from reasons supported by the evidence. On the other hand, a group of statements may have high linguistic merit and be rationally unacceptable. That would be the case of any statements that are well expressed but nonetheless deficient in either their logical connectedness, their evidential support, or both.

Rhetorical Power

Another desirable feature of statements quite independent of rational acceptability is *rhetorical power*. It is present whenever language is used persuasively. Both linguistic and nonlinguistic factors contribute to the rhetorical power of certain statements; for example, the speaker's choice of emotionally charged words, tone of voice, and accuracy in pronunciation or grammar. But nonlinguistic factors might also contribute to rhetorical power; for example, the speaker's accent, demeanor, physical appearance, or, in the case of a printed text, the publisher's imprint and even the typeface and format. Sometimes a passage or speech is emotionally loaded in overt ways, and this augments its rhetorical power. Other times rhetorical power is more insidiously "coded" in subtle ways to arouse psychological reactions of various sorts. When we ask about the rhetorical power of a putative inference, then, we're asking whether it does in fact tend to be persuasive on the basis of such factors. Yet we should bear in mind that none of those factors could make a difference to the rational acceptability of the inference.

Thus, as in the case of linguistic merit, rhetorical power also falls outside the province of logical thinking, for it can add nothing to the rational acceptability of a piece of reasoning. It is a feature of statements that may succeed in convincing the target audience, though sometimes not by strictly rational means. Some reasoning that lacks rational acceptability may in fact have a lot of rhetorical power; for example, when it is presented by a skillful speaker who knows how to "sell" an idea. On the other hand, thinking that has rational acceptability may in fact lack rhetorical power; for example, reasoning that is too complex and difficult to follow may be rejected by some audiences. This suggests that rational acceptability and rhetorical power are independent. One could exist without the other.

The upshot for the logical thinker is:

Be aware that although it may be nice to persuade an audience of the beliefs you have, you want to do it in the *right way*, which is one that has rational acceptability.

Rhetoric vs. Logical Thinking

A good rhetorician, either in writing or in speech, is one adept at convincing others. The best rhetoric is simply that which is most successful in convincing them—in winning them over. That might well, in some cases, include appeals to emotion and other factors that have no bearing at all on rational acceptability, for they can neither enhance nor undermine logical connectedness and evidential support. The political orator whose stem-winding speech arouses our feelings of patriotism and nationalism in support of a foreign war and the defense attorney who plants the defendant's aged mother in the courtroom audience during his closing argument may both succeed in convincing their audiences. But in either case, we might well doubt that the audience *has a good reason* to be convinced.

It is not logical thinking but rhetoric that studies the art of persuasion. This discipline focuses on the development of various techniques that can enhance rhetorical power. Logical thinking, on the other hand, focuses precisely on how to give good reasons to support our claims. As logical thinkers, we must care about whether we are *justified* in making a certain claim—as we would be only if the claim can *rightly* be inferred from some other statement or statements, which are in turn supported by the evidence. That is, it is rational acceptability that is the criterion of adequate reasoning—the sort that *ought to* persuade us. We must always keep an eye on the warning signs of weak and misleading reasoning so that we can avoid the snares laid by unscrupulous or careless persuaders.

Exercises

I. Review Questions

1. In what does rational acceptability consist?
2. How is logical connectedness related to the strength of an inference?
3. What does evidence have to do with rational acceptability? What is the "total evidence" for a belief?
4. How does truth differ from evidence?
5. Is rhetorical power relevant to thinking logically? And what about linguistic merit? Explain.
6. Some statements can have rhetorical power without having rational acceptability and vice versa. What does this show about the relation between rhetorical power and rational acceptability?

II. For each of the following remarks, determine whether it bears on logical connectedness, evidential support, linguistic merit, rhetorical power, or a combination of these.

1. The Declaration of Independence is clear and has just the right words.
SAMPLE ANSWER: linguistic merit

2. The best available information points to the truth of Einstein's theories of relativity. _____

* 3. The speaker was well-dressed and spoke with the right voice and gestures. _____

4. The fossil record favors neither evolution nor creation. _____

* 5. The fossil record favors evolution. _____

6. He is a lousy speaker. Always insecure. On top of it, he never looks at you when he speaks. _____

7. The belief that some mammals are whales is strongly supported by the belief that all whales are mammals. If the latter is true, the former must be true. _____

* 8. It makes no sense to think that Ellen is an ophthalmologist but not an eye doctor. Once you accept that she is an ophthalmologist, you are committed to accepting that she is an eye doctor. After all, "ophthalmologist" *means* "eye doctor." _____

9. After seeing him so devastated, I became totally convinced of his story. _____

*10. The inference was poorly expressed, in a heavily accented language. Almost a dialect. _____

11. Had you been in court this morning, you'd have been persuaded by the prosecutor's stern attitude. _____

*12. The claim that the butler doesn't have an alibi offers only weak support to the conclusion that he did it. Couldn't that claim be true but the conclusion false? _____

13. If someone is a brother, it follows that he is a male sibling. _____

14. The belief that the earth is not flat was strongly supported by Magellan's voyage. If the earth were flat, Magellan's ship couldn't have circumnavigated it. _____

*15. She couldn't have found better words to make her point. _____

III. **Each item on the left pertains to one of the four subjects on the right. Pair them accordingly.**

1. Being prolix in language
   SAMPLE ANSWER: Linguistic merit

* 2. Having good manners

3. Being concise

* 4. Finding fingerprints at the scene of a crime

5. Persuading the audience

6. Giving support for a belief

7. Citing a report of a reliable witness

A. Logical connectedness

B. Evidential support

C. Linguistic merit

D. Rhetorical power

* 8. Having a direct visual experience

9. Being inferred from other beliefs

*10. Being strongly inferred from other beliefs

11. Failing to be inferred from other beliefs

*12. Having nervous mannerisms in speech

IV. **For each group of statements below, determine whether their logical connectedness is strong, weak, or failed.**

1. Columbus was married. Therefore Columbus wasn't single.
   SAMPLE ANSWER: strong logical connectedness

2. Pierre is French. Therefore he is European. _____

* 3. The Yucatán ruins are well preserved. Therefore Yucatán is worth visiting. _____

4. Triangles have three internal angles. Isosceles triangles are triangles. Therefore cats are feline. _____

5. My dog, Fido, barks. Therefore all dogs bark. _____

* 6. She is the string quartet's first violin. Therefore she is a musician.
   _____

7. A home run has been scored. Therefore a tennis match is going on.
   _____

8. A loud sound broke the calm of night. Therefore there is some thunder in the clouds. _____

* 9. If candies are nutritious, they are not delicious. Therefore if candies are not nutritious, they are delicious. _____

10. We visit only cities that have nice weather. Last year we visited Winnipeg and Seattle. Therefore these cities have nice weather.
    _____

V. **Determine whether each of the following scenarios is possible or impossible. For each one that is impossible, explain why.**

1. A group of statements that is logically connected and it isn't.
   SAMPLE ANSWER: Impossible. This scenario is contradictory

2. A statement that is neither supported nor unsupported by the evidence. _____

* 3. A rationally acceptable group of statements that conflicts with the available evidence. _____

4. A rationally acceptable group of statements that has logical connectedness. _____

5. A rationally acceptable group of statements without rhetorical power. _____

* 6. A rhetorically powerful group of statements that has linguistic merit. _____

7. A group of statements that has logical connectedness and evidential support but lacks rational acceptability. _____

* 8. A poorly phrased passage that has linguistic merit. _____

9. A rationally unacceptable inference that lacks rhetorical power. _____

*10. An unpersuasive speech that has rhetorical power. _____

11. A speech that has neither linguistic merit nor rhetorical power. _____

12. A passage that is neither rationally acceptable nor rhetorically powerful. _____

*13. A passage that has rhetorical power. _____

14. A false statement that is supported by the evidence. _____

*15. A true statement that is unsupported by the evidence. _____

VI. Your Own Thinking Lab

1. Provide a statement that is supported by the current total evidence.

2. Provide an example of a statement that is false but was once supported by the total evidence.

3. Provide an example of a statement that is true but was once unsupported by the total evidence.

4. Provide an example of a statement that has been undermined by the total evidence.

5. Suppose you believe that there is a party in the street, but—unknown to you—your belief is false. Provide a scenario in which that belief would nonetheless be supported by the evidence.

2.3 From Belief to Statement

We've already seen that inference is the logical relation that obtains whenever at least one belief is taken to support another, and that it can also be conceived as a logical relation that obtains whenever one or more statements are offered in support of another. When thus considered, inference is often called "argument." Any argument, then, is the linguistic expression of an inference. As beliefs are the parts that make up inferences, so statements are the parts that make up an argument.

Now, what, exactly, are statements? Roughly, statements constitute the standard way to express one's beliefs by means of language. Consider:

8   Snow is white.

When someone accepts (8) in thought, the thinker entertains the belief *that snow is white*. Were (8) to be uttered, the speaker would be making the statement *that snow is white*. Either way, (8) has a certain information content—namely:

9   *That snow is white.*

As a statement, (8) could be taken to express the speaker's belief *that snow is white* provided that she is sincere and competent. The belief then has exactly the same information content as the statement: one that represents snow as being in a certain way (white). Whether a belief or statement, (8)'s information content is (9), which is complete, in the sense that it represents a state of affairs. Contents of this sort are true when things are as represented by them and false when they are not. Since any belief or statement has a content of this sort, it also has one of these truth values: it's either *true* or *false*. Clearly, that's the case of (9), whose truth value is determined by applying the rule given in Box 3. For the content of each belief or statement we are considering, we may come up with a rule along similar lines telling us its *truth*

> ### BOX 3 ■ TRUTH CONDITIONS OF (9)
>
> (9) is true if and only if snow is white and false otherwise.

conditions, which are the conditions under which that belief or statement would be true.

Propositions

We shall call "proposition" any information content with truth conditions, keeping in mind that

> Propositions
> - Are the information content of beliefs and statements.
> - Represent states of affairs.
> - Have a truth value: they are either true or false.

Consider the information content of an utterance such as

10 Snow.

(10)'s information content is an isolated *concept*. Contents of this sort are *incomplete*, in the sense that they lack a truth value: what (10) says is neither true nor false. No rule along the above lines could state truth conditions for concepts. Unlike (8), then, (10) does not express a proposition.

Note that different statements may have one and the same information content provided that they all express the same proposition. That happens when they all represent the same state of affairs and therefore have the same truth conditions. We would then say that the statements express the same proposition. For example,

11 La nieve es blanca.

12 La neige est blanche.

(11) and (12), as well as (8) above, have the same content. Suppose speakers of English, Spanish, and French sincerely uttered (8), (11), and (12), respectively. Their statements would each represent the same state of affairs and therefore express the same proposition or complete content—namely, *that snow is white*. Such speakers would, however, be making different statements. After all, (8), (11), and (12) are different sentences.

2.4 Uses of Language

Ordinarily, we use our language in a number of ways: for example, to assert or deny propositions, to ask questions, make promises, issue commands, express our feelings, greet someone, and so on. All such ways fall into one or another of three basic categories:

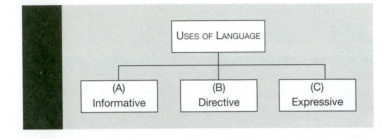

Any utterance made to convey information, as when we assert (or deny) that something is the case, report a state of affairs, describe how things are, etc., belongs to A. Since informative utterances have complete contents, they are either true or false, depending on whether things are as represented by them. Here language is put at the service of representing how things are. *B* comprises linguistic expressions such as questions, commands, and requests. In utterances falling within this category, language is put at the service of getting things to be as the speaker directs. *C* includes utterances whose function is to express that part of the speaker's inner world which is made up of feelings and psychological attitudes such as desires and fears.

Types of Sentences

The sentences of our language exemplify a variety of grammatical forms that can be grouped in four basic types: declarative, interrogative, imperative, and exclamatory. Each of these sentence types is most suited for utterances falling within one or another of the three basic uses of language. There is a straightforward connection between *declarative* sentences and the informative use of language and between *exclamatory* sentences

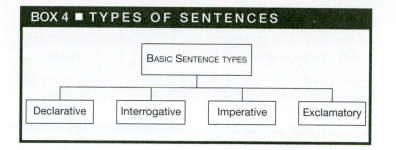

BOX 4 ■ TYPES OF SENTENCES

BASIC SENTENCE TYPES

Declarative | Interrogative | Imperative | Exclamatory

and the expressive use of language. *Imperative* sentences are the principal means of making requests and issuing commands, while *interrogative* sentences are commonly used to ask questions. Both imperative and interrogative sentences are, then, linked to the directive use of language. Exclamatory sentences constitute the primary vehicle for expressing the speaker's inner world.

By now, you may be wondering about the relations between these four sentence types and the three basic uses of language mentioned above. Given that each of the sentence types is suited to function *directly* in only one of these basic uses of language, the picture of their relations is as follows:

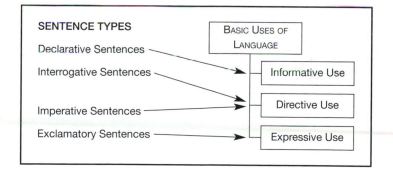

SENTENCE TYPES

BASIC USES OF LANGUAGE

Declarative Sentences
Interrogative Sentences → Informative Use
Imperative Sentences → Directive Use
Exclamatory Sentences → Expressive Use

Although *interrogative* and *imperative* sentences illustrate two different sentence types, they both serve the directive use of language. The other relations are straightforward: declarative and exclamatory sentences are more suitable to the informative and the expressive uses of language respectively.

Declarative Sentences

Of the above four sentence types, it is chiefly declarative sentences that are of interest to logical thinking. This is because

> Declarative sentences are those typically used to make statements.

We've seen that statements, like beliefs, amount to fundamental units or building blocks of reasoning. When speakers are sincere and competent, what they state is what they believe. So declarative sentences constitute the sentence type most suitable to express belief. As we shall discover, however, other types of sentences can be uttered to this end, depending on the context.

2.5 Indirect and Nonliteral Language

It is also the case that interrogative, imperative, and exclamatory sentences, although they are the standard means of the directive and expressive uses of language, each could be put at the service of other uses. Consider the interrogative sentence

13 How long do I have to wait in line?

Its direct function is that of asking a question. It therefore falls within category *B*, the directive use of language (since it's trying to get someone to give an answer or to speed up the service). Yet as we shall see in the next section, in a certain context, questions such as (13) might also express one's feelings (here, exasperation after a long wait). In the latter cases, interrogative sentences are indirectly fulfilling an expressive use of language. Similarly, consider

14 Please be punctual.

Ordinarily, an utterance of this imperative sentence would have as its typical function that of issuing a command, which falls under *B*, the directive use of language. But in a certain context it may fall under *C*, the expressive use—for example, when uttered ironically to express disapproval of the addressee's obsession with punctuality. Exclamatory sentences could also have an indirect use. Consider an utterance of

15 I wish Mike were more conversational.

Although this would ordinarily fall within the expressive category C when used directly, it could also be used indirectly–for example, to convey the information that Mike is not conversational. In that case, (15) would fall under A, the informative use. But sentences such as (13), (14), and (15) cannot be used to assert (or deny) a proposition *directly*. Thus none of them can be the direct means of making a statement.

Indirect Language

In describing the above relations between sentence types and uses of language, we are assuming direct language: one in which a sentence of any of the four types is employed with its standard link to one of the three basic uses. Moreover, we are assuming literal language: one in which a sentence is uttered (or written) to express a proposition that results from combining the concepts that make it up. But language is often used indirectly and/or nonliterally. In a case of indirect use, a sentence is uttered with a function different from that standardly associated with sentences of the same type. In a case of nonliteral use, a sentence expresses a proposition other than the one it would convey if the concepts that make it up were taken at face value. Let's consider both indirect and nonliteral uses of language in turn.

BOX 5 ■ NONLITERAL AND INDIRECT LANGUAGE

Nonliteral Language: A linguistic expression is used nonliterally when it has a content different from the one it would have when the contents of its parts and their combination are taken at face value.

Indirect Language: A linguistic expression is used indirectly when it has a function different from the one standardly associated with expressions of that type.

When used indirectly, a sentence of one type is uttered with a function often associated with sentences of another type. Consider the interrogative sentence

16 Can you pass me the salt?

When used directly, (16) asks whether the addressee is *able to pass the salt* to the speaker. Yet in a situation where it is *common knowledge* that the addressee is in such a position, (16) should be interpreted as indirectly making a request: namely, that the addressee pass the salt to the speaker. It then has a directive use, which is standardly performed by an utterance of the imperative sentence

17 Pass me the salt.

Similarly, consider the sentence

18 What would human life be without art?

It may be directly used to ask a question—for instance, by psychologists speculating about some hypothetical scenarios. But used indirectly, (18) would appear to convey the information *that art is necessary for human life*; it would therefore fall within category *A*, the informative use of language. Exactly the same function could be directly served by an utterance of the declarative sentence

19 Art is necessary for human life.

Nonliteral Language

When used nonliterally, a sentence expresses a proposition different from what it would express if the concepts that make it up were taken at face value. Metaphors constitute a common type of nonliteral use of language. For example, consider an utterance of

20 No donkey does well in symbolic logic.

In a certain context, this literally expresses a proposition about donkeys—one concerning their poor performance in symbolic logic. Yet in another context, it could metaphorically express a proposition about people—namely, one about individuals who perform poorly in symbolic logic!

As far as logical thinking is concerned, indirect and nonliteral uses of language are not welcome, for they often obscure the logical relations among statements and ultimately among beliefs. Even so, logical thinking must take account of natural language, the sort of language that makes indirect and nonliteral uses unavoidable. What, then, are we to do? We must follow these rules:

> When doing informal logic,
> 1. Be tolerant about indirect and/or nonliteral uses of language.
> 2. If possible, recast
>   - Indirect expressions as direct
>   - Nonliteral expressions as literal

A related question arises when we consider fictional language, which is the language of novels, poems, song lyrics, and the like. Here the rule is

> Even in cases where fictional sentences may appear to be informative, keep in mind that they always fall within category *C*, the expressive use of language.

Exercises

VII. Review Questions

1. What is a statement?
2. What is a proposition?
3. Could the same proposition be expressed by different statements? Explain.
4. In which sense, if any, are thought and language parallel?
5. What are the uses of language?
6. Define each of the four basic sentence types.
7. How are the uses of language related to the sentence types?
8. What is indirect language? Provide two examples of your own.
9. What is nonliteral language? Provide two examples of your own.
10. Which sentence type is commonly associated with the informative use of language? Explain.

11. Could an interrogative sentence have an informative use? If so, how? If not, why not?

12. How do logical thinkers deal with indirect language? And what about nonliteral language?

VIII. Which use of language is illustrated by each of the following?

1. At first, America was not called "America."
   SAMPLE ANSWER: Informative use

2. Why was Jane traveling alone? _____

* 3. How wonderful! _____

4. That animal is a beaver. _____

* 5. Whether you like it or not, you must move on with your life.
   _____

6. One after another, they all signed up. _____

* 7. Each person has some natural talents. _____

8. We must go to bed early tonight. _____

9. This is amazing! _____

*10. Let's hope that Boris's problems will be over soon. _____

11. Evolution vs. creation is an endless debate. _____

*12. Try a little bit harder. _____

13. There is life on Mars. _____

14. Who is telling the story? _____

*15. What an odd statement to make! _____

IX. For each of the following, determine its sentence type.

1. Fido is a dog.
   SAMPLE ANSWER: Declarative sentence

2. Snow isn't white. _____

3. God exists. _____

* 4. Please shut the door. _____

5. What time is it? _____

6. Good Lord! _____

* 7. Winter days are short. _____

8. Some dentists have clean teeth. _____

9. Not all cars need gas. _____

*10. What is your favorite dish? _____

11. How is John? _____

12. Today is Monday. _____

*13. The Amazon forest is being depleted. _____

14. The moon was a ghostly galleon, tossed upon cloudy seas.
_____

15. Keep your promise. _____

*16. Oh, my gosh! _____

17. What are you up to? _____

18. Make it short. _____

*19. I have a headache. _____

20. There is life after death. _____

X. For each sentence, identify its type and a possible indirect use. Explain.

1. Isn't it crazy to think that there is no life after death?

    SAMPLE ANSWER: Interrogative sentence. Indirect use: informative. (The speaker is, in effect, *asserting that there is life after death*.)

2. Can Jill play tennis with that old racket? _____

* 3. When are you going to stop making fun of poor Harry?
_____

4. Gosh, the bank account is empty! _____

* 5. The king is dead! _____

6. It is a sunny day. _____

* 7. Is he really sleepy? _____

8. That is not funny. _____

9. What are you doing in the dark? _____

*10. Tomorrow is another day. _____

XI. Interpret each of the following sentences in two ways: (A) literally and (B) nonliterally.

1. This room is a pigsty.

   SAMPLE ANSWER: (A) This room is used to house pigs.
   (B) This room is dirty.

2. He is Hercules. _____

* 3. Those players are robots. _____

4. A rose grows in this garden. _____

5. No parrots allowed here. _____

* 6. We are approaching a volcano. _____

7. That's the sticking point. _____

8. We are Romeo and Juliet. _____

* 9. Jim wears two hats. _____

10. I am not Bill Gates. _____

11. They went the extra mile. _____

*12. That city is an anthill. _____

13. She is a saint. _____

14. My heart told me that she was the one for me. _____

*15. He's toast. _____

XII. YOUR OWN THINKING LAB

1. Provide three sentences of your own and interpret them (A) directly and (B) indirectly.

   SAMPLE ANSWER: Isn't it time to go to bed?

   (A) Directive: to request information about whether it's time to go to bed

(B) Informative: to inform someone that it is time to go to bed

(C) Directive: to order someone to go to bed

2. Provide three sentences of your own and interpret them (a) literally, and (b) a nonliterally.

SAMPLE ANSWER: Words are cheap.

(A) Words don't cost anything.

(B) It's easier to talk than to *act* in accordance with what one says.

(C) That's easier to say than to prove.

3. Record a conversations with a friend and then identify its nonliteral and indirect uses of language.

4. Make a list of six common nonliteral expressions that you believe are overused.

2.6 The Philosopher's Corner

The Study of Language and Its Dimensions

Two contemporary disciplines, philosophy of language and linguistics, are devoted to the study of *public* or *natural* language—the languages spoken by speech communities, such as English, Chinese, Swahili, Portuguese, and so on. This common everyday sort of language is to be contrasted with *private* languages (which are devised by individuals for their own use) and also with *artificial* languages, which include Esperanto and the formal languages devised by logicians and mathematicians. Linguists often focus on *phonology*, the study of the sound structure of a language, and *syntax*, the study of its grammar, and thus devote themselves to identifying the basic elements of language and the rules that govern the permissible combinations of those elements. Philosophers, however, usually focus on other dimensions of natural language. Some are interested in *pragmatics*, the dimension that concerns various aspects affecting the *use* of linguistic expressions, such as context—that is, the circumstances in which a linguistic expression is uttered (spoken or written). But many others devote themselves to *semantics*, the dimension of language that concerns the *meaning* and *reference* of linguistic expressions. The reference of an expression is what the expression applies to, while its meaning is its information content (or what is said by it). Consider

21 The author of *Innocents Abroad* grew up in Hannibal, Missouri.

22 The author of *Huckleberry Finn* grew up in Hannibal, Missouri.

Roughly, since "The author of *Innocents Abroad*" and "The author of *Huckleberry Finn*" apply to the same person, Mark Twain, these expressions have the same reference. And since other things are equal in (21) and (22), these sentences have the same reference. Yet on a traditional view, since "The author of *Innocents Abroad*" and "The author of *Huckleberry Finn*" do not present their referent in the same way, they do not have the same meaning. Reference and meaning constitute the semantic features (or properties) of a language.

Type and Token

Some other distinctions drawn for language also matter to logic. These include those between "type" and "token" and between "use" and "mention." Let's consider the first of these. *Tokens* are instances or occurrences of a certain *type*. To understand the distinction, think about the letters that make up "kettle": the word features six letter *tokens* that are instances of four letter *types* ("k," "e," "t," and "l").

Or, consider this scenario. One day Smith awakens with a toothache in his upper left molars. He goes to see his dentist. But when he arrives in the waiting room, he finds another patient ahead of him: it's Bill Clinton. In conversation with Clinton, Smith learns that Clinton also has a toothache in his upper left molars. Bill says to Smith, "I feel your pain." Now in one sense, of course, this is true: Clinton also has a pain in his upper left molars. So he has *the same type* of pain Smith does ("your pain," in this sense, means "upper-left-molar pain"). But in another sense, it's false: Clinton can't literally feel *Smith's* pain. Only Smith can feel that! (Here, "your pain" means "your private sensation of discomfort.") In other words, Smith's *token* of upper-left-molar pain is distinct from Clinton's *token* of upper-left-molar pain, even though both tokens are of the same type.

Use and Mention

Another contrast worth drawing distinguishes expressions that are *used* in a linguistic context from those that are merely *mentioned*. The reference of an expression that is used is its customary one, while that of an expression that is mentioned is the expression itself. For example, the word "dog" is used in

23 Lassie is a dog,

while it is mentioned in:

24 "Dog" is monosyllabic.

When an expression is being mentioned rather than used, it is customary to put it within quotes, as in (24). Here is another example:

25 Although "Archie Leach" is an authentic and down-to-earth name, when the real Archie Leach went into the entertainment business, his manager thought that he would do better as "Cary Grant." But Cary Grant was originally named "Archie Leach." Since whoever was Cary Grant had also been Archie Leach, therefore "Cary Grant" and "Archie Leach" refer to the same person.

The quotes around an expression that is *mentioned* "lock it in," since whatever may be truly said of *the expression itself* might not be truly said of *that to which the expression applies* in a context where the expression is *used* instead. A failure to recognize the difference between use and mention may result in inferences that fail. For example,

26 Cary Grant is the leading actor in the film *North by Northwest*. "Cary Grant" is a stage name. Therefore, a stage name is the leading actor in "*North by Northwest*."

Exercises

XIII. Use the type/token distinction to explain what has gone wrong in each of the following exchanges:

* 1. BETH: Yesterday, we went to see *The Nutcracker*. The best part of the ballet was the scene where twenty kids dance wearing the same mouse costume.

    BOB: How could twenty kids possibly fit into the same mouse costume?

  2. JACK: I said that John is an unmarried man, not that he is a bachelor.

    JILL: But that's the same as saying that John is a bachelor.

* 3. MAY: You and Brian are reading the same book.

    MOE: Really? How can I be reading the same book that Brian is reading? I haven't seen him for a long time.

  4. SAUL: The Andersons adore Siamese cats and recently got one.

    SAM: They then have the same cat as their neighbors.

XIV. The use/mention distinction can account for the invalidity of the following arguments. Explain how.

  1. To be a sister is to be a female sibling. "Sister" has six letters. Therefore, "female sibling" has six letters.

* 2. This glass contains what Walter would call "water." Water is H_2O. Thus, this glass contains what Walter would call "H_2O."

  3. "Mark Twain" is a pen name. Samuel Langhorne Clemens and Mark Twain are the same. It follows that "Samuel Langhorne Clemens" is a pen name.

* 4. In 1888, Londoners feared that Jack the Ripper would strike again. "Jack the Ripper" is a name given to the unidentified perpetrator of those sensational murders. Thus, in 1888, Londoners feared that a name given to the unidentified perpetrator of those sensational murders would strike again.

XV. In each of the following passages, put quotes as needed.

* 1. For some philosophers, the expressions mercy killing and voluntary active euthanasia mean the same. But others argue that there is no such thing as voluntary active euthanasia. If they are right, then voluntary active euthanasia is a misleading expression, and the

practice sometimes called euthanasia cannot be the same as what's called mercy killing.

2. What is called mind could very well be nothing over and above what's called brain—perhaps also including what's called nervous system. But from this, it doesn't follow that the mind is the brain.

3. Even though water is H_2O, that is not equivalent to saying that the word water means the same as the chemical formula H_2O. If water and H_2O meant the same, then speakers who don't know that water is H_2O could not use the word water competently.

* 4. Suppose that the term knowledge is equivalent in meaning to the expression, justified true belief. In addition, suppose that we have a clear idea of what true and belief each means. Even so, to know what knowledge means we would need to know what justification means.

■ Writing Project

Write a long email (about 300 words) to a hypothetical friend, where you inform her or him about a rhetorically skillful yet unscrupulous speaker you've seen in action recently. First describe the speech and its context in detail, then assess it critically in light of what you've learned about rational acceptability and warn your friend of the dangers of being misled by such speakers.

■ Chapter Summary

Standards for Rationally Acceptable Beliefs

1. Logical connectedness: Beliefs must be connected in the right way. If some are entertained as reasons for another, we should ask whether they really do provide such reasons.

2. Evidential support: In the case of a great number of beliefs, what matters also is whether they agree with the total evidence.

Standards that Fall Beyond Rational Acceptability

1. Linguistic merit

2. Rhetorical power

Evidence for a Belief must Not Be Confused with Its Truth

1. Some beliefs might be *supported by the evidence yet **false.***

2. Other beliefs might be *unsupported by the evidence yet **true.***

3. This suggests that the question of *what it is for a belief to **be** true* is different from the question of *what evidence counts as a reason for thinking that* some particular belief is true.

Statements Express Beliefs (when the speaker is sincere and the circumstances are normal)

1. The information content of beliefs and statements are PROPOSITIONS.

2. Any propositional content has **truth conditions.**

3. Statements and beliefs have **truth values**—each is either **true** or **false.**

Uses of Language and Types of Sentence

1. | **Sentence Type:** | **Uses of Language:** |
   |---|---|
   | DECLARATIVE | INFORMATIVE |
   | INTERROGATIVE | DIRECTIVE |
   | IMPERATIVE | EXPRESSIVE |
   | EXCLAMATORY | |

2. In logic, our concern is chiefly with the **informative function**; hence, with **declarative sentences.**

Indirect Language

Sentences of one type are used to serve the purpose of a *different* type.

Nonliteral Language

Sentences are used metaphorically or ironically.

The Dimensions of Language

1. *Syntax* concerns the relation among expressions of a language. This dimension is captured by rules of grammar

prescribing how to form and transform the expressions of that language.

2. *Semantics* concerns the meaning and reference of simple and compound expressions. The **meaning** of an expressions is its content, and its **reference** is, if anything, what the expression is about.

3. *Pragmatics* concerns aspects of an expression that arise from its use. This dimension is captured by rules prescribing how to employ expressions of a language.

Type vs. Token

Tokens are instances or occurrences of a certain *type*.

Use vs. Mention

The reference of an expression that is used is its customary one, while that of an expression that is mentioned is the expression itself.

■ Key Words

Logical connectedness
Evidential support
Truth value
Truth conditions rule
Proposition
Rhetorical power
Linguistic merit
Informative use
Directive use
Expressive use
Exclamatory sentence

Declarative sentence
Interrogative sentence
Imperative sentence
Indirect language
Nonliteral language
Syntax
Semantics
Pragmatics
Use/mention
Type/token

3 | CHAPTER

The Virtues of Belief

This chapter looks more closely at the nature of belief, noting that beliefs are the building blocks of our inferences. In connection with this you'll learn about such topics as

- Belief, disbelief, and nonbelief, understood as different psychological attitudes.
- Crucial *virtues* of belief that are to be cultivated: accuracy, truth, reasonableness, consistency, conservatism, and revisability.
- The *vices* of belief that are to be avoided: inaccuracy, falsity, unreasonableness, inconsistency, dogmatism, and relativism.
- The difference between empirical reasons and conceptual reasons.

- The concept of contradiction and the notion of logically possible worlds.
- The way in which rationality and irrationality amount to a "supervirtue" and a "supervice," respectively.
- The philosophical problems raised by evaluative beliefs when such beliefs are expressed in evaluative sentences: in particular, the problem of whether such sentences can express propositions.

3.1 Belief, Disbelief, and Nonbelief

A belief is one of the many psychological attitudes a person may have toward a proposition—which, as we have seen, is a content that represents a certain state of affairs. Consider, for example, the proposition that

1   Dogs are carnivorous.

Anyone who believes (1) has the psychological attitude of accepting *that dogs are carnivorous*. The person takes that content to be the case. Under normal circumstances, if asked whether (1) is true, she would assent. Assuming she's sincere and competent, she would voice her belief by stating (1). In fact, she could also state

2   *It is true* that dogs are carnivorous.

3   *It is the case* that dogs are carnivorous.

And she might state many other sentences that are logically equivalent to these (that is, sentences that are logically the same as these).

If we use "*S*" to stand for a subject (or person), "*P*" for a proposition, and "believing *that P*" for the psychological attitude of accepting *that P*, we can define belief as in Box 1.

Note that the definition of belief in Box 1 invokes normal circumstances and the speaker's sincerity. In their absence, it may be that none of the described parallels between what a person *S* believes and says do obtain, even in cases where *S* believes *that P*. Because there are deceivers (whose words misrepresent the beliefs they actually have) and self-deceivers (who

BOX 1 ■ BELIEF

Assuming normal circumstances and *S*'s sincerity, *S* has a belief *that P* if and only if

- *S* accepts *that P*.
- If *S* is asked, "Is *P* true?" *S* would assent.
- If *S* is asked, "What do you make of *P*?"
  S would assert sentences such as
  ✔ "*P*."
  ✔ "*P* is true."
  ✔ "It is the case *that P*."

deny the beliefs they actually have), we must assume the *speaker's sincerity* when we draw these distinctions. And because sometimes *S* might, out of coercion, delusion, or other impairment say something she doesn't in fact believe, we must assume *normal circumstances*. These include the speaker's being *competent*—that is, not mentally compromised or impaired in any way.

But what about those who simply don't have a certain belief—say one with the content (1) above? The psychological attitude of anyone who does not believe that

1 Dogs are carnivorous.

may be either a *disbelief* or a *nonbelief* involving that content. Let's first consider a disbelief about (1), which is a belief with content such as

4 Dogs are *not* carnivorous.

5 *It is false* that dogs are carnivorous.

or

6 *It is not the case* that dogs are carnivorous.

Under normal circumstances, a person who holds any of these beliefs has the psychological attitude of rejecting (1). If asked whether (1) is true, she would dissent. And to voice her disbelief, she would deny (1)—for example, by asserting (4). Disbelieving *that P*, then, amounts to having the psychological attitude of rejecting *that P*.

BOX 2 ■ DISBELIEF

Assuming normal circumstances and *S*'s sincerity, *S* has a disbelief *that P* if and only if

- *S* rejects *that P*.
- If *S* is asked, "Is *P* true?" *S* would dissent.
- If *S* is asked, "What do you make of *P*?"
  S would deny sentences such as
  - ✔ "*P*."
  - ✔ "*P* is true."
  - ✔ "It is the case *that P*."

What about those who neither believe nor disbelieve that dogs are carnivorous? They have a *nonbelief* involving that content. Under normal circumstances, they would neither accept nor reject it. If asked whether that content is true, they might shrug, giving no sign of assent or dissent. Box 3 summarizes all these reactions, which are important for determining whether someone has a nonbelief about a certain proposition.

Nonbelieving *that P*, then, amounts to lacking any belief or disbelief about *P*. The corresponding psychological attitude is

BOX 3 ■ NONBELIEF

Assuming normal circumstances and *S*'s sincerity, *S* has a nonbelief *that P* if and only if

- *S* neither accepts, nor rejects, *that P*.
- If *S* is asked, "Is *P* true?" *S* would neither assent nor dissent.
- If *S* is asked, "What do you make of *P*?"
  S would neither assert nor deny sentences such as
  - ✔ "*P*."
  - ✔ "Not *P*."
  - ✔ "*P* is true."
  - ✔ "*P* is false."

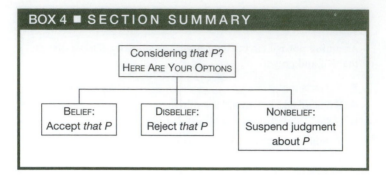

BOX 4 ■ SECTION SUMMARY

Considering *that P*?
HERE ARE YOUR OPTIONS

| BELIEF:
Accept *that P* | DISBELIEF:
Reject *that P* | NONBELIEF:
Suspend judgment
about *P* |

that of suspending judgment about it. We should bear in mind that whenever we are considering whether to accept or reject a content (such as *that dogs are carnivorous*), there is also the option of withholding belief, which amounts to suspending judgment. The outcome of any such situation is outlined in the summary in Box 4.

Whether we hold a belief, disbelief, or nonbelief toward a proposition, thinking logically can help in developing the attitude that would be most adequate. This is important, since our beliefs are the building blocks of our reasoning. Here the rule is that, to keep the whole edifice sound, one must use high-quality building blocks, and do regular maintenance. How, then, are we to tell which building blocks of reasoning are high-quality and which aren't? That is the topic of our next section.

Exercises

I. Review Questions

1. What is a belief? And what sort of content is eligible for being the content of a belief?
2. What is the difference between a disbelief and a nonbelief?
3. Is nonbelief a kind of belief? If yes, why? If not, why not?
4. Think of two scenarios of your own where a person has a nonbelief.
5. Is disbelief a kind of belief? If yes, why? If not, why not?
6. In what does suspending judgment consist?
7. To report a speaker's belief on the basis of her statement, her *sincerity* is a necessary assumption. Explain why.
8. To report a speaker's belief of the basis of her statement, her *competence* is a necessary assumption. Explain why.

II. **Assuming that each of the following is a sincere state-ment made under normal circumstances, indicate whether it expresses a belief, disbelief, or nonbelief:**

1. I accept that the earth revolves.

   SAMPLE ANSWER: Belief

2. I reject that the Pope is in Rome. _____

* 3. I neither accept nor reject that God exists. _____

4. It is false that cats are feline. _____

* 5. It is the case that Newton was smart. _____

6. It is not the case that the moon is bigger than the earth. _____

* 7. I suspend judgment about the belief that there is life after death. _____

8. I neither accept nor reject the belief that there are UFOs. _____

* 9. Dick Cheney is bald. _____

10. No zealots can be trusted. _____

III. **Suppose that, under normal circumstances, a sincere and competent speaker utters the sentences below. Report the belief, disbelief, or nonbelief thus expressed. If two or more equivalent reports are possible, include at least two.**

1. The earth is a planet.

   SAMPLE ANSWER: The belief that the earth is a planet.

2. The earth is not a star. _____

3. It is false that earth is a star. _____

* 4. It is neither true nor false that the sun will rise tomorrow. _____

5. Either the earth is a star or it isn't. _____

* 6. It is not the case that the earth is not a planet. _____

7. It is not the case that the earth is a planet. _____

* 8. It is neither true nor false that galaxies are flying outward. _____

9. Triangles are not figures. _____

*10. I am thinking. _____

11. I am not thinking. _____

*12. Is there life after death? I cannot say. _____

13. UFOs do not exist. _____

*14. I am agnostic about whether humans are the product of evolution or Divine creation. _____

15. If Pluto isn't a star, then it is a planet. _____

IV. YOUR OWN THINKING LAB

* **1.** Explain why normal circumstances and the speaker's sincerity are needed assumptions in exercises (II) and (III) above.

2. Provide two examples of belief.

3. Report each of your two examples in a different yet logically equivalent way.

4. Provide two examples of disbeliefs and two of nonbeliefs.

5. Report in two different yet logically equivalent ways your examples of disbeliefs and nonbeliefs.

* **6.** Suppose you were considering the proposition *that there is life after death*. What attitudes are your options? Report those attitudes.

3.2 Belief's Virtues and Vices

Among the traits or features of beliefs, some contribute to good reasoning and others to bad. We may think of the good-making features as virtues and of the bad-making ones as vices. Prominent among such features are rationality and irrationality, whose significance in logical thinking justifies considering them a supervirtue and a supervice, respectively. Why are they so significant? Because rationality marks the limits of acceptable reasoning. Irrational beliefs are beyond that limit. In their case, the aims of reasoning are, as we shall see, no longer achievable. In this section, we take

BOX 5 ■ SOME OF BELIEF'S VIRTUES AND VICES

Virtues	Vices
Accuracy	Inaccuracy
Truth	Falsity
Reasonableness	Unreasonableness
Consistency	Inconsistency
Conservatism	Relativism
Revisability	Dogmatism

up some virtues and vices of belief, leaving rationality and irrationality for the next section. The features of beliefs in our agenda are listed in Box 5.

First, note that since logical thinkers wish to avoid beliefs with bad-making features, someone might think that it is advisable to have only nonbeliefs, for if we didn't have any beliefs (or disbeliefs) at all, we wouldn't have any beliefs with bad-making features! But this advice is self-defeating, for it is not possible to have only nonbeliefs. Assuming the speaker's sincerity, the claim that logical thinkers are better off without beliefs (and disbeliefs) itself expresses a belief. As logical thinkers, we must have some beliefs, so our aim should be simply to have as many beliefs with good-making features and as few with bad-making features as possible. Our aim, in other words, is that of maximizing the virtues and minimizing the vices in our beliefs. To say that a belief has a virtue is, of course, to praise it—while to say it has a vice is to criticize it. In what follows, we'll take up each of the virtues and vices listed above.

3.3 Accuracy and Truth

Accuracy and Inaccuracy

To have an acceptable degree of accuracy, a belief must either represent, or get close to representing, the facts. In the former case, the belief is true; in the latter, it is merely close to being true or approximately true. We may have the belief that

BOX 6 ■ ACCURACY AND INACCURACY

When a belief is true, it has maximal accuracy; when it is false, it has maximal inaccuracy.

    7   Brasilia is the capital of Brazil.

This belief represents things as they actually are, and it is therefore true. True beliefs have the highest degree of accuracy. On the other hand, one may have a false belief such as

    8   Rio is the capital of Brazil.

False beliefs have the highest degree of inaccuracy, simply because they neither represent, nor get close to representing, things as they actually are.

    At the same time, there may be related disbeliefs, such as

    9   Rio is *not* the capital of Brazil.

    10 *It is false* that Rio is the capital of Brazil.

These are true and therefore maximally accurate.

Truth and Falsity

Ideally, as logical thinkers, we believe what is true and disbelieve what is false. But it is often difficult to tell which beliefs are true and which are false. Thus, sometimes we end up mistakenly believing what is false—as when people in the Middle Ages believed that

    11 The sun revolves around the earth.

Such people were, of course, later shown to be mistaken. Note, however, that (11) was also never *accurate*, since its content not only failed to represent the facts truly but (most crucially) never even got close to representing them. A belief can be more or less accurate depending on how close it is to representing the facts as they are—that is, depending on how close it is to getting the facts right. Any such belief is *merely* accurate, since it falls short of being true. For example,

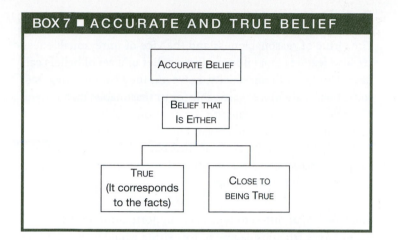

BOX 7 ■ ACCURATE AND TRUE BELIEF

ACCURATE BELIEF

BELIEF THAT
IS EITHER

TRUE
(It corresponds
to the facts)

CLOSE TO
BEING TRUE

12 France is hexagonal.

(12) is roughly accurate but not accurate enough to count as strictly true (e.g. not good enough for a cartographer). Similarly,

13 Lord Raglan won the Battle of Alma.[1]

(13) is accurate. But should we say it's true? Well, it's *approximately* true. In fact the conclusion of that Crimean War battle was to some degree ambiguous, although the British did seem to have the upper hand. It's not *clearly wrong* to say that Lord Raglan "won" it. On our definition, accuracy is plainly a matter of degree, for it depends on the contents of beliefs, and some contents are closer to representing the facts than others. Some beliefs are thus more accurate than others.

Yet truth and falsity are not a matter of degree at all: each belief is either true or false. It makes no sense to say of a belief that it is "more true" or "less true" (or "false") than another belief. A belief is either true or it isn't. At the same time, both accuracy and truth are virtues that either a single belief or a set of beliefs may have (likewise for the vices of inaccuracy and falsity). But individual beliefs and groups of beliefs may lack such virtues and still be *reasonable*. How is this possible? To answer that, let us consider reasonableness.

---

[1] *These two examples (12 and 13) we owe to J. L. Austin, who used them in "Performative-Constative"* (La Philosophie Analitique, Cahiers de Royaumont, 1962).

3.4 Reasonableness

The virtue of reasonableness and the vice of unreasonableness are also features that either a single belief or a set of beliefs can have. Unlike truth and falsity, however, they come in degrees: some beliefs are more reasonable (or unreasonable) than others. Their degree of reasonableness depends on *how their contents are supported* or on *what their grounds are*. We may say that

THE VIRTUES OF BELIEF

> A belief is reasonable if and only if it is well supported. Otherwise, it is unreasonable.

Since beliefs of different types are supported differently, how a belief might attain its degree of this virtue would vary according to its type.

Empirical and Conceptual Reasonableness

In other words, what's required for a belief to be reasonable varies according to what sort of belief it is. For example, consider empirical (or observational) beliefs such as these:

14 Fido is barking.

15 Dogs bark.

What's required for them to be reasonable differs from what's required for nonobservational beliefs to be reasonable, such as

16 Ophthalmologists are eye doctors.

17 A Brother is a male sibling.

The grounds for (16) and (17) are conceptual: it is sufficient to understand the concepts involved to realize that each of the contents expressed by these sentences is true. The truth of (16) is clear to anyone who has mastered the concepts "ophthalmologist" and "eye doctor"—as is the truth of (17) to anyone who has mastered the concepts "brother" and "male sibling." Thus (16) and (17) are both reasonable, since each is supported conceptually. For conceptual beliefs, reasonableness can be defined as follows:

> A conceptual belief is reasonable if and only if its content is such that to understand it is to realize that it is true.

Reasonable conceptual beliefs, then, are those that *go without saying* to anyone who understands their contents.

By contrast, (14) and (15) are not eligible for this kind of support. Still, such beliefs would clearly be reasonable in some circumstances and unreasonable in others. How, then, can we draw this distinction for beliefs like (14) and (15)? Suppose that someone believes falsely that her dog, Fido, is barking now. That is, she believes (14), even though she knows that Fido has been mute for many years. When challenged, she engages in what is plainly a case of *wishful thinking*: her desire that Fido could bark somehow makes her believe that the dog is barking. In this scenario, (14) would be unreasonable, simply because the standard rule here is

> To be reasonable, empirical beliefs must be supported either by evidence or by inference from evidence.

Call "evidence" the outcome of the sensory experience of seeing, hearing, touching, tasting, and/or smelling. Thus, if as a result of *seeing* Fido's barking behavior and *hearing* him barking one comes to believe (14), then under normal circumstances that sensory experience itself would be evidence for (14), which would therefore render it a reasonable belief. Trustworthy testimony also counts as evidence, since we may rightly take it to be vicarious observation. Being supported by the evidence, then, is all that's usually needed for a belief like (14) to be reasonable.

On the other hand, to score high in reasonableness, beliefs such as (15) (*that dogs bark*) must be supported *in part* by the evidence and *in part* by other beliefs or inference. Evidence is understood here as before: the outcome of observation—which, for (15), consists in seeing and hearing a number of dogs barking. But (15) is the same as

15' *All* dogs bark.

Therefore one would need more than simply the first-hand evidence from observing some barking dogs to support it. After all, it is impossible to observe *all* barking dogs. Yet (15) seems well supported and therefore reasonable. What else, apart from evidence, is contributing to its support? Other beliefs are required, such as:

18 A great number of dogs have been observed.

19 They all barked.

On the basis of (18) and (19), it is reasonable to think *that dogs bark*. But if (15) is supported by (18) and (19), then the relation among these is that of inference: (15) is inferred from (18) and (19) in the nonconclusive sense of "inference" discussed in Chapter 1.

For empirical beliefs, then, evidence and inference are the two standard routes to reasonableness. Generally, when such beliefs lack the support of either of these two, they could then be said to have instead a substantial degree of unreasonableness. Yet keep in mind that for beliefs of other types, the criteria of reasonableness may be different.

3.5 Consistency

Accuracy, truth, and reasonableness are virtues that a single belief may have. Consistency, on the other hand, is a virtue that only a *set* of beliefs, two or more of them, can have—and likewise for the vice of inconsistency. But what does "consistency" mean?

Defining "Consistency" and "Inconsistency"

A good place to start for a definition of "consistency" is "*inconsistency*," since these two words are interdefinable: once one of them is defined, the other can be defined by putting in place the necessary negations. Let's begin with "inconsistency," defined thus:

> A set of beliefs is *inconsistent* if and only if its members *could not all be true at once*.

Consider, for example, the beliefs that

20 Dorothy Maloney is a senator.

21 Dorothy Maloney is a jogger.

(20) and (21) could *both be true* at the same time: Dorothy Maloney could be both a senator and a jogger. But suppose we add the belief that

22 Dorothy Maloney is *not* a public official.

Examples (20), (21), and (22) make up an *inconsistent* set, since it is impossible for all its members to be true at the same time: clearly, no one could be a senator while at the same time failing to be a public official.

Now we can define "consistency" in this way:

> A set of beliefs is *consistent* if and only if it is not inconsistent.

But a closer look at this definition would show it equivalent to this one:

> A set of beliefs is *consistent* if and only if its members could all be true at once.

To say that some beliefs are consistent is to say that they are compatible. Compatible beliefs need not *in fact* be true: it is sufficient that they *could* all be true at once. Beliefs that are actually false could make up a perfectly consistent or compatible set. We'll now examine how.

Logically Possible Propositions

Consider, for example, a set made up of the following propositions:

23 Arnold Schwarzenegger is a medical doctor.

24 Pigs fly.

(23) and (24) *could* both be true at once in some logically possible world or scenario (our world, which we'll call the "*actual world*," is just one among many such worlds). Note that the expression "could," as used here, alludes to what is *logically possible* in the sense of being *thinkable at all*. For a situation or scenario to be thinkable at all, it must be coherent (more on this in "Consistency and Possible Worlds" below).

> ## BOX 8 ■ LOGICALLY POSSIBLE PROPOSITION
>
> A proposition is logically possible if and only if there is a coherent scenario where it is true.

Logically Impossible Propositions

Propositions that are not thinkable at all are *logically impossible*, *necessarily false*, or *absurd*. For example,

25 All pigs are mammals but some pigs are not mammals.

26 Arnold Schwarzenegger is a medical doctor and he isn't.

27 Arnold Schwarzenegger is a married bachelor.

Each of these is necessarily false or logically impossible: that is, false not only as a matter of contingent fact in the actual world, but false in any possible world. Propositions of this sort are also known as "self-contradictions."

> ## BOX 9 ■ SELF-CONTRADICTION
>
> Self-contradiction: A necessarily false proposition–that is, a proposition that is false in any logically possible world.

Examples (25), (26), and (27) each illustrates a *self-contradiction*: each is *logically impossible* or *necessarily false* due to its own content or form. A quick inspection of (25) and (26) shows that there is no possible world in which either one could be true, simply because they have, respectively, these logical forms

25' **All** such-and-such are so-and-so, but **some** such-and-such **are not** so-and-so.

26' X **has** a certain feature and **does not have** it.

Each of these exhibits a certain arrangement of logical expressions (boldface above) that make it impossible for any proposition with the same arrangement to be true. Each is therefore logically self-contradictory. On the other hand, we may say that

(27) is *conceptually contradictory*: given the concepts involved, there is no possible world where (27) could be true. No one could literally be a **married bachelor**, just as no **triangle** could have **four internal angles**. Any proposition with such contents would be *absurd* or nonsensical, in the sense of *unthinkable*, since it would be impossible to comprehend its content.

Other logically impossible propositions are those that are logically incompatible or contradictory in that, if one is true, the other must be false, and vice versa. The propositions that Dorothy Maloney is a senator and that she is not a public official illustrates such contradictory propositions. By the definition of inconsistency and contradiction, any set consisting of contradictory propositions is inconsistent.

Consistency and Possible Worlds

Let's now reconsider the following set:

23 Arnold Schwarzenegger is a medical doctor.

24 Pigs fly.

These propositions, though actually false, are nonetheless consistent. For there are *possible worlds* (i.e., scenarios involving no contradiction) where they could be compatible. In those possible worlds, they are both true at the same time: for example, a world where Arnold Schwarzenegger never became a movie star but became a medical doctor instead, and where also pigs were anatomically equipped to overcome the law of gravity so that they could fly.

In light of these considerations, "consistent" and "inconsistent" may be recast alternatively as

A set of beliefs is *consistent* if and only if

- There is a logically possible world where its members could all be true at once.

A set of beliefs is *inconsistent* if and only if

- There is *no* logically possible world where its members could be all true at once.

Consistency in Logical Thinking

Given the above definitions, no set of contradictory beliefs is eligible for consistency. Inconsistency, or failure of consistency, amounts to a serious flaw, since it offends against our intuitive sense of what is logically possible and, to that extent, thinkable at all. Inconsistent beliefs are to be avoided completely. Whenever a set of beliefs is found to be inconsistent, logical thinkers must first ask whether it can be made consistent, and if it can, then they must take the necessary steps to make it so. How? By revising it in a way that eliminates the source of inconsistency. Recall our inconsistent set:

20 Dorothy Maloney is a senator.

21 Dorothy Maloney is a jogger.

22 Dorothy Maloney is not a public official.

To remove the inconsistency here requires that either (20) or (22) be abandoned.

Note, however, that although consistency is a virtue, it is not a guide to accuracy or even to reasonableness. Beliefs that could all be true in some possible scenario might, as we have seen, in fact be false and even quite preposterous in our actual world. Furthermore, like truth and falsity, neither consistency nor inconsistency comes in degrees. No set of beliefs can be "sort of consistent": it's either consistent or inconsistent. Finally, keep in mind that consistency is related to conservatism, another virtue of beliefs to which we now turn.

3.6 Conservatism and Revisability

Conservatism Without Dogmatism

Conservatism or *familiarity* is a virtue that beliefs have insofar as they are consistent with other beliefs we already have. That is, beliefs have this virtue if they *fit in* with the beliefs we presently hold. Suppose that in a circus performance we observe that

28 A person inside a box was cut in two halves, later emerging unharmed.

Shall we accept (28)? That would seem reasonable but inconsistent with beliefs we already have, such as that

29 No one who has been cut in two halves could emerge unharmed.

(28) and (29) cannot both be true. Given conservatism, (28) must be rejected. To accommodate (28) in our edifice of beliefs, we may take it to report nothing more than a clever illusionist's trick.

Yet conservatism has to be balanced with *revisability,* to which we'll turn below. Otherwise, conservatism could lead to accepting *only* what is consistent with what we already believe, whether the evidence supports it or not, which would be not only unreasonable but dogmatic.

Dogmatism is the vice that some revisable beliefs may have when they are held immune to revision. Those who hold beliefs with a significant share of this vice are *dogmatists.* Dogmatism conflicts with revisability, which is needed for the accuracy, reasonableness, and consistency of our beliefs: for our beliefs to have these virtues, they must be revised often in light of new evidence.

BOX 11 ■ CONSERVATISM VS. ACCURACY

We must not be *too* strict about conservatism, for sometimes beliefs that seem *not* to be conservative turn out to be accurate—or even true!

Revisability Without Relativism

Revisability is the virtue that beliefs have insofar as they are open to change. It comes in degrees, as do accuracy and reasonableness. But, unlike them, revisability has an upper limit: too much revisability may lead to *relativism,* the view that some contradictory beliefs could all be true at the same time. This makes sense only when beliefs are taken to be "true for" a group of people, rather than "true period." With the qualification "true for," the relativist can say that, for example, the belief that the earth doesn't move was *true for* people in antiquity. At the same time, it is not true for us. And there is no contradiction here.

But it seems that the relativist cannot explain away some common intuitions. One is that

> A belief is **true** if and only if it corresponds to the facts.

Another intuition is that it strikes us as plain false that the earth didn't move in antiquity. That belief did not correspond to the facts then, just as it doesn't correspond to the facts now. Moreover, given relativism, "true" is actually "*true for...*," where the dots could be filled in according to the relativist's preferred parameter (culture, social group, historical period, etc.). This leads to the relativist's acceptance of at least some contradictions, since opposite beliefs may be "true for" different cultures. But a strong view in the West since antiquity is that contradiction makes dialogue among logical thinkers impossible.

How much revisability, then, counts as a virtue? In fact, this varies according to belief type. Consider mathematical and logical beliefs such as

30 6 is the square-root of 36.

31 Either Lincoln is dead or he isn't.

These may perhaps be counted as needing very little of that virtue at all. And similarly for

32 Lawyers are attorneys.

Other beliefs of these types, which are all supported by reasoning alone, may also be only marginally revisable. They will typically have the highest degree of conservatism and the lowest degree of revisability (if any at all).

On the other hand, consider empirical and memory beliefs such as

33 The John Hancock Building is Chicago's tallest building.

34 I visited the John Hancock Building in 1996.

These have a great share of revisability. And (33), a belief supported by observation, can be contrasted with evidence (it is in fact false)–as can (34), a belief that could be an instance of a false memory. Given the possibility of such tests, beliefs of either type are open to change (provided that they are not held dogmatically).

3.7 Rationality vs. Irrationality

Rationality is the supervirtue characteristic of all beliefs within the limits of reasoning, while irrationality is the vice characteristic of all beliefs beyond that limit. Although a person's actions may also be said to be rational in some cases and irrational in others, here we shall consider these features only insofar as they apply to beliefs. Rational belief requires the conditions listed in Box 12.

Condition (1) limits the range of beliefs to which (2) and (3) apply: not all of them, but just the beliefs a thinker is *presently and consciously* considering. Typically, as thinkers we have many beliefs, but only some of them are the focus of conscious attention at any given time. Since the vast majority of them are, so to speak, in the back of our minds, then given condition (1), those beliefs can be neither rational nor irrational. Current *conscious* beliefs, on the other hand, must be either rational or irrational, depending on whether or not they satisfy conditions (2) and (3). Given (2), the rationality of beliefs requires that the thinker have some reasons for them. Given (3), rationality requires that the thinker *not* be aware of her beliefs' *failing* in any of the specific virtues listed above (accuracy, truth, reasonableness, consistency,

---

BOX 12 ■ RATIONAL BELIEF

A belief is rational only if

1. It is currently, consciously held by a thinker.
2. A reason for having it is available to the thinker.
3. The thinker is *not* aware of the belief's failing in any of the virtues discussed above.

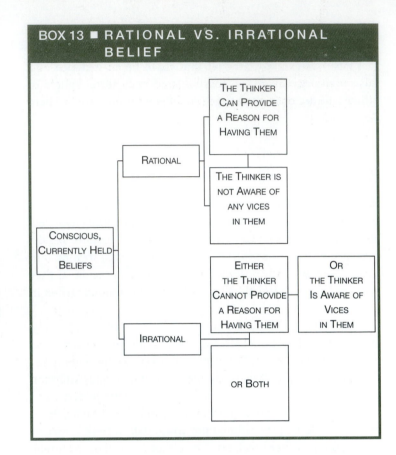

BOX 13 ■ RATIONAL VS. IRRATIONAL BELIEF

conservatism, and revisability). Suppose a thinker is currently, consciously entertaining these beliefs:

35 My neighbor Sally Chang died and was resuscitated.

36 No person can die and be resuscitated.

37 (35) and (36) are not consistent.

These beliefs are irrational, for, as we've seen, consistency is an important virtue that beliefs should have. Here, however, the thinker is aware of her beliefs' lack of consistency and does nothing to revise them to restore consistency. Thus her beliefs are irrational. Similarly, they would be irrational if, once challenged, the thinker could produce no reason whatsoever for holding those beliefs. Derivatively, the thinker herself may in both cases be said to be irrational.

Exercises

V. Review Questions

1. When is a belief accurate? How is truth related to accuracy?
2. Why does belief type matter for reasonableness?
3. Does consistency come in degrees? Explain.
4. When are beliefs consistent? How is consistency related to truth and possible worlds?
5. When is a belief revisable? How is revisability related to conservatism?
6. What is dogmatism? Give a reason why it should be avoided.
7. What is relativism? Give a reason why it should be avoided.
8. How does the relativist understand truth?

VI. Indicate which of the following is clearly accurate, inaccurate, or neither. Explain your choice.

1. The earth is flat.

   SAMPLE ANSWER: Inaccurate. The statement is false.

2. The earth is not flat. _____

* 3. New York City is the capital of the United States. _____

4. New York City is located in the state of New York. _____

* 5. George W. Bush is tall. _____

6. A week has 8 days. _____

* 7. Hip hop is better than jazz. _____

8. Everybody likes Picasso's paintings. _____

9. Killing animals for food is wrong. _____

*10. Homicide is illegal in the United States. _____

11. The Vikings were the first Europeans to visit North America. _____

12. All members of the Texas legislature are space aliens from another galaxy. _____

*13. High blood pressure is a dangerous medical condition. _____

14. The Amazon river is located in Russia. _____

*15. You must stop at red lights. _____

VII. In the above exercise, the statements that turn out to be neither accurate nor inaccurate are so because they each lack a truth value. Explain, for each of these, why it lacks a truth value.

VIII. The contents listed in (VI) above are either reasonable, unreasonable, or nondecidable on the basis of empirical evidence. Determine which is which.

IX. The following are sets of beliefs, each marked with braces. Some are consistent, others inconsistent. Indicate which is which and explain your choice. (Tip: Remember that the actual world is one among many logically possible worlds that matter for consistency.)

1. {The fetus is a person and abortion is wrong. Convicts on death row are also persons, but capital punishment is not wrong.}

SAMPLE ANSWER: Consistent. By modifying "person" with "innocent" in the first case and "guilty" in the second, any appearance of contradictory beliefs is eliminated.

2. {God exists. There is no deity.}

* 3. {All students in Phil. 101 are juniors. Some students in Phil. 101 are freshmen.}

4. {John is a bachelor. John is married.}

* 5. {Helen is a sister. Earth is a waterless planet.}

6. {The present king of France is bald. Triangles have four internal angles.}

* 7. {The earth is flat. The earth is not flat.}

8. {New York City is the capital of the United States. New York City is in the state of New York. Snow is white.}

* 9. {Some people don't like Picasso's paintings. Everybody likes Picasso's paintings.}

10. {Fido is an old dog. Fido is a puppy.}

*11. {It is false that there is a number that is the largest number. Bachelors are unmarried men.}

12. {Lincoln was not assassinated. Homicide is legal in the United States.}

*13. {Bert was once in Romania. Bert was never in Romania.}

14. {In some countries abortion is illegal. But in those countries, execution is legal.}

*15. {2 + 2 ≠ 4. Sisters are male siblings.}

X. For each of the following statements, determine whether its content is empirical, conceptual, or other. For each that is "other," explain why it is in that category. (Hint: In each case, ask yourself, How would we go about determining whether it's true?)

1. Abraham Lincoln was assassinated.

SAMPLE ANSWER: Empirical

2. "Sister" means "female sibling." _____

* 3. 5 + 7 = 12 _____

4. Madonna is taller than Michael Jackson. _____

* 5. If Everest is taller than Aconcagua, then Aconcagua is not taller than Everest. _____

6. Some mushrooms are tasty. _____

* 7. Poverty is inhumane. _____

* 8. There is no life on Mars. _____

9. Jazz is intolerable. _____

10. There are UFOs. _____

*11. Cookies are delicious. _____

12. A straight line is the shortest path between two points. _____

*13. Earth is the center of the universe. _____

14. Some forms of non-Western medicine are worth considering.

_____

*15. There is life after death. _____

XI. Given the state of our knowledge today, each of the following beliefs is either conservative or nonconservative. Indicate which is which.

1. We are all aliens from another planet.

   SAMPLE ANSWER: Nonconservative

2. 2 + 2 = 4 _____

* 3. The earth will stop revolving tomorrow. _____

4. All pigeons are robots in disguise. _____

* 5. If a figure is a rectangle, then it is not a circle. _____

6. Puppies are young dogs. _____

* 7. Whales are fish. _____

8. The earth is flat. _____

* 9. Chickens can't fly long distances. _____

10. The lines of your palm contain information about your future. _____

*11. There are no witches. _____

12. Water is H_2O. _____

*13. George W. Bush is a Democrat. _____

14. Alabama is a southern state. _____

*15. There are out-of-body experiences. _____

XII. For each of the following combinations of beliefs, determine whether it is rational or irrational.

1. I know that a bachelor can't be married. Yet I'm a married bachelor.

   SAMPLE ANSWER: Irrational

2. I'm aware that Jane was childless in 1979, but now she has four grandchildren. _____

* 3. That elephants are extinct is unreasonable. Yet I do believe they are. _____

4. God does not exist—and neither do angels. _____

* 5. Although there's no evidence for believing that the end of the universe is coming, I believe it is. _____

6. I believe that all cats are felines and that some cats are not felines. Furthermore, I believe that these beliefs are contradictory. _____

* 7. As a zoologist, I have no doubts that cats are felines and that all felines are mammals. I'm not aware of these belief's being defective.
_____

8. I have never seen muskrats. Moreover, I have never acquired any information whatsoever about them. As far as I'm concerned, they are rodents. _____

* 9. There is no evidence that there is an afterlife, yet I prefer to believe that there is. _____

10. I believe that Mario and Lucille have a romantic relationship. Yes, Brian says that they do, but he is not a reliable source of information about who is dating whom. Yet I learned about it from a trustworthy source. _____

XIII. YOUR OWN THINKING LAB

1. Give three examples of irrational belief.

2. Explain why your examples for (1) above are irrational. What would be required to make them rational?

3. Provide a scenario in which a thinker is a dogmatist.

4. Provide a scenario in which a thinker is a relativist.

5. Write three sets of inconsistent beliefs.

6. Protagoras of Abdera (Greek, c. 490–421 B.C.E.) argued that "man [i.e., human beings] is the measure of all things—of things that are, that they are, and of things that are not, that they are not. As a thing appears to a man, so it is." How does this amount to a *relativist* position? What sort of objections might be brought against it?

3.8 The Philosopher's Corner
Evaluative Reasons

Statements that make *evaluative* claims are often thought to pose a special puzzle for philosophers. As we have seen, a statement is a declarative sentence used to express a proposition. And a proposition amounts to a content with a truth value: each proposition is either true or false. Propositions have truth values because they are meant to represent things as they are. If a proposition agrees with the facts, that proposition is true; otherwise, it is false. This seems straightforward enough, yet it runs into problems, because some declarative sentences are meant to express *evaluative* judgments—claims about *good* and *bad*, *right* and *wrong*, and what we *ought* or *ought not* to do. They may be about specific things or individuals, as in

38 Hitler's genocidal acts were evil.

39 Egypt has art that is worth seeing.

Or they may be generalizations, such as

40 Genocide is wrong.

41 Egyptian art is worth seeing.

Related to evaluative sentences are sentences that attempt to express a norm or prescription, such as

42 Genocide ought to be condemned unconditionally.

43 People should see Egyptian art.

We shall call "evaluative" any sentence such as (38) through (43). Evaluative sentences are those that can be used to evaluate things, actions and agents and to prescribe what ought (or ought not) to be done. And all of this has seemed to many philosophers somehow not quite the same as making judgments that express propositions.

Now, in fact, this is a topic of considerable controversy. Whether evaluative sentences can *also be used to represent the facts* is currently a matter of dispute among philosophers. To say that they can do so is to say that such sentences express propositions and therefore have truth values. A common argument offered in favor of the view that evaluative sentences do *not* express propositions takes note of the fact that there is pervasive disagreement among people about the truth of many such sentences. If people are often unable to agree about whether such sentences are true, that may be because, when we look to see what it is they describe, we find that *there is no* fact of the matter. And this has led some philosophers to conclude that moral sentences, though seeming to express propositions, actually express only our personal attitudes of commitment or our feelings of approval or disapproval.

Whatever we may conclude about that, one thing is clear: evaluative sentences do have something special about them, and that extra dimension must somehow be accommodated. One widely accepted view has it that only arguments already containing evaluative statements among their premises can actually support evaluative conclusions. Such arguments often have among their premises a general principle stipulating criteria of evaluative justification, so that it's made clear what counts as right or wrong, good or bad, just or unjust, etc. For example, one sort of moral principle—what's sometimes called "consequentialism"—would run

44 Where an action has several expected directly caused effects, some good and some bad, the action is justified only if the good effects outweigh the bad ones.

An alternative moral principle might run

45 An action with more than one effect is justified provided the agent is doing his best to bring about results that ought to be achieved and to avoid other foreseen results that, all things being equal, ought not to be achieved.

Obviously these are only two examples. They are not the only sort of principles one might find in an argument that aims to support an evaluative conclusion. But having *some* such premise would make an argument of that sort vastly easier to defend. What's controversial is whether an argument with *no* evaluative premise at all could support an evaluative conclusion. For more on this topic, see the Philosopher's Corner in Chapter 4.

Exercises

XIV. In the passage below, the American philosopher Judith Thomson (b. 1929) summarizes a common antiabortion argument before offering her own qualified defense of abortion. Once you've read that argument, (a) explain why its conclusion expresses a moral belief and (b) state a reason an objector might offer against its premise.

Most opposition to abortion relies on the premise that the fetus is a human being, a person, from the moment of conception.... We are asked to notice that the development of a human being from conception through birth into childhood is continuous; then it is said that to draw a line, to choose a point in this development and say "before this point the thing is not a person, after this point it is a person" is to make an arbitrary choice.... It is concluded that the fetus is... a person from the moment of conception.[2]

XV. In the reconstructed argument below, British philosopher R. M. Hare (1919–2002) articulates his own reasons against abortion.[3] Identify the moral principle contained in the premises and explain how that principle is required by the argument's conclusion.

1. An action is right for me to take in a certain situation only if it would be right for anyone else to take in a similar situation.

2. Since I am (for the most part) glad to be alive, I have to say that my life is (on the whole) a good thing.

3. But then I am committed to saying that my mother, when she was pregnant with the fetus that later became me, did the right thing in not having an abortion.

4. From this it follows that I must also say that it would have been wrong for my mother to have had an abortion in that case.

5. But then I also have to conclude that any other similarly situated woman would do wrong to have an abortion...(i.e., where the person who comes into being if the pregnancy is brought to term would be likely to be glad to be alive, as I am).

XVI. Some philosophers hold that there is a "fact-value gap": no sentence can express both a fact and a value. The American philosopher Hilary Putnam (b. 1926) rejects this view. Reconstructed below is one of Putnam's arguments against the fact-value gap. But is Putnam's argument effective? Raise an objection to it.

1. The view that no moral sentence can express both a fact and a value rests on one basic assumption: that if something is a *fact*,

---

[2] *Page 507 in Judith Jarvis Thomson, "A Defense of Abortion" (reprinted in* Moral Philosophy, *edited by B. N. Moore and R. M. Stewart, Mountain View, CA: Mayfield, 996, 507-517).*
[3] *Page 6 in R. M. Hare,* Essays on Bioethics *(Oxford: Clarendon Press, 1993).*

then that is just to say that *it could be proved* to any intelligent person.

2. But evaluative sentences cannot be proved in this sense. For,

   a. If they could, then, since Hitler was an intelligent person, it should have been possible to convince even Hitler himself that he was evil.

   b. But this is crazy. No such thing could have been done.

3. So the "basic assumption" mentioned in (1) is false.

4. From this it follows that some moral sentences *do* after all express both a fact and a value, so that there is no fact-value gap.[4]

■ Writing Project

Choose one of the following two projects and write a short composition:

1. A nonsense essay, where you describe three logically impossible scenarios and then explain why they are logically impossible.

2. After you've read Lewis Carroll's *Alice in Wonderland*, identify two scenarios in the story that are *logically impossible* and another two that are *logically possible but simply false in our actual world*. Write a short paper about this, explaining the logical impossibility in the first two cases and the logical possibility in the second two.

■ Chapter Summary

1. A belief is a psychological attitude of accepting that something is the case.

2. A disbelief is a psychological attitude of rejecting that something is the case.

3. A nonbelief is the lack of a psychological attitude of accepting or rejecting that something is the case.

4. The virtues of belief: common features of beliefs that contribute to *good reasoning*.

5. The vices of belief: common features of beliefs that contribute to bad reasoning.

---

[4] *Page 68 in Hilary Putnam,* The Many Faces of Realism, *(La Salle, Illinois: Open Court, 1987).*

6. It's important to distinguish these good-making and bad-making characteristics:

Virtues	Vices	
Accuracy	Inaccuracy	(A matter of degree.) How close does the belief come to being true? Is it approximately right? Or far-fetched?
Truth	Falsity	(NOT a matter of degree.) Does the belief correctly represent the facts? Or not?
Reasonableness	Unreasonableness	(A matter of degree.) Is the belief well supported? Does the available evidence render it plausible?
Consistency	Inconsistency	(NOT a matter of degree). Of some *set* of beliefs, could they all be true at once? Is there some imaginable world in which it would be logically possible for them all to be true? Or are they contradictory, either in themselves or with each other?
Conservatism		(A matter of degree.) Beliefs are conservative insofar as they **fit in with other beliefs we already hold.** The more outlandish a belief is, the less conservative it is.
Revisability		(A matter of degree.) Beliefs are revisable insofar as **they can be modified or rejected on the basis of new evidence**.

7. Beliefs with *too little revisability* have the VICE of DOGMA-TISM. But too much revisability poses a danger of a different kind. If we allow our beliefs to be changed too easily and too frequently, we may end up thinking that contradictory beliefs could all be true at once—or that "true" just means "true for me" or "true for you." This is the *vice* of RELATIVISM.

8. A supervirtue: RATIONALITY. A supervice: IRRATIONALITY.

   A belief is RATIONAL if:

   1. It is currently, consciously held.
   2. There is some reason(s) to support it.
   3. The thinker is not aware of its failing in any of the *virtues of belief.*

   If a belief is **rational**, we have a compelling reason to accept it.

   A belief is IRRATIONAL if:

   1. It is currently, consciously held.
   2. It fails on either conditions (2) or (3) above or on both.

   If a belief is **irrational**, we have a compelling reason to reject it.

■ Key Words

Belief	Contradiction
Belief's vices	Disbelief
Belief's virtues	Dogmatism
Conservatism	Inconsistency
Consistency	Revisability
Truth	Irrationality
Rationality	Nonbelief
Reasonableness	Accuracy
Relativism	
Self-contradiction	

Reason and Argument

Tips for Argument Analysis

This chapter considers some techniques for argument reconstruction. Here you'll learn about

- The roles of faithfulness and charity in reconstructing arguments.
- Arguments that have missing premises.
- Recognizing extended arguments and each of their parts.
- The distinction between deduction and induction, drawn on the basis of that between conclusive and nonconclusive reasons.
- Evaluative arguments and missing evaluative premises.
- The philosophical question of whether evaluative conclusions can follow deductively from purely factual premises.

93

4.1 A Principled Way of Reconstructing Arguments

That we endorse a certain claim or reject it is never the primary aim of argument analysis. Rather, its aim is to decide whether a certain claim should be accepted or rejected on the basis of the premises (reasons) offered for it. But this requires that we first get clear about two aspects of argument reconstruction. One is *faithfulness*, the other *charity*—that point to the concerns listed in Box 1.

Faithfulness

Being faithful to the arguer's intentions is crucial to argument reconstruction. To meet this requirement, we must observe the principle of *faithfulness* in interpretation, which recommends that we strive to put ourselves in the shoes of the arguer. That is, we must try to represent her argument exactly as she intends it. Failing that, we're not dealing with the actual argument under discussion, but some other one we have made up!

Charity

Another crucial requirement of argument analysis is that we make the argument as strong as possible. That is, we must observe a second principle, that of *charity* in interpretation, which recommends that we reconstruct an argument in the way that maximizes the truth of its parts and the strength of their logical relation. We must, in other words, try to give "the benefit of the doubt" to the arguer, and take her argument to be as strong as possible. Maximizing truth requires that we interpret an argument's premises and conclusion in such a way

---

BOX 1 ■ TWO CONCERNS IN ARGUMENT RECONSTRUCTION

1. How to read the argument so that it captures the arguer's intentions
2. How to read the argument so that it comes out as strong as possible

BOX 2 ■ FAITHFULNESS AND CHARITY

In reconstructing an argument, keep in mind:

- The principle of faithfulness
    - ✔ It recommends that we try to set out as carefully as possible exactly what the arguer meant to say
- The principle of charity
    - ✔ It recommends that we take the argument seriously, giving it the benefit of the doubt and maximizing the truth and logical connectedness of its parts

that they come out true, or at least close to true. And maximizing the strength of an argument requires that we interpret the relation of inference among its premises and conclusion in a way that is as strong as possible. In an argument where that relation is the strongest of all, if its premises are true, its conclusion must also be. But as we shall see, not all arguments can be interpreted as consisting in a relation of that sort. For a summary of the two requirements for adequate reconstruction of arguments, see Box 2.

When Faithfulness and Charity Conflict

Although faithfulness and charity are both indispensable to argument analysis, these two principles do, nevertheless, sometimes come into conflict. This happens when maximizing the one implies minimizing the other. Let's consider some examples. First, one where faithfulness and charity get along well. Someone argues

> **1** House rules do not allow dogs in the lobby, but dogs are there. So there has been a breach of house rules.

The second premise may be recast as "Dogs are in the lobby," which could be interpreted in two ways: it is either referring to (a) all members of the species *dogs* or (b) just some members of that species. Which one should we choose? Charity and faithfulness both suggest that we choose (b), since otherwise the premise would be false and also say something that doesn't capture the arguer's intentions. Thus our interpretation would be failing charity and faithfulness. Reconstructed without these shortcomings, (1) reads

> **2**   1. House rules do not allow dogs in the lobby.
> 2. Some dogs are in the lobby.
> _____
> 3. There has been a breach of house rules.

Here, then, charity and faithfulness don't clash. But let's consider an argument where the two principles do seem to pull in different directions:

> **3**   The following two reasons absolutely prove that witches do not exist: (1) there is no evidence that they exist and (2) to invoke witches doesn't really explain anything.

Here faithfulness pulls us toward interpreting this argument as one in which the conclusion is supposed to follow *with necessity* from the premises. That's precisely what "absolutely prove" amounts to. Under this interpretation, however, the argument fails: it is plainly false that its conclusion follows necessarily from its premises, since the premises could be true (as in fact they are in this case), and the conclusion false.

On the other hand, charity pulls us toward reading (3) as making the weaker claim that its conclusion is a reasonable one *on the basis of the argument's premises*. Under this interpretation, the argument may be recast as

> **3'**   The following two reasons *suggest* that witches do not exist: (1) there is no evidence that witches exist and (2) to invoke witches doesn't really explain anything.

We have now maximized the argument's strength, since although (3')'s premises could be true and its conclusion false, the former give good reasons for the latter: the conclusion is likely to be true if the argument's premises are true. Instead of failing, (3') turns out to provide support for its conclusion. But maximizing charity comes at the price of minimizing faithfulness: (3') simply isn't what the arguer seems to have had in mind in proposing (3)! Yet since faithfulness always trumps, here we should stick to our first reading of (3), which is the one that maximizes faithfulness.

> ## BOX 3 ■ FAITHFULNESS
>
> You can't simply change what the arguer had in mind in order to make an argument as strong as possible. The price of doing that is to end up analyzing an argument that is altogether different from the one actually proposed.

Compare the argument,

4 Contemporary biologists believe that there are microorganisms. From this, *it follows necessarily* that there are microorganisms.

If we focus on (4)'s premise and conclusion, they both seem plainly true. But here again, once we prioritize faithfulness in reconstructing (4), we must also say that the argument fails simply because its conclusion, though reasonable, does not follow *necessarily* from its premise. After all, although the possibility that *all* biologists have got it wrong about microorganisms might be an exceedingly remote one, it is still a possibility. On the other hand, if we prioritize charity in our reconstruction of (4), its premise would be taken as merely providing a reason for its conclusion—and the argument would therefore consist in a weaker relation, such as

4' Contemporary biologists believe that there are microorganisms. This supports the conclusion that there are microorganisms.

But should we recast (4) as (4')? No—for recall that when the two principles come apart in reconstructing an argument, the rule is *always prioritize faithfulness*. In other words, faithfulness is more stringent than charity. The rationale for this rule is given in Box 3.

4.2 Missing Premises

Charity and faithfulness sometimes require that any missing (but implicit) premise be restored. Recall one of the arguments discussed in Chapter 1:

5 I think, *therefore* I am.

To make this argument as strong as possible without compromising the arguer's intentions, we must add a missing premise, something to the effect that *anything that thinks exists*. With this extra premise, the inference is much stronger, for the argument could then be reconstructed as (5'):

> **5'** 1. I think.
> 2. Anything that thinks exists.   ← MISSING PREMISE
> 3. I exist.

It is now such that if its premises are true, its conclusion has to be true. Here is another argument with a missing premise:

> **6** 1. Mary is my sister.
> 2. Mary has a sibling.

(6) is a strong inference, since if its premise is true, its conclusion must be true. Yet a connection between the premise and the conclusion is left implicit. A version of (6) that makes that connection explicit would read

> **7** 1. Mary is my sister.
> 2. Anyone who is a sister   ← MISSING PREMISE
>   has a sibling.
> 3. Mary has a sibling.

4.3 Extended Arguments

Sometimes the conclusion of an argument serves as a premise of another argument. In such a case, we may speak of an *extended argument*. Here is an extended argument that has as its starting point our previous argument (5):

> **8** 1. I think.
> 2. Anything that thinks exists.
> 3. I exist.
> 4. If I exist, then there is at least one thing (rather than nothing).
> 5. There is at least one thing (rather than nothing).

In (8) we have in fact two arguments: one offers two premises to support the first conclusion, statement 3, and the other takes

BOX 4 ■ EXTENDED ARGUMENT

When you are presented with an extended argument, bear in mind that

- You are in fact presented with at least two conclusions.
- The conclusion of one is often a premise of the other.
- Any conclusion that itself fails to be supported by the premises of an extended argument cannot succeed in supporting further conclusions of that argument.

statement 3 as a premise, adds premise 4, and draws the argument's second conclusion, statement 5. Since (8) has more than one conclusion, it is an extended argument. The reconstruction and evaluation of extended arguments proceed according to the principles of faithfulness and charity recommended above.

Exercises

I. Review Questions

1. What are the two main requirements of argument reconstruction?
2. In what respects do the principles charity and faithfulness differ?
3. Why are charity and faithfulness important in argument analysis?
4. What should the logical thinker do in a case where charity and faithfulness come apart?
5. What is a missing premise?
6. What is an extended argument?
7. What is the relevance of missing premises to argument analysis?
8. According to the principle of charity, in reconstructing an argument, we must do which of the following?
   A Make that argument as strong as possible
   B Try to capture the author's intentions
   C Suspend judgment

II. Each of the following arguments has a missing premise. Identify that premise.

1. On paydays Jack often goes home at 11:00 P.M., therefore he will not be home tonight until 11:00 P.M.

   SAMPLE ANSWER: Today is payday.

2. The Bible says that God exists. Thus, God exists. _____

* 3. Rolf is European, for he was born in Germany. _____

4. Probably Michael is not a heavy drinker. After all, he is an athlete. _____

5. If the papers find out, she won't be promoted. So if the papers find out, she'll feel miserable. _____

* 6. The Federal Reserve Board predicts a trend among U.S. banks to raise their prime interest rates. Thus we may expect that U.S. banks will be raising their prime interest rates in the near future. _____

7. Since she moved to this town, Pam has frequently gone to the doctor. Hence, she is seriously ill. _____

8. Buzz will probably not major in one of the sciences, because his grades in mathematics have always been rather low. _____

* 9. Either she is telling the truth or she is committing perjury. We must conclude that she is committing perjury. _____

10. If she has a truck, she can move herself out. Therefore she can move herself out. _____

11. No dolphins are fish. Therefore no dolphins are creatures with gills. _____

*12. Tony is Canadian. Thus he is used to cold weather. _____

13. Mary did not come for lunch. For had she come, the maid would have noticed it. _____

14. Isosceles triangles have three internal angles. After all, they are triangles! _____

*15. According to a survey, more than 90 percent of cell phone users cannot get through the day without using their phone. Thus, Jane cannot get through the day without using hers. _____

16. Socrates is human. Therefore Socrates is mortal. _____

*17. Since creation science is a religious theory, creation science should not be taught in biology courses in public schools. _____

18. The earth is a planet and has carbon-based life. This suggests that Mars has carbon-based life. _____

19. My cousin has good vision, for people who don't wear eyeglasses have good vision. _____

*20. Canaries are birds and have feathers. Thus pelicans probably have feathers. _____

III. Underline the conclusions of the following arguments and determine which argument is simple and which extended.

1. Since I'm happy to be alive, my mother did the right thing in not having an abortion when she was pregnant with the fetus that became me. It follows that I must oppose abortion.

   SAMPLE ANSWER: Since I'm happy to be alive, <u>my mother did the right thing in not having an abortion when she was pregnant with the fetus that became me.</u> It follows that <u>I must oppose abortion.</u> Extended argument.

2. Teens who sleep only a few hours a day often report psychological problems. Tom is a teenager who sleeps about two hours a day. As a result, he is likely to report psychological problems.

* 3. No real vegetarian eats meat. Mary is a real vegetarian. Thus she doesn't eat meat. Hence there is no point in taking her to the steak house.

4. Tonight I'll be working extra hours. Whenever I work extra hours, I'm home late. It follows that tonight I'll be home late. All days when I'm home late are days when I don't see my kids. Thus I won't see my kids today.

* 5. If the ocean is rough here, there will be no swimming. If there is no swimming, tourists will go to another beach. Thus if the ocean is rough here, tourists will go to another beach.

6. Fluffy is a feline, for cats are felines and Fluffy is a cat. Since felines are carnivorous, Fluffy is carnivorous.

* 7. No Democrat votes for Republicans. Since Pam voted for Republicans, she is not a Democrat. Thus she won't be invited to Tom's party, for only Democrats are invited to his party.

8. Either we'll go by car or we'll fly there. If we go by car, it will take us four hours, but we'll save money. If we fly to that location, we'll spend more money, and it will take us a little more than three hours from the time we leave the house until we arrive at the hotel. This suggests that we should go by car.

* 9. To understand most web pages you have to read them. To read them requires a good amount of time. Thus, to understand web

pages requires a good amount of time. Since I don't have any time, I keep away from the web and, as a result, I miss some news....

10. If whether the fetus is a person is controversial, then whether abortion is morally permissible is also controversial. It is in fact controversial whether fetuses count as persons. Therefore whether abortion is morally permissible is controversial.

IV. Your Own Thinking Lab

1. Use the following argument in an extended argument of your own: "If I get a good review, I'll be promoted. Therefore if I get a good review, I'll have a better salary."

2. State the missing premise in (1).

3. Provide two arguments of your own with missing premises.

4.4 Types of Reason and Types of Argument

Deductive vs. Inductive Arguments

We have seen that an argument consists of a conclusion that makes a claim of some sort and one or more premises intended as support for that conclusion. But there are two different ways such support can be offered, depending on whether the premises aim at guaranteeing the truth of the conclusion or at simply providing some reasons for it. So far, we have distinguished the former from the latter as cases, respectively, of *conclusive* and *nonconclusive* relations of inference. But we can now be more precise and say that a conclusive relation between certain premises and a claim is the mark of a deductive argument, a nonconclusive relation that of an inductive argument. All arguments exemplify either the one or the other of these two relations.

A deductive argument is one in which the truth of the conclusion is supposed to follow *necessarily* from the premises. The following illustrate such arguments:

9 1. If today is Monday, then we have logic class.
   2. Today is Monday
   3. We have logic class.

10 1. All dogs bark.
    <u>2. Fido is a dog.</u>
    3. Fido barks.

11 <u>1. Today is cloudy and warm.</u>
    2. Today is cloudy.

In each of these, if the premises are all true, the conclusion *must* be true too (it *cannot* be false). So they are all plainly deductive. Now compare

12 <u>1. Most university students have studied plane geometry.</u>
    2. Some students in this class have studied plane geometry.

13 1. Many cats are docile.
    <u>2. Felix is a cat.</u>
    3. Felix is docile.

Both (12) and (13) illustrate arguments where the premises provide at most nonconclusive reasons: they all fall short of guaranteeing the truth of the conclusions they attempt to support. In each of them, the conclusion could be false even if the premises are true. Thus we count such arguments as inductive.

In argument analysis, it's useful to keep in mind the distinctions represented in the summary below. We must always decide

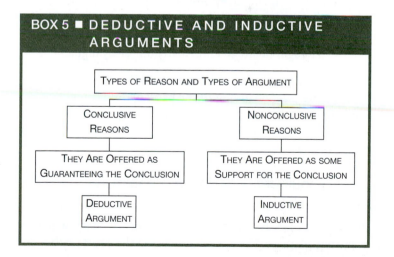

BOX 5 ■ DEDUCTIVE AND INDUCTIVE ARGUMENTS

whether a given argument is deductive or inductive, since the standards of evaluation vary accordingly. Many arguments are defective if evaluated as deductive but quite good if evaluated as inductive. When in doubt, what should we do? Simply ask yourself: Could all the premises be *true* and the conclusion *false* at the same time? If so, then the argument can be considered *inductive*. If not, it's *deductive*.

4.5 Evaluative Arguments With Missing Premises

Evaluative Arguments

Earlier in this chapter, we saw that when arguments are presented in everyday language, they sometimes have missing premises. Logical thinkers will be alert to one especially common way in which this may happen in evaluative arguments. These are arguments for the conclusion that something has a certain *value*, such as good or bad, right or wrong, just or unjust, beautiful or ugly, and the like. Also, arguments for the conclusion that something is permissible (may be done), obligatory (ought to be done), or forbidden (should not be done) may be classified as belonging to this type. Consider

14 1. One ought to obey one's parents.
2. My parents told me not to go to the party on Friday night.
3. I ought not to go to the party on Friday night.

The conclusion of (14) is an evaluative sentence, since it represents a certain action (going to the party on Friday night) as being forbidden. That's sufficient to make the argument evaluative. But (14)'s premise 1, which expresses a principle of obligation, is also evaluative.

Moral Arguments and Moral Principles

When casual speakers or writers present evaluative arguments, they sometimes leave out a crucial premise: one that is a general evaluative sentence. These are sentences to the effect that actions or things of a certain kind are right or wrong, ought to be done, etc. Among such general sentences are some that are common in *moral arguments*. A moral argument is an inference about how various agents, whether individuals or institutions, should behave in order to do what is right or avoid what is wrong. Those general sentences are often called "*moral principles*" because they state a broad rule such as

15 An action is right to take only if it produces, for all those affected by it, more overall good or less overall harm than some alternative action would.

16 An action is right to take only if it is fair to persons, in the sense that it respects them as one would oneself want to be respected.

17 A trait of character is good to have only if it manifests the moral virtues, such as wisdom, courage, moderation, and justice, among others.

Many moral arguments, however, do not invoke any of these moral principles, either explicitly or implicitly. Furthermore, although a moral argument may sometimes feature one or another principle in its premises, it can also have no such principle at all. Either way, as noted above, what makes an inference a moral argument is its conclusion: it always consists of a claim that some action, practice, or thing is *right* (or *wrong*), obligatory, permissible, forbidden, etc., for a certain agent or group.

Implicit Evaluative Premises

Only some evaluative arguments are moral arguments. Evaluative arguments can also have nonmoral conclusions that consist in aesthetic, legal, or prudential claims. Any arguments whose conclusions express value judgments or purport to give normative guidance (i.e., guidance about what to do) can be considered evaluative in a broad sense. Whatever their type, evaluative arguments may have *missing premises* that are evaluative general sentences such as "Keeping promises is right," "Slavery is unjust," or "One ought to obey the law." Here are some examples of such arguments. As you read them, try imagining what they'd sound like with the general evaluative premise left out.

18 Legal argument:

1. Driving faster than 55 miles per hour on the Taconic Parkway

    is forbidden by law. ← EVALUATIVE GENERAL PREMISE

2. Yesterday I drove faster than 55 miles per hour on the Taconic Parkway.

3. Yesterday I did what I ought not to do, according to the law.

19 Aesthetic argument:

1. Music that consists of only a random collection of honks,

    bleats, and screeches is ugly. ← EVALUATIVE GENERAL PREMISE

2. Professor Murgatroyd's "Traffic Jam Serenade" consists of only a random collection of honks, bleats, and screeches.

3. Professor Murgatroyd's "Traffic Jam Serenade" is ugly.

20 Prudential argument:

1. You ought to do whatever would best serve

    your own self-interest. ← EVALUATIVE GENERAL PREMISE

2. Agreeing with your boss whenever possible would best serve your own self-interest.

3. You ought to agree with your boss whenever possible.

21 Moral argument:

1. Lying is wrong. ← EVALUATIVE GENERAL PREMISE
2. Failing to report income on your tax return is lying.
3. Failing to report income on your tax return is wrong.

These arguments cannot really be conclusive unless evaluative premises, of the sorts marked here as *evaluative general premises*, are made explicit (together with whatever other reasons are given in each argument's premises). Now the point to be noticed is that evaluative arguments of the sort one is likely to meet in

BOX 6 ■ EVALUATIVE ARGUMENTS WITH MISSING PREMISES

- Evaluative arguments often leave out general evaluative reasons.
- Faithfulness and charity require that such reasons be made explicit in argument analysis.
- The bottom line is that a careful logical thinker will want to be sure that *all* of an argument's premises are in place, since only in that way can a fair assessment be made of the argument's conclusiveness or nonconclusiveness.

everyday life very often fail to include among their premises the relevant evaluative general principles—since such premises are often taken for granted, as in

19' Professor Murgatroyd's "Traffic Jam Serenade" consists of only a random collection of honks, bleats, and screeches; thus Professor Murgatroyd's "Traffic Jam Serenade" is ugly.

20' Agreeing with your boss whenever possible would best serve your own self-interest, so you ought to agree with your boss whenever possible.

In (19'), "music that consists of only a random collection of honks, bleats, and screeches is ugly" is the missing premise. What's left out is the *evaluative general premise* that purports to say *what "ugliness in music" is.* In (20'), the missing premise is "you ought to do whatever would best serve your own self-interest"—again, an evaluative general premise, this time holding that *serving one's self-interest* is a sufficient reason to justify an action.

Exercises

V. Review Questions

1. Could the premises of an argument provide conclusive reasons? If so, how? If not, why not?
2. What is a deductive argument? Provide two equivalent definitions.
3. How do deductive arguments differ from inductive ones?
4. Should all inductive arguments be avoided?

5. Could a deductive argument with true premises have a false conclusion? Explain.
6. Could an inductive argument with true premises have a false conclusion? Explain.
7. What is an "evaluative argument"?
8. When an evaluative argument has a missing premise, what sort of premise is it that's likely to be left out?

VI. Read each of the following arguments carefully, adding any missing premise if needed, and then determine whether it is deductive or inductive.

1. The defendant is not guilty. After all, his mother says he wasn't at the scene of the crime.

   SAMPLE ANSWER: Inductive

2. Tina Turner has no problems. She is a famous singer, and no famous singer has problems. _____

* 3. Pigeons fly. Sparrows fly. Even ducks fly. It follows that all birds fly.
   _____

4. The Wisconsin Badgers will win this season because they have trained hard. In the past, anytime they trained hard they won.
   _____

5. If whales are mammals, then they are animals. Hence if whales are not animals, then they are not mammals. _____

* 6. Joe will fail philosophy 100 because he never goes to class, and most students who don't go to class fail. _____

7. Gold expands under heat. Aluminum expands under heat. Copper expands under heat. It follows that all metals expand under heat.
   _____

* 8. All metals expand under heat. Gold is a metal. So gold expands under heat. _____

9. George will have lung problems, because a high percentage of smokers develop lung problems, and he is a smoker. _____

*10. Lawyers are attorneys. Rumpole is a lawyer. Therefore Rumpole is an attorney. _____

11. Cats are furry animals. It follows that all pets are furry animals.
    _____

*12. Coffee is a common beverage and contains caffeine. Tea is a common beverage and contains caffeine. Coca-Cola is a common beverage and contains caffeine. In sum, all common beverages contain caffeine.

_____

13. Mary is a mother. Therefore she is married. _____

14. Mary is a lawyer, therefore she is an attorney. _____

*15. Mary is a lawyer, therefore she drives a Mercedes-Benz.

_____

16. The reality show's winner will either meet the president or he will meet the vice-president. It is not the case that he'll meet the vice-president. Therefore he'll meet the president. _____

17. Whenever people meet in a chat room, there is a chance that a relationship built on intellect may develop. I met someone in a chat room. Hence there is a chance that a relationship built on intellect may develop between us. _____

*18. Some Texans are tall. Billy Bob is a Texan. Therefore Billy Bob is tall.

_____

19. No sharks are friendly. White sharks are sharks. Therefore, no white sharks are friendly. _____

*20. Columbus was either Spanish or Italian. He was not Spanish, therefore he was Italian. _____

VII. Each of the following arguments has at least one missing *evaluative* premise. Write in that missing premise or premises.

1. Voluntary euthanasia reduces suffering. Thus voluntary euthanasia is ethically justified.

   SAMPLE ANSWER: Whatever reduces suffering is ethically justified.

2. Cambodian dictator Pol Pot brought misery and death to millions of people. Therefore what Pol Pot did was wrong. _____

* 3. The new Hearst Building was designed by Sir Norman Foster; therefore the Hearst Building is beautiful. _____

4. Everybody agrees that one is better off safe than sorry. Therefore you should stop playing games that are not safe. _____

5. Mendoza & Co. are honest brokers. After all, their dealings with me have always been fair. _____

* 6. On the R train, it would take you twenty minutes to travel the same distance that it now takes you forty minutes on the local bus. Thus you are better off taking the R train. _____

7. That witness is committing perjury. Therefore he should be prosecuted. _____

8. Cookies are full of sugar. As a result, they are not good for you.
_____

* 9. Sandy deals poorly with her financial problems. Thus she ought to get married. _____

10. Having a college degree will improve your earning potential, so you should finish your degree. _____

11. Spreading false rumors about one's competitors is a form of lying; therefore spreading false rumors about one's competitors is wrong.
_____

*12. Elton John's songs are the best. After all, his songs are always hits.
_____

13. Since the ocean is rough today, swimming is not a smart idea.
_____

14. SUVs pollute the atmosphere worse than cars, so they are bad for the health of Americans. _____

*15. Jason ought to report for active duty in Iraq. After all, Jason is a member of the Army Reserve, and his commanding officer ordered all the soldiers in his unit to report for active duty in Iraq. _____

16. Since *The Sopranos* is watched by millions, it follows that it's great television. _____

17. Everybody knows that Bill betrayed his wife Hillary in his affair with Monica, so Bill is a reprehensible character. _____

*18. Capital punishment deters criminals from committing murder. Therefore capital punishment is ethically justified. _____

19. A former president is a big fan of Kinky Friedman's novels. So Kinky Friedman's novels are great literature. _____

*20. You ought to pay that traffic ticket right away. After all, that's the law.
_____

VIII. **The following arguments are evaluative, where this includes moral, aesthetic, prudential, legal, or a combination of some of these types. In each case, indicate which is which.**

1. Thelonious Monk's music is great jazz because it has subtle harmonic phrasing and tonal complexity that distinguish it from all other jazz.

   SAMPLE ANSWER: (1) Aesthetic

2. It is in your self-interest to succeed in college. Besides, that's what you promised to your parents. It follows that you must try to succeed in college. _____

3. Senator Jones favors legislation legalizing embryonic stem cell research. Embryonic stem cell research is immoral. Therefore Senator Jones favors immoral legislation. _____

* 4. Julia Roberts's performances are well crafted. Comparing hers with those of other Hollywood actresses today, we must acknowledge that hers are the best and that she deserves an award.

   _____

5. Benito Mussolini had many of his opponents shot. So he was an evil man. _____

* 6. Wal-Mart uses partially hydrogenated oil in its food products, and these oils are a health hazard. Furthermore, it has questionable labor practices. It follows that I ought not to buy at Wal-Mart.

   _____

7. Nancy favors a woman's right to choose on the question of abortion. Our laws require that those who favor women's rights speak up. Furthermore, their views can improve our society. Therefore, Nancy should speak up. _____

8. Five-year-old Tyler must get his vaccinations. After all, he needs to start school with the other children, and the law requires children to be inoculated if they're going to attend school. _____

* 9. Since you're going to smoke, you must step outside the restaurant.

   _____

*10. I know my boss has been breaking the law with his illegal stock trading. But since nothing could be gained by reporting this, I should keep quiet about it. _____

11. If there is freedom of speech in the Unites States, defamation laws cannot be used to stifle comments on the Internet. And there is freedom

of speech in the United States. Therefore defamation laws cannot be used to stifle comments on the Internet. —————————

12. Landis was found to have used a banned substance. Thus what he did was wrong, and—according to Tour de France's regulations—someone else should be declared champion. —————————

*13. Recently polar bears and hippos were added to the list of threatened species. This suggests that we should take the necessary steps to preserve biodiversity: it is good for its own sake and it could, in the long run, only benefit us. —————————

14. Since consumers are wrestling with higher interest rates and other increased household costs on a monthly basis, we should adopt new sales strategies. —————————

*15. Welcome aboard! Our museum promotes the arts and thus contributes toward making our city a more beautiful place to live in. So join us: these are worthy goals. —————————

IX. Some of the following are evaluative arguments and some are nonevaluative. Indicate which is which.

1. The Internet gives a huge opportunity to waste time web surfing while at work. It follows that the Internet is not such a great invention.

   SAMPLE ANSWER: Evaluative

2. Plain and simple: the European Union did the right thing. For funding for stem cell research should not be banned when so many lives could be saved and so much suffering with debilitating illnesses could be stopped. —————————

* 3. If you are consistent, you cannot be opposed to the "deaths" of unborn innocent children and be OK with the deaths of innocent men, women, and children by way of "collateral damage" in war. Hence, you are not consistent. —————————

4. If cell technology develops, then people afflicted by certain illnesses could be cured, which is intrinsically good. Thus any restriction on stem cell research makes no sense. —————————

* 5. The challenge for us is reducing the impact of greenhouse gas emissions on the climate. For such emissions are eroding ecodiversity, which we want to preserve. —————————

6. If we are serious about helping the developing world, new kinds of energy are needed. Since we do want to help the developing world, it follows that new kinds of energy are needed. _____

* 7. We should either save money or the environment. Attempts to save the environment cannot succeed, scientists say. Therefore we should save money. _____

8. If you care about switching to broadband, you also care about freeing your phone line and speeding Internet access. But neither matters to you. So why bother with switching to broadband? _____

* 9. One liter of seawater can contain more than 20,000 different types of bacteria, according to an international project attempting to catalogue all ocean life. As a result, microbial biodiversity is now considered much greater than previously thought. _____

10. It's clear that unless we can control carbon dioxide emissions, we'll run into dangerous climate change sooner than expected. But we cannot control carbon dioxide emissions. It follows that sooner than expected we'll run into dangerous climate change. _____

*11. Sign up! We won't judge you. If you don't wish to risk your own safety in the future, you should be one of us. _____

12. Taxpayers' money should not be used to help build more laboratories to carry out tests on animals for medical research. After all, many taxpayers are against such research. _____

*13. The first commercial trip around the moon for "space tourists" will cost an estimated $100 million. So each space tourist will have to pay a great deal of money. _____

14. A recent survey reveals that while 75 percent of people think it is rude to use a cell phone during dinner, only 9 percent of respondents said it was unreasonable to do so on a train. Therefore, although it is rude to use a cell phone during dinner, it is reasonable to use it on a train. _____

*15. Whenever a species is in the news, that species is at risk of disappearing. So polar bears and hippos might disappear, since they have recently been in the news. _____

X. YOUR OWN THINKING LAB

1. Consider the claim "Ray has at least one sibling." Write two arguments for it, one deductive (i.e., providing conclusive reasons) and the other inductive (i.e., providing nonconclusive reasons).

2. Write an argument with a missing evaluative premise, and then identify the type of evaluative sentence that it exemplifies.

3. Consider the claim "There is life after death." Write an argument for it and one against it. Discuss whether these arguments are conclusive or nonconclusive.

4. Suppose you're in the checkout line at the supermarket. The cashier asks you, "Paper or plastic?" What sort of evaluative reasons could be relevant in answering this question? Discuss.

5. What is wrong with arguing that because Oscar Schindler was disloyal to his superiors, he behaved badly? We don't want to say *that*! Can you see what the problem is here? What kind of word is "disloyal"? [Schindler was a German industrialist in the 1940s and a member of the Nazi Party, but he helped many Jews escape the death camps.]

4.6 The Philosopher's Corner

Can "*Ought*" Follow Deductively from "*Is*"? Hume's Position

The sort of inference at work in certain moral arguments has long been a matter of controversy in philosophy. These are arguments that have evaluative sentences as their conclusions even though their premises consist entirely of sentences about facts (or putative facts). Let's call sentences of the latter kind "*Is*-sentences" and those of the former "*Ought*-sentences." The content expressed by an *Is*-sentence is factual or descriptive. But that expressed by an *Ought*-sentence is evaluative, since it involves saying that a certain action or thing is good/bad, right/wrong, ought to be done/ought not to be done, etc. Clearly, the content of an *Is*-sentence such as

> **22** Abernathy and Ferguson both live on Mudd Street,

seems to involve only facts. But compare this *Ought*-sentence:

> **23** Abernathy ought to apologize for breaking his promise to Ferguson.

(22) appears to involve more than mere facts. Sentences of these two types seem very different, and some philosophers even think that *Ought*-sentences cannot be used to make *statements* at all—that is, that they cannot be used to say anything with a truth value. But that's an issue we'll not pursue here.

Instead we'll ask: Is it possible for an argument to be *conclusive*—that is, *deductive*—when all of its premises are factual (i.e., they are *Is*-sentences) and its conclusion is evaluative (i.e., an *Ought*-sentence)? The influential Scottish philosopher David Hume (1711–1776), in his *Treatise of Human Nature* (1739), held that the answer is *no*. Judgments about what *ought to be done*, he noted, seem entirely different from judgments about *what is the case*; therefore it seems impossible that *Ought*-sentences could be correctly deduced from *Is*-sentences. Why is this? Because any argument with exclusively *Is*-sentences as premises and an *Ought*-sentence as a conclusion could have true premises and a false conclusion.

On this issue, Hume appears to be pointing to a problem that arises given a certain difference between *Is*- and *Ought*-sentences. Let's call that problem the "*Is/Ought* problem" and consider Hume's position on this. If he is right, then it is not possible to infer *Ought*-sentences conclusively from *Is*-sentences. To support Hume's point, note that

- For any conclusive (deductive) argument, its premises and conclusion have absolute logical connectedness.
- As a result, accepting any such argument's premises and rejecting its conclusion inevitably amounts to a contradiction.

We'll have more to say about conclusive arguments in Chapter 5, when we discuss deduction in greater detail. For our purpose here, it is enough to note that since, given Hume's point, no contradiction arises when an argument's *Is*-premises are accepted and its *Ought*-conclusion rejected, any such argument would fail to be conclusive.

Let's illustrate what Hume is up to here with an example. First, consider an argument that draws an evaluative conclusion from a purely factual premise, such as

24 1. Punishing people for crimes they have committed increases happiness in the world.

     2. Punishing people for crimes they have committed is always morally right.

To assess the import of Hume's point, suppose we accept (24)'s premise 1 but rejects its conclusion 2. In this case we would be saying

25 Punishing people for crimes they have committed increases happiness in the world.

But

26 It is not the case that punishing people for crimes they have committed is always morally right.

Although holding both (25) and (26) at the same time might seem odd, these sentences aren't logically contradictory. After all, their contents could have exactly the same truth value: they could be both true or both false. A view along the lines of (24) and (26) is in fact held by "transitionalists" in political philosophy. They hold that, for the sake of national reconciliation—for example, in countries where there are many individuals who have committed crimes under a despotic former regime, as in South Africa or Chile—there should not be absolute justice but only "transitional justice," where some criminals of the deposed regime are permitted to go unpunished in the interests of facilitating national "healing" and concord. Those who disagree with transitionalists might muster a number of reasons against them. But the one thing they *cannot* do is charge that (25) and (26) are contradictory.

Searle's Reply

In any case, careful logical thinkers will want to ask: Is Hume right about the Is/Ought problem? Or is there a confusion lurking here? Some contemporary philosophers dispute Hume's doctrine.

One is the American philosopher John Searle (b. 1932),[1] who has argued that *Ought*-sentences *can* after all be deduced from *Is*-sentences. His argument is roughly this:

> 1. Jones says "I hereby promise to pay Smith $5."
>   *Therefore*
> 2. Jones has promised to pay Smith $5.
>   *Therefore*
> 3. Jones owes Smith $5.
>   *Therefore*
> 4. Jones ought to pay Smith $5.

Searle contends that this is an extended deductive argument, with exclusively *Is*-sentences as its premises and an *Ought*-sentence as its ultimate conclusion, 4. Since Hume denies that an *Ought*-sentence can be deduced from *Is*-sentences alone, he and Searle are plainly saying *opposite* things. They can't *both* be right. Has the "*Is/Ought* problem" been solved by Searle's argument? If we accept that it has, then that would be the same as accepting that *there is no* deductive gap between fact sentences and value sentences.

Yet Searle's argument faces a number of objections. One of these is related to a topic discussed earlier in this chapter: arguments with missing premises. Our objection to Searle's argument is not simply that it has a missing premise, one that would have to be added for the argument to support its conclusion, because that often happens with successful arguments. Our objection is rather that there is a missing *evaluative* premise. Once we insert it, the argument becomes

> 0. We ought to keep our promises (MISSING PREMISE)
> 1. Jones says "I hereby promise to pay Smith $5."
>   *Therefore*
> 2. Jones has promised to pay Smith $5.
>   *Therefore*
> 3. Jones owes Smith $5.
>   *Therefore*
> 4. Jones ought to pay Smith $5.

---

[1] *"Deriving 'Ought' from 'Is'."* Pp. 175–198 in John R. Searle, Speech Acts *(Cambridge, UK: Cambridge University Press, 1969).*

Without the hidden premise o, the conclusion that Jones ought to pay Smith $5 does not follow deductively from the other premises of the argument. But premise o is already an *Ought*-sentence. So Searle's argument fails to be a counterexample to Hume's point: that an *Ought*-sentence cannot be deduced from premises made up exclusively of *Is*-sentences. Rather, it seems that with arguments of this sort, the *Is/Ought* problem remains unresolved.

But our objection, if successful, has shown only that *Searle's* argument fails to solve the *Is/Ought* problem, not that *no argument at all* could solve it! Logical thinkers interested in pursuing this topic may well find other responses to Hume that stand a better chance of success. In any case, as this debate illustrates, all missing premises relevant to a certain conclusion must be in place before we attempt any critical pronouncement on whether the inference is conclusive. And nowhere is there a greater need for vigilance on this detail than with arguments that purport to deduce evaluative conclusions from purely descriptive premises.

Exercises

XI. For each of the following, determine whether it is an *Is*-sentence or an *Ought-sentence*.

1. Euthanasia should be permitted in some cases of terminal illness.

   SAMPLE ANSWER: *Ought*-sentence

2. Don't do to others what you don't want done to you. _____

3. You ought to tell the truth when they ask you about that traffic ticket. _____

* 4. Some mathematical equations are quite complex. _____

5. The Hollywood Freeway is busy at rush hour. _____

6. Bill Sykes is a disgusting character. _____

* 7. Trent Lott has served a good twenty years, at least, in the United States Senate. _____

* 8. Failure to report income on your tax return is dishonest. _____

9. The cold front is sure to bring relief to these overheated regions when it comes through. _____

*10. Some books have words in them that require a dictionary to understand. _____

11. Web pages help to develop comprehension skills, which are fundamental to understanding. _____

*12. Dr. Martin Luther King was an authentic American hero.

_____

13. Many employers distrust their staff too much to allow them to work at home. _____

14. It is difficult to collect information on the relationship between radiation exposure and the subsequent risk of thyroid disease. _____

*15. It is contradictory to say "Fuel-efficient vehicles are popular and they are not popular." _____

XII. In *some* of the following arguments, an attempt is made to draw an evaluative conclusion from a purely factual premise. For each argument below, indicate whether or not it runs into Hume's *Is/Ought* deductive problem.

1. New York's Central Park was designed by Olmstead and Vaux. Therefore, Central Park is beautiful.

   SAMPLE ANSWER: *Is/Ought* problem

* 2. Labrador retrievers are highly intelligent dogs. Therefore Labrador retrievers will recognize when you're in trouble. _____

3. Mendelssohn's music makes use of beautiful harmonic qualities. Therefore Mendelssohn's music is superior art. _____

* 4. Mendelssohn's music was written in the nineteenth century. Therefore Mendelssohn's music is superior art. _____

5. Senator Snort supported Joint Resolution 553. Therefore Senator Snort believes in compromise. _____

* 6. Global warming is causing odd weather patterns throughout the world. Therefore we ought to take steps to reduce global warming.

   _____

7. O'Brien arrived late to work today. Therefore O'Brien is a bad man.
   _____

8. Sheila works at the telephone company. Therefore she is a member of an employee health plan. _____

* 9. Some jaguars are found in the rain forests of Central America. Therefore some jaguars are not in captivity. _____

10. Mayor Mufkin will not confront the governor and his powerful friends. Therefore Mayor Mufkin is a spineless coward. _____

*11. Tahiti is a tropical island in French Polynesia. Therefore Tahiti is a gorgeous place for a vacation. _____

12. Madonna's music is played on radio stations all over the world. Therefore Madonna's music is really great. _____

13. The last local election was filthy. No one elected in a filthy election should be allowed to govern. Therefore no one elected in the last local election should be allowed to govern. _____

*14. Energy may become more scarce in the near future. We ought to save energy. _____

15. Start pestering your friends to save the environment. If we don't begin to do something about the environment now, it is doomed to collapse. _____

XIII. **Suppose someone sympathetic to Searle's argument above reasons as follows:**

Given the *Is/Ought* problem, no *Ought*-sentence can be deduced from an *Is*–sentence. But from my sincere utterance "I apologize," it follows that I did something *wrong*. Hence, there is no *Is/Ought* problem.

What could a Humean reply to this?

■ Writing Project

Consider the claim "Killing another human being is always wrong." Write a short essay (about three pages) offering at least one argument for it and at least one against it. Then discuss which sentences making up those arguments are evaluative. Finally, in light of Hume's position, determine whether the arguments themselves could be conclusive or not.

■ Chapter Summary

In argument analysis, keep in mind the following:

1. The principle of *faithfulness*.

   At all times, try to reconstruct an argument in a way that captures the arguer's intentions—that is, premises and conclusion should say just what the arguer intends them to say.

2. The principle of *charity*.

   At all times, make the argument as strong as possible—maximize the truth of premises and conclusion, and the strength of the relation among them.

3. The rule for balancing faithfulness and charity.

   When there is a conflict between these two, faithfulness takes priority.

4. In argument reconstruction, missing premises, if any, must be restored.

5. An argument could have more than one conclusion. In any such case, the argument is *extended*.

6. When needed, decide whether a given argument is deductive or inductive on the basis of whether the argument's premises are offered as guaranteeing the conclusion or only as providing some support for it.

7. An evaluative argument is an argument for the conclusion that something has a certain value or is permissible (may be done), obligatory (ought to be done), or forbidden (should not be done). An evaluative argument could be moral, aesthetic, prudential, legal, or a combination of these, depending on its conclusion.

8. Evaluative arguments often leave out general evaluative premises that should be restored in accordance with faithfulness and charity.

■ Key Words

Principle of charity	Principle of faithfulness
Conclusive reasons	Evaluative argument
Nonconclusive reasons	Evaluative general premise
Inductive argument	Missing premise
Deductive argument	Extended argument
Is/Ought problem	

Evaluating Deductive Arguments

In this chapter, you'll look more closely at deductive reasoning, focusing first on the concept of validity and then on related topics, including

- The difference between valid and invalid arguments.
- Some common ways to determine validity.
- The concept of argument form.
- The difference between propositional and syllogistic argument forms.
- The concept of soundness.
- The concept of deductive cogency.
- The normative implications (or "cash value") of validity, soundness, and cogency.
- Two ways in which the premises of a valid argument may be justified namely, *a priori* or *empirically*.

5.1 Valid Arguments

As we've seen, a deductive argument is one in which the conclusion is supposed to follow necessarily from the premises—so that if the premises were all true, the conclusion would be too. A deductive argument that actually has this feature is *valid*. In such an argument, there is *entailment*: when a deductive argument is valid, its premise or premises entail its conclusion—which is another way to say that if its premises are true, then its conclusion cannot be false. Since in any argument that meets the entailment or validity requirement the truth of its premises is transferred to its conclusion, the argument can also be said to be *truth-preserving*. Any argument that fails to have this feature would be one whose premise/s could be true and its conclusion false at once. Such an argument is, by definition, *invalid*.

BOX 1 ■ ENTAILMENT

There is *entailment* in an argument if and only if the truth of the argument's premises guarantees the truth of its conclusion. Such an argument is *valid* and therefore truth-preserving.

Now notice that we are using "valid" and "invalid" in a special sense here. Sometimes people do use these words loosely, where "valid" means "acceptable" or "reasonable" and "invalid" means "unfounded" or "insupportable," but these are not what we mean by "valid" and "invalid" in logical thinking. Only deductive arguments are capable of being valid, and they are actually valid only when the premises do entail (i.e., necessitate) the conclusion.

At this point, it is important to notice that we have introduced some different expressions that mean the same. To say that an argument is valid is equivalent to saying that its premise/s entail its conclusion. And both of these are equivalent to saying that the argument is truth-preserving and that its conclusion follows necessarily from its premise or premises. The cash value of these concepts for logical thinkers is simply this:

> If you accept the premises of a valid argument (that is, if you think that they are true), then you are committed to accepting its conclusion. If you reject it, then your beliefs are contradictory.

Once you accept a valid argument's premises, were you to reject its conclusion (that is, think that it is false), that would be contradictory or nonsensical. *Contradictory beliefs* cannot have the same truth value: if one is true, the other is false (and if one is false, the other is true). For example, consider this valid argument:

1 It's warm and sunny. *Therefore* it's sunny.

You cannot accept that it's warm and sunny and at the same time deny that it's sunny: that would be contradictory. It would make no logical sense.

Now, notice a further point: because validity is very demanding, some arguments that count as invalid by this standard may yet be OK by a less demanding one. Some arguments in which the conclusion fails to follow with necessity from the premises may yet be arguments in which it follows with probability. That is, some arguments in which the premises fall short of guaranteeing the conclusion may nevertheless make it likely. And many of these arguments may be very useful to us—for example, if they support certain generalizations about the workings of nature or of human societies. Recall inductive arguments: although their premises might provide some reasons for the conclusion, they would never entail it. Note that, according to this definition, all inductive arguments fail to meet the standard of validity. But the premises of some such arguments may yet provide strong reasons for believing their conclusions, even when they fall short of entailing them. We shall examine this type of argument later. For now, it is enough to note that, when it comes to valid arguments, the criteria are straightforward: whether certain premises entail a given conclusion is never a matter of degree but instead one of *all or nothing*. An argument cannot be "sort of valid." It's either valid or it's not.

To tell whether a given argument is valid, simply apply this test: As you read the argument, ask yourself, Could the conclusion be false with all the premises true at once? If so, then, on the above definition of validity, the argument flunks the test: it's invalid. But if not, then you may accept it as valid. Let's consider some examples. Suppose we ventured to predict what next summer in Baltimore will be like. We might say,

2 Next summer there will be some hot days in Baltimore. After all, according to Baltimore's records for the last 100 years, summers have included some hot days.

Or imagine that we want to decide what to expect on our European vacation. We might reason,

3 Yves is a Parisian and speaks French. The same is true of Odette, Mathilde, Marie, Maurice, Gilles, Pierre, Jacques, and Jean-Louis. So, all Parisians speak French.

Now clearly in both arguments the conclusion could be false and all premises true. Although the likelihood of that may seem exceedingly remote, it is possible. Both arguments are therefore invalid. In claiming that such situations are "possible," we have in mind *logical possibility*. Whether (2) and (3) would be likely to have true premises and false conclusion in our actual world, with things being as they are, is beside the point. Rather, if there is some scenario, *possible* in the sense that it implies no internal contradiction, in which these argument's premises could be true and their conclusion false at once, then the arguments are invalid.

At the same time, notice another thing: whether an argument is valid or not is entirely a matter of whether its conclusion follows necessarily from its premises. The actual truth or falsity

---

BOX 2 ■ VALIDITY AND POSSIBLE WORLDS

Determining whether it is *logically possible* for a given argument to have all true premises and a false conclusion often requires that we imagine a scenario that is "possible" in the wide sense of *involving no contradiction*. The actual world is only one among many such possible scenarios called "possible worlds."

of premises and conclusion in isolation is irrelevant to an argument's validity. What matters is whether the premises could be true and the conclusion false, because that would determine the invalidity of the argument. Thus, a valid argument could have one or more false premises and a true conclusion, as in

4   1. All dogs are fish.
    2. All fish are mammals.
    3. All dogs are mammals.

Here, although the conclusion is not false, both premises are false. But (4) is valid, for its conclusion is entailed by its premises: if these were true, the conclusion would have to be true. Furthermore, it is even possible for an argument to be made up entirely of false statements and yet be valid. Consider this one:

5   1. All Democrats are vegetarians.
    2. All vegetarians are Republicans.
    3. All Democrats are Republicans.

In (5), all three statements are false. But the argument is valid. This is because, as in the case of (4), the argument follows a form or pattern that guarantees that when premises are true, the conclusion has to be true. That underlying form is

6   1. All *A* are *B*
    2. All *B* are *C*
    3. All *A* are *C*

In any argument exemplifying this form, if its premises are true, then its conclusion cannot be false. It is in that relationship, which we have called "entailment," between premises and conclusion that validity consists, and nothing more. The fact that an argument might have one or more false premises, then, is irrelevant to its validity, since validity is entirely a matter of entailment: when this relationship obtains between premises and conclusion, the argument is valid; when it doesn't, it's not.

Finally, notice that it is possible for an argument to be invalid even though its conclusion is true. For instance,

7   1. All famous politicians are public figures.
    2. Arnold Schwarzenegger is a public figure.
    3. Arnold Schwarzenegger is a famous politician.

Valid vs. Invalid Argument

■ Arguments may be divided into two groups: those that are *valid* and those that are *invalid*.

■ Only valid arguments are *truth-preserving*: If their premises are true, then it is not possible for their conclusion to be false.

■ Only in a valid argument do the premises *entail* the conclusion.

■ The cash value of validity is:

✔ A logical thinker who accepts the premises of a valid argument cannot reject its conclusion without contradiction. But this doesn't happen in the case of an invalid argument.

(7)'s conclusion is true (indeed, all three statements are true), but the argument is invalid because the conclusion is not entailed by the premises–that is, it does not follow necessarily from them, as can be seen from the fact that we can imagine a scenario where the conclusion is false and both premises true. (That would be so if, for example, Schwarzenegger had chosen to remain a movie star and not gone into politics.)

"Validity" as a Technical Term

Notice another consequence of the above discussion. As we have been using the word "valid" here, there is no such thing as a "valid statement." This is because "valid" is a technical term that applies not to a single statement but to a group of statements (two or more) so related that one of them follows necessarily from the others. Only some *relations* among statements, then, may be valid or invalid. A group of statements would together have the feature of validity if and only if they were related in such a way that one of them—the conclusion—followed necessarily from the other/s. Thus validity is a feature of (some) sets of statements (i.e., of some arguments), though not of individual statements. It makes no sense to say that a statement is valid or invalid. At the same time, it makes no sense to say that an argument has a truth value: arguments can't be "true"—or "false." Keep in mind, then, that

Statements are
- Either true or false
- But neither valid nor invalid

Arguments are
- Neither true nor false
- But either valid or invalid

Exercises

I. Review Questions

1. When is an argument invalid? When is an argument valid?
2. What is entailment? How is entailment related to validity?
3. If we know that an argument is valid and has true premises, we can then know the truth value of the conclusion. Why is this?
4. If the premises of a valid argument are known to be false, can we then know the truth value of the conclusion? If so, how? If not, why not?
5. What does it mean to say that "validity" is a technical term?
6. What does it mean to say that a valid argument is "truth preserving"?
7. What is an argument form? And how does an argument differ from an argument form?
8. Could an argument be an instance of more than one argument form? If so, how? If not, why not?
9. Could different arguments be instances of the same argument form? If so, how? If not, why not?
10. Define validity and invalidity in terms of argument form.

II. Determine whether the following "types of arguments" are logically possible or impossible. For each that's logically possible, give an example.

1. A valid argument whose premises are true and conclusion false.

   SAMPLE ANSWER: Logically impossible

2. An invalid argument whose premises are true and conclusion false.

   _____

* 3. An invalid argument whose premises are true and conclusion true.

   _____

4. An invalid argument form that cannot have true premises and a false conclusion. _____

* 5. A valid argument whose premises are false and conclusion false. _____

6. A valid argument whose premises are false and conclusion true. _____

7. An invalid argument whose premises are false and conclusion false. _____

* 8. An argument that is more or less valid. _____

III. Determine which of the following arguments is valid.
Tip: For each argument, ask yourself: Could all the premises be true with the conclusion false? If so, the argument is invalid. Otherwise, it is valid.

1. No successful movie stars are poor. Queen Latifah is a successful movie star. It follows that Queen Latifah is not poor.

   SAMPLE ANSWER: Valid

2. New York, Toronto, Denver, Boston, Chicago, Minneapolis, Pittsburgh, Montreal, and Detroit are all big cities in North America, and all of these cities have snow in winter. We may infer that all big North American cities have snow in winter. _____

3. Since Mr. and Mrs. Gunderson are Republicans, their son Mark must be a Republican too. _____

* 4. All squares are polygons, for all squares are rectangles, and all rectangles are polygons. _____

5. All whales are fish, and some whales are members of the Conservative Party. Thus, some fish are members of the Conservative Party. _____

6. Isaac Newton wrote a book called *Principia Mathematica*, which was published in England. Alfred North Whitehead and Bertrand Russell wrote a book called *Principia Mathematica* which was published in England. Hence, Russell, Whitehead, and Newton were collaborators. _____

* 7. No people who wear sweaters are cold. So Mr. Rogers is never cold, because Mr. Rogers always wears a sweater. _____

8. Since beavers are nocturnal, we may infer that badgers, weasels, and wolverines are too, for all of these are small, fur-bearing mammals found in the upper Midwest. _____

9. Seven-year-old Jason has contracted chickenpox. This occurred only a week after his three younger sisters, Gertrude, Samantha, and Hermione were stricken with chickenpox. So, Jason caught the chicken pox from his sisters. _____

*10. Bart Simpson cannot run for governor of California because Bart Simpson is a cartoon character, and no cartoon characters are citizens of California. Only citizens of California are eligible to run for governor of California. _____

11. Every winter there has been some rain in Vancouver. This has been true for as long as records have been kept. It follows that next winter there will be some rain in Vancouver. _____

12. Since Shaquille O'Neal and Michael Jordan are tall, we may infer that at least two basketball stars are tall, for Shaquille O'Neal and Michael Jordan are basketball stars. _____

*13. Since this is a freshman-level course, it is an easy course, for all freshman-level courses are easy. _____

14. It is unlikely that Joe will be a senator. Most senators are people who win public debates, and so far Joe has lost every one. _____

15. If my computer keeps crashing, then it must have picked up a virus somehow. Therefore it must have a virus, because it keeps crashing. _____

*16. The Washington Redskins is a football team that has thousands of enthusiastic fans. The same is true of the Denver Broncos, the New York Jets, the Minnesota Vikings, and the Dallas Cowboys. It follows that all American professional football teams have thousands of fans. _____

17. Since no health-conscious people are sedentary couch potatoes, no marathon runners are sedentary couch potatoes, for all marathon runners are health-conscious people. _____

18. The Dow Jones average is falling every day. If the Dow Jones average is falling every day, then stocks seem not to be a good investment. Thus, stocks seem not to be a good investment. _____

*19. We'll either watch a DVD or dine out. If we watch a DVD, we'll be amused. If we dine out, we won't have to cook. Thus, either we'll be amused or we won't have to cook. _____

20. Sally is always happy because she is a singer, and many singers are always happy. _____

21. Nat is not a spy. All spies have espionage training, and he has never had such training. _____

*22. JJ's doesn't have the support of the Chamber of Commerce, for the Chamber of Commerce usually supports local firms, and JJ's is from out of state. _____

IV. For each of the above arguments that are invalid, offer a counterexample.

V. YOUR OWN THINKING LAB

1. Give three valid arguments.

2. Give three invalid arguments.

3. What would be a *valid* argument for the conclusion "Joan is married"?

4. What would be an *invalid* argument for the conclusion "Joan is married."

Some Valid Propositional Argument Forms

As we have seen, another way to refer to valid arguments is as arguments that are truth-preserving. This is the same as saying that if their premises are true, then their conclusions must also be true—or, equivalently, that the truth of their premises guarantees the truth of their conclusions. Being truth-preserving is a characteristic a valid argument has in virtue of the form or pattern it illustrates. Some arguments have the characteristic of being truth-preserving because the statements that constitute their premises and conclusion are connected in certain ways, forming distinctive patterns of relationship that transfer the truth of the premises (if they are true) to the argument's conclusions. Other arguments have it because within the statements that constitute their premises and conclusions there are some expressions, which we shall call "terms," that bear certain relationships to each

BOX 4 ■ PROPOSITIONAL AND SYLLOGISTIC ARGUMENTS

Some Intuitive Cues

When you see certain connections between propositions such as "Either...or..." and "If...then...," the argument is probably better reconstructed as propositional. On the other hand, when you see in the premises certain words indicating quantity, such as "All," "No," and "Some," the argument is probably better reconstructed as syllogistic.

other which make the argument's conclusions true (if the premises are true). Arguments of the former type are *propositional*, while those of the latter type are *syllogistic* (in a broad sense).

We'll examine each type in more detail later, but before we go on, it's important to be clear about what we mean by "proposition." Recall that a *proposition* is the *content* of a belief or statement which has a truth value: it is either true or false. Let's now consider some propositional arguments—that is, those for which being truth-preserving hinges on relations between the propositions that constitute their premises and conclusions. For example,

8   1. If my cell phone is ringing, then it is making noise.
    2. My cell phone is ringing.
    3. My cell phone is making noise.

(8) is a valid argument because of the relation among the propositions that make it up. Its first premise features a compound of two simple propositions connected by "if...then...;" its second premise features the first of those two simple propositions. After replacing each simple proposition in this argument with capital letters used as symbols, keeping the logical connection *if...then...*, (8)'s argument form becomes apparent. It is

8'   1. If C, then M
     2. C
     3. M

where C stands for "My cell phone is ringing," and M for "My cell phone is making noise." (8') is not an argument but an argument

BOX 5 ■ SOME VALID ARGUMENT FORMS

Modus Ponens

If *P*, then *Q*

P

Q

Hypothetical Syllogism

If *P*, then *Q*

If *Q*, then *R*

If *P*, then *R*

Contraposition

If *P*, then *Q*

If not *Q*, then not *P*

Modus Tollens

If *P*, then *Q*

Not *Q*

Not *P*

Disjunctive Syllogism

Either *P* or *Q*

Not *P*

Q

Either *P* or *Q*

Not *Q*

P

form showing a certain relation between premises and conclusion that is known as *modus ponens*. Any argument with this form illustrates a modus ponens. For example,

9 1. If thought requires a brain, then brainless creatures cannot think.
2. Thought requires a brain.
3. Brainless creatures cannot think.

Let's now consider other propositional argument forms. This argument has the logical form *modus tollens*:

10 1. If there is growth, then the economy is recovering.
2. But the economy is not recovering.
3. There is no growth.

which is revealed by symbolizing it as

10′ 1. If *G*, then *E*
2. Not *E*
3. Not *G*

Box 5 above offers a short list of some propositional argument forms, which we'll revisit in Chapter 12. For now, let's illustrate other forms in Box 5.

11 1. If inland temperatures increase, then crops are damaged.
2. If crops are damaged, then we all suffer.
3. If inland temperatures increase, then we all suffer.

Argument (11) is an instance of a *hypothetical syllogism*, for it has the form

11' 1. If *I*, then *C*
2. If *C*, then *A*
3. If *I*, then *A*

And as you can prove for yourself, (12) and (13) below illustrate the two versions of *disjunctive syllogism* in Box 5, while (14) illustrates *contraposition*:

12 1. Either American Dennis Tito or South African Mark Shuttleworth was the first space tourist.
2. South African Mark Shuttleworth was not the first space tourist.
3. American Dennis Tito was the first space tourist.

13 1. Either American Dennis Tito or South African Mark Shuttleworth was the first space tourist.
2. American Dennis Tito was not the first space tourist.
3. South African Mark Shuttleworth was the first space tourist.

14 1. If Persia was a mighty kingdom, then Lydia was a mighty kingdom.
2. If Lydia was not a mighty kingdom, then Persia was not a mighty kingdom.

All these arguments are *substitution instances*, that is, examples (or simply, *instances*) of one or another of the argument forms in Box 5, which are all valid. This means that in any argument that is an instance of one of these forms there is entailment, no matter what actual statements the symbols stand for. That is, no actual arguments of the forms listed in Box 5 could have true premises and a false conclusion. There are many such forms, but again, we'll examine this topic at greater length in Chapter 12.

Some Valid Syllogistic Argument Forms

Many arguments, however, are clearly valid, even though they don't fit into any form of propositional logic. Consider

15   1. All dentists have clean teeth.
     2. Dr. Chang is a dentist.
     3. Dr. Chang has clean teeth.

Argument (15) is plainly valid, for if its premises are true, then its conclusion must be true. Now suppose we replace its parts by letter symbols, treating the argument as if it were an instance of an argument form in propositional logic. We would then get this form:

16   1. D
     2. C
     3. E

But (16) is an invalid form, since it is easy to imagine substitution instances of this form with true premises and a false conclusion. Such instances are called "counterexamples" because they show the invalidity of a form. A counterexample to (16) is

17   1. Whales are mammals.
     2. George W. Bush was president of the United States in 2006.
     3. The earth is flat.

(17) is all we need in order to show the invalidity of any argument of the form (16). It amounts to a counterexample to any such argument. A counterexample to any given argument is an argument of the same form with true premises and a false conclusion. (17), whose form is (16), clearly has true premises and a false conclusion. Now recall that this form was supposed to represent argument (15), which seems *valid*! Something has gone wrong here.

What has gone wrong is that the validity of (15) is lost when the argument is taken to be an instance of (16), where each letter symbol stands in for a proposition. In other words, (16) is too coarse-grained to serve as the correct argument form of (15), where the entailment hinges on relations among *certain expressions within the propositions* that make up that argument, rather than on relations among the propositions themselves that constitute premises and conclusion. In (15) the entailment depends on relations among terms such as "all," "Dr. Chang," "dentist," and "clean teeth."

A more fine-grained representation is needed for arguments such as (15). We shall represent their forms by adopting the following conventions:

> 1. Use "to be" in present tense as the main verb in each premise and conclusion.
> 2. Make explicit any logical expressions, such as "all," "some," and "no."
> 3. Replace expressions such as "dentist" and "clean teeth" with capital letters.
> 4. Replace expressions for specific things or individuals, such as "Dr. Chang," "Fido," "I," and "that chair" with lowercase letters.

In this language, the logical form of (15) is similar to that of

18 1. All soda companies are businesses that prosper.
    2. Pepsi is a soda company.
    _____
    3. Pepsi is a business that prospers.

Example (18)'s argument form is

18' 1. All A are B.
    2. c is an A
    _____
    3. c is a B

where "A" stand for the term "soda companies," "B" for "businesses that prosper" and "c" for "Pepsi." We can also represent in this language arguments such as

19 1. All ophthalmologists are doctors.
    2. Some ophthalmologists are short.
    _____
    3. Some doctors are short.

(19) is a plainly valid argument: it is a substitution instance of a valid syllogistic argument form. Another is as that of

20 1. All red squirrels are rodents.
    2. Some red squirrels are wild animals.
    _____
    3. Some wild animals are rodents.

No. 1

1. All *A* are *B*
2. No *B* are *C*
3. No *C* are *A*

No. 2

1. Some *A* are *B*
2. All *A* are *C*
3. Some *C* are *B*

No. 3

1. No *A* are *B*
2. All *C* are *A*
3. No *C* are *B*

No. 4

1. All *A* are *B*
2. All *C* are *A*
3. All *C* are *B*

(For more syllogistic argument forms
that are valid, see Chapter 14.)

20'   1. All *A* are *B*
      2. Some *A* are *C*
      3. Some *B* are *C*

Here "*A*" stand for "red squirrels" (or "ophthalmologist"), "*B*" for "rodents" (or "doctors"), and "*C*" for "wild animals" (or "short").

Let's now recall a point made at the beginning of this section: that another way to understand validity is to say that whether an argument is valid or not is simply a matter of whether it has a valid form. Consider

21   1. No Peloponnesians are Euboeans.
     2. All Spartans are Peloponnesians.
     3. No Spartans are Euboeans.

Even someone who knew nothing at all about Greek geography could nevertheless see that the argument is valid, because it is an instance of the valid form No. 3 in Box 6. No argument with this form could have true premises and a false conclusion. Similarly, the following argument is valid even when its premises are false. Why? Simply because it has valid form No. 4 above:

22   1. All apples are oranges.
     2. All bananas are apples.
     3. All bananas are oranges.

Validity, then, is entirely a matter of argument form. The same could be said for the other examples above. This brings us to another important point: for each form that is valid, all of the arguments that have it will be valid; similarly, for each invalid form, all of the arguments that have it will be invalid.

> SUGGESTION: In this section, there are a number of valid argument forms. For quick reference and to gain familiarity, construct a card with these forms. Write down on one side those where validity hinges on relations among propositions and on the other side those where validity hinges on relations among terms.

The Cash Value of Validity

Logical thinking has goals, such as learning, understanding, and solving problems. Each of these requires argument analysis, and sometimes refutation, the process by which a given argument is shown to fail. But, far from being among logical thinker's primary goals, refutation is a result of argument analysis unavoidable in some cases. Achieving logical thinking's primary goals greatly depends on charitable and faithful reconstruction of arguments. For those that are deductive, charity recommends making them as strong as possible, maximizing the truth of their premises and conclusion and the validity of their forms—while faithfulness recommends trying to capture the arguer's intentions. In all of this, logical thinkers strive to capture the form of an argument correctly, adding missing premises when needed. Once they have properly reconstructed an argument, they then move on to evaluate it, keeping in mind rules such as

- Do not criticize/accept an argument by focusing solely on its conclusion.
- Direct each objection to the argument form or to a clearly identifiable premise.
- Use the evaluative criteria offered here. Do not make unsubstantial criticisms, such as that "that is a matter of opinion."

Any challenge to validity is a challenge to the argument form. If the premises of an argument with a certain form could be true and its conclusion false, then the argument is invalid because it has an invalid form. To prove that an argument is invalid, logical thinkers sometimes use the method of counterexample discussed above. Yet finding an argument invalid is not a conclusive reason to reject it, since it could still be a good inductive argument (more on this in Chapter 6). Once an argument is found valid, logical thinkers must move on to check whether its premises are true—which brings up the topic of soundness, to be taken up later in this chapter.

The cash value of standards for argument evaluation, such as validity, is simply their *normative impact*: knowing whether an argument meets them or not determines the attitude we should have about its conclusion on the basis of its premises. Validity, which is a matter of argument form, has cash value. When an argument meets this standard, its form is valid—and if we know this, then we know that its conclusion cannot be false if all its premises are true. Therefore asserting that argument's premises and denying its conclusion at the same time would be a contradiction. For example, since argument

23 1. If Felix is a cat, then it is a feline.
2. Felix is a cat.
3. Felix is a feline,

is valid, we cannot accept its premises and deny its conclusion without falling into contradiction. For if an argument is valid, then if you assert (or accept) the argument's premises, you must logically assert its conclusion. Asserting (23)'s premises and denying its conclusion would amount to saying something like this,

24 If Felix is a cat, then it is a feline. And Felix is a cat. But it is not a feline.

Clearly, these three statements cannot all be true at once. (24) should be rejected, since its three statements are a logically impossible set: there is no possible world where all its members could be true.

What about the cash value of invalidity? It is this:

> If you know that an argument is invalid, you know that its premises could all be true and its conclusion false at once.

Note, however, that

> If *all* you know about an argument is that it is invalid, then you *don't know* that its premises are in fact true and its conclusion in fact false.

You know *only* that such a scenario *could* be the case: the argument form makes that *possible* (something that could not happen with a valid argument form). As discussed above, in all cases of invalidity, arguments fail to be truth-preserving—so that then *any* arrangement of truth values in premises and conclusion would be logically possible.

Exercises

VI. Review Questions

1. What does it mean to say that an argument's form is propositional?
2. What does it mean to say that an argument's form is syllogistic?
3. What is the convention for representing propositional argument forms?
4. What is the convention for representing syllogistic argument forms?

VII. For each of the following arguments, determine whether it is propositional or syllogistic.

1. All living creatures need liquid water. My cat is a living creature. Thus, my cat needs liquid water.

   SAMPLE ANSWER: Syllogistic argument

2. There is no extraterrestrial intelligence. After all, if there were extraterrestrial intelligence, we should have evidence of it by now. But we don't have it. _____

* 3. No desert is humid. Atacama is a desert. Therefore, Atacama is not humid. _____

4. Doctors are exposed to agents that cause ailments. Jane is a doctor. Hence she is exposed to agents that cause ailments. _____

* 5. If the Orinoco crocodile is a rodent, then the Chinese alligator is also. But the Chinese alligator is not a rodent. Therefore, the Orinoco crocodile is not a rodent. _____

6. Euripides enjoyed tragedy. After all, all fifth century Greeks enjoyed tragedy and Euripides was a fifth century Greek. _____

* 7. All mammals that hibernate slow their breathing in the winter. Since polar bears hibernate, they slow their breathing in the winter. _____

8. If one has poor health, one goes to the doctor. If one goes to the doctor, one spends money. Thus, if one has poor health, one spends money. _____

* 9. Chris will take summer courses, for either he takes them or he'll have to wait until next fall for graduation, and he won't wait that long. _____

10. All Diesel engines produce exhaust gases. Each school bus has a Diesel engine. Thus, each school bus produces exhaust gases. _____

*11. The universe can act as a magnifying lens, since if relativity theory is correct, that would be the case. And relativity theory is correct. _____

12. People who drink a glass of warm milk before going to bed are able to sleep well. Given that Beth never misses hers, I'm sure she is able to sleep well. _____

*13. Chameleons could be scary, since they are lizards that change their color, and any such lizard could be scary. _____

14. Crocodiles either wallow in mud holes or are caught by hunters. If the former, they get diseases. But if the latter, they often lose their lives. So they either get diseases or often lose their lives. _____

*15. No Ohio farmer grows papayas, for no northern farmer grows papayas and Ohio farmers are northern farmers. _____

VIII. For each of the following arguments, give its form. (Hint: First, reconstruct the argument and then replace propositions or terms by the symbols inside parentheses according to the conventions outlined above.)

1. If the defendant's car was used in the robbery, then the car was at the scene of the crime. But it was not at the scene of the crime. Thus, the defendant's car was not used in the robbery. (D, C)

   SAMPLE ANSWER: If D, then C
   <u>Not C   </u>
   Not D

2. If these snakes are cobras, then they're poisonous. Therefore, if these snakes are not poisonous, then they are not cobras. (C, O)

3. If offenses against the innocent are punished, then we have a fair system of justice. If we have a fair system of justice, then the guilty are treated as they deserve. So if offenses against the innocent are punished, then the guilty are treated as they deserve. (O, J, G)

* 4. Since all computers are mechanical devices, no computers are things that can think, for no things that can think are mechanical devices. (C, D, H)

5. Archie doesn't eat chicken, for he is a vegan, and if he is a vegan, then he doesn't eat chicken. (A, C)

* 6. If Massachusetts does not allow gay marriage, then its laws governing marriage are conservative. In fact, its laws governing marriage are not conservative. So, Massachusetts does allow gay marriage. (M, L)

7. Either doctors favor the new health program or the uninsured suffer. But doctors do not favor the new health program. Hence the uninsured suffer. (D, N)

8. All accountants are good at math. Greg is not an accountant. Therefore he is not good at math. (A, M, g)

* 9. If a flower is an orchid, then it is costly. Therefore, if a flower is not costly, then is not an orchid. (F, C)

10. Since no tropical country has blizzards and Venezuela is a tropical country, Venezuela doesn't have blizzards. (C, B, v)

*11. All babies are infants. Some babies are good at crawling. Therefore, some infants are good at crawling. (B, I, C)

12. If you eat a lot of carrots, then your eyesight improves, since if you eat a lot of carrots, you get plenty of vitamin A, and if you get plenty of vitamin A, then your eyesight improves. (C, A, E)

*13. No schoolchildren are college graduates. All college graduates have a college diploma. Therefore no schoolchildren have a college diploma. (*C, G, D*)

14. If penguins are birds, then they are likely to have feathers. Since it is the case that penguins are birds, we must conclude that they are likely to have feathers. (*B, F*)

*15. Our planet is not special, for either Earth is the center of the universe or our planet is not special. And Earth is not the center of the universe. (*E, C*)

16. Anne is Mario's wife. That means that Mario is not a bachelor. For if Anne is his wife, then he is not a bachelor. (*A, B*)

17. Nathan's girlfriend, Adelaide, will leave him for good this time; because either Nathan will stop spending all of his paycheck at the racetrack or Adelaide will leave him for good. But Nathan will not stop spending all of his paycheck at the racetrack! (*N, A*)

*18. If oxygen is the lightest element, then oxygen is lighter than hydrogen. But oxygen is not lighter than hydrogen. Therefore oxygen is not the lightest element. (*O, H*)

19. If Winston Churchill was English, then he was not Brazilian. But if he was not Brazilian, then he was not South American. Thus if Winston Churchill was English, then he was not South American. (*E, B, A*)

*20. Melissa will either pledge Gamma Phi or she will not join a sorority at all this year. Accordingly, she will not join a sorority at all, since she will not pledge Gamma Phi. (*M, J*)

IX. **For each of the above arguments, indicate whether it is syllogistic or propositional, and if the latter, give the name of its form.**

SAMPLE ANSWER: 1. Propositional argument, modus tollens

X. **Indicate whether each of following is true or false. Discuss.**

1. A valid argument cannot have a false conclusion.

SAMPLE ANSWER: False

2. A valid argument cannot have a false premise. _____

* 3. A valid argument cannot have true premises and a false conclusion.
_____

4. Invalid arguments always have true premises and false conclusions. _____

* 5. A valid argument could have a counterexample. _____

6. All valid argument forms are truth-preserving. _____

* 7. An invalid argument could never have a true conclusion. _____

8. An invalid argument could never have true premises. _____

* 9. If there is entailment in an argument, then that argument is truth-preserving. _____

10. An invalid argument could have no counterexample. _____

XI. **The following syllogistic arguments are invalid. After symbolizing their forms accordingly, show invalidity in each case with a counterexample. (Tip: Use the same counterexample for arguments exemplifying the same invalid form. When the given argument plainly has true premises and a false conclusion, you can simply point that out in lieu of a counterexample.)**

1. All female college students are students. Some students are smokers. Therefore, some female college students are smokers.

    SAMPLE ANSWER: All *F* are *D*
                             Some *D* are *M*
                             Some *F* are *M*

    Counterexample: *F*, *D*, and *M* stand for "fish," "animal," and "mammal." [All fish are animals. Some animals are mammals. Thus, some fish are mammals.]

2. All giraffes are mute. That animal is mute. Thus that animal is a giraffe.

3. Most American citizens are permitted to vote in the United States. Michael is not permitted to vote in the USA. So Michael is not an American citizen.

4. Roses are flowers. Some flowers are daffodils. Thus roses are daffodils.

* 5. No SUVs are easy to park. Some SUVs are speedy vehicles. Hence no speedy vehicles are easy to park.

6. Some days are rainy days. Some days are sunny days. Therefore some rainy days are sunny days.

* 7. Fido is a dog. Some dogs bark. Therefore Fido barks.

8. Most Mexicans speak Spanish. Some Texans speak Spanish. Therefore some Texans are Mexicans.

* 9. All intellectuals support stem cell research. Barbra Streisand supports stem cell research. Therefore Barbra Streisand is an intellectual.

10. No desktop computer is light. My computer is not light. Hence my computer is not a desktop.

XII. Your Own Thinking Lab

1. Explain in your own words the relation between "invalidity" and "counterexample."

2. Explain in your own words the claim that validity is a matter of argument form.

3. Give two arguments of your own for each of the following valid argument forms: modus ponens, modus tollens, hypothetical syllogism, disjunctive syllogism, and contraposition.

4. Give a counterexample to the following argument: Horses are domestic animals. Trigger is a domestic animal. Therefore Trigger is a horse.

5. Provide two arguments illustrating each of these argument forms:

   1. All A are B

     All B are C

     All A are C

   2. All A are B

     Some A are not C

     Some B are not C

   3. No As are Bs

     All C are A

     No C are B

   4. All A are B

     Some A are C

     Some B are C

5. All *A* are *B*

   <u>*c* is not a *B*</u>

   c is not an *A*

6. All *A* are *B*

   <u>*c* is an *A*</u>

   c is a *B*

6. For each form in (XII) above, provide an argument *with true premises* that exemplifies it.

5.2 Sound vs. Unsound Arguments

Must we then always accept the conclusions of valid arguments? No, for there may still be something wrong with them (as is clear in some of the examples above). To evaluate an argument, validity is the first criterion we use, but not the only one. After we have decided that an argument is valid, we must also determine whether it is *sound*, bearing in mind that

> An argument is sound if and only if it is valid and all of its premises are true.

Thus, consider some arguments given earlier:

21 1. No Peloponnesians are Euboeans.
    2. <u>All Spartans are Peloponnesians.</u>
    3. No Spartans are Euboeans.

(21) is sound, while (4) and (5) are unsound

4 1. All dogs are fish.
   2. <u>All fish are mammals.</u>
   3. All dogs are mammals.

5 1. All Democrats are vegetarians.
   2. <u>All vegetarians are Republicans.</u>
   3. All Democrats are Republicans.

BOX 7 ■ SOUND ARGUMENT

1. An argument is *sound* if and only if it is valid and all of its premises are true.
2. An argument is *unsound* if it lacks either validity or true premises or both.
3. Unsoundness is a reason to reject an argument even if it's valid.
4. The conclusion of a sound argument is true.
5. Given (4), a sound argument's conclusion cannot be rejected without falsity.

This is the case because if an argument lacks either validity or true premises (or both), then it is unsound. The problem with (4) and (5) is that their premises are false, thus rendering the arguments unsound, even though, as we have seen, both are valid. Important things to remember are, first, that if even one of an argument's premises is false, then the argument is unsound, whether it's valid or not. Second, since validity is a necessary condition of soundness, an argument can also be unsound because its form is not valid. For example,

25   1. Horses have four legs.
    2. Felix has four legs.
    3. Felix is a horse.

BOX 8 ■ SOUNDNESS

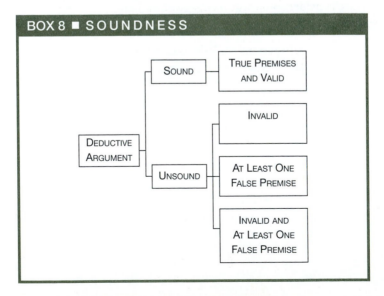

Here we may assume the premises to be true. Yet the argument is unsound because it is invalid: in a scenario where Felix is a four-legged cat, its premises are true and its conclusion false.

Validity *and* true premises, then, are the necessary conditions for soundness. Of course the question of whether premises are in fact true or false is another matter entirely, which usually cannot be answered by logic alone. Many such answers belong rather to the sciences, or to the investigations of historians, geographers, and other factfinders. To be sure, a good logical thinker will want to get her facts straight! But this is where she must head for the library or the laboratory and consider the evidence for the premises of arguments that purport to be sound.

The Cash Value of Soundness

Why, then, is soundness so important? Why is soundness a desirable characteristic in arguments? Because if one is aware of an argument's soundness, then not only is one fully justified in accepting its conclusion, one *has to* accept it. As defined above, all valid arguments are truth-preserving in that, if their premises are true, their conclusions must be true. If an argument is valid and also has true premises, it is sound; and that means that the truth of the premises transfers to the conclusion. Thus there is no denying the conclusion of any such argument without falsity, since the truth of that conclusion is guaranteed.

Thus soundness involves more than just validity, for it implies also that the premises of a valid argument are true. To establish an argument's soundness, it is not enough that it has been found valid: we still have to determine whether the argument's premises are in fact true. If even one premise is not clearly true, that's sufficient to doubt an argument's soundness (although, of course, more than one premise might fail to be true—or even all of them). Thus, validity and soundness are crucial evaluative criteria. They have a normative impact or worth because they support general norms telling logical thinkers what to make of any given argument that meets or fails to meet these standards. Stronger than validity, the cash value of soundness is more significant—for, as we've seen, an argument to be sound, must be not only valid but also have true premises. In any argument that meets this standard, *the conclusion must be true.* Thus, the cash value of soundness is twofold:

When an argument is sound, then

1. Given its validity, you can't assert its premises and deny its conclusion without saying something contradictory.
2. Given its validity and its true premises, you can't deny its conclusion without saying something false.

What about *unsoundness*? What is its cash value for logical thinkers? When an argument is unsound because its premises are false, it fails to provide good reasons for the conclusion. Thus logical thinkers should not accept that conclusion solely on the basis of such premises. But, as mentioned before, an argument that is unsound because it lacks a valid form may still provide good reasons for the conclusion (more on this in Chapter 6).

It is important to keep in mind, however, that when it comes to evaluating deductive arguments that are valid, soundness is far from being the final word. Even a sound argument could still let thinkers down in an important way. To this we now turn.

5.3 Cogent vs. Noncogent Arguments

Valid arguments might still fail in an important way even if they are sound: namely, they could lack *cogency*. A valid argument is cogent if and only if it is rationally persuasive—that is, if and only if it can rationally move a thinker to the acceptance of its conclusion. For an argument to have this feature, validity is a necessary condition but not a sufficient one. In addition to being valid, the cogent argument must also have premises that are not only acceptable but more clearly acceptable than the conclusion they are offered to support. Here is a summary of the conditions an argument must satisfy to be cogent:

1. Recognizable entailment (validity)
2. Acceptable premises
3. Premises that are more clearly acceptable than the conclusion

Given condition 1, to be cogent, an argument's validity must be recognizable to the thinker. Furthermore, conditions 2 and 3 require the *acceptability* of the argument's premises, not their truth. Thus this falls short of requiring that the cogent argument be sound: that is, an *unsound* argument could be *cogent* provided that, unbeknownst to the thinker, at least one of its premises turned out to be false. Consider, for example,

26   1. If the general theory of relativity is false, then it is false that the gravitation of large celestial bodies causes light rays to bend.

     2. But it is not false that the gravitation of large celestial bodies causes light rays to bend.

     3. The general theory of relativity is not false.

This argument has a recognizably valid form (modus tollens) and its premises appear not only acceptable but more clearly acceptable than the conclusion. In fact, astronomical observations support premise 2. Yet that premise could turn out to be false, making the argument unsound. Nevertheless, the argument seems cogent: someone who doubted its conclusion at first might be persuaded by the argument to accept it, provided that the person found its premises more acceptable and worked out the entailment.

The important thing to note is that sound arguments might sometimes lack cogency. For having validity and true premises is not enough for an argument to be compelling. Consider,

27   1. The earth is not flat and is not the center of the universe.

     2. The earth is not the center of the universe.

Argument (27) is plainly valid, since if its premises are true, its conclusion cannot be false. Moreover, since its premises are true,

BOX 9 ■ COGENCY

The standard of cogency is met by a given valid argument if and only if the argument is such that anyone who recognizes its validity and accepts its premises is thereby rationally compelled to accept its conclusion.

the argument is also sound. But could (27) move someone who reasonably doubts its conclusion to accept it? Imagine that the argument was offered in the Middle Ages, when all available evidence pointed to the falsity of that conclusion. Surely, people then did not *know* that premise 1 is true and would have found the whole argument noncogent or unpersuasive. Thus even sound arguments might sometimes fail to be cogent when their premises fail to be more acceptable than the conclusion they attempt to support. In any such case, the thinker would not be rationally compelled to accept the conclusion on the basis of the argument.

The Cash Value of Cogency

A valid argument meeting the high standard of cogency is one whose premises can transfer their acceptability to its conclusion. It is only then that its conclusion is rationally compelling (or simply, "compelling") to anyone who accepts the argument's premises and works out the entailment. What does it mean to say that a thinker is *rationally compelled* to accept the conclusion of a cogent argument? It means that if she were to reject it, that rejection would be irrational. Although failures of rationality sometimes happen, logical thinkers should be on guard for them and strive to avoid them altogether. The important thing to keep in mind here is that if, *unbeknownst* to the thinker, at least one premise of a certain seemingly sound argument turns out false, the argument could still meet the standard of cogency provided that the thinker were *not aware* of the flaw and she accepted the conclusion by deductive reasoning from premises found more acceptable. We'll have more to say about the cash value of cogency in Chapter 8, where we'll discuss begging the question, a mistake in reasoning that makes a valid argument noncogent.

Exercises

XIII. Review Questions

1. What does it mean to say that a deductively cogent argument is rationally compelling?
2. Explain the difference between soundness and cogency.

3. Given a certain standard for deductive arguments, it is contradictory to assert the premises of an argument that satisfies it and yet at the same time deny the conclusion. What standard is that?

4. What is the effect of denying the conclusion of sound argument?

5. What is the effect of denying the conclusion of an argument that one recognizes as cogent?

6. Must the conclusion of an invalid argument always be rejected? Explain your answer.

XIV. Of the following, which are possible types of argument and which are impossible?

1. An unsound argument with a valid form

    SAMPLE ANSWER: Possible

* 2. A sound argument whose premises are all false _____

3. A sound argument with only one false premise _____

* 4. A sound argument that is invalid _____

5. An unsound argument with a true conclusion _____

* 6. A sound argument with a false conclusion _____

7. A sound argument with true premises and true conclusion
    _____

* 8. An unsound argument with a false conclusion _____

XV. What's the matter with the following arguments? Explain.

1. An argument whose premises entail its conclusion is valid. Hence, one should accept the conclusion of any valid argument.

    SAMPLE ANSWER: Such an argument could be noncogent, or have false premises and thus be unsound.

* 2. Only sound arguments guarantee the truth of their conclusions. Thus, entailment and *therefore* validity are of no importance.

3. Logical thinking books make too much fuss about soundness. After all, unsound arguments may also have true conclusions.

* 4. Validity doesn't matter in science, for science values truth, and there is no relation between validity and truth.

XVI. Indicate whether the following scenarios are logically possible or impossible.

1. An unsound argument where there is entailment

   SAMPLE ANSWER: Logically possible (a valid argument with at least one false premise)

2. An unsound argument with a false conclusion _____

3. A valid argument where there is no entailment _____

* 4. A sound argument that is not truth-preserving _____

5. An argument that is an instance of a valid form _____

* 6. An invalid argument with true premises and a false conclusion

   _____

7. A sound argument with false premises and a false conclusion

   _____

* 8. An unsound argument with false premises and a false conclusion

   _____

9. A sound argument where there is no entailment _____

*10. A cogent argument that is not rationally compelling _____

11. A cogent argument that is invalid _____

*12. A cogent argument that is unsound _____

XVII. Your Own Thinking Lab

1. For any possible arguments in the previous exercise, provide an example of your own.

2. Give two examples of your own to illustrate the following: modus ponens, contraposition, and disjunctive syllogism.

3. Explain why your examples above are valid.

4. Explain each of the following claims:

   A. Denying the conclusion of a cogent argument is irrational.

   B. Asserting the premises while denying the conclusion of a valid argument is contradictory.

   C. Some valid arguments might not be cogent.

   D. Some unsound arguments might not be cogent.

E. Some unsound arguments might be cogent.

F. A deductively valid argument might yet be clearly unsound.

5. Illustrate each of the statements above with an example, supplying the context when needed.

6. The following extended argument is valid and has seemingly true premises. But is it cogent? If so, how? If not, why not?

   1. If the evidence supports the evolution of species, then evolutionary theory is correct.

   2. The evidence supports the evolution of species.

   3. Evolutionary theory is correct.

   4. If evolutionary theory is correct, then human beings evolved over time.

   5. Human beings evolved over time.

5.4 The Philosopher's Corner

Deductive Arguments and the A Priori/Empirical Distinction

A belief may be said *justified* if good reasons can be given in support of it. According to a traditional view in epistemology, the branch of philosophy concerned with human knowledge, one's beliefs can be justified in one or the other of two ways: either by reasoning alone or by observation. The former is the mark of *a priori* justification, the latter of *a posteriori* justification. Either way, beliefs so justified, if true, amount to *knowledge* in some sense. A priori knowledge is sometimes referred to as "armchair knowledge," while *a posteriori* knowledge, based on observation, is also known as "empirical knowledge." The standard prime candidates for a priori knowledge include propositions involving mathematical and logical truths, such as

   28 $2 + 2 = 4$

   29   *P* and *Q* entails *P*

But propositions that are true given the concepts alone, such as

   30   Puppies are young dogs.
   and
   31   To be a brother is to be a male sibling.

are also prime candidates for a priori knowledge. On the other hand, propositions traditionally considered knowable only *empirically* include those based on observation—whether this be our own or someone else's. For example,

32 The capital of Minnesota is St. Paul.

33 Water quenches thirst.

Whenever *all* premises of a valid argument can be known a priori, the argument's conclusion is also knowable a priori—that is, just by thinking. A person who works out the entailment can come to know the conclusion of the argument "without leaving her armchair." By extension, any such argument may be said to be a priori derivatively. But in the case of a valid argument with at least one premise knowable only *empirically*, no one could come to know its conclusion a priori just by working out the entailment in the argument. That is, a priori knowledge transmits from premises knowable a priori to a conclusion also knowable in that way only if the argument is *valid* and contains no *empirical* premises.

Exercises

XVIII. Which of the following is true and which is false?

1. "Water is H_2O and can be found in the vicinity" is knowable a priori.

   SAMPLE ANSWER: False

2. "Water is H_2O or it isn't" is knowable a priori. _____

* 3. "Water is H_2O" is knowable empirically. _____

4. Mathematical truths can be known a priori. _____

* 5. "It is not the case that water is H_2O and it isn't" is knowable empirically.

   _____

6. *Empirical* knowledge can be obtained just by thinking.

   _____

* 7. "P is identical to P" is knowable a priori. _____

8. "Grass is green" is knowable a priori. _____

* 9. "To be a sister is to be a female sibling" is knowable empirically.

_____

10. "A priori" means *knowledge that depends on experience*.

_____

XIX. Determine whether each of the following arguments would, if sound, provide an priori or an empirical justi-fication for its conclusion.

1. The cat is on the mat, since the cat is either on the mat or at the window, and it is not at the window.

   SAMPLE ANSWER: Empirical

* 2. A total of 100 swans have been observed to be white. Therefore, there are at least 100 white swans. _____

3. If p is true, and p implies q, it follows that q. _____

* 4. There is scientific evidence that the brain is the bodily organ that controls thoughts, feelings, and other mental phenomena. This suggests that the mind is the brain. _____

5. Many animals enjoy the company of humans and are capable of solving problems. Intelligence and joy are present only in creatures that have minds. Therefore many animals have minds. _____

* 6. By the definition of "disbelief," *to disbelieve that p* is *to believe that p is false.* _____ .

XX. The following passages present rough outlines of some famous philosophical arguments offered to prove the existence of some specific entities. Each of these would, if sound, provide a justification for its conclusion. But is the intended justification a priori or empirical? For each case, indicate which it is. Discuss.

1. In order to prove the existence of a world external to our minds, British philosopher G. E. Moore (1873–1958) argued along these lines:

   | 1 | Here is a hand. | (Image Moore holding up one of his hands in good light, clear-minded, with eyes open, etc.) |

2 If here is a hand, then there is an external world.

> (For hands are objects in a world external to the mind.)

3 Therefore, there is an external world.[1]

SAMPLE ANSWER: Empirical, for its first premise rests on observation

* 2. The concept of God is the concept of the greatest being possible. If the greatest being possible didn't exist, then there would be a being that is greater than the greatest being possible. But it is conceptually impossible that there could be a being greater than the greatest being possible. Therefore, God, the greatest being possible, exists.

3. Things are in motion in the world. Anything that is in motion is moved by something else—namely, a mover. But it is not possible that there be an infinite number of movers. Therefore, there is a First Mover: a Being that originates all motion but is not itself moved by anything else.

* 4. The propositions that an omnibenevolent (all good), omniscient (all knowing), and omnipotent (all powerful) God exists and that there is evil in the world are logically inconsistent. Obviously there is evil in the world, since many innocent people suffer. Therefore God does not exist.[2]

5. I am now thinking that tigers are carnivorous. If I'm thinking that tigers are carnivorous, then I have the concept "tiger." But to have that concept, I myself, or at least some members of my linguistic community, must have been in contact with tigers in the world. How else could I have acquired the concept "tiger"? It follows that there are (or have been) tigers in the world.[3]

XXI. Select two arguments from the previous exercise, one vulnerable to the objection of invalidity and the other to that of unsoundness. In each case, discuss why the argument would be vulnerable in that way.

[1] G. E. Moore, "Proof of an External World." Proceedings of the British Academy Vol. 25, 1939.
[2] Cf. J. L. Mackie's "Evil and Omnipotence" (included in God and Evil, N. Pike ed., New York: Prentice-Hall, 1964).
[3] Michael McKinsey has argued that a current view in philosophy would allow inferences of this sort. See his "Anti-individualism and Privileged Access," Analysis 51 (1991a): 9-16.

■ Writing Project

Go to a news source on the web or consult a newspaper or magazine and find an argument that you suspect of being invalid. Reconstruct it, keeping in mind the principles of faithfulness and charity and following all the steps of argument reconstruction. If it turns out valid after all, repeat this process with another argument you suspect of invalidity and continue searching in this way until your analysis reveals a genuine example of an invalid argument. Then write a short paper (a page should be enough) in which you (1) write out all the parts of this argument one by one and (2) present a counterexample that plainly reveals this argument as one that could have a false conclusion with all its premises true at once.

■ Chapter Summary

- ■ Deductive arguments may be classified as belonging to one or the other of two different kinds, either **propositional** arguments or **syllogistic** arguments.

- ■ In **a propositional argument**, the relation of inference hinges on relations among the propositions that make up its premises and conclusion.

- ■ In **a syllogistic argument**, the relation of inference hinges on relations among the terms **within** premises and conclusion.

- ■ SOME VALID FORMS OF PROPOSITIONAL ARGUMENTS

  modus ponens

  modus tollens

  hypothetical syllogism

  disjunctive syllogism

  contraposition

- ■ In logic, validity, soundness, and cogency are criteria for evaluating deductive arguments. The words used for such criteria are technical terms, and must therefore be applied as defined below.

Criteria of Evaluation for Deductive Arguments

VALIDITY

Condition

1. Entailment (i.e., having no counterexamples or having a truth-preserving form).

Cash Value

- It is not possible that the argument's premises be true and its conclusion false at once.
- But the latter could be false, if at least one of the premises is.
- It is, then, contradictory to accept a valid argument's premises and reject its conclusion.

SOUNDNESS

Conditions

1. Entailment.
2. True premises.

Cash Value

- The argument's conclusion must be true: to deny it is to say something false.
- Furthermore, to assert its premises and deny its conclusion is contradictory. But it is not irrational, unless the thinker has recognized the argument's soundness.

COGENCY

Conditions

1. Recognized entailment.
2. Acceptable premises.
3. Premises that are more acceptable than the argument's conclusion.

Cash Value

- Any argument that satisfies conditions 1 through 3 is rationally compelling, in the sense that it would move the thinker to accept its conclusion (provided she accepts its premises and works out the entailment).
- It would be irrational for the thinker to reject the conclusion of that argument.

■ Key Words

Validity
Entailment
Truth-preserving argument
Argument form
Propositional argument
Syllogistic argument
Soundness
Justified belief
Counterexample

Substitution instance
Cogency
Epistemology
A priori
A posteriori
Armchair knowledge
Empirical knowledge

Analyzing Inductive Arguments

6.1 Reconstructing Inductive Arguments

Since we have already dwelt at some length on deductive arguments, in this chapter we turn to inductive ones, which are crucial to ordinary and scientific reasoning. As we have seen, an argument is either deductive or inductive, depending on what sort of inferential support its premises are supposed to provide: premises could either *guarantee the truth* of a conclusion, or simply *provide some reason* for it. The former sort of support is the mark of deductive arguments, the latter of inductive ones.

There are a number of related tests that may help in recognizing an inductive argument. First, in the case of any such argument, ask yourself

Could the premises of the argument be asserted and the conclusion denied without logical contradiction?
- If yes, the argument is inductive.
- If no, the argument is deductive.

Let's consider some examples. First, a simple deductive argument:

   1 Pam is energetic and athletic. Therefore Pam is athletic.

The first test recommends trying to see what happens when (1)'s premises are asserted and its conclusion denied. The test yields

   2 Pam is energetic and athletic. But Pam is not athletic.

This is contradictory. There is no logically possible scenario in which the statements that make up (2) could all be true (or all false). In light of such a result, argument (1) above is deductive. By contrast, consider

3   1. Pam is athletic.
   2. Most of those who are athletic don't eat junk food.
   3. Pam doesn't eat junk food.

Argument (3)'s premises could all be asserted and its conclusion denied without contradiction. After all, there are possible scenarios in which these premises are true and the conclusion false. For example, a scenario in which Pam is athletic and most athletic people do not eat junk food, but Pam eats junk food. Thus, (3) is inductive. Similarly,

4   1. Many horses are friendly.
   2. Mr. Ed is a horse.
   3. Mr. Ed is friendly.

This is inductive, given that its premises could be asserted and its conclusion denied without contradiction, as can be seen in (5).

5   Many horses are friendly. Mr. Ed is a horse. But Mr. Ed is *not* friendly.

Compare (4) with

6   1. All horses are friendly.
   2. Mr. Ed is a horse.
   3. Mr. Ed is friendly.

Of the two, only (6) is deductive, since it is not possible to assert its premises and deny its conclusion without contradiction. If we try to do it, then we would be saying something contradictory, namely,

7   All horses are friendly. Mr. Ed is a horse. But Mr. Ed is not friendly.

There is no possible scenario where all three of these statements could be true at once, for clearly, if it is true that *all* horses are friendly and that *Mr. Ed is a horse*, it must be false *that he is not friendly*. Thus, since argument (6)'s premises cannot be asserted and its conclusion denied without contradiction, the argument is deductive.

Notice that an inductive argument always involves an *inferential leap*, for its conclusion invariably has more information content than what is given in the premises. Thus the former is not strictly contained in the latter. But this feature makes inductive arguments ideally suited for the empirical (i.e., observational) sciences such as physics and biology, where scientists often make causal connections or reach general conclusions on the basis of only a sample of observed cases. Thus, the observation that a great number of metals expand under heat plays a role in our inductively concluding that *all* metals do so, as does research on the habits of people with lung disease in our concluding that smoking increases the risk of contracting such ailments.

Another distinctive feature of inductive arguments is that newly acquired evidence could always make a difference in the degree of support for their conclusions, strengthening it in some cases, weakening it in others. Consider

8   1. Ninety-eight percent of State College students are involved in politics.
    2. Heather is a State College student.
    3. Heather is involved in politics.

Argument (8) is inductive. Its premises, if true, would provide some support for its conclusion. New evidence to the effect that Heather is indifferent to politics, however, could undermine that support. Once that evidence is added, the argument then is

9   1. Ninety-eight percent of State College students are involved in politics.
    2. Heather is a State College student.
    3. Heather never votes.
    4. Heather is involved in politics.

A quick comparison of (8) and (9) shows that in the latter, support for the claim *that Heather is involved in politics* has been undermined by the addition of the third premise.

The features of inductive arguments so far reviewed suggest that there is no entailment in them: their premises, even in cases

BOX 1 ▪ INDUCTIVE ARGUMENTS

What sort of argument counts as inductive?

▪ Any argument whose premises may provide evidence for its conclusion or hypothesis, but do not guarantee it.

How does one determine whether an argument is inductive or not?
By using one or the other, or both, of these tests:

▪ Check whether it would be possible for an argument with the same form to have true premises and a false conclusion.

▪ Test whether one can assert its premises and deny its conclusion without contradiction.

If in either case the answer is yes, then the argument is inductive.

where they succeed in supporting their conclusions, could never *necessitate* them. That is, no inductive argument is truth-preserving. Although an inductive argument may in fact have true premises and a true conclusion, what makes the argument inductive is that an argument of the same type *could* have true premises and a *false* conclusion—which, again, is the same as saying that the premises of an inductive argument do not entail its conclusion. Yet, as we shall see in this chapter, the lack of entailment in inductive arguments does *not* mean that they cannot offer support for their conclusions. In fact, they often make their conclusions probably true, or reasonable to believe, by providing evidence for them, even though such premises always fall short of necessitating their conclusions. This is why it is common to refer to the premises of inductive arguments as "evidence." At the same time, since the conclusions of such arguments may be supported but are never completely proved true by their premises, such conclusions have the status of *conjectures* and are often called "hypotheses."

Given these features, inductive arguments are *plausibility arguments*. That is, although the evidence that any such argument may provide for its hypothesis never entails it, when successful, the argument can make it plausible. To say that a claim is plausible is to say that it is likely to be true, probably true, or at least, reasonable to accept. We shall look closely at the standard for successful induction once we have examined some common types of inductive argument. Before leaving this section, however, it is important to emphasize that, regarding any such argument, there are two basic questions that you must ask—namely, those in Box 1 above.

6.2 Some Types of Inductive Argument
Enumerative Induction

Here we'll be discussing four of the several types of inductive argument. The first of these is *enumerative induction*. In an enumerative induction, one or more premises state that *some* things of a certain kind have a certain feature, and this is offered as evidence for the conclusion that *all* things of the same kind have that feature. The conclusion of any such argument, often called an "inductive generalization," is a *universal generalization*.

A universal generalization

- Is a statement asserting that all of the members of a certain class have (or don't have) a certain feature.
- May be expressed by a great number of different patterns of sentence. Some standard patterns are "All ... are ...," "Every ... is ...," "No ... is ...."

Consider

10 Roses blossom in the summer.

Unless more information is provided here, (10) should be read as saying "*All* roses blossom in the summer," which illustrates the standard pattern "All *As* are *Bs*."

To support (10) with an enumerative induction, we may adopt one or the other of two equivalent strategies. First, offer a single premise to the effect that, for example, many roses have been observed to blossom in the summer. That would be a _nonuniversal generalization_, where

The argument would run

11 1. Many roses have been observed to blossom in the summer.

   2. All roses blossom in the summer.

This conclusion consists in a universal generalization asserting that _all things_ of a certain kind (roses) have a certain feature (blossoming in the summer). Here are other such generalizations:

12 Every metal expands when heated.

13 Any potato has vitamin C.

14 Each body falls with constant acceleration.

15 All bodies attract each other in proportion to their masses and in inverse proportion to the square of the distance between them.

16 No emeralds are blue.

17 No seawater quenches thirst.

18 No mules are fertile.

Our list illustrates common universal generalizations in two contexts: scientific and everyday. Following the above strategy, we could attempt to support these generalizations by enumerative induction. Each of our arguments would have a premise that would be a nonuniversal generalization to the effect that things of the relevant kind have (12 through 15) or do not have (16 through 18) a certain feature.

An alternative yet equivalent strategy to support these universal generalizations by enumerative induction would have *specific statements* as premises, where

> A specific statement is a statement about an *individual* thing or person. For example: "Benjamin Franklin founded the University of Pennsylvania," "That oak is infested," "Mary's cap is waterproof," and "The U.N. is in session."

If we wish to use this strategy to support the conclusion that roses blossom in the summer, our argument may run

19   1. Rose 1 has been observed to blossom in the summer.
       2. Rose 2 has been observed to blossom in the summer.
       3. Rose 3 has been observed to blossom in the summer .....
       4. Rose n has been observed to blossom in the summer.
       5. All roses blossom in the summer.

When n is a large number (say, billions) of individual roses, the universal generalization in the argument's conclusion (statement 5) would be supported by premises that are about individual roses found to blossom in the summer. This strategy is equivalent to the one used in (11) above, given that (19)'s premises spell out what (11)'s premise summarizes. Similar to (11) is

20   1. Every raven *so far observed* has been black.
       2. Ravens are black.

Argument (20)'s conclusion is a universal generalization ascribing a certain feature (blackness) to *all* ravens. Like other inductive arguments, this too makes an inferential leap: from *a number* of ravens' having a certain feature, it draws the conclusion that *all* ravens have that feature. Its premise, if true, supports the claim that *a great number* of ravens have that feature, but it cannot conclusively support (i.e., guarantee) the claim that *all* do. After all, nobody can observe *all* past, present, and future ravens! Argument (20)'s conclusion, then, goes beyond the information given in its premise. Inductions of this sort run along the lines of (21).

21   1. A number, n, of *As* have been observed to be *Bs*
       2. All *As* are *Bs*

Clearly, any argument along such lines could have a true premise and a false conclusion, since it is always possible that some unobserved *A*s lack the feature of *being a B*. Even in cases when *n* is a very large number, this could happen. Note that if *n* were taken to involve *all* cases, the argument would be deductive. Furthermore, notice that (20)'s hypothesis is a universal generalization—namely,

> **22** All ravens are black.

Therefore a single raven that is observed *not* to be black would be a counterexample proving (22) false. Similarly, were a single whale observed to be a cold-blooded animal, that would be a counterexample to

> **23** No whale is a cold-blooded animal.

Here the rule is

> Any exception to the conclusion of an enumerative induction has the status of a *counterexample*. That is, it proves that conclusion false.

Counterexamples have consequences for scientific laws such as those of physics and biology, which are universal generalizations of the sort exemplified by Galileo's law of free fall and Newton's law of gravitation in (14) and (15) above. If counterexamples to such scientific generalizations were found, then the scientific theories built on them would be in need of revision.

Another familiar use of enumerative induction is to predict the future and to explain the past—as, for example, when someone reasons,

> **24** 1. In the past, most animal species have survived by adaptation.
> ———————————————————————————
> 2. Animal species will continue to survive by adaptation.

Imagine some naturalists who offer (24)'s conclusion. They may defend their claim, a universal generalization about future events, by insisting that for millions of years in the past many species of animals have survived by adaptation. Yet that premise is a nonuniversal generalization, which can be defended only by listing cases of species that have been observed to survive by adaptation. At the same time, the case of any species found *not* to have survived by adaptation would be a counterexample, in light of which our naturalists would be forced to revise their theory.

Statistical Syllogism

A statistical syllogism is an inductive argument whereby a certain feature is ascribed to some case or cases on the basis of their being subsumed within a larger class of things, some of which, perhaps many, have the ascribed feature. For example,

25   1. Most surgeons carry malpractice insurance.
      2. Dr. Hagopian is a surgeon.
      3. Dr. Hagopian carries malpractice insurance.

Crucial to this argument is the generalization in premise 1, which is a nonuniversal one, since it is not about *all* surgeons. Thus (25)'s form is

26   1. Most *As* are *Bs*
      2. *h* is an *A*
      3. *h* is a *B*

Compare the form

27   1. All *As* are *Bs*
      2. *h* is an *A*
      3. *h* is a *B*

Clearly, (27) is a deductive form, while (26) isn't. An inductive argument along (26)'s lines is a statistical syllogism. Like other inductive arguments, statistical syllogisms are common, both in ordinary and scientific reasoning. Their general premises could be put at the service of explaining the past, as in

28   1. Most famous battles involved careful strategy.
      2. Trafalgar was a famous battle.
      3. Trafalgar involved careful strategy.

Or predicting the future, as in

29   1. Eighty percent of police officers have antiterrorism training.
      2. Michael will be a police officer.
      3. Michael will have antiterrorism training.

> ### BOX 2 ■ UNIVERSAL AND NONUNIVERSAL GENERALIZATIONS
>
> 1. A **universal generalization** involves *all* members of a certain class. It may be expressed by linguistic devices such as "all" and "no."
> 2. A **nonuniversal generalization** involves only *some* members of a certain class. It may be expressed by "some," "most," "many," "a few," "lots of," "*n* %," etc.

Argument (29) illustrates a common pattern of statistical syllogisms, that is,

30   1. *n* % of *As* are *Bs*
      2. *m* is an *A*
      —————————
      3. *m* is a *B*

But argument (28) illustrates pattern (26). The scope of the nonuniversal generalization in a statistical syllogism matters for the argument's reliability: the greater the size, the more reliable the argument. At the same time, as noted above, the generalization must be nonuniversal, since otherwise, the argument would be deductive rather than inductive. Recall that these two types of generalization differ in the ways described in Box 2. In an argument by statistical generalization, there is always one premise that is a nonuniversal generalization. Keep in mind that, when that generalization is expressed as

31   *n* percent of *As* are *Bs*

then for the argument to be inductive, "*n*" has to be a number smaller than 100.

Causal Argument

In a *causal argument*, one or more premises are offered to support the hypothesis that a certain event is causally related to another event. Such arguments often involve eliminating other events as possible causes (or effects) in favor of the one that is taken to be the more likely cause (or effect). Their conclusions count as inductive because they have the status of *hypotheses*. Their premises always fall short of entailing those hypotheses.

The question of what it means to say that two events are related as cause and effect, or of when we can confidently say that such a relationship obtains, is a difficult philosophical problem that is largely beyond the scope of our concern here. The word "cause" itself is ambiguous. It could mean different things in different contexts. Sometimes it is used to talk about an incident or action that has a certain event as its outcome. For example,

32   1. There was a power blackout in our region yesterday.
      2. Many computers in our region crashed yesterday.
      3. Yesterday's blackout caused many computers to crash.

Here 'cause' is a sufficient cause for the occurrence of an event, and it also has that use in the following:

33   Heating causes metals to expand.

Other times, "cause" is used to mean the necessary cause of an event, as in

34   HIV causes AIDS.

This is to say that, in the absence of HIV, AIDS cannot occur.

One conceptual requirement that seems fundamental to our notion of causation is that a cause must regularly precede its effect. If it is a matter of well-documented observation that whenever in the past a flame came in contact with combustible substances this was invariably followed by a fire, then we may safely conclude that Jim's lighting a match this morning near the gas was the cause of the fire that immediately erupted. In making such claims, however, it is often assumed that cause and effect are uniformly connected: that is, that once some apparent causal relation has been established, any similar cause C will have a similar effect E. But C is not the cause of E if, other things being equal, C does at some point occur without E. This is the so-called *regular conjunction* view, which falls short of defining the relation between cause and effect. As famously noted by Thomas Reid (1710–1796), although day regularly follows night, it makes no sense to say that the latter is the cause of the former. Causation must be *something* over and above mere regular conjunction, but it is not so easy to say *what*.

In his *System of Logic* (1843), John Stuart Mill (1806–1873) attempted to capture ordinary intuitions about cause/effect relations.

BOX 3 ■ TWO OF MILL'S METHODS

- *Agreement and Difference*: What different occurrences of a certain phenomenon have in common is probably its cause. And factors that are present only when some observed phenomenon occurs are probably its cause.

- *Concomitant Variation*: When variations of one sort are highly correlated with variations of another, one is likely to be the cause of the other, or they may both be caused by something else.

He proposed five methods to determine when two events are causally related. The basic principle is this: whenever something occurs, it is often possible to narrow the range of acceptable hypotheses about its likely cause—or about its effect—by eliminating plainly irrelevant factors until at last we find the hypothesis most likely to be the actual cause (or effect). Here we'll consider two of Mill's methods, the so-called *method of agreement and difference*, and *method of concomitant variation*. The basic ideas underwriting these methods are summarized in Box 3.

The Method of Agreement and Difference

Suppose a coach wants to find out why Mick, Jim, and Ted, three of his best players, often perform poorly on Friday afternoons. After collecting some data about what each player does before the game, the coach reasons along these lines:

35 1. Mick, Jim, and Ted have been performing poorly on Friday afternoons.
2. Going to late parties on Thursday is the one and only thing that all three do when and only when they perform poorly.
3. Going to late parties on Thursday likely causes their poor game performance.

The pattern of causal argument underlying (35) is that of "agreement" roughly,

36 1. X has occurred several times.
2. Y is the one and only other thing that precedes all occurrences of X.
3. Y causes X.

But to make a more precise cause/effect claim, the coach should also reason by "difference": first, he should compare the players' performance when they've been going to late parties and when they haven't, and then, if they perform poorly only in the former cases, he should conclude that *that difference* also points to going to late parties as the likely cause of their poor performance. In fact, although the methods of agreement and difference are independent, they are usually employed jointly for the sake of greater precision.

The Method of Concomitant Variation

When variations in one phenomenon are highly correlated with variations in another phenomenon, one of the two is likely to be the cause of the other, or they may both be caused by some third factor. Suppose now the coach reasons:

37 1. The more fit the players are, the better their performance.

2. Probably, being fit causes their better performance, or their better performance causes their being fit, or something else causes both their better performance and their being fit.

The underlying reasoning is roughly

38 1. X varies in a certain way if and only if Y varies in a certain way.

2. Y causes X, or X causes Y, or some Z causes both X and Y.

Analogy

Analogy is a type of inductive argument whereby a certain conclusion about an individual or a class of individuals is drawn on the basis of some similarities that an individual or class has with other individuals or classes. For example,

39 1. Mary's vehicle, a 2007 SUV, is expensive to run.

2. Jane's vehicle is a 2007 SUV and is expensive to run.

3. Simon's vehicle is a 2007 SUV and is expensive to run.

4. Peter's vehicle is a 2007 SUV.

5. Peter's vehicle is expensive to run.

Here the arguer attempts to make her conclusion reasonable by analogy: Peter's vehicle shares two features with Mary's, Jane's, and Simon's: *being a 2007 model and an SUV*. This provides some reason to think that it may also have in common a third feature, that of *being expensive to run*. Let m, j, s, and p stand respectively for Mary's vehicle, Jane's vehicle, Simon's vehicle, and Peter's vehicle and A, B, and C for the ascribed features: *being a 2007 model, being an SUV* and *being expensive to run*. Then (39)'s pattern is,

39′   1. m is A, B, and C
       2. j is A, B, and C
       3. s is A, B, and C
       <u>4. p is A and B</u>
       5. p is C

Any argument along these lines would fall short of entailing its conclusion. Yet if its premises were true, they might count as evidence for it, depending on the specific case. Analogies can make their conclusions plausible provided that they meet the standards for all inductive arguments, which we'll discuss below. Among the specific factors that matter for the success of analogies are those presented in Box 4.

BOX 4 ■ FACTORS THAT AFFECT THE SUCCESS OF AN ANALOGY

1. **The number of things and the number of features held to be analogous.**
   - ■ Greater numbers here would make an analogy stronger.
2. **The degree of similarities and dissimilarities among those things.**
   - ■ More of the former and less of the latter would make an analogy stronger.
3. **The relevance of ascribed features to the hypothesis.**
   - ■ Greater relevance would make an analogy stronger.
4. **The boldness of the hypothesis with respect to the evidence.**
   - ■ Modesty in the hypothesis would make an analogy stronger.

Now consider

40 Extensive research on polar bears and hippos has shown that they have a great number of relevant features in common with other animals listed as threatened species. These species might disappear. So polar bears and hippos might disappear.

The pattern of reasoning underlying this analogy is

> 1. **Things a and b have n relevant features in common with x, y, and z.**
> 2. **x, y, and z also have feature $n + 1$.**
> 3. **a and b probably have feature $n + 1$.**

If polar bears and hippos do in fact share a number of features with threatened species, and such features are truly relevant to the conclusion of this argument, then (40) can be said to succeed in rendering its conclusion plausible.

Exercises

I. Review Questions

1. How do inductive arguments differ from deductive ones?
2. Is it contradictory to assert the premises of an inductive argument and deny its conclusion? If so, why? If not, why not?
3. What is an enumerative induction?
4. Why are the premises and conclusion of an inductive argument called "evidence" and "hypothesis" respectively?
5. What does it mean to say that a hypothesis is "plausible"?
6. What is an inductive generalization?
7. What's the difference between universal and nonuniversal generalizations?
8. How can a universal generalization be proved false?
9. Explain the reasoning involved in statistical syllogism.
10. Explain the reasoning involved in causal argument.
11. Why is the word "cause" ambiguous?
12. Explain the reasoning involved in analogy.

II. Determine whether the following arguments are deductive or inductive.

1. Many whales observed in this region are white mammals. Therefore any whale in this region is a white mammal.

   SAMPLE ANSWER: Inductive argument

2. Triangles have exactly three internal angles. Rectangles have exactly four internal angles. Therefore rectangles are not triangles.

   _____

* 3. If all roses have a scent, then the roses in the vase have a scent. But they don't. It follows that it isn't true that all roses have a scent.

   _____

4. Buying a house is a good investment. After all, that's exactly what statistics have shown for the last 10 years. _____

5. In all samples of water so far tested, the composition is H_2O. Thus water is H_2O. _____

* 6. The Crusades were bloody, for most medieval wars were bloody, and the Crusades were medieval wars. _____

7. Surely the earth is not flat. If it were flat, then Magellan could not have circumnavigated it. But he did! _____

8. Jane is a dentist and has clean teeth. Bruce is a dentist and has clean teeth. Therefore all dentists have clean teeth. _____

* 9. Cars are mechanical devices. No mechanical devices are easy to fix. Thus no car is easy to fix. _____

10. Many medical doctors care about their patients. Tom is a medical doctor. Thus he cares about his patients. _____

11. Mary doesn't like being denied a salary increase, for she is a state worker, and no state worker likes that. _____

*12. To be an ophthalmologist is to be an eye specialist MD. My new neighbors are eye specialist MD's, so they are ophthalmologists.

   _____

13. Children riding in school buses always arrive punctually. Jill rides in a school bus. Therefore Jill always arrives punctually.

   _____

14. Carl is divorced. Therefore Carl was married. _____

*15. White feathers in pigeons are likely to be an adaptation against predators, for such feathers have been observed to distract falcons and other attackers in the air. _____

III. **For each of the arguments in the previous exercise that is *inductive*, make it deductive by modifying premises and conclusion accordingly. (Tip: Add premises if necessary.)**

> SAMPLE ANSWER: 1. All whales observed in this region are white mammals.
> Therefore, no whale observed in this region has not been a white mammal.

IV. **For each of the following inductive arguments, determine whether it is an enumerative induction, an analogy, a statistical syllogism, or a causal argument.**

1. Dinosaurs were warm-blooded animals, since the fossil record supports that hypothesis by showing a large number of dinosaurs in heat-conserving poses typical of such animals.

   SAMPLE ANSWER: Enumerative induction

* 2. Of a group of 250 seventh graders, only those who received fruits rich in zinc performed well in cognitive tasks. Thus, zinc may be good for boosting cognitive acuity. _____

3. People who drink a warm glass of milk before going to bed always sleep well. Therefore drinking a warm glass of milk before going to bed helps a person sleep well. _____

4. Infants like baby talk. This is supported by recent experiments on 2000 infants led by cognitive psychologists at Columbia University.
   _____

* 5. The earth is a planet with carbon-based life. The three elements required for carbon-based life are carbon, liquid water, and energy. These elements appear to be, or to have been, present in Mars, which is also a planet. This suggests that Mars could have had carbon-based life. _____

6. Eighty-four percent of the students quit smoking after seeing in health class films of smokers' blackened lungs. Therefore, visually demonstrating how a drug affects one's body is conducive to avoidance of that drug. _____

7. Like you or me, doctors are human beings. Hence, they are also exposed to ordinary "wear and tear," as well as to common agents that cause ailments. _____

* 8. The Orinoco crocodile belongs to the species *Crocodilia* and is critically endangered. The Chinese alligator belongs to the species *Crocodilia* and is critically endangered. The Philippine crocodile belongs to the species *Crocodilia* and is critically endangered. The Nile crocodile belongs to the species *Crocodilia*. It follows that the Nile crocodile is critically endangered. _____

* 9. Dalinsky's Drugstore is a small business and therefore affected by current increase in household costs. After all, most small businesses are wrestling with such costs. _____

10. Appearances are misleading. For example, the landscape looks lifeless in Atacama, a Chilean desert thought to be lifeless until very recently. But satellite images have identified geological formations there that contain minerals similar to those in the Sahara desert, where microbes sometimes nestle. Thus make no mistake: microbes may nestle in the Atacama desert. _____

*11. People who have a high percentage of folic acid in their diets also have a lower incidence of Alzheimer's disease. But these are people who generally have more healthy habits. Thus, either a high percentage of dietary folic acid causes a lower incidence of Alzheimer's disease or having healthy habits cause both. _____

12. During repeated experiments of consumption of high-flavonoid cocoa, researchers measured significant improvements in blood flow and the function of endothelial cells. They concluded that high-flavonoid cocoa may help blood pressure and blood flow. (*New York Times*: "Science Times," p. D5, February 17, 2004.) _____

13. Smaller, more fuel-efficient vehicles are now quite popular among many college students. My roommate is about to buy a vehicle. I predict that he'll buy a small, fuel-efficient, car. _____

*14. Anyone wishing to be a space tourist will have to pay $100 million. For, according to my records, each space tourist has recently paid $100 million for traveling in space. _____

15. Russia's Olympic champion Natalia Sadova has been banned for two years after testing positive for an anabolic substance. A great number of athletes who are banned for illegal substance consumption never regain popular support. Therefore Natalia Sadova is unlikely to regain popular support. _____

1. Provide the following extended argument: an enumerative induction whose conclusion is a premise in a deductive argument used to draw another conclusion.

2. Explain the reasoning underwriting Mill's methods of agreement and difference, and of concomitant variation. Support your explanation with two arguments illustrating each of these methods.

3. Write an inductive generalization and imagine what would be a counterexample to it. Explain how your counterexample would undermine the generalization.

6.3 Evaluating Inductive Arguments

Inductive Reliability

Suppose we try to reconstruct many of the above arguments as if they were deductive and then proceed to evaluate them according to deductive standards, such as validity, soundness, and cogency. That would plainly conflict with charity and faithfulness, since no such argument could pass that evaluation. Yet some such arguments do *support their conclusions* provided that their premises are true. This suggests that we need standards other than the deductive ones to assess inductive arguments. Chief among these is *inductive reliability*. It concerns the form of an argument and may be defined as follows:

> An inductive argument is *reliable* if and only if its form is such that, if its premises were true, it would be reasonable to accept its conclusion as true.

When an inductive argument is reliable, it has a form that makes its conclusion plausible *provided that its premises are true.* Consider

41   1. Ninety-nine percent of guitar players also play other musical instruments.

2. Phong is a guitar player.

3. Phong also plays other musical instruments.

This inductive argument seems pretty reliable: its form is such that, if its premises were true, its conclusion would be *plausible*. Compare

> **42** 1. Fifty-nine percent of guitar players also play other musical instruments.
>
> 2. Phong is a guitar player.
> _____
> 3. Phong also plays other musical instruments.

This is less reliable than (41), but more reliable than

> **43** 1. Thirty-nine percent of guitar players also play other musical instruments.
>
> 2. Phong is a guitar player.
> _____
> 3. Phong also plays other musical instruments.

Inductive reliability is, then, a matter of degree. An inductive argument of the form

> **44** 1. Fifty-nine percent of *A*s are *B*s
>
> 2. *p* is an *A*
> _____
> 3. *p* is a *B*

is more reliable than one of the form

> **45** 1. Thirty-nine percent of *A*s are *B*s
>
> 2. *p* is an *A*
> _____
> 3. *p* is a *B*

The cash value of inductive reliability for logical thinkers can be better appreciated by comparing it to the cash value of deductive validity. Both standards are related to argument form. Both concern the support an argument's conclusion may have *provided that its premises are true*. In the case of a valid argument, if its premises are true, its conclusion *must be true*. In that of a reliable one, if its premises are true, its conclusion is *likely to be true*. As we saw in Chapter 5, a valid deductive argument is truth-preserving. By contrast, a reliable inductive argument is not. Even so, inductive reliability is one of the two desirable features that ordinary and scientific arguments should have.

Inductive Strength

Strength is another desirable feature for inductive arguments; thus we may use it to evaluate such arguments. An inductive

BOX 5 ■ STRONG INDUCTIVE ARGUMENT

When an inductive argument is *strong*, it has a reliable form and its premises are true. It is then reasonable to accept its conclusion as true.

argument is strong if and only if it (a) is reliable and (b) has true premises. When an inductive argument is strong, it is reasonable to accept its conclusion. That is, it is reasonable to think that the conclusion is true. We may think of this standard in terms of competition: given the structure of an inductive argument, rival conclusions are always logically possible. Imagine a case where a professor in Biology 100 has just received an email from one of her new students whose name is Robin Mackenzie. She is trying to decide whether she should begin her reply, "Dear Mr. Mackenzie" or "Dear Ms. Mackenzie." Let's assume that it is true that 80 percent of the students in Biology 100 are women and reason through the steps of this inductive argument:

46　1. Eighty percent of the students in Biology 100 are women.
　　2. Robin is a student in Biology 100.
　　3. Robin is a woman.

Since (46) is an inductive argument, the conclusion, statement 3, may in fact fail to be true, even if both premises are true. After all, a person named "Robin" could be a man. Even so, given the evidence provided by the premises, it seems that conclusion 3 is more plausible than the other competing hypothesis (i.e., that Robin is a man). But imagine a different scenario: suppose that we knew that 80 percent of the students in Biology 100 were men. Then, among the competing hypotheses, the conclusion that is most likely to be true on the basis of that information is that Robin is a man. The argument now is

47　1. Eighty percent of the students in Biology 100 are men.
　　2. Robin is a student in Biology 100.
　　3. Robin is a man.

We may alternatively define inductive strength in this way:

> An inductive argument is *strong* if and only if its hypothesis is the one that has the greatest probability of being true on the basis of the evidence.

In the same way that inductive reliability can be contrasted with deductive validity, *inductive strength* can be contrasted with *deductive soundness*. For one thing, the latter does not come in degrees, since it depends on validity and truth, neither of which is itself a matter of degree (there's no such thing as a "sort of true" premise or a "sort of valid" argument). Hence, just as any given deductive argument is either valid or invalid, so too is it either sound or unsound. On the other hand, inductive strength does come in degrees, for it depends in part on reliability, which is a matter of degree. What about the cash value of these standards? When an argument is deductively sound, its conclusion is *true*—and must be accepted by any logical thinker who recognizes the argument's soundness. But the conclusion of any inductively strong argument can be, at most, *probably true*—and thus reasonable to accept by a logical thinker who recognizes the argument's strength. For each of the two criteria by which we assess inductive arguments, then, we may summarize its cash value as follows:

Inductive Reliability's Cash Value

- If an argument has a good share of reliability, then it would be reasonable to accept its conclusion *only if its premises were also true.*

Inductive Strength's Cash Value

- If an argument has a good share of inductive strength, then it's reasonable to accept its conclusion, since it has a reliable form and its premises *are* true.

What, then, of inductive arguments that *fail* by one or the other of these two criteria? Of course, not all inductive arguments are good arguments. It's important, then, to investigate common reasons why some may fail. In the next chapter, we'll have a look at some such reasons.

Exercises

VI. Review Questions

1. What are the two standards for evaluating an inductive argument? Define each.
2. Does inductive reliability depend on the form of an argument? What about strength?
3. What question should we ask to determine whether an inductive argument is reliable?
4. Assuming that an inductive argument is reliable, when would it be strong?
5. Does the cash value of deductive validity differ from that of inductive reliability? Explain.
6. What factors are relevant to determining whether an enumerative induction is reliable?
7. What factors are relevant to determining whether an enumerative induction is strong or weak?
8. What factors are relevant to determining whether an analogy is reliable?

VII. Identify whether the arguments below are enumerative inductions, analogies, causal arguments, or statistical syllogisms and determine which are reliable and which are not. For any argument whose reliability cannot be determined, explain why not.

1. There is consensus among experts that heavy drinking is linked to liver disease. Therefore heavy drinking leads to liver disease.

   SAMPLE ANSWER: Causal argument, reliable

2. Millions of fish so far observed have all been cold-blooded animals. Thus, all fish are cold-blooded animals. _____

* 3. Most South American coffee beans are dark. Brazilian coffee beans are South American coffee beans. Hence Brazilian coffee beans are dark. _____

4. Nancy lives downtown and pays a high rent. Bob lives downtown and pays a high rent. Pam pays a high rent. Thus Pam probably lives downtown. _____

5. Forty percent of college students sleep less than eight hours a day. Peter is a college student. Therefore Peter sleeps less than eight hours a day. _____

* **6.** Every pizza eater I have met liked mozzarella. Thus pizza eaters like mozzarella. _____

7. Betty's pet is carnivorous, and so are Lois's, Brenda's, and John's pets. It follows that all pets are carnivorous. _____

8. Senegal is an African nation and has a forest. Nigeria is an African nation and has a forest. Since Egypt is also an African nation, it probably has a forest. _____

* **9.** Caffeine is related to poor memory. All recent studies have shown that people can improve their memory by reducing their daily consumption of caffeinated drinks. _____

10. The Matsuda family has lived in Spring Valley for ten years, and they like it there. The same is true of the Levines, the Robertsons, the Wilsons, the Al-Habibs, the Garcias, the Mahoneys, and the Mazzinis. My family will move to Spring Valley. So my family will like it there too. _____

11. Since their discovery, microorganisms have been observed to be present in all infections. Thus microorganisms are responsible for infections. _____

* **12.** Mike sells junk food, for he owns a fast food restaurant, and that's what most fast food restaurants sell. _____

13. Frank Sinatra sang in a 1950s movie wearing a tuxedo. Sammy Davis, Jr., Peter Lawford, and Joey Bishop were all in tuxedos in that movie with Frank, and they made up 90 percent of the male actors cast in it. Since Dean Martin also sang in the same movie, he must have worn a tuxedo. _____

14. From 1951 to 2001, Sir Richard Doll documented the mortality rate of British male doctors born between 1900 and 1930. Eighty-one percent of nonsmokers lived to at least age seventy, but only 58 percent of smokers lived to that age. Cigarette smoking stood out in Doll's findings as the only major factor distinguishing these two groups of doctors. Thus, the shorter survival rate in the second group was a result of smoking. _____

* **15.** Chase is a bank and makes home finance loans. Citibank is a bank and makes home finance loans. Wells Fargo is a bank and also makes home finance loans. This suggests that all U.S. banks make home finance loans. _____

16. After an extensive study involving major research universities, scientists discovered that poison ivy grew there at 2 1/2 times its normal rate when they pumped carbon dioxide through pipes into a pine forest. Their work suggests that atmospheric carbon dioxide is at least partially responsible for the higher growth rate of poison ivy. _____

17. I'll be accepted. Let's not forget that 98 percent of applicants with my qualifications get accepted. _____

*18. Given that Tina Turner is a famous singer and has an insurance policy on her legs, Queen Latifah probably has one too. After all, she is also a famous singer. _____

19. Ninety-two percent of computer owners cannot get through a typical day without using their computer. John is a computer owner, thus he probably cannot get through a typical day without using his computer. _____

20. It'll cool off soon, for these winds from the northeast usually bring a cool front. _____

*21. Wood can be made to rot by breaking down lignin, the compound that holds plant tissue together. This is in fact what fungus does to lignin. It has been proved that the molecular structure of lignin and construction glues is similar. Therefore fungus can be used to breakdown construction glues. _____

22. Most people with low levels of "good" cholesterol are at risk of heart disease. John has low levels of good cholesterol. Therefore, John is at risk of heart disease. _____

*23. According to a new study by naturalists, African elephants rarely climb hills. This is because climbing hills is too costly for them in terms of energy. _____

24. Some people aged between eighteen and forty say that cars have improved their lives. Betty and Miguel are both nineteen years old. Therefore, Betty and Miguel both probably think that cars have improved their lives. _____

*25. We will all have to pay more for manufactured goods. The reason is well known: U.S. producers' prices are pushed up by the price of fuel. _____

VIII. The following inductive arguments are not reliable. In each, introduce any change needed to make it reliable. Use your imagination!

1. Chickens are birds, and they cannot fly. Ostriches are birds, and they cannot fly. Rheas are birds. Therefore rheas cannot fly.

    SAMPLE ANSWER: Chickens are heavy birds adapted for ground motion and they cannot fly. Ostriches are heavy birds adapted for ground motion and they cannot fly. Rheas are heavy birds adapted for ground motion. Therefore rheas cannot fly.

2. A few birds can fly. Sparrows are birds. Therefore sparrows can fly. _____

3. Some fictional characters don't exist in real life. Since Cinderella is a fictional character, she doesn't exist in real life. _____

4. John F. Kennedy International Airport has tight security. Minneapolis/St. Paul is also an international airport. Hence, Minneapolis/St. Paul has tight security. _____

5. Sodium burns orange. After all, an experiment recently performed has shown that it does. _____

6. San Francisco is on the coast and it's a diverse, densely populated city in the United States. Miami is on the coast and it's a densely populated U.S. city. Therefore Miami is diverse. _____

7. All muscles turn to fat when one stops working out. After all, that's what happened to me last year when I stopped working out due to a small accident. _____

8. Avoid scorpions: Some such creatures observed in the Arizona desert sting you with poison. _____

9. Mechanical problems have been found in a few Lockheed L-1011s. The plane I'm now riding in is an L-1011. So the plane I'm now riding has mechanical problems. _____

10. Theodore Roosevelt ran for president without the endorsement of a major party and he was defeated. Since Ted Smith is running for president without the endorsement of a major party, he'll be defeated. _____

1. Select the standard for deductive arguments that is more adequately contrasted with inductive strength and discuss the cash value of each.

2. Select the standard for deductive arguments that is more adequately contrasted with inductive reliability and discuss the cash value of each.

3. Propose a strong analogy and a weak analogy. Identify which is which and explain in either case what makes it strong or weak.

6.4 The Philosopher's Corner

Is Natural Science Inductive?

Earlier in this chapter we saw that no inductive argument is truth-preserving: no matter how strong an inductive argument is, its premises could be true and its conclusion false—which amounts to saying that in inductive arguments there is no entailment. By contrast, consider the following deductive arguments:

48 Since all triangles have three internal angles, and isosceles triangles are triangles, it necessarily follows that isosceles triangles have three internal angles,

49 That all whales are mammals entails that some mammals are whales.

These arguments guarantee the truth of their conclusions provided that their premises are true. A great part of our ordinary and scientific reasoning, however, seems not to involve arguments of this sort at all but rather *inductive* arguments. As a result, even when we start out with true premises, that never suffices to *guarantee* the truth of our conclusions, for although we may take these conclusions to be true, they in fact amount only to hypotheses, even in cases where our premises are good evidence for such conclusions. Earlier we noted that a common form these arguments may take is enumerative induction, whereby we infer a universal generalization from evidence about a finite number of past observations. For example,

50   A vast number of ravens have been observed to be black. Therefore ravens are black.

Since (50)'s conclusion amounts to an inferential leap with regard to its premise, the conclusion of this argument could be false. This is clearly bad news for science, because a great number of scientific inferences appear to be inductive, just as (50) is.

Call "inductivism" the view that the natural sciences are based on induction. According to inductivism, a scientific theory originates in direct observations and other ways of gathering empirical evidence that is then used to infer, by induction, a general conclusion. Given inductivism, the universal generalizations of science could turn out false. This would include even well-known scientific laws, such as Galileo's law of free fall and Newton's law of gravitation [see (14) and (15) above]. The reasoning underwriting such laws and theories faces what has come to be known as "the problem of induction." In a nutshell, this is the problem that inductive reasoning cannot be adequately justified either empirically (by induction) or a priori (just by philosophical thinking).

Considerations of this sort have led some philosophers to advocate *deductivism*, the rival doctrine that science proceeds by deduction rather than induction. How could scientific method be deductive? On a prominent deductivist account, it proceeds as follows:

1. Scientists propose a theory that includes some universal generalizations, which have the status of a hypothesis.
2. The theory is used to predict some observable phenomena, which are in turn tested empirically by experiments.
3. If the observable phenomena are as predicted, then the theory has passed the tests, and scientists can continue to hold it (though as only provisionally confirmed).
4. But if the observable phenomena are *not* as predicted, then the theory has been refuted and must be abandoned (since any attempt to continue holding it would render the theory nonscientific).

On this model, then, justifying the acceptance of a theory would indeed appear to rest on deductive reasoning. For it seems to unfold as a modus tollens: a theory, call it T, is advanced as implying certain observable phenomena O. If O is not what scientists observe in their experiments, then they conclude that T is false. The reasoning, then, is

51 1. If T, then O
   2. not O
   —————
   3. not T

which is a modus tollens. According to the deductivist model of scientific method, this is what happens in *most* scientific experiments. Many, many hypotheses are falsified in turn. On the other hand, suppose the theory T passes the test, which means O comes out as predicted by T. The reasoning here is

52 1. If T, then O
   2. O
   —————
   3. T

To deductivists, instances of (52) confirm T, but only provisionally. After all, (52) exemplifies a notoriously invalid argument form (more on this in Chapter 12). In consequence, reasoning along the lines of (52) would always fall short of proving T even if O is as predicted by T. Compare

53 1. If you take the 6:00 P.M. bus, you'll make it home by 7:00 P.M.
   2. Today you made it home by 7:00 P.M.
   —————
   3. Today you took the 6:00 P.M. bus.

If in fact you didn't take the bus but got home by 7:00 P.M. by carpooling with a friend instead, (53)'s premises would be true and its conclusion false.

Thus, if deductivism is correct, then no scientific theory can ever be conclusively confirmed by the evidence, though a theory could be conclusively falsified by genuine contrary evidence. And this means that no matter how well-accepted a scientific theory is, it never amounts to anything more than a *conjecture* or hypothesis. This is perhaps deductivism's most vulnerable aspect, as its critics have been quick to point out. Those who find the view implausible might object along these lines:

54 1. As an alternative to the ancient Ptolemaic conception of the universe (which held that the earth was its center, with the sun and other planets orbiting the earth), Copernicus proposed a heliocentric theory in which *all* planets orbit the sun.
2. Given deductivism, however, a theory such as Copernican heliocentrism is still only a conjecture (it's merely been "provisionally confirmed").
3. But, after centuries of intricate observations by astronomers in which predictions based on the Copernican model have been borne out, it is implausible that that theory is merely a conjecture. Surely, the solar system, as understood by modern science, is a *fact* if anything is!
4. Deductivism is implausible.

However, inductivism, the rival view about the justification of scientific theories, is itself not objection-free: as we have seen, it faces the formidable *problem of induction*. At this point, we may wonder who's got it right? Obviously, we are in no position to resolve a disputed question of this magnitude simply on the basis of the information provided here. Logical thinkers interested in pursuing it further should consider the study of philosophy of science, one of whose central topics is the analysis of arguments on either side of this debate.

Exercises

X. Discuss the following questions. Provide a correct answer for each, taking account of the above explanation.

1. Crucial to the justification of scientific theories is observation. What is its role according to deductivism?

2. How does observation enter into inductivism's account of the justification of scientific theories?

3. Does deductivism accept that scientific theories can be conclusively confirmed? If not, why not? And if so, what account of it is provided?

4. What's the matter with the following argument?
   Inductivists and deductivists agree that all scientific theories are mere hypotheses. Thus, we may validly conclude that all scientific theories are mere social constructs and thus neither true nor false.

5. According to Avogadro's law, all gases contain the same number of molecules per unit volume at the same temperature and pressure. How, according to inductivists, would scientists go about justifying this law? And what would deductivists say?

6. Could deductivists consistently hold that modern evolutionary biology is true? If yes, how? If not, what must they say? Assess their answer.

7. In the nineteenth century, Karl Marx proposed a theory that came to be known as historical materialism. One claim of that theory was that socialist revolutions would first break out in countries that were part of the industrialized world (western Europe and the United States). Suppose you were a deductivist assessing Marx's theory. What would you say about its scientific status?

XI. **The following passages relate to some aspects of the above discussion. Explain in your own words what's at issue in each of them.**

1. "Take the humblest generalization from observation: that giraffes are mute, that sea water tastes of salt. We infer these from our observations .... The principle involved here, far from being self-evident, does not always lead to true generalizations ...."[1]

2. "The obvious way of testing a hypothesis is to test its consequences .... But its truth is far from established thereby. It has merely withstood the challenge."[2]

XII. **Are these arguments persuasive? If so, how? If not, why not?**

1. David Hume noted that, even when the evidence from past experience suggests that the sun will rise tomorrow, one could accept that evidence yet consistently maintain that the sun will *not* rise tomorrow.

2. In his *Logic of Scientific Discovery*, Karl Popper is skeptical about induction for reasons that we may reconstruct as follows:

   1   That induction is a good guide to true belief is a principle that can be justified only in one or the other of two ways: *empirically* or *by reason alone* (i.e., just by thinking).

---

[1] p. 64 in W. V. Quine and J. S. Ullian, The Web of Belief (New York: McGraw-Hill, 1978).
[2] p. 96 in The Web of Belief.

2   The attempt to justify induction empirically is circular, since it requires induction (after all, why think that the future will be like the past?).

3   The attempt to justify the principle of induction by reason alone is hopeless, since the principle is not a conceptual truth.

4   Therefore the principle of induction is unjustifiable.

3. According to deductivism, the justification of a scientific theory is entirely a deductive process that requires us to ask questions, such as: Is the theory consistent? And are the observed phenomena as predicted by the theory? Affirmative answers to the latter question, however, would provide only temporary support for the theory (subsequent observations might yet falsify it). No induction is used in answering these questions.

■ Writing Project

Write a short essay (about 2 pages) in which you explain in your own words the difference between "inductivism" and "deductivism" as rival theories about how science works. Contrast and compare these competing accounts of scientific method and say what you take the dispute to be about. In doing this, you'll want, for instance, to contrast the two theories' differing views on the *steps* of scientific method, and you'll also need to explain the relative strengths and weaknesses of each of the two opposing views. If you conclude that one side makes a stronger case than the other, give reasons to support your view. Be sure to give full references for any sources you cite.

■ Chapter Summary

1. **Inductive argument:** Its premises, if true, could at most provide evidence for its conclusion, but could not entail it (since it is logically possible for the premises to be true, and the conclusion false). The conclusion of such an argument always has the status of a hypothesis.

2. Two criteria for evaluating inductive arguments: **reliability and strength.**

3. **Inductive reliability:**

   A. Has to do with **argument form**. In a reliable argument, the relation of premises to conclusion is such that if all the premises were true, then it would be reasonable to accept the conclusion.

B. Is **a matter of degree.**

C. Can be contrasted with deductive validity.

4. **Inductive Strength**

    A. Applies to an inductive argument with a reliable form and all true premises.

    B. Means it's **reasonable to accept the conclusion of any such argument.**

    C. Can be contrasted with deductive soundness.

5. **Types of Inductive Argument:** causal argument, analogy, statistical syllogism, enumerative induction

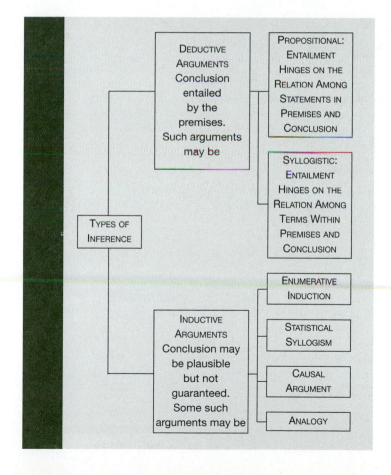

■ Key Words

Induction
Evidence
Hypothesis
Analogy
Enumerative induction
Statistical syllogism
Empirical science
Inductive
  generalization
Causal argument

Inductive reliability
Inductive strength
Nonuniversal generalization
Universal generalization
Inductivism
Deductivism
Method of agreement and
  difference
Method of concomitant
  variation
Problem of induction

Informal Fallacies

CHAPTER 7

Some Ways an Argument Can Fail

Chapter Objectives

This chapter introduces the notion of fallacy as represented in common patterns of defective argument and proposes a possible way of classifying twenty of the so-called informal fallacies. It then considers how inductive arguments can fail in at least five different ways, each of which illustrates one of the fallacies of the abuse of induction. Here you'll find discussions of

- How to define and classify twenty informal fallacies.
- The fallacy of hasty generalization.
- The fallacy of weak analogy.
- The fallacy of false cause and three of its more common forms: post hoc ergo propter hoc, non causa pro causa, and oversimplified cause.
- The fallacy of appeal to ignorance.
- The fallacy of appeal to unqualified authority.
- Appeals to authority that aren't fallacious.

■ Descartes's argument for mind/body dualism and the appeal to ignorance: How a philosophical argument can be undermined by fallacy.

7.1 What Is a Fallacy?

We have seen that arguments do sometimes go wrong by failing to meet deductive standards, such as validity and soundness, or inductive ones, such as reliability and strength. We'll now look more closely at some *informal fallacies*, which are types of defect that arguments may have. This is a topic of great importance, since we can learn quite a lot about what *good reasoning* is by paying close attention to some clear examples of how reasoning can go badly. In this and the next three chapters, therefore, we'll be studying different types of fallacy. But before we go any further, let's first be clear about what we do *not* mean by "fallacy."

The defects in reasoning referred to as "fallacies" consist not simply in erroneous beliefs or mistaken opinions—as, for example, when in everyday language someone speaks of the "fallacy" that animals do not feel pain. Rather, fallacies are *defective arguments*. Fallacies are worth studying, not only because they can cause an argument to draw an *erroneous* conclusion but also because they may render it *misleading*. They may affect an argument in subtle ways, so that it will seem OK when we first read or hear it. But the more we think about the argument, the more we will come to suspect that something has gone wrong. The so-called informal fallacies represent a number of different types of defect in reasoning. Some may affect deductive arguments, others inductive arguments, and some both. Our first step, however,

---

BOX 1 ■ THE CASH VALUE OF AVOIDING FALLACIES

Logical thinking requires *knowing how to avoid fallacies*—that is, how to recognize when someone else's argument commits a fallacy (so as not to be fooled) and how to keep one's own arguments from committing them.

must be to provide some assistance in site navigation by offering a tentative classification of those fallacies.

7.2 Classification of Informal Fallacies

There is more than one way to classify the informal fallacies, but some fallacies are more important than others. In this book, you'll find a fairly standard list, which includes the following.

Fallacies of Failed Induction

1. hasty generalization
2. weak analogy
3. false cause
4. appeal to ignorance
5. appeal to unqualified authority

Fallacies of Presumption

6. begging the question
7. begging the question against
8. complex question
9. false alternatives
10. accident

Fallacies of Unclear Language

11. slippery slope
12. equivocation
13. amphiboly
14. confused predication

Fallacies of Relevance

15. appeal to pity
16. appeal to force

17 appeal to emotion

18 ad hominem

19 beside the point

20 straw man

We'll consider each of these subcategories one by one, looking carefully at each of the informal fallacies grouped under them. Since we've just finished (in Chapter 6) discussing inductive reasoning, let's look first at fallacies that may arise through the abuse of induction.

7.3 When Inductive Arguments Go Wrong

Hasty Generalization

The fallacy of *hasty generalization* may affect enumerative induction. Earlier we saw that any argument of this sort starts out with premises asserting that certain things have (or lack) some feature and then draws a general conclusion about *all* things of that kind, to the effect that they have (or lack) that feature. The conclusion of the argument is a universal generalization, such as "All leopards are carnivorous," "No leopard is carnivorous," and the like. Thus an enumerative induction might go like this:

1   All leopards so far observed have been carnivorous.
    All leopards are carnivorous.

When a *representative sample* of leopards have been observed to be carnivorous, the conclusion of this inductive argument is well supported. Similarly, if we've observed a representative sample of leopards and found them all to be wild animals, we would be justified in drawing the general conclusion that leopards are wild animals on the basis of those observations. Our inductive argument would be

2   1. Every leopard observed so far has been a wild animal.
    2. All leopards are wild animals.

BOX 2 ■ HOW TO AVOID HASTY GENERALIZATIONS

In evaluating an enumerative induction, keep in mind that it would avoid hasty generalization if and only if

1. The sample on which its conclusion is based is large enough. In examples (1) and (2), the arguer has to have observed quite a few leopards.
2. The sample is both comprehensive and randomly selected among the target group. In (1) and (2), the arguer has to have observed typical leopards under a variety of different circumstances from all the regions of the world where leopards are found.

But in order for any such inductive conclusion to be justified, the conditions listed in Box 2 must be met. If either of those two conditions, or both, are unfulfilled, then the argument commits the fallacy of hasty generalization and therefore fails.

> Hasty generalization is the mistake of trying to draw a conclusion about *all* things of a certain kind's having a certain feature on the basis of having observed too small a sample of the things that allegedly have it, or a sample that is neither comprehensive nor randomly selected.

Suppose that a team of naturalists were to observe 500,000 leopards, which all turned out to be wild animals. Yet they were all observed in India during the first week of August, at a time when these animals were about to eat. The sample seems large enough, and the observers might therefore draw the conclusion that

3   All leopards are wild animals.

However, they would be committing a hasty generalization, since leopards are also found in other parts of the world. And they are found at other times of the year and in other situations. Clearly, the sample lacks comprehensiveness and randomness.

Argument (2) would fail to provide a good reason for its conclusion. On the other hand, suppose that the naturalists directly observed patterns of wild behavior among leopards in all parts of the world where such animals are found, at different times of the year and in many different situations. Yet the sample now consists of only thirty-seven leopards. Do the naturalists have better grounds for concluding (3) above? No, because although the comprehensiveness and randomness criteria are now met, the sample is too small. The charge of hasty generalization would similarly apply in this scenario.

It is, however, not only naturalists and other scientists who will need to beware of this sort of blunder. Logical thinkers will want to be on guard for hasty generalization in many everyday situations. Among these is the familiar mistake of stereotyping people. Suppose someone from the Midwest visits California for the first time. He becomes acquainted with three native Californians, and it happens that all three practice yoga. Imagine that, on his return home after his vacation, he tells his friends,

4 All Californians practice yoga.

If challenged, he would offer this argument

5 1. I met Margaret Evans, who is a Californian and practices yoga.
2. I met Alisa Mendoza, who is a Californian and practices yoga.
3. I met Michael Yoshikawa, who is a Californian and practices yoga.
4. All Californians practice yoga.

The reasoning in (5) is again an instance of hasty generalization. Furthermore, it stereotypes Californians: on the basis of the sample described by the premises, the conclusion is simply unwarranted.

Now imagine a different scenario: suppose that an anthropologist visits California with the intention of studying the folkways of modern Californians. Suppose she goes to southern California, northern California, the San Joaquin Valley, the Bay area, all regions of the state, and meets Californians from all walks of life, all social groups, all religions, all ethnic groups—from cities, suburbs, small towns, and rural areas. Suppose she talks to thousands, and suppose she discovers that *all* of these people practice yoga! (This is unlikely, but suppose it happened.) Then it would *not* be a fallacy to draw conclusion 4: assuming the thoroughness and breadth of the study, this conclusion would be a reasonable outcome of a strong enumerative induction. But notice how different this argument is from the earlier (5) above! A conclusion about *all Californians* based only on three instances is plainly unreasonable. It is a mockery of enumerative induction and an offensive stereotype to boot. To avoid stereotyping, together with the fallacy of hasty generalization that always underlies it, logical thinkers should keep in mind that

> No conclusion about a class or group could gather support from a sample that is either
> - Too small, or
> - Insufficiently comprehensive and random, or both

Weak Analogy

Weak analogy is another way an inductive argument could fail to support its conclusion. The underlying pattern of reasoning in analogy is something like this:

6   1. f and j are alike in that both have features n.
    2. f also has feature $n + 1$.
    _____
    3. j also has feature $n + 1$.

But whether an argument of this form can succeed depends very much on whether it passes the test outlined in Box 3. If the test shows that $n + 1$ may be features that only f has, then the things thought to be analogous would actually be disanalogous and the argument would commit the fallacy of weak analogy, which we may summarize as follows:

> To succeed, an analogy must make reasonable that the things alleged to be alike in the premises are in fact analogous in ways relevant to its conclusion. Any failure to do so counts as a fallacy of weak analogy.

In evaluating an argument of (6)'s form, we should ask these
questions:

- How *large* is number *n*? And are these *n* features *relevant* to the
  analogy's conclusion? (Here we want to know whether the
  premises provide an *exhaustive* account of the features relevant
  to the claim being made in the analogy's conclusion.)
- Are the things alleged in the premises to be alike *really* alike, in
  that they all have features *n*? (Here we want to know whether
  the similarities alleged in the premises are in fact present.)

Imagine this scenario: there are two siblings, a boy five years old
and his sister, who is thirteen. One evening it's little Johnny's
bedtime, and his mother says to him, "Johnny, it's nine o'clock.
Time for bed!" But Johnny replies, "You let Susie stay up late."
Could Johnny rightfully claim unfair treatment here? His argument may be reconstructed as follows:

7   1. Susie and I are alike in a number of features.
    2. Susie is not supposed to go to bed at 9:00 P.M.
    3. I'm not supposed to go to bed at 9:00 P.M.

This, however, is a weak analogy, since it takes for granted that
Susie's situation and Johnny's are relevantly similar. Yet they are
not. Although they live in the same house, attend the same school,
and have the same parents, there is a feature relevant to this argument that they don't share: the same age. Johnny is only five
years old while Susie is thirteen. When it comes to staying up late,
the mother may reasonably respond: *What I allow for a thirteen-
year-old differs from what I allow for a five-year-old.* In this respect, the
two cases are relevantly dissimilar; thus Johnny's argument is too
weak an analogy to support its conclusion.

Of course not all cases of weak analogy are as clear-cut as this,
and often there is room for disagreement about whether a certain
analogy is a fallacy at all. Some analogies are weak, but others are
strong. Still others are borderline cases whose degree of strength
or weakness is hard to assess. Moreover, analogy is one of the

most common forms of argument in everyday reasoning. It's a form widely used in political rhetoric. Logical thinkers are advised to beware of attempts by politicians to treat certain analogies as obviously strong when in fact they are debatable. Was the threat from Saddam Hussein's Iraq really analogous to that of Hitler's Germany? Is the Iraq War really analogous to the Vietnam War? When we think logically about current affairs, we will want to do careful research into the facts of the matter before we decide that an analogy is strong or weak. And obviously this is the kind of argument on which much may depend in real-life decisions. When presented with an argument to the effect that j has feature D because j and f are similar in having some other features A, B, and C in common, and because f also has feature D, we should

Accept the argument's conclusion only if

- Having A, B, and C is relevant to also having D; and
- No available evidence suggests that f and j differ in some important respect relevant to whether or not both have D.

False Cause

We saw earlier that a causal argument occurs when, on the basis of having observed two constantly conjoined events, it is inferred that they are causally related to each other or to some other event. Some such arguments can be inductively strong. If Jane comes down with the chickenpox only a week after her sisters, Penelope

BOX 4 ■ HOW TO AVOID FALSE-CAUSE ARGUMENTS

Causal arguments can fail in two basic ways:

1. The argument concludes that there is a cause-effect connection between two phenomena where there is none at all.
2. The argument mistakenly identifies some phenomenon as a sufficient (or determining) cause when in fact it's only a contributory cause (i.e., one among many) of some observed effect.

and Bernice, had chickenpox, and if Jane has been in contact with Penelope and Bernice during that time, we may reasonably infer that she caught the chickenpox from her sisters. Given what we know about how infectious diseases are transmitted, this inductive conclusion seems supported. But not all causal arguments are strong. When either of the two types of error listed in Box 4 occurs, a fallacy of *false cause* has been committed.

> False cause is simply the mistake of arguing that there is a significant causal connection between two phenomena when in fact the connection is either minimal or nonexistent.

Let's consider three different variants of the fallacy of false cause that may occur. One is

> ***Post hoc ergo propter hoc*** ("after this, therefore because of this"): The fallacy of concluding that some earlier event is the cause of some later event when the two are in fact not causally related.

The inclination to commit this fallacy in everyday life rests on the fact that when we see two events constantly conjoined—so that they are always observed to occur together, first the one, then the other—it may eventually seem natural to assume that the earlier is the cause of the later. But it is not difficult to imagine cases of precisely this sort where an imputation of causal connection would be absurd. Suppose we saw a bus passing the courthouse in the square just before the clock in the tower struck 9:00 A.M. and we then continued to see the exact same sequence of events day after day. Do we at last want to say that it's the bus's passing the courthouse that *causes* the clock to strike 9:00 A.M.? Of course not! And yet, in our experience, the two events have been constantly conjoined: the clock's striking has *always* been preceded by the bus's passing.

Clearly it would be preposterous to argue, in that case, that, from the evidence of constant conjunction between the bus's passing and the clock's striking 9:00, it follows that the former causes the latter. But similarly absurd arguments are in fact sometimes heard in everyday life. Now suppose that Hector and Barbara are not getting along and one of their friends ventures to explain the source of the problem:

8
1. Hector was born under the sign of Capricorn.
2. Barbara was born under Pisces.
3. They're not getting along because Capricorns and Pisces are not compatible.

Argument (8) fails to support its conclusion simply because it claims a causal connection for which the argument gives no good evidence—nor, in this case, should we expect good evidence to be forthcoming. After all, there's no good reason to think that configurations of stars and other celestial events really do affect the courses of our lives, and whatever the cause of this couple's troubles might be, it's probably traceable to something else. Argument (8) is a fallacy of *post hoc ergo propter hoc*—a form of false cause, for it assumes a cause-effect relation between being born on a day when celestial bodies have a certain configuration (i.e., under a certain zodiac sign) and subsequently growing up to develop certain personality traits. But there is no reason to think that these two sequential events are actually casually related.

Another way *false cause* may occur is

> **Non causa pro causa** (roughly, what is *not* the cause is mistaken *for* the cause): A fallacy in which the error is not an imputation of causality in a temporal sequence of events (as in *post hoc ergo propter hoc,* where an earlier event is wrongly thought to be the cause of a later one) but rather the simple mistake of misidentifying some event contemporaneous with another as its cause when in reality it's not.

One form of this error occurs when cause and effect are confused. An early nineteenth century study of British agriculture noted that, of farmers surveyed, all the hard-working and industrious ones owned at least one cow, while all the lazy ones owned no cows. This led the researchers to conclude that productivity could be improved overall and habits of industry encouraged in the lazy farmers by simply giving them each a cow!

Now plainly there is something wrong in that reasoning. But what? It seems to rest on an extended argument along these lines:

9 1. All of the observed industrious farmers are cow-owners.
 2. None of the observed lazy farmers is a cow-owner.
 3. All and only cow-owning farmers are industrious.
 4. There is a positive correlation between cow-owning and industriousness.
 5. It's cow-owning that causes industrious farmers to be industrious.

If we grant, for the sake of discussion, that the sample of British farmers in the study was large enough and that it was also comprehensive and randomly selected, then premises 1 and 2 support conclusion 3 and its restatement, conclusion 4. But 5's claim about cause and effect fails to be supported! It's industriousness that is probably the cause of cow-owning and not the other way around. By confusing cause with effect, (9) commits *non causa pro causa*.

Finally, there is a version of false cause in which the source of the mistake is something rather different from what we've seen so far:

Oversimplified cause:
The fallacy of *overstating the causal connection* between two events that do have some causal link.

Suppose a vice-president, campaigning for reelection, argues

10 1. At the beginning of this administration's term, the national economy was sluggish.
 2. At the end of this administration's term, the national economy is booming.
 3. White House economic policies do have an effect on the nation's economy.
 4. The improvement in the economy is due to this administration's policies.

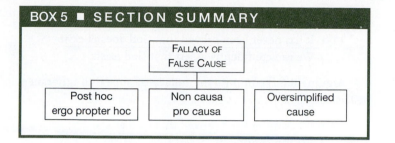

BOX 5 ■ SECTION SUMMARY

FALLACY OF
FALSE CAUSE

| Post hoc ergo propter hoc | Non causa pro causa | Oversimplified cause |

Argument (10) fails to support its conclusion. Let's assume that the premises are true. Even then, the causal relation asserted in premise 3 is merely one of *contributory cause*—i.e., one causal factor among others—which amounts to a rather weak sense of "cause." But 4 grandly asserts as the conclusion something much more than that: namely, that the actions taken by the incumbent administration are a *sufficient cause* of the improvement in the economy. Now surely this is an exaggeration. The campaigning vice-president commits a fallacy of oversimplified cause by taking full credit for the nation's economic turnaround, thereby overstating the sense in which his administration's policies "caused" it. Of course many politicians are quite prepared to take credit for anything good that happens while they're in office, but proving that it was due entirely to their efforts is something else again. The logical thinker should be on guard for this and any of the other versions of false cause as representing different ways in which a causal argument may fail.

Appeal to Ignorance

As we've seen, when inductive arguments go wrong, they may commit readily identifiable fallacies. Another of these is *appeal to ignorance* (or *ad ignorantiam*): an argument that commits this fallacy might conclude either that some statement *is true* because it has never been proved false or that it *is false* because it has never been proved true. More generally,

The fallacy of appeal to ignorance is committed by any argument whose premises attempt to support the conclusion that something is (or isn't) the case by appealing to *the lack of evidence to the contrary*.

Suppose someone reasons

11 1. It has never been proved that God doesn't exist.

2. We can confidently assert that God exists.

Argument (11) commits the fallacy of appeal to ignorance, just as does (12):

12 1. It has never been proved that God exists.

2. We can confidently assert that God doesn't exist.

Similarly, a believer in "extrasensory perception" might argue

13 1. No one has ever been able to prove that ESP *doesn't* exist.

2. It's reasonable to believe that there is ESP.

Clearly the only reason offered by (13) to support its conclusion is the absence of contrary evidence. But from that premise, all that can be supported is that *we don't know what to say about ESP!* The conclusion given—that "it's reasonable to believe that there is ESP"—is far too strong to be supported by such a flimsy premise. Reasoning along similar lines could also be used to demonstrate the failure of (11) and (12).

We must, however, add a note of caution. Suppose that the attempt to prove some claim has occasioned rigorous scientific investigation, and that these efforts have repeatedly turned up no evidence in support of the claim. Furthermore, suppose that the claim doesn't serve the purpose of explaining anything. In that

---

BOX 6 ■ HOW TO AVOID THE APPEAL TO IGNORANCE

- Notice that any argument whose premises merely invoke the lack of evidence against a certain conclusion commits the fallacy of appeal to ignorance. Such premises are *bad reasons* for the conclusion they attempt to support, and the argument therefore fails.

- Why? Because the mere lack of negative evidence does not in itself constitute positive evidence for anything! It justifies nothing more than an attitude of nonbelief toward the conclusion.

case, it is *not* a fallacy to reject that claim out of hand. Here we have to proceed case by case. Consider the claim,

14 There are witches.

Although there is of course a long history of claims that witches exist, all efforts to prove those claims have so far failed for lack of evidence. Furthermore, the concept of a witch has no serious explanatory function in any scientific theory: the existence of witches doesn't explain anything that happens in the natural world. These considerations suggest that it is *not* a fallacy to conclude

15 Probably there are no witches.

Inductive conclusions of this sort are rendered plausible by the absence of reliable empirical evidence after thorough investigation and must not be confused with the fallacy of appeal to ignorance.

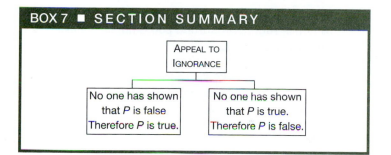

BOX 7 ■ SECTION SUMMARY

APPEAL TO IGNORANCE

No one has shown that *P* is false. Therefore *P* is true.

No one has shown that *P* is true. Therefore *P* is false.

Appeal to Unqualified Authority

Another fallacy of weak induction that may prevent an argument from supporting its conclusion is *appeal to unqualified authority*, also known as *ad verecundiam*.

When an argument commits the fallacy of appeal to unqualified authority, its premises attempt to support the conclusion by invoking alleged authorities who in fact have no expertise relevant to the claim that's being made.

Years ago, a television commercial in New York City featured the great New York Yankees baseball star Joe DiMaggio touting the Bowery Savings Bank. Suppose that a viewer, inspired by the sports hero's message, argued

16 The Bowery Savings is the best bank because Joe DiMaggio said so.

Argument (16) is an appeal to unqualified authority. DiMaggio, though undoubtedly an expert baseball player, was never an authority on banks. The television commercial was merely exploiting DiMaggio's immense popularity. But note that in this case it's not DiMaggio committing the fallacy—it's the television ad and the viewer speaking in (16), who wrongly thinks that the sports hero's testimony supports a claim about the Bowery Savings' being the best bank. Had he instead cited a view for which there is consensus among experts on the topic of the commercial (such as eminent bankers, financiers, or the chairman of the Federal Reserve) in support of the claim, the argument would not have committed this fallacy.

Now notice another important point: not all appeals to authority are fallacious. Consider,

17 To prevent tooth decay, the American Dental Association recommends daily flossing, so daily flossing is a good way to prevent tooth decay.

Although (17) appeals to an authority, the ADA, it does not commit the fallacy under discussion. Since the ADA is a *qualified*

BOX 8 ■ HOW TO AVOID FALLACIOUS APPEALS TO AUTHORITY

To avoid fallacious appeals to authority, keep in mind the way it differs from appeals to authority that aren't fallacious. The difference hinges on whether the authority cited in support of a claim

- Does indeed have expertise in the relevant field; and
- Is expressing a view well represented (perhaps the prevailing one) among the experts on the topic

---

authority on the topic of the conclusion, that conclusion is supported by (17)'s premise.

Thus appeals to authority are sometimes open to dispute—and may be fallacious—*only* when the invoked source is not authoritative on the subject of the claim an argument makes, or when a genuine authority's views are presented as representing expert consensus when in fact they do not. If we say,

18 Harvard Law School is a great place to study law, because Uncle Jack says so,
this appeal would be fallacious unless Uncle Jack were an authority expressing a view well represented among experts on law schools (see Box 8). By contrast, the appeal to authority is *not* fallacious in

19 Many eminent jurists and law professors hold Harvard Law School in high regard.

Harvard Law School is a great place to study law.

Argument (19) appeals to the view of experts on the topic of the conclusion, which is supported—provided that the premise is true. Since appeal to authority is often needed for the justification of many claims, it is crucial that we distinguish between authorities who are legitimate and have expertise relevant to the claim being made and those who aren't. The rule is:

> In evaluating an argument of the form "**A says that P**; **therefore P**," check whether *A* is a genuine authority expressing a view on *P* that is well represented among the experts on *P*. If *A* is not, then the argument fails to support its conclusion and must be rejected.

For example, beliefs about history are more reasonable when put forward by reputable historians than when proposed by amateur ones. If we want to have reasonable, well-founded beliefs about the French Revolution, the Ming Dynasty, or the presidency of Theodore Roosevelt, we should look to reliable sources. Similarly, for beliefs about nature, it goes without saying that respected journals in the natural sciences are dependable sources of information, unlike supermarket tabloids that describe miracle cures for cancer and "evidence" of mental

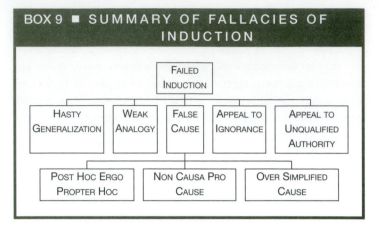

BOX 9 ■ SUMMARY OF FALLACIES OF INDUCTION

FAILED INDUCTION

- HASTY GENERALIZATION
- WEAK ANALOGY
- FALSE CAUSE
- APPEAL TO IGNORANCE
- APPEAL TO UNQUALIFIED AUTHORITY

False Cause:
- POST HOC ERGO PROPTER HOC
- NON CAUSA PRO CAUSE
- OVER SIMPLIFIED CAUSE

telepathy. For logical thinkers, an important competence is the ability to tell the difference between real experts and bogus ones, since it is often on that distinction that the difference between legitimate appeals to authority and the fallacy of appeal to unqualified authority turns.

Exercises

I. Review Questions

1. What is a fallacy?
2. What is the point of studying fallacies, as far as logical thinking is concerned?
3. What is the fallacy of hasty generalization?
4. Are all generalizations to be avoided?
5. What is stereotyping? And how is this related to hasty generalization?
6. What is the fallacy of weak analogy?
7. The fallacy of false cause has at least three different forms. What are these? And how are these all variations of the same kind of mistake?
8. What is the fallacy of appeal to ignorance?
9. What is the fallacy of appeal to unqualified authority?
10. What is the difference between the legitimate use of appeal to authority and the fallacy of appeal to unqualified authority?

II. Name the fallacy or fallacies committed by each of the following arguments.

1. I'm an Aquarius, so I love doing lots of projects at once.

   SAMPLE ANSWER: False cause

2. There is no evidence linking industrial waste in our rivers with the higher incidence of birth defects in this area. Thus something else is responsible for such defects. _____

3. A TV viewer interviewed by the local newspaper said "U2 would have made more money touring had they not been forced to postpone their tour of New Zealand, Australia, Japan, and Hawaii until the end of the year." That's precisely why U2's concerts have not been profitable lately. _____

4. Drinking and smoking are not harmful for anyone. After all, Winston Churchill smoked cigars and drank whiskey every day and he lived to be ninety years old. _____

* 5. Remarking on the usefulness of violence in producing social change, a twentieth-century political leader once observed, "In order to make an omelette, it is necessary to break some eggs."

   _____

6. Some people can cure heart disease by meditation. I know it because the coach of my son's soccer team told me. _____

7. Irving Berlin ate beet soup every day, and he lived to be 101. Since I want to live a long life, I should eat beet soup every day.

   _____

* 8. Wage and price controls will not work as a means of controlling the rate of inflation. After all, no economist has ever been able to give conclusive proof that such controls are effective against inflation.

   _____

9. Most HIV patients are young. Thus, youth causes HIV.

   _____

10. Yogi Berra, an Italian American, was one of the greatest baseball players of all time. So, no doubt about it, Italian Americans are great baseball players. _____

*11. I ought to wait before deciding whether or not to take that job in California, because my friend Mack, who is a professional astrologer, told me to wait. _____

12. Notre Dame will win the game today, because every time their coach wears his green tie, they win. And today he is wearing the green tie. _____

13. Foreign wars are good for a nation, just as exercise is good for the body. In the same way that exercise keeps the body fit, foreign wars keep a nation fit as a society. _____

14. In the election of 2004, every time I went for a walk in New York City, I saw many "John Kerry" buttons but no "G. W. Bush" buttons. I concluded that no American would support G. W. Bush.

_____

*15. Bud had a stomachache before he was to take the LSAT test to qualify for law school. He failed the test and went on to become a taxi driver. Thus a stomachache caused Bud to become a taxi driver.

_____

16. According to Britney Spears, the chances for stability in the Middle East will continue to improve. Therefore the chances for stability in the Middle East will continue to improve. _____

17. When W. V. Quine began studying philosophy as a young man, he also began losing his hair. The more philosophy he read, the balder he became. After years of study, he was completely bald. We may infer that Quine could have avoided baldness if he hadn't studied philosophy. _____

*18. Since attorneys for the prosecution were not able to establish beyond a doubt that Hinckley was sane when he fired at President Reagan, we have no choice but to conclude that he was insane.

_____

19. Do I really think I can drive all the way from Miami, Florida, to Fairbanks, Alaska, in a few days? Of course! Just a few months ago, I drove from Dallas to Houston, and that took four hours.

_____

20. A diet rich in cholesterol is not healthy. After all, people who really care about me have told me that. _____

*21. My grandfather never went to a doctor in his life. He went to a healer who practiced folk medicine. As a result, granddad lived to be ninety-four. So folk remedies always work. _____

22. All the stories in the newspaper about Zheng's resignation are false. For one thing, some interested parties tried to prove them true and did not succeed. _____

23. Some years ago, after not having seen my twin for months, we met for lunch and were surprised to find that our clothes and hairstyles were the same! This could have happened only because of our being twins. _____

*24. A recent poll of regular churchgoers showed that all surveyed believed that taxpayers' dollars should not be used to fund laboratories that carry out tests on animals for medical research. Why, then, do we go on spending taxpayers' dollars for that purpose? _____

25. I think you're giving up on advanced calculus too easily. Since you can do simple arithmetic, you can also do advanced calculus. _____

26. Every rainy day I have a pain in my elbow; so it must be the damp climate that's responsible for this pain. _____

*27. Angela Merkel, the first woman chancellor of Germany, is not doing a good job. This suggests that women are not fit to govern a country. _____

28. The Internet is a great technological advance and is available to many people. Space travel is another great technological advance. Thus, space travel is available to many people. _____

29. The top-ten biggest earners in music include Aerosmith, Coldplay, and Sir Paul McCartney, and they all play popular music. Since Aerosmith and Coldplay are bands, we may infer that Sir Paul McCartney is a band. _____

30. Several television personalities on the David Letterman Show the other night said that they had decided to invest in gold. So, it's probably a good idea to buy gold now. _____

*31. Drinking always leads to death. A simple example supports this conclusion. Between 1650 and 1850, a significant majority of the populations of Europe and North America consumed alcohol every day. And *all* of those people are now dead! _____

32. Professor Amy Hart, of Texas A&M, told the *Austin American-Statesman* website that so far no test supports the long-standing suspicion that bats harbor Ebola virus. Therefore bats do not harbor Ebola virus. _____

33. The local radio station has played an important part in protecting our environment. It is all very simple: the media always promote public awareness of the problems that affect all of us as a community.

_____

34. There is extraterrestrial intelligence. After all, what reason could we offer for the view that intelligence is exclusive to human beings?

_____

35. The odds are against the development of human settlements in the Atacama desert. Look at the Sahara: settlements there have proved not only difficult but impossible. _____

III. **For each of the above arguments, explain** *how* **it commits one or more fallacies.**

IV. **Assuming that the premises of the following arguments are true, determine which commits a fallacy of appeal to unqualified authority and which doesn't.**

1. We must accept that Landis was the best American rider in the last Tour de France since that's precisely what Tour director Jean-Marie Leblanc reported as an opinion shared by all the judges of this important event.

   SAMPLE ANSWER: Not a fallacy

2. Leonardo DeCaprio is the best American actor this year—a pronouncement widely supported by national opinions polls of movie goers. _____

3. The national census shows that Latinos are the fastest-growing ethnic group, representing the largest minority in the country. Therefore Latinos are the fastest-growing ethnic group, representing the largest minority in the country. _____

4. There is reason to suspect that Mel Gibson may have been involved in drunk driving, since a spokesman for the sheriff's department confirmed that Gibson has been charged with driving while intoxicated. His bail was set at $5000. _____

5. The secretary of defense sees signs of growth in our economy. Thus our economy is recovering. _____

6. The universe can act as a magnifying lens. One of the best current physical theories, Einstein's, says so. _____

7. It is simply false that cell phones create the risk of developing a brain tumor. Five well-established cell phone companies surveyed this

issue extensively, all reaching the same conclusion: no such risk exists. More details on this are available at the companies' web pages. _____

8. There is nothing wrong with drinking coffee. Many U.S. presidents, including Theodore Roosevelt, are known to have been coffee drinkers. _____

9. Although much can be said against diets low in carbohydrates, one thing is decisive: the shared view among leading neuroscientists is that calories from carbohydrates enhance cognitive tasks.

   _____

10. Our kids should avoid riding in the school bus. In the last meeting at Emerson School, the treasurer of the Parents' Association remarked that the exhaust gases produced by diesel vehicles harm the children's respiratory systems. _____

V. YOUR OWN THINKING LAB

The following arguments may or may not commit a fallacy. For each, provide a scenario where it commits a fallacy and one where it doesn't. Add any missing premise.

1. Every tiger so far observed has been fearless. Therefore all tigers are fearless.

2. My mother and her circle of friends think that species have evolved. Therefore species have evolved.

3. Nobody has ever observed a centaur. Therefore centaurs do not exist.

4. Ellen and Jose are both college students who vote. Both are also prelaw majors. Jose is also interested in golf. Therefore Ellen is interested in golf.

7.4 The Philosopher's Corner

Appeal to Ignorance in Philosophical Arguments

What do we really know *for sure* about the world of our everyday experience? Do we actually know that the earth existed for many years before we were born? Or that there is anything at all outside of our own minds? Do we know that we have minds and bodies and that there are trees, rivers, and mountains? Extreme skeptics are persuaded that we don't really know *for certain* any of these things that we commonly take ourselves to know. After all, they argue, we could all be victims of some illusion, hallucination, or dream—or even be tricked into thinking that our beliefs about such things are true when in fact they've been planted in us by some diabolical scientific genius or other powerful being whose purpose is to deceive us.

In his *Meditations on First Philosophy* (1641), the French philosopher René Descartes (1596–1650) famously set out to reject extreme skepticism by examining the skeptics' reasons and proposing his own counterarguments. In doing this, he thought that he had proved conclusively an important doctrine in philosophy of mind. This is *mind/body dualism*, the view that mind and body are radically different, with only the latter being material and located in space. Given dualism, mind (which Descartes calls "soul") is something nonphysical and separable from the body. One of his arguments for this doctrine may be reconstructed as

20 1. I'm certain that I have a mind (after all, I'm now thinking).
   2. I'm not certain that I have a body (after all, I could be deceived about this).
   3. Mind and body are not same.

Argument (20) correctly assumes that if two things are exactly the same, then they must share all their features. By "certain," Descartes means "not open to doubt." So mind and body appear to have different features, since it's open to doubt by him that he has the latter, but not the former. What Descartes seems to mean here might be expressed as this extended argument:

20′ 1. My mind doesn't have the feature of being open to doubt by me.
   2. My body does have the feature of being open to doubt by me.
   3. Mind and body don't have exactly the same features.
   4. Things that are the same must have exactly the same features.
   5. Mind and body are not the same.

Has Descartes succeeded in supporting mind/body dualism with (20′)? Hardly, since a closer look at this argument reveals that it commits the fallacy of appeal to ignorance. Premise (2), after all, is needed to support its first conclusion (3), which functions as a premise for conclusion (5), the doctrine of dualism. In light of the above skeptical arguments, Descartes claims (2): he *does not know* whether he has a body. No such premise could, however, be invoked in support of a conclusion such as (3). Why? Because (3) makes a claim about the way mind and body *actually are*, not about the way the arguer takes them to be. Clearly, it sometimes happens that things that appear different are actually the same and we merely fail to notice it. Fiction abounds with cases of precisely this sort—think of Superman/Clark Kent, or Dr. Jekyll/Mr. Hyde. If we're ready to accept that there could be such unrecognized identities, why not think that Descartes himself might have overlooked the similarity of mind and body?

Exercises

VI. The following arguments all commit the fallacy of appeal to ignorance. For each, explain its weakness.

* 1. According to commonsense realism, tables, trees, dogs, and other middle-sized objects exist independent of human perception—that is, independent of our minds. But the only things that one could really be certain about are *the data of one's experience*, such as a green patch in one's field of vision, the sensation of cold, or the loud sound that one is now consciously perceiving. From this, it follows validly that commonsense realism is false.

2. Consider the case of a glass cube that appears to be pink through and through. There is no evidence, however, that color is a feature homogeneously present in objects at the atomic level. Thus the cube is not pink.

3. The history of the attempt to prove that God exists includes the arguments not only of well-known philosophers but also of eminent theologians. Yet no such attempt has ever really succeeded. It follows that God does not exist.

* 4. There is a long and varied history of scholars offering arguments to the effect that God does not exist. But none of these arguments has really been absolutely conclusive. Therefore God does exist.

5. Although the desk in front of me appears to be a solid object, it has not been proved that this is so. In fact, contemporary physics says

just the opposite: what seem to us solid objects are mostly empty space. It follows deductively that the desk in front of me is not a solid object.

* 6. No one has shown that moral judgments are grounded in some objective standard. Therefore moral judgments are not grounded in any objective standard.

7. There is no way to justify induction. For clearly no attempts to do so have succeeded.

■ Writing Project

Find at least three examples of questionable analogy arguments used by public figures—either of the present day or historical figures—and write a short essay in which you discuss whether these do actually amount to fallacies of weak analogy. In cases where you think they do, explain exactly why the analogy fails. In cases where you think the analogy is strong after all, explain why you think it should be allowed to stand. (Tip: the language of politicians and journalists makes frequent use of analogy.)

■ Chapter Summary
Fallacies of Failed Induction

1. **Appeal to unqualified authority** (*ad verecundiam*)

    A fallacy committed by any argument whose conclusion rests on the testimony of some "authority" who is really *not an authority at all* in the relevant field. Note: Not all appeals to authority are fallacious.

2. **Appeal to ignorance** (*ad ignorantiam*)

    A fallacy committed by any argument whose conclusion rests on nothing more than *the absence of evidence to the contrary.*

3. **Hasty generalization**

    The fallacy of trying to draw a conclusion about *all* things of a certain kind on the basis of having observed *only a few* of them, or some unrepresentative sample of them. This fallacy is committed by any enumerative induction whose conclusion rests on a sample that either is too small or lacks comprehensiveness and randomness, or both.

Note: The mistake of *stereotyping people* is one form of Hasty Generalization.

4. **False cause**

   In a fallacy of false cause, one makes the mistake of *thinking that there is a significant causal connection between two events when in fact there is either a minimal causal connection or none at all*. This fallacy can be committed in three different ways:

   I.   *Post hoc ergo propter hoc*

   II. *Non causa pro causa*

   III. *Oversimplified cause*

   Note: Not all causal arguments are fallacious.

5. **Weak analogy**

   Whether an analogy is strong or not depends chiefly on *whether the things alleged to be alike really are alike in relevant ways*. Any analogy where the things alleged to be alike may *in fact not be very much alike in relevant ways* commits the fallacy of weak analogy.

   Note: Not all arguments from analogy are fallacious.

■ Key Words

Fallacy	Hasty generalization
Informal fallacy	Commonsense realism
Weak analogy	Mind/body dualism
False cause	Skepticism
Appeal to ignorance	Appeal to authority
Appeal to unqualified authority	

Avoiding Ungrounded Assumptions

8.1 Fallacies of Presumption

Now we're ready to look at some fallacies that can be grouped together because arguments committing them rest on some presumption that is in fact debatable. Presumptions are strong assumptions: background beliefs often taken for granted. Arguments commonly rest on some such implicit beliefs that create no fallacy of presumption at all. But when an argument takes for granted some belief *that is in fact debatable*, it commits a fallacy of presumption. The presumption at work in any such argument may *seem* to be accurate or acceptable, though in reality it is neither.

8.2 Begging the Question

In Chapter 5 we saw that deductive soundness is a tough standard to meet. If a deductive argument is invalid or if any of its premises are false (or even dubious), then the argument is *unsound*. Furthermore, when a thinker *is aware* that either of these problems affects a deductive argument, that argument becomes noncogent. But cogency could also fail in a valid argument whose premises are true or beyond doubt. How? Imagine that we intend to convince you rationally to accept a certain claim—say, that

1 We care about logical thinking.

We offer you this reason as a premise:

2 It is not the case that we don't care about logical thinking.

The argument is

3 1. It is not the case that we don't care about logical thinking.
    _____
    2. We care about logical thinking.

BOX 1 ■ COGENT ARGUMENT

Cogent argument = Rationally compelling or persuasive argument

Argument (3) lacks cogency, since it cannot move anyone to accept conclusion 2 on the basis of recognizing the argument's validity and accepting premise 1. Why not? Because the premise is *not* more acceptable than the conclusion that it is offered to support. It simply amounts to a restatement of that conclusion. Consider, more generally, any argument with this form:

4 1. It is not the case that not-P
<hr>
2. P

or any other equivalent form such as

5 P
<hr>
P

Such an argument would be valid and, if its premise is true, also sound. Yet it would lack cogency, for it would be viciously circular. Any argument exhibiting this defect *begs the question* and thus commits a fallacy (sometimes called *petitio principii*). When a valid (or even a sound) argument begs the question, its premises cannot offer compelling reasons for accepting its conclusion. The conclusion of a question-begging argument may in fact be quite acceptable, but this would be for reasons other than those offered by such a fallacious argument.

Sometimes, however, a failure in cogency is not so easy to detect. Suppose we now argue

6 1. It is not the case that the Democrats are indifferent to education.
<hr>
2. The Democrats care about education.

Whether or not a valid argument is cogent depends in part on its premise's being better accepted than the conclusion it is offered to support. In (6), assuming that "not being indifferent to" means roughly the same as "caring about," that condition for cogency remains unfulfilled, since here again the premise is just a restatement of the conclusion it is supposed to be supporting. Thus, the premise falls short of providing a compelling reason for (6)'s conclusion.

Now consider

7 1. Homer wrote the Odyssey.
<hr>
2. Homer existed.

Is (7) cogent? If its premise would require the previous acceptance of the conclusion it is attempting to support, then the answer would be no. For in that case (7) would fail to offer a reason that could compel logical thinkers to accept its conclusion, even if its premise were true and the argument valid. And a close look at that premise reveals that it does in fact require the previous acceptance of (7)'s conclusion: no one who disputes the latter would be moved to accept it on the basis of the former. The argument is viciously circular and therefore begs the question. The point to keep in mind is,

> An argument begs the question if and only if one or more of its premises can be accepted only if the conclusion has already been accepted. Since, in any such argument, at least one premise assumes the conclusion, that premise cannot be a reason for accepting that conclusion. The argument is said to "beg," rather than to support, its "question" or conclusion.

A valid argument whose premises assume its conclusion, in the sense that they are acceptable only if the conclusion is already deemed acceptable, begs the question. Begging the question is a failure in the cogency of a deductive argument that amounts to a fallacy arising from *viciously circular reasoning*. If the premises of a valid argument are found acceptable only because the conclusion has already been accepted, how could they compel a thinker to accept that conclusion? Thus whenever an argument begs the

BOX 2 ■ HOW TO AVOID BEGGING THE QUESTION

- The fallacy of begging the question can be avoided only by cogent arguments.
- The bottom line is that, given a circular valid argument with acceptable premises, you must ask yourself whether these amount to reasons that render its conclusion acceptable. If yes, it's a cogent argument. If no, it's question-begging.

question, it lacks cogency—the important virtue of valid arguments discussed in Chapter 5.

To put it another way, the premises of any viciously circular argument are not able to transfer their acceptability to the conclusion. The thinker finds herself reasoning in a vicious circle, unable to obtain from the premises a reason for the conclusion.

Circular Reasoning

Not all circular arguments beg the question. The context of a circular argument, together with the type and degree of circularity in it, can help to determine whether it begs the question. Let's try to clarify this by having a brief look at circular arguments. Now clearly any valid argument has some degree of circularity, due either to its form, the concepts involved, or both. The following two arguments are affected by circularity hinging on *argument form*:

8   1. Today it's cloudy and breezy.
     2. Today it's breezy.

9   1. The Pope is in Rome.
     2. The Pope is in Rome.

Clearly, the circularity afflicting these arguments hinges on their forms—which are

8' 1. $C \& B$
    2. B

9' 1. E
    2. E

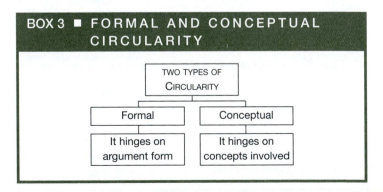

BOX 3 ■ FORMAL AND CONCEPTUAL CIRCULARITY

TWO TYPES OF CIRCULARITY

Formal	Conceptual
It hinges on argument form	It hinges on concepts involved

Any argument with either of these forms is valid, for if its premise is true, then its conclusion must also be. But in each case the conclusion has to be true for its premise to be true. As a result, no one who doesn't already accept the conclusion would come to accept it on the basis of working out the validity of the argument and the acceptability of the premise.

Yet circularity could also be conceptual, hinging on the *meaning or concepts expressed.*

Consider

10 1. If Michael Jordan is basketball player, then he plays basketball.
2. Michael Jordan is basketball player.
3. Michael Jordan plays basketball.

11 1. If someone is a concert violinist, then that person is a musician.
2. Anne-Sophie Mutter is a concert violinist.
3. Anne-Sophie Mutter is a musician.

Given the concepts involved in (10) and (11), no logical thinkers who grasp them but doubt the argument's conclusions could come to accept those conclusions on the basis of their premises, for in each argument the premises presuppose the conclusion they are supposed to support and therefore fail to support them. As in (8) and (9) above, these arguments too are affected by circularity that renders them fallacious. Whether formal or conceptual, circularity comes in degrees: *too much of it* causes an argument to beg the question.

Benign Circularity

But circularity does not always make an argument question-begging. Compare,

12 1. If the mind is the brain, then the mind is organic matter.
2. If the mind is organic matter, then it perishes with the body.
3. If the mind is the brain, then it perishes with the body.

Here the argument form is

12' 1. If M, then O
2. If O, then B
3. If M, then B

In an argument with this form, there is some formal circularity, since the propositions represented as M and B appear not only in the conclusion but also in the premises. Yet (12) does not beg the question, because finding its premises acceptable and recognizing the argument's validity could provide reasons to move logical thinkers to accept its conclusion. Anyone who accepts the argument's premises and works out the entailment appears thereby compelled to accept conclusion 3. By contrast with other formally circular arguments, such as (8) and (9) above, since (12)'s conclusion is not explicitly contained in its premises, deducing it from those premises amounts to a cognitive achievement.

Let's now compare some conceptually circular arguments, such as,

13 1. Salsa is music for dancers.
2. Salsa is music for those who dance.

14 1. John is a bachelor.
2. John is unmarried.

15 1. She has drawn an isosceles triangle.
2. She has drawn a triangle.

All three of these arguments are valid: if their premises are true, their conclusions must be true as well. Yet each begs the question, for in each argument acceptance of its premise requires a previous acceptance of the conclusion. No logical thinker who disputed the conclusion would be compelled to accept it on the basis of the argument's premise and recognition of the argument's validity. But consider,

16 1. The moon orbits the earth.
2. Any large celestial body that orbits a planet is a satellite.
3. The moon is a satellite.

Although in (16) there is some conceptual circularity between the concepts "satellite" and "large celestial body that orbits a planet," this does not make the argument question-begging. For a logical thinker who lacked some basic astronomical knowledge and initially doubted claim 3 might be persuaded to accept it on the basis of deducing it from 1 and 2 provided that she were led to recognize the acceptability of those premises and the validity of the argument. Finally, note that

> Logical circularity, whether formal or conceptual, comes in degrees. Some valid arguments have more circularity than others. The more logically circular an argument is, the more its conclusion follows trivially from its premises and is likely to beg the question.

The Burden of Proof

The expression "burden of proof" occurs most often in a *dialectical context*, which is the context of a debate, controversy, or deliberation on a disputed question between opposing sides defending incompatible claims. It refers to the obligation to take a turn in offering reasons, which, at any given stage of the deliberation, is on one side or the other (except for the paradoxical situations discussed below). A deliberation commonly follows this pattern: one party, C, makes a claim. The other party, O, replies by raising some objections to it. If these objections are adequate, the burden of proof is now on C, who must get rid of (or "discharge") it by offering reasons for her claim. If she comes

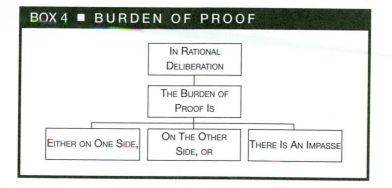

BOX 4 ■ BURDEN OF PROOF

In Rational Deliberation

The Burden of Proof Is

Either on One Side, | On The Other Side, or | There Is An Impasse

---

BOX 5 ■ WHERE IS THE BURDEN OF PROOF?

In the following debate, $\otimes$ shows the burden of proof and $\odot$ an impasse.

1. A rejects a claim made by B, which is a commonly held belief. $\otimes$ A
2. A defends her rejection with an argument that begs the question against B. $\otimes$ A
3. A recasts her argument so that it now seems cogent. $\otimes$ B
4. B offers an argument that turns out to be clearly invalid. $\otimes$ B
5. B's argument is modified and now seems as cogent as A's. $\odot$
6. A provides further strong evidence in support of her view. $\otimes$ B
7. B replies by offering weak evidence for his view. $\otimes$ B
8. B offers further evidence which is equally strong as A's. $\odot$

---

up with a sound or strong argument that outweighs O's argument, the burden of proof then switches to O, who must try to discharge it by offering the appropriate arguments.

It may happen, however, that the arguments on both sides appear equally deductively sound (or inductively strong). As a result, there would then be a dialectical impasse, or standoff in the deliberation. No progress can be made until new reasons are offered to resolve the conflict. Except for these situations, however, we may expect that the burden of proof will, at any given stage of a deliberation, be on either the one side or the other. As the deliberation progresses, it will likely switch from the one to the other more than once, always falling upon the participant whose claim is more in need of support.

Another thing to notice is the *privileged standing* with respect to the burden of proof enjoyed by *commonsense beliefs* or claims, which are those generally taken for granted as true and justified: whoever challenges them has, at least initially, the burden of proof. For example, the belief that the Earth has existed for more than five minutes belongs to common sense. If someone challenges it, the burden of proof is on the challenger, who must now offer adequate reasons against that commonsense belief. But even that advantage can be overridden by further considerations if available.

Knowing where the burden of proof is at any given stage of a debate has this *cash value*:

> - If you know that the burden of proof is on you, you should try to discharge it by offering an adequate argument in support of your claim.
> - If you know that the burden of proof is on others, you should ask them to give reasons for their claims.
> - If you know that you are defending a claim that is part of common sense, then you also know that the burden of proof is on any challenger; so you must act accordingly: request appropriate reasons.

Finally, note that some deliberation is inner: it goes on "internally," for example, when a person reflects upon which of two opposite theories is correct. If, in the course of inner deliberation, a thinker is fair-minded, then the burden of proof will tend to shift from one side to the other, following the same general considerations outlined above.

8.3 Begging the Question Against

A common way to beg the question is by failing to discharge the burden of proof. Suppose that we assert "Not *P*" (that is, that *P* is false), but someone else, Jane, has just offered us some good reason for thinking that *P* is true.

The burden of proof is now on us, and we must discharge it by offering an adequate argument against *P*. The failure to do so—by assuming that *P* is false without offering a reason for this—commits the fallacy of begging the question against Jane.

> **BOX 6 ■ HOW TO AVOID BEGGING THE QUESTION AGAINST**
>
> Don't include any controversial statement among your premises without first offering adequate reasons for it.

> **BOX 7 ■ BEGGING THE QUESTION AND BEGGING THE QUESTION AGAINST**
>
> 1. When an argument begs the question, at least one premise assumes the conclusion being argued for.
> 2. When an argument "begs the question against," at least one premise assumes something that is in need of support.

For it amounts to implicitly reasoning in either of these viciously circular forms:

17 1. *P* is false.
2. *P* is false.

or

18 1. Not *P*
2. Not *P*

The fallacy of begging the question against (your opponent) is often committed in everyday arguments on controversial topics. For example, when someone maintains

19 1. In abortion, the fetus is intentionally killed.
2. A fetus is an innocent person.
3. Intentionally killing an innocent person is always homicide.
4. Abortion is always homicide.

although 1 seems unobjectionable, 2 and 3 are controversial premises that cannot be employed unless good reasons have already been offered to back them up. Premise 2 begs the question against the view *that a fetus is not a person*—a view that can be supported in a number of ways (as most parties to the current popular debate over the morality of abortion now recognize). But begging the question against can be difficult to detect, for it involves presupposing the truth of premises that, although controversial, are sometimes inadvertently taken for granted. To avoid this fallacy, always abide by the rule in Box 6.

Exercises

I. Review Questions

1. What is a circular argument? And what types of circularity have been distinguished in this section?
2. Would any circular argument beg the question? Explain.
3. Why is begging the question a fallacy?
4. Why is begging the question *against* a fallacy? And against whom is the question begged in any argument that commits this fallacy?
5. Must the conclusion of a question-begging argument be false? If yes, how? If not, why not?
6. How is the burden of proof related to commonsense beliefs?

II. For each of the following circular arguments, determine whether its circularity is formal, conceptual, or both.

1. John is a brother. Therefore John is a male sibling.

   SAMPLE ANSWER: Conceptual

2. Capital punishment is cruel, for it is cruel and unusual punishment. _____

* 3. The mind is immaterial and different from the body. Hence, the mind and the body are not the same. _____

4. The number 2 is smaller than any other even number. Therefore 2 is not an odd number. _____

* 5. It is false that demons exist. Therefore demons do not exist. _____

6. The present king of France is bald. Therefore the present king of France is either bald or he colors his hair. _____

* 7. Since Fred is a hunter and all hunters hunt, it follows that he is someone who hunts. _____

8. Neither the U.S. president nor the British prime minister supports the treaty. As a result, it is not the case that both the U.S. president and the British prime minister support the treaty. _____

* 9. Given that unless Oprah switches into the publishing industry, she stays on television, it follows that she either goes into the publishing industry or stays on television. _____

10. The first witness is not trustworthy, since he is not reliable.

    _____

*11. If that geometrical figure is a circle, then it is not a rectangle. Therefore if the figure is a rectangle, then it is not a circle. _____

12. Mount Aconcagua is taller than Mount Whitney. As a consequence, Mount Whitney is not taller than Mount Aconcagua.

    _____

III. **Each of the following arguments begs the question, begs the question against, or does both. Assuming ordinary circumstances, determine which of these fallacies is committed.**

1. Women are less productive than men. Hence women should receive lower wages.

   SAMPLE ANSWER: Begs the question against.

2. Euthanasia is murder and is wrong. So euthanasia is wrong.

   _____

* 3. Fido is a puppy. Therefore Fido is a young dog. _____

4. A woman has an absolute right to control her own body. Therefore abortion is morally permissible. _____

* 5. Since the Democrats lost the '04 presidential election, it is simply false that they didn't lose. _____

6. Hillary Clinton has an insurance policy on her cars, for it is not the case that her cars lack such a policy. _____

* 7. The fetus is an unborn baby. Therefore it is not the case that the fetus is not an unborn baby. _____

8. Anyone who is an idealist is also a loser. Thus idealists are losers.

   _____

9. John is a bachelor. Therefore John is unmarried. _____

*10. Infanticide is always morally wrong. Therefore infanticide is never morally right. _____

11. If materialism is true, then the mind is the same as the body. But the mind is different from the body. Hence materialism is not true.

    _____

12. The right to life is God's will. Therefore the right to life is the will of Divine Providence. _____

*13. If atheists are right, God doesn't exist. But it is not the case that He doesn't exist, so the atheists are not right. _____

14. Pat got a *B* on her philosophy paper this semester. Therefore she turned in a philosophy paper this semester. _____

15. There is life after death. Therefore there is an afterlife. _____

*16. Since no person should be denied freedom and Betty is a person, it follows that Betty is entitled to freedom. _____

17. Mary is a sister. Therefore she is a female. _____

18. Since capital punishment is murder, capital punishment is wrongful killing. _____

19. Northfield is not far from Minneapolis. Thus Northfield is close to Minneapolis. _____

20. Socialism is an unjust system of government. Unjust systems of government must be abolished. Therefore, socialism must be abolished. _____

IV. Determine whether the following arguments are possible or impossible.

1. A cogent argument that is not rationally compelling.

   SAMPLE ANSWER: Impossible

2. A valid argument that is noncogent. _____

3. A sound argument that is noncogent. _____

* 4. A question-begging argument that is not circular. _____

5. A circular argument that is not fallacious. _____

* 6. A cogent argument that begs the question against. _____

7. A sound argument that is cogent. _____

* 8. A question-begging argument that is sound. _____

9. A question-begging argument that is rationally compelling. _____

*10. An argument that begs the question against without having the burden of proof. _____

V. **In the deliberation described below, determine where the burden of proof lies at each stage: if on Carolyn, write *C*; if on Karl, write *K*; and if there is a dialectical impasse, write *I*.**

1. *C* rejects a commonsense belief held by *K*.

   SAMPLE ANSWER: *C*

2. *C* defends her rejection with an argument that begs the question against *K*. _____

3. *C* recasts her argument in a way that makes it clearly unsound.
   _____

* 4. *C* offers a new argument that turns out to be invalid. _____

5. *C*'s argument undergoes another recast that makes it cogent.
   _____

* 6. *K* advances a valid yet question-begging argument against *C*.
   _____

7. *K* offers a nonquestion-begging argument with clearly false premises. _____

* 8. *K* recasts his argument so that it is now as cogent as *C*'s.
   _____

VI. **In the following deliberation, either *S* or *O* has the burden of proof. Identify which has it at any given stage in the deliberation and mark dialectical impasses. *Explain your choice.***

1. *S* makes a claim that challenges a commonly held belief.

   SAMPLE ANSWER: BURDEN OF PROOF on *S*. When commonsense beliefs are at issue, the burden of proof is on the challenger.

2. *S* attempts to support her claim by offering an inductively weak argument. _____

3. *S* recasts her argument so that it is now clearly valid but unsound.

   _____

4. *S* recasts her argument again so that it is now sound but question-begging. _____

5. *S*'s argument undergoes another recast that makes it deductively cogent. _____

6. *O* responds with a valid argument that begs the question against *S*.

   _____

7. *O* recasts her argument so that it is now nonquestion-begging but plainly unsound. _____

8. *O* recasts her argument once more so that it is now deductively cogent. _____

VII. Your Own Thinking Lab

* **1.** Consider the following argument: "Marriage can be only between two persons of different sexes. Therefore gay couples cannot be married." What's the matter with this argument?

2. Provide an argument that both begs the question and begs the question against.

3. Provide an argument that begs the question without begging the question against.

4. Provide an argument that begs the question against without begging the question.

* **5.** Discuss the conditions an argument must meet to be deductively cogent.

* **6.** An argument that is invalid always falls short of being rationally compelling, but could such an argument be cogent? Must its conclusion be rejected? Explain your answers.

7. Imagine a debate in which two rival claims are equally well supported by observational evidence. Of the two, one agrees with common sense, the other doesn't. Does this make a difference? Where is the burden of proof? Explain.

8. Discuss what's wrong with an argument that begs the question.

9. Discuss what's wrong with an argument that begs the question against.

*10. Suppose you are engaged in a rational debate. Your opponent has just offered a seemingly adequate argument for a claim that you wish to reject. Where is the burden of proof? What does "burden of proof" mean?

8.4 Complex Question

Another fallacy of presumption is *complex question*. Here, the *question* of concern is literally an interrogative sentence: a question is being asked of someone. But it is a loaded question, since

> A complex question is a question phrased in such a way that it presupposes some claim that has not been supported at all.

Commonly, the presupposition of a complex question is something bad about persons or things being queried. In a standard example, a man is asked

20 Have you stopped beating your wife?

Here a yes is just as bad as a no, because it seems to *follow* from this question that the addressee was engaged in wifebeating. Often phrased so that a direct answer can be only a yes or a no, questions of this sort are unfair, since the person queried will convict himself with either answer. Consider another example: A young man who was never a marijuana user has arrived to pick up his date for the evening. He meets her father, who regards him with suspicion and says,

21 Before you take my daughter to the movies, I must ask you this: do you intend to conceal from me your history of marijuana use?

Now what is the correct answer to this? Obviously, the young man doesn't want to answer yes. But if he answers no, then that is equally *to admit to marijuana use* (something he's innocent of). Either answer will convict him. Notice, however, that that is only

BOX 8 ■ HOW TO AVOID COMPLEX QUESTION

Beware of any questions presupposing that, if you answer it yes, a certain proposition *P* is true, and if you answer it no, *P* is also true.

because the question itself is unfair. It *assumes*—without anything in the context making it plausible—that the young man *has* used marijuana!

It's not difficult to see the mistake here. But how is this an *argument*? First, the question asks whether or not the addressee intends to conceal his history of marijuana use. If he does, then he has a history of marijuana use. And if he doesn't, then he also has a history of marijuana use. Assuming that he either does or doesn't, it follows that he has a history of marijuana use. But there is a problem with these premises, since they rest on an unproved assumption—namely, that the person queried *does have a history of marijuana use.*

Yet not all arguments that commit the complex question fallacy may be intended specifically to trap an individual. For example, some consist simply in questions phrased so that *any* answer a respondent gives must necessarily endorse an unsupported assumption built into the question itself. Suppose that a politician, in a speech, asks

22 Does my opponent agree with the president's disastrous economic policy, which is now leading our nation to ruin?

Because the question is phrased in such a way that it assumes (without anything in the context making it plausible) that the president's economic policy *is* "disastrous," and that it *is* "leading our nation to ruin," anyone who responds to (22) either in the affirmative or in the negative will be implicitly endorsing those views! Again, a fallacy of complex question has been committed, in this case by the politician. To a complex question, it seems, any answer is a wrong answer. But that is only because there is something wrong with the question itself. It is phrased so that it assumes something not yet supported.

8.5 False Alternatives

False alternatives is a defect in reasoning that might affect an argument containing a disjunction as a premise.

> An argument commits the fallacy of false alternatives if and only if one of its premises wrongly assumes that a certain disjunction between propositions
> - Is exclusive, when in fact it is inclusive
> - Involves only two propositions when in fact it involves more than two

Recall that a disjunction is a compound proposition with two members or "disjuncts." An exclusive disjunction has the form

23 Either *P* or *Q* (but not both).

Here *P* and *Q* represent propositions standing as *exclusive* alternatives, because if one is true, the other is false and vice versa. For example,

24 Either the groundhog hibernates during the winter or it continues in a state of animation.

This is an *exclusive disjunction,* since it presupposes that exactly one of the alternatives is true. By contrast, consider the *inclusive disjunction*

25 Apples that are either too small or too ripe are discarded.

This has the form

25' Either *P* or *Q* (or both).

That is, (25) presupposes that any apple that is both too small and too ripe is also discarded. Another thing to notice about these disjunctions is that they present the alternatives as being *exhaustive.* For example, (24) presupposes that hibernation (or suspended animation) and animation are the only two possible states a groundhog could enter in winter.

When an arguer offers a disjunctive premise as presenting exhaustive, exclusive alternatives, we must determine whether these are really so. This involves checking premises of (23)'s form to be sure that P and Q exhaust all the alternatives and could not both be true—provided that the disjunction is intended to be exhaustive and exclusive. A fallacy of false alternatives would be committed, for example, by any argument such as (26), whose premise 1 is intended as exhaustive, when in fact there are more alternatives than the two expressed in that premise.

26 1. Either you're a Catholic or you're a Buddhist.
    2. You are not a Buddhist.
    <u>   </u>
    3. You are a Catholic.

Or, again, suppose that a political activist is trying to convince us to agree with her. She appeals to our sense of civic duty and says,

27 You must join my party, the only one that offers a solution to the homelessness problem. For you're either part of the solution or part of the problem.

But these options seem unduly restrictive. Why are *just those* the only choices? Perhaps we are neither part of the problem (since we did not really contribute to causing it) nor part of the solution (since our participation might not make any difference). Or perhaps we are *both* part of the problem *and also* (potentially) part of its solution—isn't that equally possible? So, in this example, the activist commits the fallacy of false alternatives. Once all missing premises are stated, her extended argument is:

28 1. There is a problem of homelessness.
    2. Either you are part of this problem or part of its solution.
    3. It is wrong for you to be part of the problem.
    4. You must be part of the solution.
    5. To be part of the solution, you must join my party.
    <u>   </u>
    6. You must join my party.

Assuming that other premises are true, premise 2 rests on an inaccurate assumption: namely, that our choice is limited to

> **BOX 9 ■ HOW TO AVOID FALSE ALTERNATIVES**
>
> In evaluating an argument with a disjunctive premise, check that premise to be sure that (A) there are at most two disjuncts and/or (B) the alternatives are really incompatible when they are meant to be so.
>
> If either (or both) of these conditions is not met, then the argument commits the fallacy of false alternatives.

either the one or the other of the two mutually exclusive alternatives offered there—that is, to being *either* part of the solution *or* part of the problem. Since that is *false*, the argument should be rejected on the ground that it commits the fallacy of false alternatives.

Yet not all arguments featuring exhaustive, exclusive disjunctions commit this fallacy, for there are situations that do appear to present us with such a choice. It is plausible to say that citizens of France in 1940 really did have to make a decision between only two mutually exclusive alternatives: either collaborate with the puppet government imposed by Hitler's invading armies or resist it in some way. And a southerner in the United States in 1961 really did have to choose whether or not to support the integration of schools, churches, and lunch counters—a movement that was then challenging racially discriminatory laws. But most everyday situations are not likely to be as dramatic as these. Therefore, for the most part, one is well advised to be skeptical when someone claims that there is a choice of *only two* extreme alternatives. (It may be so, but probably not.)

8.6 Accident

Accident is another fallacy of presumption that can undermine arguments; it is committed when some *accidental* or exceptional feature of a case at hand is overlooked.

> The fallacy of accident is committed by an argument if and only if the argument presupposes that a case falls under a general rule or principle when the case in fact counts as an exception to it.

Suppose someone reasons as follows:

29 1. Dogs are friendly animals.
2. Otto [my Rottweiler, which has already bitten six people] is a dog.
3. Otto is a friendly animal.

Although it's true in general that "dogs are friendly animals," that rule does not apply to Otto. Thus, (29) commits the fallacy of accident. As in other arguments committing this fallacy, here the arguer fails to notice that some principle that is *generally* true may not be *always* true, so that he fails to allow for an exception to the rule in a case where an exception is warranted.

Now imagine that Smith invites Perkins to lunch one day. "Come on, let's go to lunch," he says. "We can go to the corner delicatessen, and I'll treat you." Perkins is about to accept, but then thinks to himself, "Wait a minute! *There's no such thing as a free lunch!*" Now this judgment results from the fallacious reasoning involved in accident. Although part of the problem is that a familiar cliché is being taken too literally, the larger mistake is that some principle that is *generally true* is being misapplied. Of course, for the most part, it is true that "there's no such thing as a free lunch" (meaning that things ostensibly free of charge ordinarily come with hidden costs we must pay), but if Smith is *inviting*

BOX 10 ■ HOW TO AVOID ACCIDENT

Logical thinkers must bear in mind that even the best principles usually have exceptions, and that if a principle is applied inappropriately—i.e., to a case that is rightly an exception—then a fallacy of accident has been committed.

BOX 11 ■ SUMMARY OF FALLACIES OF PRESUMPTION

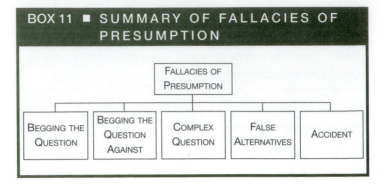

Perkins to lunch, then this is an exception. *Usually* there's no free lunch. But today there is. Perkins is simply being obtuse.

Or again, suppose Jones believes that one should always tell the truth. In general, this is of course a good rule to follow. One day Jones meets his next-door neighbor in the supermarket. She says, "How do you like my new hat?" Jones look at the hat, and thinks to himself, "Always tell the truth *no matter what*." So he says, "I think it looks ridiculous," thereby hurting her feelings and contributing slightly toward increasing the unhappiness in the world. Now, wouldn't we say here that Jones is simply being too fanatical about truth telling? Yes, one should usually tell the truth. But surely this was a case in which a small lie was called for! No one would have been treated unfairly or otherwise wronged by doing so, and a small degree of happiness would thereby have been produced. By not recognizing this, Jones has committed a fallacy of accident. He has failed to understand that, although the rule prescribing veracity is in general a good one, there are justifiable exceptions; and here he has not allowed for an exception where an exception was warranted.

Exercises

VIII. Review Questions

1. What do all fallacies of presumption have in common?
2. What does it mean for an argument to be "circular"? Is all circularity bad?
3. What is the fallacy of "begging the question against"? How does it differ from begging the question?
4. How does complex question differ from begging the question?

5. What is meant by "the burden of proof"?

6. What is the fallacy of accident?

7. Consider the following claim: All arguments employing a disjunction (an "either ... or ..." statement) commit the fallacy of false alternatives. Is this true or false? Explain.

IX. The following arguments are instances of complex question, false alternatives, and accident. Determine which is which.

1. Are you still in agreement with the senator's unpatriotic view that tax cuts will help the economy?

   SAMPLE ANSWER: Complex question

2. Jorge plans to apply to the University of Texas, where one can major in biology or in history. But since he cannot stand history, he'll major in biology. _____

* 3. Since people generally survive influenza, you shouldn't worry about your eighty-eight-year-old grandfather's catching it. _____

4. Have you stopped cheating on your taxes? _____

5. Neither Roman Catholics nor Protestants have a religion suitable for me. Therefore there is no religion suitable for me. _____

* 6. I'm sure that Jane avoids eating at night, for she has been losing weight without dieting. And to lose weight, one either diets or avoids eating at night. _____

7. Professor Wilson almost never gives F's in her classes. So I'm sure I won't get an F this time, even though I've missed all but one of her class sessions and failed all three exams. _____

8. South Texas farmers grow either grapefruits or oranges. Miguel is a South Texas farmer who doesn't grow oranges. Thus Miguel is a South Texan farmer who grows grapefruits. _____

* 9. How could smart people such as the HP board of directors support that crazy search for extraterrestrial intelligence? _____

10. Although environmentalists argue that the Orinoco crocodile is critically endangered, these animals are after all crocodiles, a species that is not critically endangered. This suggests that the Orinoco crocodile is not critically endangered. _____

X. **The following arguments are instances of begging the question, begging the question against, complex question, false alternatives, or accident. Determine which is which. Indicate when an argument commits more than one of these fallacies.**

1. Jane has to come to work. She may be sick, as she says, but she is needed in the office. Whenever an employee is needed in the office, she must show up.

   SAMPLE ANSWER: Accident

2. Women should not be drafted, because no woman should be expected to serve in the military. _____

3. We've had record hot weather for two weeks. In a heat wave as bad as this, there are only two options: either one spends all day complaining about it or one shuts up and goes about one's work. _____

* 4. Can you get on line with that obsolete PC? _____

5. Everyone should get some strenuous physical exercise every day, like running a mile before breakfast. So, my Uncle Olaf, who is ninety-seven years old, ought to run a mile every day before breakfast. _____

* 6. To be wealthy, you have to be either a Wall Street financier or a drug dealer. You are wealthy but you are not a Wall Street financier. It follows that you are a drug dealer. _____

7. Some James Bond fans are not happy with the choice of actor Daniel Craig to take over the role of Agent 007. The website, www.craignotbond.com, asks "How can a short, blond actor with the rough face of a professional boxer and a penchant for playing killers, cranks, cads, and gigolos pull off the role of a tall, dark, handsome, and suave secret agent?" _____

8. Sarah had better marry Dombrowsky. For either she marries him or ends up single. _____

* 9. In general, any one traveler's statistical chance of being a victim of terrorism is so small that it's not even worth considering. So I'm not worried about traveling in the Middle East next week. _____

10. Did Mary manage to get along with Jim? _____

11. Was he able to stay out of trouble during his last visit?

   _____

*12. Murderers don't have a right to life. Since Joe is a murderer, he doesn't have a right to life. _____

13. Certainly there is life after death, since there are many well-known people who have lived previous lives and have memories of those earlier selves long ago. _____

14. The law clearly states that all citizens must pay their taxes or they'll be prosecuted. So my four-year-old cousin Egbert should be prosecuted! After all, I happen to know that he paid no taxes last year.

   _____

*15. Do you support Senator Krank's ridiculous school appropriations bill, which would bankrupt our state government? _____

16. Either you're studying business administration or you're studying engineering. Since you're not studying engineering, you must be studying business administration. _____

17. It will surely be in the interest of the United States to abolish tariffs on commerce with nations south of the Rio Grande, for free trade with Latin America can only be in the interest of the United States.

   _____

18. Do you really want to pass up your chance of a lifetime to invest in Swampwood Estates, Florida's most exclusive and luxurious new residential neighborhood? _____

19. Were you sober last weekend? _____

*20. I can say whatever I want about my neighbor O'Connor. Whether it's true or not, I can say it, and no one can stop me! After all, the First Amendment guarantees freedom of speech in the United States. _____

21. Since we've seen no economic growth in our country for nearly a year, we're to the point where only two things could happen: either there will be disruptive social upheaval or the military will overthrow the government. _____

*22. I always tell the truth. For Smith can testify to this, and whatever he says is the case is so. I can vouch for it myself. After all, I never lie.

   _____

23. There is a good reason to think that children riding to school inhale exhaust gases, for they ride to school either by bus or in private cars. If they ride to school by bus, they inhale exhaust gases. And if they ride to school in private cars, they also inhale exhaust gases.

_____

24. Since media literacy is a proven tool against crime, it could be used to reform convicted murderers. What are we waiting for? Why are we spending taxpayers' dollars on prisons when we could provide murderers the required literacy and return them to society?

_____

*25. Is Betty still complaining endlessly about intractable insomnia? A warm glass of milk before going to bed should end the problem. After all, it helps others to sleep well. _____

XI. YOUR OWN THINKING LAB

1. "If a principle has proved to be *generally* true or reliable, it's probably true or reliable most of the time." Should we agree with this rule?

2. Suppose we find in an argument some premise that itself depends on the conclusion's being true. What's wrong with the argument? Explain the fallacy that it commits.

3. Provide two circular arguments, one that begs the question and one that doesn't.

4. Ask a complex question and explain why it is a fallacy.

8.7 The Philosopher's Corner

Is the "Open Question" Argument Viciously Circular?

Since the end of the nineteenth century, it has sometimes been thought that some areas of study claimed by philosophy are in fact more properly part of the sciences. Fueling this view is the conviction that only science can provide knowledge of the natural world, given that all that exists is natural and that all causes are natural causes. Some philosophers, the so-called naturalists, have endorsed this view. With regard to ethics, the branch of philosophy that studies morality, naturalists deny that it is a philosophical discipline with a subject matter and method entirely independent of the sciences. Some ethical naturalists, whom we'll call "content naturalists," hold the following view:

30 Value words such as "good," "right," and "ought to do" are completely synonymous with descriptive words such as "maximizes well-being," "what we desire on reflection," and "maximizes enjoyment."

To say that any two expressions are synonymous is to say that they are *equivalent in content*, or mean the same. For example, in

31 "Sister" means *female sibling.*

the expressions "sister" and "female sibling" are said to be synonymous, just as are "puppy" and "young dog" in

32 "Puppy" is content-equivalent to *young dog.*

At the beginning of the twentieth century, the English philosopher G. E. Moore (1873–1958) set out to refute this and other versions of ethical naturalism by proposing the so-called *open question argument*, which we'll call *OQA* and reconstruct as an argument *against* content naturalism:

33 1. If content naturalism is true, then a value expression such as "good" is synonymous with a descriptive expression such as "well-being–maximizing."
    2. If "good" is synonymous with "well-being–maximizing," then the question "Granted, this action is well-being–maximizing, but is it good?" is closed (i.e., makes no sense to ask).
    3. But the question, "Granted, this action is well-being–maximizing, but is it good?" is open (i.e., makes sense to ask).
    4. "Good" is not synonymous with "well-being–maximizing."
    5. Steps (1) through (4) can be repeated for each attempted naturalistic definition of a value expression in terms of descriptive expressions.
    6. No value expression is synonymous with descriptive expressions.
    7. Content naturalism is false.

Premise 1 states the main claim of content naturalists. In premises 2 and 3, the terms "closed" and "open" could be interpreted in this way:

34 For any competent user *u* of a value expression *V* and a descriptive expression *D*, the question "Granted this action is *D*, but is it *V*?" is *closed* (or *settled*) for *u* if and only if the expressions *D* and *V* are synonymous; otherwise it is *open* (or *unsettled*) for *u*.

So the first part of *OQA* can be read as arguing that if "good" and "well-being–maximizing" were synonymous for a competent user, then the question

35 Granted this action is "well-being–maximizing," but is it good?

would be closed. But it seems *not* to be closed, since it does seem to make sense to ask the question. Because the question is open, then, it follows that "good" and "well-being–maximizing" are not synonymous.

This line of reasoning, however, has encountered the objection[1] that it begs the question against content naturalists, which amounts to the charge that at least one of *OQA*'s initial premises takes for granted as true something that is in fact controversial. If the objector is right, the culprit would appear to be premise 3, which assumes that the relevant question is open. After all, a question such as (35) would in fact be *closed* for content naturalists who take "good" and "well-being–maximizing" to mean exactly the same (or at least to apply to the same actions). Moreover, because premise 5 of *OQA* holds that the strategy of asking such questions could be repeated for other synonymity claims of content naturalists, the argument seems hopelessly flawed.

Yet surely, just *who* is doing the question-begging-against here is determined by where the burden of proof lies. To illustrate this, let's begin by imagining that content naturalists propose a definition of "good" as "enjoyment-maximizing." Now suppose that Mort is an avid fan of television's *Jerry Springer*

---

[1] *The objection is fully spelled out in W. K. Frankena, "The Naturalistic Fallacy" (Mind 48, 192 (1939): 464–77).*

Show, even though he does not really *like* the fact that he enjoys it. Although making fun of vulnerable people has considerable entertainment value, Mort thinks, it is achieved at a morally questionable price. Mort now sincerely asserts

36 *The Jerry Springer Show* maximizes enjoyment, but it is not good.

Content naturalists willing to take Mort's words "good" and "enjoyment-maximizing" to be synonymous would face a problem without a clear solution. For if that synonymity claim is right, then (36) would be as contradictory as

37 Mary is a sister, but she is not a female sibling.

To explain what's going on with Mort's assertion (36), content naturalists would have to deny at least one of the following:

A. That Mort knows what's he is talking about (i.e., that he is a competent speaker of English)
B. That he is sincere (i.e., that he means what he says and/or is serious), or
C. That he is rational (i.e., that he would avoid defective thinking if he could do so)

But it is difficult to see how any of these three assumptions could be plausibly denied, since they seem independently supported by other common scenarios similar to the one we are now imagining. Suppose we were to report what Mort believes on the basis of (36). We would simply say

38 *Mort believes* that The Jerry Springer Show *maximizes enjoyment but that it is not good.*

And suppose Mort utters (37) and we were to report it. We would say

39 Mort asserts *that Mary is a sister, but that she is not a female sibling.*

To make sense of Mort's assertion in the latter case, we must deny one or the other of the above three assumptions. Since other common scenarios could be imagined which would arouse an intuition similar to that aroused by Mort's utterance (36)–namely, the sense that in calling something "good" one does something more than merely describe it in naturalistic terms–this suggests that it is the content naturalists who have the burden of proof. They need to dispel that common intuition before they can justify their claim that terms such as "good" and "enjoyment-maximizing" are synonymous. Merely insisting that they are won't do. After all, OQA rests on the common intuition that if two expressions of these sorts are indeed synonymous, then a user who is rational, sincere, and competent and who has reflected long enough about their meaning ought to be able to recognize it.

Exercises

XII. In each of the following dialogues, an arguer A begs the question while a respondent R provides a tip about how that is done. Reply to A in a way consistent with R's tip.

* 1. *A:*   Death is the worst thing that could happen to a person. Thus killing a person, even at his own request, is never morally justified.

    R: Consider the case of a hopelessly ill person who is in great pain. Death may, in that case, be less bad than enduring further suffering.

2. *A:*   Induction is well justified. For any strong inductive argument makes its conclusion probable.

    R: Your premise can be supported only inductively.

3. *A:*   Skepticism about perceptual beliefs is well founded. After all, sense perception cannot provide conclusive justification for beliefs of that sort, which never amount to knowledge. Thus, one is never justified in claiming—and therefore does not know—that there is a plate of spaghetti with red sauce before one on the table, even when all the current evidence of one's senses point to there being such a plate.

    R: If I believe that there is a plate of spaghetti with red sauce on the table on the basis of seeing the plate as well as smelling it and tasting its contents, then my belief is completely justified and, if true, amounts to knowledge in some sense.

*4. *A*: The skeptic about perceptual beliefs entertains the possibility of scenarios in which a person is having all the usual sensations as if, for example, there were a plate of spaghetti with red sauce before her on the table while in reality she is asleep in bed. But such scenarios of perfect deception should be rejected. After all, it is always possible to figure out whether things are part of a dream. How? Simply by asking others whether one is awake!

R: Skeptics about perceptual beliefs can reply by insisting that, to entertain the possibility of a perfect-deception dream scenario, it is enough that at least some dreams could appear real to the dreamer.

5. *A*: Given the long history of people encountering God, we may conclude that God exists.

R: You mean "people *reporting* having encountered God," right?

6. *A*: The expression "good" just means "what the most informed people desire upon reflection." What either of these exactly amounts to could be decided only by sociologists. It follows that ethics, the discipline that examines value expressions such as "good," must be a part of sociology.

R: If "good" just meant "what the most informed people would desire upon reflection," then the question "Granted, this thing is what the most informed people would desire upon reflection, but is it good?" would be as trivial as saying "Granted, Jane is a sister, but is she a female sibling?"

■ Writing Project

Research three types of source: (1) advertising; (2) journalism, either print or electronic; and (3) the language of politicians and other public figures and find three examples of the fallacy of false alternatives and three examples of the fallacy of complex question. Write a three-page paper entitled "Some Fallacies of Presumption in Everyday Life," describing how these fallacies were committed in the examples you cite. Be sure to explain for each example why it amounts to a *bad* argument (i.e., what, exactly, is *wrong* with it).

■ Chapter Summary

Fallacies of Presumption

Arguments that commit any of these fallacies fail because they have some *unwarranted* assumption built into their premises. Such an argument seems to work only as long as the assumption is taken for granted.

1. **Begging the Question**
   - ■ An argument that commits this fallacy fails because it is viciously *circular*: one of its premises assumes the truth of the conclusion.

2. **Begging the Question Against**
   - ■ An argument that commits this fallacy fails because it contains at least one premise that is just as controversial as the conclusion, and the questionable premise is treated as obviously true when in reality it is not.
   - ■ It typically involves the *failure to discharge the burden of proof.*

3. **Complex Question**
   - ■ An argument that commits this fallacy fails because it involves a *loaded question*: a question that has an unfair assumption built into it—so that one cannot give any answer to it without implicitly endorsing the questioner's preferred claim (any answer will be the wrong answer).

4. **False Alternatives**
   - ■ An argument that commits this fallacy fails because it presents a disjunction as either being *exclusive*, when in fact both disjuncts could be true, or as offering *the only two alternatives*, when in fact there are more than two.

5. **Accident**
   - ■ An argument that commits this fallacy fails because it does not allow for an exception to a rule when an exception is warranted. Any such argument assumes that because some principle is generally true, therefore it must be true also in *this* case (even though that case is an exception).

■ Key Words

Complex question
Begging the question
Vicious circularity
Formal circularity
Conceptual circularity
Burden of proof
Exclusive disjunction
Naturalism

Begging the question
 against
Accident
False alternatives
Commonsense belief
Presumption
Content naturalism
Open question argument

From Unclear Language to Unclear Reasoning

Chapter Objectives

This chapter considers some common forms of unclarity in language and the ways in which they lead to unclarity in reasoning. Its topics include

- Vagueness.
- Ambiguity.
- Confused predication.
- The sorites paradox.
- The fallacy of slippery slope.
- The fallacy equivocation.
- The fallacy of amphiboly.
- The fallacy of composition.
- The fallacy of division.

- Semantic definitions, as an antidote to semantic unclarity.
- Real and conceptual definitions.
- Philosophical analysis.

9.1 Unclear Language and Argument Failure

Vagueness, ambiguity, and *confused predication* are three different sources of unclear language. Each may lead to argument failure, and we shall find, rooted in these defects, several types of informal fallacy as well as a type of puzzling argument. When an expression is vague to a significant degree, it is unclear whether it applies to certain things. For instance, it's unclear whether "rich" applies to Betty, who has $900,000 in her bank account. She's certainly doing well, but she's not even a millionaire, much less a billionaire! The problem is that "rich" is a vague word: for some cases it's not clear what (or who) counts as being rich. By contrast, when an expression is *ambiguous* to a significant degree, it has more than one *meaning* and *reference,* and it is unclear which ones are intended by it. For example, it is unclear whether "challenging arguments" means *the act of disputing some arguments* or *complex arguments that are difficult to follow.* Roughly, the reference of an expression is what the expression applies to, while its meaning is its content. Consider

1   The sum of $1 + 1$

2   The smallest even number

Both (1) and (2) may be used to refer to the same thing, since they both apply to the same number—namely, the number 2. Yet (1) and (2) don't have the same *content,* which is equivalent to saying that they don't have the same *meaning,* for

MEANING = CONTENT

Since reference and meaning belong to the *semantic dimension* of a language, vagueness and ambiguity are two different forms of *semantic* unclarity. Each may undermine an argument by affecting some of the *terms* or *concepts* that make up its premises and conclusion.

BOX 1 ■ THE SORITES PARADOX AND SOME FALLACIES OF UNCLEAR LANGUAGE

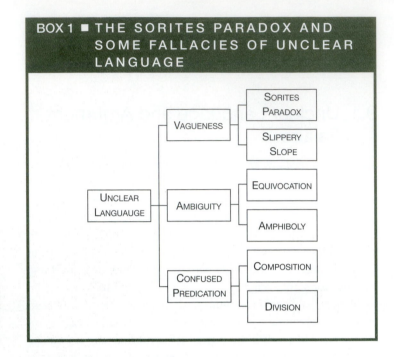

Confused predication, on the other hand, also amounts to semantic unclarity, but it can arise only at the level of relations between *statements* in an argument. That is, confused predication is a fallacy involving a certain error committed in using some *predicate*, or expression that attributes some feature or quality to a thing. For example "occupying 60 percent of the surface of the earth" in the conclusion of this argument:

3   Since oceans occupy 60 percent of the surface of the earth and the Mediterranean is an ocean, therefore the Mediterranean occupies 60 percent of the surface of the earth.

While "occupying 60 percent of the surface of the earth" might be truly predicated of *all oceans* taken collectively, it obviously fails to be true of the Mediterranean Sea. The confusion in (3) is a common type of mistake that stems from an erroneous inference involving a predicate (we'll have more to say about predicates later in this chapter).

Linguistic unclarity rooted in any of these phenomena (confused predication, vagueness, and ambiguity) can render an argument fallacious. Yet before we examine common ways in which this may happen, we must ask why such mistakes matter to logical thinking at all. Two millennia ago, Greek philosophers pointed out that unclarity in language is a sign of unclarity in reasoning. Today we'd say much the same. Assuming that speakers are sincere, what they say is what they believe. And since beliefs are the building blocks of their reasoning, it is then quite likely that any unclarity in what they say results from unclarity in how they reason (for more on this topic, see Chapters 2 and 3).

9.2 Semantic Unclarity

Vagueness and ambiguity are forms of semantic unclarity that may affect linguistic expressions of different kinds as well as the logical relations between them. When a term is *vague*, it is unclear whether or not certain cases fall within its reference; while when it is *ambiguous*, it is unclear which of its meanings or referents is the intended one. Suppose someone says

> **4** She got the cup.

This is said in a room where there are several women, without pointing to anyone in particular. In this context, it is unclear to whom the word "she" applies. At the same time, the term "cup" is clearly ambiguous, since it may equally mean and refer to either "bowl-shaped drinking vessel" or "sports trophy." Furthermore, if we assume that it is used to refer to a drinking vessel, it is unclear just how wide the range of its application may be. Does it apply, for example, to coffee mugs? What about beer tankards? These seem *borderline* cases about which "cup" neither definitely applies nor

---

BOX 2 ■ VAGUENESS AND AMBIGUITY

- When an expression is vague, there are borderline cases where it is unclear whether the expression applies.
- When an expression is ambiguous, it has more than one meaning and sometimes more than one reference.

definitely fails to apply. Hence, "cup" is not only ambiguous but also to some degree vague.

Vagueness and ambiguity can, however, both also be found at a higher level in the statements that make up arguments. Here the worst-case scenario is one where a defect of either type renders an argument *misleading*. In any such argument, although its conclusion might at first appear acceptable on the basis of the argument's premises, a closer look could show that in fact it's not. The premises would provide *no* support for it.

> Logical thinkers should be alert for misleading arguments and try, through careful, case-by-case scrutiny, to unmask fallacies lurking behind vague or ambiguous language.

These two forms of semantic unclarity are unavoidable features of many everyday arguments. Such arguments are, after all, cast in a natural language, which, unlike a formal language, is rich in semantic connotations. For example, suppose that a college instructor, on the day of an examination, receives this phone message:

5   This is Mary. I was at the bank during the test, so I'd like to take the makeup.

Unable to recognize the voice and aware of several financial institutions as well as a river nearby, the instructor cannot make much

---

BOX 3 ■ HOW TO AVOID AMBIGUITY AND VAGUENESS

Ambiguity and vagueness are a matter of degree. Although they affect most expressions in natural languages (which is in part why symbolic logic has developed formal languages to study logical relations such as inference), the fog they raise can often be thinned by looking at the *context*—that is, other linguistic expressions surrounding the affected ones, and factors in the arguer's environment. When we are engaged in argument reconstruction, the principles of charity and faithfulness recommend that we check the context, when available, to gain semantic clarity.

of (5). First, of the several students named "Mary" who missed the exam, it is unclear who the caller in (5) is. Second, of the two meanings of "bank" possible in (5), either "financial institution" or "side of a river," it is unclear which one is intended.

Suppose the student who left the message later sends a note from the local Citibank branch attesting that, on the date of the exam, she, Mary McDonald, had to go there to refinance her mortgage. Putting two and two together, the instructor reasons

6   Mary McDonald was the student who reported her absence. She can prove she was at the local Citibank branch the day of the exam. Thus, she qualifies for the makeup.

No ambiguity remains now: a look at contextual information has eliminated the semantic unclarity in (5) above.

Yet sometimes semantic unclarity bearing on the soundness or strength of an argument persists even after we have engaged in a charitable and faithful reconstruction of the argument. In that case, we must reject the argument on the ground that its premises provide no support for its conclusion, even though they might at first appear to support it. As we shall presently see in detail, each of these two types of semantic unclarity can render an argument misleading.

9.3 Vagueness

Vagueness is at the root of some philosophically interesting, puzzling arguments and also of many fallacious ones. Later in this section, we'll examine some cases of each. But first, let's consider a shortcoming common to all arguments affected by vagueness: *indeterminacy*.

When either the premise or conclusion of an argument is significantly vague, that statement is indeterminate: neither determinately true nor determinately false. Such indeterminacy undermines the argument as a whole.

BOX 4 ■ WHAT'S WRONG WITH ARGUMENT 7?

1. It uses the expression, "young," which has no clear cutoff point between the cases to which it determinately applies and those to which it determinately does not apply.
2. Tom Cruise is among the borderline cases of people about whom it is *indeterminate* whether that word applies or not. He is neither determinately young nor determinately not young.

This is because, as you may recall, to be deductively sound or inductively strong, an argument must have premises that are determinately true. Without that, it counts as neither. Consider

7 1. Young people are independent-minded.
    2. Tom Cruise is young.
    ―――――――――――――――――――――
    3. Tom Cruise is independent-minded.

This argument seems valid, since if its premises are true, its conclusion cannot be false. At the same time, it also seems *unsound*, for soundness requires determinately true premises, and premise 2 suffers from a significant degree of vagueness. *No* contextual information is available to reduce the vagueness of that premise, which results from the two facts described in Box 4. Yet couldn't we stipulate a *cutoff* point between the cases to which "young" determinately applies and those to which it determinately does not? Couldn't we say that anyone 25 years old or less is young and otherwise not young? That would be rather arbitrary, for if a 25-year-old person is young, it seems reasonable that a 26-year-old is too. But if a 26-year-old person is young, so is a 27-year-old. And if a 27-year-old person is young.... As we can see, in the case of this vague term, one borderline case seems to lead to another. At some point we'll reach other cases in which the term "young" clearly doesn't apply at all, such as that of a person 90 years old. But no clear cutoff between the two types of cases is available.

When a statement has a vague term applied to a borderline case, that statement is neither determinately true nor determinately false. Try this yourself: run another series with, for example, "cold," beginning with the determinately true statement, "A temperature

BOX 5 ■ SUMMARY OF VAGUENESS

When a term is vague,

- It is indeterminate whether it applies or not to certain border-line cases.
- There is no *cutoff* between the cases to which it determinately applies and those to which it determinately does not.

When a statement is vague, it is neither determinately true nor de-terminately false.

of zero degrees Fahrenheit is cold" and continuing to a point where you cannot draw the line. Is it 47 degrees? 48 degrees? 50? Again, any cutoff point in the series would be rather arbitrary.

Keep in mind, however, that vague terms may have nonvague occurrences. Compare

8 Tom Cruise is young.

9 A 12-year-old is young.

10 A 90-year-old is young.

While (8) is indeterminate, (9) seems determinately true and (10) determinately false.

The Sorites Paradox

Arguments illustrating the *sorites paradox* are every bit as puzzling to us today as they were to the philosophers of ancient Greece who discovered them. Any sorites (from the Greek, "soros," *a heap*) trades on the vagueness of some term, beginning with seemingly true premises and ending with a false conclusion. For example,

11 1. One grain of sand is not a heap.
    2. If 1 grain of sand is not a heap, then 1 + 1 grains of sand are not a heap.
    3. If 2 grains of sand are not a heap, then 2 + 1 grains of sand are not a heap.
    4. If 3 grains of sand are not a heap, then 3 + 1 grains of sand are not a heap.

5. If one grain of sand is not a heap, then $n + 1$ grains of sand are not a heap.

6. $n + 1$ grains of sand are not a heap.

Since n could be replaced by a number as large as we please, (11)'s conclusion is preposterous. It amounts to the obviously false claim that no matter how many grains of sand there are, they never make up a heap. There is something very puzzling about (11), because

> (A) The argument seems valid, (B) its premises seem true, but (C) its conclusion seems false.

Given A and B, (11)'s conclusion couldn't be false. Yet its conclusion is plainly false. What is going on here? Like other sorites arguments, (11) raises a *paradox*, for A, B, and C cannot all be true, but it is difficult to say which of them is false.

> A paradox is a puzzle without apparent solution involving claims that cannot all be true at once, even when each seems independently true. Standardly, a paradox may be dealt with in one or the other of two ways: it may be solved or it may be dissolved. To solve a paradox, at least one of its claims must be shown false. To dissolve it, it has to be shown that the claims are not really inconsistent.

Until we do either the one or the other, the sorites paradox remains. Since antiquity, this paradox has resisted many attempts of both kinds, all of which have turned out to be flawed in one way or another.

Let's now use our earlier example of a vague word, "young" to run a simplified sorites paradox.

12 1. A 1-year-old is young.
   2. If a 1-year-old is young, then an $n + 1$ year-old is young.
   3. An $n + 1$ year-old is young.

Again, the argument seems valid, its premises true, and its conclusion false. This would be so, for instance, when n is replaced by a large number, such as 110. Premise 2 supports a series of premises such as

13 If a 1-year-old is young, then a 1 + 1 year-old is young.

14 If a 2-year-old is young, then a 2 + 1 year-old is young.

The series eventually reaches borderline cases such as "30-something"-year-old people and "40ish" people, about whom the term is neither determinately true nor determinately false. Since the term is vague, there is no cutoff point between these and the previous cases or between these and the cases about which the term is determinately false, such as

15 A 110-year-old person is young.

More needs to be said about sorites arguments if we are to succeed in determining what's wrong with them. On the basis of our discussion, we should suspend judgment on whether or not they commit a fallacy. Our more modest conclusion here should be

- Any instance of sorites is a paradox: an argument seemingly valid, but with true premises and a false conclusion.
- The paradox arises from the vagueness of one of the terms occurring in the argument's premises and conclusion.

The Slippery Slope Fallacy

Arguments that commit the *slippery slope fallacy* are not paradoxical but plainly misleading. Any such argument moves through a continuum of cases from a premise involving a certain (covertly vague) expression that seems determinately true to a conclusion that appears to be the unavoidable result of sound reasoning. Yet close scrutiny often shows that it isn't sound. Whether deliberately or not,

In the slippery slope fallacy, the arguer misleads by creating the illusion that if one accepts the initial premise, one is ultimately saddled with the conclusion that some obviously false claim must be accepted.

Since, given that initial premise, some disastrous result appears unavoidable, the arguer attempts to show that the premise should be rejected. Let's consider an example. Suppose you arrive 5 minutes late to a wedding without making much of it. Someone tries to convince you that such a delay is unacceptable by offering the following extended argument:

16 1. If arriving 5 minutes late to a wedding is acceptable, then arriving 6 minutes late is also acceptable.
2. If arriving 6 minutes late to a wedding is acceptable, then arriving 7 minutes late is also acceptable.
3. If arriving 7 minutes late to a wedding is acceptable, then arriving 8 minutes late is also acceptable.
4. If arriving 5 minutes late to a wedding is acceptable, then arriving n minutes late is acceptable.
5. Arriving n minutes late to a wedding is not acceptable.
6. Arriving 5 minutes late to a wedding is not acceptable.

Here n would be some large number, such as 100,000. Argument (16) is intended to persuade you to reject the premises apparently leading to the preposterous conclusion 4. Given (16), you'd be convinced that arriving 5 minutes late to a wedding is not acceptable! But instead, you should reject the whole argument on the grounds that it is nothing more than an instance of the slippery slope fallacy.

A quick look at the sort of assumption at work in instances of that fallacy shows how it operates. The argument's structure is essentially this:

17 1. If a case A is not significantly different from a case B, then something that is true of A, call it T, is also true of B.
2. If B is not significantly different from C, then T is also true of C.
3. If D is not significantly different from C, then T is also true of D.
4. T is true of n (where n is a case far removed from A).

The background assumption here seems to be that a sequence of small differences can never amount to a substantial difference between any two points in the sequence. And that's plainly false. Small differences can sometimes add up to a big difference in the end. Furthermore, even in the comparison of two similar cases, it may turn out that some predicates are true of one without being true

BOX 6 ■ HOW TO AVOID SLIPPERY SLOPE ARGUMENTS

Reject the principle fueling a slippery slope argument, for that something is true of some given case doesn't guarantee that it's likewise true of any other similar case. Although it is reasonable that similar cases share many predicates, small differences in a *series* of cases can add up to a big difference between the initial case and the one featured in the slippery slope argument's conclusion. The slippery slope arguer fails to take this into account.

of the other. For example, on some highways the law stipulates a speed limit of 70 miles per hour. Now there is no significant difference in speed between 70 miles per hour and 71 miles per hour; but because of the law, driving at 70 miles per hour on those highways is legal while driving at 71 is technically illegal. So the predicate "legal" truly applies in one case but not in the other, even though they are otherwise not substantially different. We may conclude that any argument committing the slippery slope fallacy rests on this *false* principle:

The slippery slope principle

What is true of *A is* also true of *Z*, provided there is a series of cases *B*, *C*, ..., *Y* between *A* and *Z* that differ from each other only minimally.

9.4 Ambiguity

Vagueness must be distinguished from *ambiguity*. As we have seen, a word or phrase is vague if its reference is indeterminate, so that it is unclear whether or not it applies to a certain case. But ambiguity is a different kind of semantic unclarity that is apt to cause havoc in arguments and therefore is equally likely to mislead. A word is ambiguous if it has more than one meaning and a given context makes unclear which meaning is intended.

> When an ambiguous word occurs in an argument's premise, it may be uncertain whether the argument's conclusion is supported by it at all.

Consider,

> **18** Entertainment Television features news about stars. So, probably many astronomers watch Entertainment Television.

Here "star" is the ambiguous word occurring in the premise, which as a result provides no support for the argument's conclusion. For the argument to succeed, we would need to know whether the intended meaning of "star" is "celestial body seen as a small fixed point of light" or "celebrity entertainer." If the former, then—assuming that that's known—the premise would give a reason for the conclusion provided that the premise is true. But if the latter, then it wouldn't (for in that case the premise and conclusion would be completely unrelated). Yet as it stands, since in (18) "star" is ambiguous and the context leaves the intended meaning unclear, the argument fails to support its conclusion. We'll now look more closely at some types of defective reasoning where arguments are fallacious by virtue of containing ambiguous expressions.

Equivocation

The fallacy of *equivocation* is always rooted in ambiguous expressions, whether words or phrases, occurring either in an argument's premises or in its conclusion.

> Equivocation arises when some crucial expression is used with more than one meaning over the course of an argument—for example, in one place it means one thing, in another something else—and the argument appears to support the conclusion *only as long as we don't notice* that there has been this shift in meaning.

BOX 7 ■ HOW TO AVOID EQUIVOCATION

In evaluating an argument, check thoroughly to be sure that its crucial expressions

1. Have unambiguous meaning
2. Have the same meaning in each occurrence in the argument.

Suppose, for instance, someone argues,

> **19** 1. All laws require a lawmaker.
> 2. Galileo's principle of inertia is a law.
> _____
> 3. Galileo's principle of inertia requires a lawmaker.

Here two different meanings of the word "law" are conflated. In the first premise, it means "statute"–or a codified public regulation enacted by a legislature or decreed by a sovereign. But in the second premise, it means "scientific generalization based on observed regularities of nature." Because the word is being used with two different meanings over the course of the argument, the argument is an instance of the fallacy of equivocation. As such, its premises fail to provide adequate support for the conclusion, and the argument fails.

Be on guard against ambiguous expressions used with different meanings in different places in an argument, which thereby make it unclear whether its conclusion follows from those premises. To detect (and avoid) the fallacy of equivocation, follow the rule in Box 7.

Amphiboly

Another form of misleading argument where ambiguity is the source of the problem is the fallacy of *amphiboly*.

In amphiboly, it's the awkward construction of sentences— the confusing way their words are arranged—that renders them unclear and so invites drawing the wrong conclusion from them.

We say "wrong" because the conclusion of an amphibolous premise either doesn't clearly follow from it or doesn't follow from it at all. To see the fallacy at work, consider the following dialogue, adapted from a routine by the comedian Fyvush Finkel:

> **20** *patient*: Doctor, doctor! My arm hurts in two places! What should I do?
>
> *doctor*: Don't go to those places!

We smile when we read or hear amphibolous sentences like the patient's, where a clumsy word order causes it to have a hilarious double meaning. Of course, the sentence *by itself* is not an argument, but if its ambiguity leads the "doctor" to draw the wrong conclusion from it, then the dialogue contains an implicit argument. How, then, does that argument commit the fallacy of amphiboly? Plainly, it is defective by virtue of ambiguity caused by word order. The argument runs

> **21** 1. Your arm hurts in two places.
>
> 2. Pain is to be avoided.
> _____
> 3. You shouldn't go to those places where your arm hurts.

Assuming that premise 2 is true, even so, since premise 1 is amphibolous, (21) fails to support statement 3. Fortunately for those who want to be alert for this fallacy, there is a distinguishing characteristic that may help to recognize it: in all cases of amphiboly, the ambiguity can be eliminated by recasting the sentence. For example, in (20), the patient's complaint is not amphibolous if recast as

> **22** There are two places on my arm that hurt.

To detect (and avoid) the fallacy of amphiboly, the rule is to inspect an argument's premises as directed in Box 8. If you find ambiguous word order in a premise, recast that premise, when possible, in a

---

BOX 8 ■ HOW TO AVOID AMPHIBOLY

In evaluating an argument, be alert for ambiguous word order in the premises that leaves uncertain whether they do in fact support the argument's conclusion.

way that removes the ambiguity. In doing so, be sure to follow the principles of charity and faithfulness for argument reconstruction.

9.5 Confused Predication

We must now turn our attention to two types of informal fallacy that are rooted in a confusion involving predication. First, let's explain terminology. What, exactly, is "predication"? Consider, for example,

23 Dick Cheney is bald.

Of the two terms in (23), "bald" and "Dick Cheney," only the former is uncontroversially a predicate—in this case, one that attributes the property of *being bald* to Dick Cheney. Predicates are often used to describe individual entities as being in certain ways. But they may also be used to attribute properties to complex entities such as classes, groups, and wholes. Those entities may involve either a *class of things* (e.g., yellow cars), a *collective group* (e.g., the Cleveland Orchestra), or a *whole* made up of parts (e.g., a computer). Classes and collective groups have members while wholes have parts. Predicates are used to attribute properties and relations to individual things or persons and also to such complex entities. Consider the following:

24 Those cars are fashionable.
25 The Cleveland Orchestra is first rate.
26 My new computer is well designed.

Here "being fashionable," "being first rate," and "being well designed" are the properties attributed by the predicates. There

---

BOX 9 ■ WHAT IS A PREDICATE?

The smallest meaningful components of statements are *terms* or *concepts*, which divide into two categories: singular, used to talk about individual things, and general, used to attribute properties or qualities, such as being *tall*, *amused*, or *a philosopher*. General terms have the logical role of predicates. To assign a predicate is, in many cases, to describe something.

is, of course, nothing wrong with using predicates in these ways to describe individual things or classes, collectives, and wholes. We couldn't do without these types of descriptions.

But sometimes a confusion in predication leads to defects in reasoning that happen when the arguer fails to notice either of these:

1. Some properties that apply to a *whole*, a *class of things*, or a *collective group* as stated in an argument's premises, do not apply to each *part* of the whole or each *individual member* of the class or group as stated in its conclusion.
2. Conversely, some properties that apply to a *part* of a whole, or an *individual member* of a class or a group as stated in an argument's premises, do not apply to the entire whole, class, or group as stated in its conclusion.

Whether it is an individual thing that is said to have a property or a class of things (or a collective group or a whole) matters for clarity in reasoning. When this important distinction is ignored, an argument may, for example, fallaciously attribute a certain property to a class of things in the premises and to a member of that class in the conclusion, as in argument (3) at the beginning of this chapter:

3 Since oceans occupy 60 percent of the surface of the earth and the Mediterranean is an ocean, therefore the Mediterranean occupies 60 percent of the surface of the earth.

We shall now look closely at two informal fallacies of confused predication known as *composition* and *division*.

Composition

Confused predication underlies the informal fallacy known as "composition."

Composition rests on the mistake of thinking that, since each of the *parts* of some whole, or each of the members of a class or group, has a certain property, therefore the whole, class, or group itself also has that same property.

BOX 10 ■ HOW TO AVOID THE FALLACY OF COMPOSITION

Bear in mind that,

■ It is one thing to predicate a property of each individual member of a team, class, etc., but quite another to predicate it of the team itself. What may be true in the one case might not be so in the other.

■ If an argument concludes that a whole itself has a certain property *on the basis* of its parts' each having that property individually, it commits the fallacy of composition and should be rejected.

For example, consider

> 27 1. Each player for the Chicago Cubs is an excellent player.
> _____
> 2. The Chicago Cubs are an excellent team.

It is very likely that (27)'s premise *is* true (in baseball, one has to be very good to get into the major leagues!). Yet even if each player for the Cubs is excellent, that wouldn't support the claim that the team *as a group* is excellent. For an excellent team is more than just a collection of excellent individual athletes. It's one that functions well as a coordinated group. Argument (27) then, is defective, even if the premise and conclusion are both true. Why? Because it commits the fallacy of composition through overlooking the crucial distinction in Box 10.

Similarly, consider

> 28 1. Each part of a computer consumes very little energy.
> 2. A computer consumes very little energy.

Argument (28) *falls short* of being deductively valid or even inductively strong. A research lab supercomputer would make its premise true and its conclusion false. Again, the root of the problem is in thinking that because each of the parts individually has a certain property (namely, that of running with little energy), therefore *the whole* made up of all of those parts must have it too.

Division

Another fallacy of confused predication is *division*.

> Division rests on the mistake of thinking that, because the whole has a certain property, therefore each of the parts or members that make it up has that same property.

Unlike composition, division makes the mistake of thinking that what can be truly predicated of the whole can likewise be truly predicated of the parts that make it up. Suppose someone argues

29 1. The U.S. Congress represents every state in the Union.
  2. Each member of the U.S. Congress represents every state in the Union.

Here the premise is uncontroversially true, but the conclusion is plainly false. What has gone wrong is that a simple principle has been ignored: that a property can be truly predicated of some collective group provides no guarantee that it can also be truly predicated of each member of that group. In (29), someone's being a member of a body that represents every state in the Union is taken to support the conclusion that *that person individually* represents every state in the Union. Thus, the argument commits the fallacy of division.

Now consider

30 1. The taxicabs in Washington, D.C., are numerous.
  2. Each taxicab in Washington, D.C., is numerous.

Does (30) also commit the fallacy of division? To answer this, we must note that the argument makes an inferential move from a

---

BOX 11 ■ HOW TO AVOID THE FALLACY OF DIVISION

- In evaluating an argument, check whether it concludes that each part of a whole has a certain property *on the basis* of the whole's having that property.
- If it does, the argument commits the fallacy of division and should be rejected.

> ## BOX 12 ■ SUMMARY OF CONFUSED PREDICATION
>
> In evaluating an argument, check whether
>
> ■ It concludes that each part of a whole has a certain property *on the basis* of the whole's having that property.
>
> ■ It concludes that a whole itself has a certain property *on the basis* of its parts' each having that property individually.
>
> If either of these is the case, then the argument commits one of the fallacies of confused predication and must therefore be rejected.

predicate's being true of a *class of things* (i.e., Washington taxicabs) in the premise, to that predicate's being true of each individual Washington taxi in the conclusion. Thus this *is* an instance of division. It is only *classes of things* that can (collectively) be numerous. Individuals can't be, so the conclusion in (30) is just nonsense! As we've seen, the fact that some collective entity has an attribute does not provide a good reason to conclude that the same attribute can rightly be ascribed to any part of it.

Logical thinkers, then, should beware of the informal fallacies that can arise through confusion in predication and be able to distinguish the two different types of confusion that underlie division, on the one hand, and composition, on the other. To detect and avoid these fallacies, follow the rules in Boxes 10 and 11.

Exercises

I. Review Questions

1. Explain the difference between vagueness and ambiguity.
2. What is the difference between meaning and reference?
3. What is a paradox?
4. Traditionally, one can get around a paradox in only one or the other of two ways. What are these? Explain.
5. What is the sorites paradox?
6. Explain what a slippery slope fallacy is. Why should such arguments be rejected?
7. What is the fallacy of equivocation?
8. In a fallacy of amphiboly, what is the source of the confusion?

9. In any genuinely amphibolous sentence, the amphiboly can be removed in a simple way. What way?
10. What are predicates? And what is meant by "predication"?
11. Why might composition be said to be a fallacy of confused predication?
12. What is the fallacy of division?

II. Some of the following are clearly vague and some are not. Determine which is which.

1. Hot day

   SAMPLE ANSWER: Clearly vague

2. Tall _____

* 3. Equilateral triangle _____

4. Leopard _____

* 5. Bachelor _____

6. Lawyer _____

* 7. Poor _____

8. Populous _____

* 9. Parallel lines _____

10. Odd number _____

11. The U.N. _____

*12. Person _____

III. For each of the above terms that is clearly vague, show its vagueness by constructing a sorites paradox involving that term.

IV. For each of the following expressions, show that it can be used ambiguously by constructing a sentence that could have different meanings. Provide the context of use.

1. Sub

   SAMPLE ANSWER: "My recent experience with subs has been a disaster." In one context, "sub" may mean a type of naval vessel; in another, a type of sandwich; in still another, a substitute worker.

2. Snake in the grass

3. Fraternity

4. Siren

5. Birthday

6. Desert

7. Pirate

8. Honey

9. Plateau

V. Identify the informal fallacy committed by each of the following arguments.

1. The one who testified against Tony Soprano was a rat. A rat is a rodent of the genus *Rattus*. It follows that the one who testified against Tony Soprano was a rodent of the genus *Rattus*.

   SAMPLE ANSWER: Equivocation

2. Donors to the Philharmonic's fund-raising campaign have given the orchestra millions of dollars this year. My neighbor Mrs. Martinez was one of these donors. We may infer that Mrs. Martinez gave the orchestra millions of dollars. _____

* 3. Phil is taking six courses this semester, and they're all three-credit courses. But each course is easy, so Phil will have an easy semester. _____

4. Leon Kass, chairman of the President's Council on Bioethics, argues for a ban or moratorium on human cloning. Permitting such cloning, he insists, can only lead to abuse. "Today, cloned blastocysts for research; tomorrow, cloned blastocysts for babymaking"—*New York Times*, February 17, 2004. _____

5. Perhaps you think that 12 is an even number? Well I can prove that it is odd. Consider my Uncle Horace. He was born with 5 toes on one foot and 7 toes on the other, which gives him 12 toes. Now I'm sure you'll agree that 12 toes is an odd number of toes for a man. Therefore, 12 is an odd number. _____

6. If we continue to permit abortion, then we'll soon be allowing euthanasia on demand. This line of reasoning leads straight to justifying mass exterminations of any "unwanted" people. At last we'll be

led to death camps and outright genocide. Therefore abortion should not be permitted. _____

* 7. Sue: "The Department of Traffic Control announced last month that in Boston a pedestrian is hit by a car once every thirty-seven minutes." Sam: "Wow! That guy must be in bad shape!" _____

8. The manager told me she would lose no time in looking at my resume. So I'm sure she will read it immediately. _____

9. With competition from European film makers, Hollywood is in trouble. Superman can rescue those who are in trouble. *Superman* is doing well at the box office. Therefore *Superman* can rescue Hollywood. _____

*10. Handgun registration laws are a bad thing. Once we start registering our weapons, where will that lead? To the government's having a list of all the weapon owners! And what will happen next? All the guns will be confiscated! From there it is but a short step to the inevitable: a despotic dictatorship and the end of freedom. _____

11. The Rolling Stones toured more frequently in the first half of the year than any other band. Keith Richards is one of the Rolling Stones' guitarists. Hence, Keith Richards toured more frequently in the first half of the year than any other guitarist. _____

12. One way to lose weight would be to fast: that is, to give up eating certain foods for a while. Of course, you would not have to give up *everything*—some foods you could continue to eat. But what foods? Well, foods appropriate to a fast, I suppose. McDonald's and Burger King are well known fast-food restaurants. Therefore if I want to lose weight, I should eat only at McDonald's or Burger King. _____

*13. After seeing this newspaper item, "The current pastor of Old South Church, now 333 years old, is the Rev. James W. Crawford," I concluded, "Funny, he doesn't look a day over fifty!" _____

14. Mother says Uncle Ryan is a couch potato. Since potatoes are vegetables, it follows that Uncle Ryan is a vegetable. _____

15. Dissenters must be suppressed at once, to ensure that they do not undermine presidential authority. One dissenter today means millions of dissenters tomorrow. If even a single person is allowed to dissent, this will be the first step that will lead ultimately to anarchy. _____

16. Since flying is more expensive than driving, birds will stop flying south for the winter. _____

*17. You can eat that chocolate chip cookie if you want, but I say you're asking for trouble. Next you'll be eating ice cream, then hot fudge sundaes. Soon it'll be double cheeseburgers, fried chicken, and layer cakes! Stroke and a heartattack are waiting for you without a doubt. _____

18. The chemical designation for common table salt is *sodium chloride* (NaCl). Salt is a compound of sodium and chlorine. And since salt is, of course, edible and not at all poisonous, it follows that sodium and chlorine are both edible and not at all poisonous. _____

19. A "cybersquatter" misused a web address containing Tom Cruise's name, which must be returned to the actor since the arbitrators have determined that the actor owns It. _____

*20. Ice cream is an enjoyable food. Beer is an enjoyable drink. Therefore, ice cream and beer would make an enjoyable lunch. _____

21. The government should do whatever it can to ensure that housing prices continue to go up. For if there is a slowdown in the price of real estate, then that would adversely affect retail spending. With a slump in retail spending, the economy would collapse.
_____

22. In the ancient world, Persia was a mighty kingdom. But the Greek king, Croesus, also ruled a mighty kingdom in Lydia. When Croesus asked the Delphic Oracle for advice, she told him, "If Croesus crossed the river Halys (i.e., invaded Persia) he would destroy a mighty kingdom." Croesus was delighted with this news and concluded that he should immediately invade Persia, which he did. As a result, Lydia was destroyed. _____

23. Some who read the *New York Times* headline "ON DRUGS, BUSH AIMS FOR A MEETING OF THE MINDS AT LEAST" concluded that the president was on drugs! _____

*24. Residents of San Francisco come from every country in the world. Ms. Solomon is a resident of San Francisco. It follows that Ms. Solomon comes from every country in the world. _____

25. A candidate for Congress introduces himself as follows: "My name is Henry G. Honest, and I believe you should vote for me. I'm the only candidate in this election who can truly call himself honest."
_____

26. Announcement in church bulletin: "For those of you who have children and may not know it, there is a nursery available in the parish hall during worship services." Thus it seems that some members of the church have children and don't know it! _____

*27. The average American family has 2.5 cars. The Johnsons are an average American family. Therefore the Johnsons have 2.5 cars.

_____

28. Taxpayers' dollars are dollars. There is nothing wrong with using dollars to buy myself a trip to Europe. Thus, there is nothing wrong with using taxpayers' dollars to buy myself a trip to Europe. _____

29. Only cardinals can vote to elect the Pope. The St. Louis Cardinals will play in the World Series this year. Therefore some voters to elect the Pope will play in the World Series this year. _____

*30. An online news source recently ran the headline, "Slain Preacher's Wife to Testify at Murder Trial." We may infer that a dead person will give testimony in court! _____

VI. Your Own Thinking Lab

1. Are coffee mugs cups? Discuss what sort of semantic unclarity is involved in expressions containing the word "mug." Is it vagueness, ambiguity, or both? Provide sentences that illustrate the sort of semantic unclarity that may affect the uses of this word.

2. What's the matter with these arguments?

    A. If euthanasia is made legal, then people would use it to get rid of ailing relatives. But if people used it to get rid of ailing relatives, then there would be no difference between what we do in our society and what totalitarian regimes have done with firing squads and death camps. Therefore euthanasia must not be made legal.

    B. If execution is rejected as cruel and unusual punishment, then life in prison without parole will be too. But this line of reasoning leads eventually to proposing that dangerous criminals go free, and that would create social chaos. It follows that execution should not be rejected as cruel and unusual punishment.

9.6 Semantic Definition: An Antidote to Unclear Language

As we have seen, one of the chief obstacles to semantic clarity is ambiguity. Semantic clarity is, however, crucial for clarity in reasoning. We may often be able to minimize, and sometimes to eliminate, ambiguity by putting together adequate semantic definitions. Definitions of this sort either clarify or revise the semantic features of a linguistic expression, which are its meaning and reference. Because such definitions have the function of indicating how linguistic expressions should be understood, they are essential to argument reconstruction. In this section, we'll introduce some such definitions: the so-called *reportive*, *ostensive*, and *contextual* ones. There are, however, more classes of semantic definitions than those we can discuss here. Furthermore, many definitions do not have a semantic function at all. We'll discuss some of these in the Philosopher's Corner.

Reconstructing Definitions

Definitions illustrate the directive use of language. Consider semantic definitions. They amount to *prescriptions* about how to use/interpret single words or larger expressions. As a result, the question of whether any such definition is "true or false" does not really arise. Rather, the definition could be said to be adequate or inadequate, correct or incorrect, and the like. But before we can evaluate a definition of any type, it's best to reconstruct it first, so that we may grasp what is being defined and what provides the definition. This requires distinguishing the two sides of a definition: the *definiendum* (that which is to be defined) and the *definiens* (that which provides the definition). In reconstructing a definition, its *definiendum* is listed first, on the left-hand side, and its *definiens* last, on the right-hand side. Here we'll adopt the practice of placing the symbol "=df." (which reads "equal by definition") between *definiedum* and *definiens*. Once a definition has been reconstructed, it looks like this:

31	Puppy	=df.	Young dog
32	Triangle	=df.	Plane figure with exactly three internal angles
33	Cube	=df.	Three-dimensional object with six sides, all of which are flat and square

In each of these definitions, the expression listed on the left is its *definiendum*, that on the right its *definiens*. Everyday definitions hardly look like (31), (32), and (33), since they are phrased in many different ways—as can be seen in the familiar case of the language learner who knows the meaning of a certain English word but is uncertain about that of a synonymous word. Let's say he masters "lawyer" without mastering "attorney." If he asks us about the meaning of the latter, we may offer a definition such as

34 To be an attorney is to be a lawyer.

34' To say that a person is an attorney is to say that the person is a lawyer.

34" "Attorney" means "lawyer."

Each of these has "attorney" as its *definiendum* and "lawyer" as its *definiens*. It could therefore be reconstructed in the way suggested above.

Reportive Definitions

Examples (34) through (34"), all equivalent in their content, are "reportive" definitions. Definitions of this sort give the everyday meaning of a word or of some larger linguistic expression. They are the type of definition commonly found in dictionaries and translation manuals. Since some such definitions succeed and others fail, we shall say that when they succeed, they are *adequate*, and when they fail, *inadequate*—where adequacy consists in the following:

> A reportive definition is *adequate* if and only if its two sides are synonymous or *meaning-equivalent* (i.e., they mean the same). Otherwise, the reportive definition is inadequate.

BOX 13 ■ COUNTEREXAMPLES AND THE INADEQUACY OF SOME REPORTIVE DEFINITIONS

- When presented with a certain reportive definition, if we could consistently describe a scenario where something satisfied one of its sides without satisfying the other that would amount to a counterexample showing the definition to be inadequate. For it would show that its two sides are not synonymous or meaning-equivalent.

- If such a scenario is *not* possible, the proposed reportive definition is adequate. Here we use the principle: *Adequate because there are no counterexamples to it.*

Among the defects that would make a reportive definition inadequate are its being too broad,

> **35** Sister   =df.   Female person

Or too narrow,

> **36** Sister   =df.   Adult female sibling

Or too broad and too narrow at the same time,

> **37** Sister   =df.   Adult sibling

Thought Experiments and Counterexamples

Counterexamples are the standard way to show that a certain reportive definition is inadequate. A single counterexample is enough to show the inadequacy of any such definition. The test proceeds as described in Box 13. A female person who is not a sibling is counterexample to (35). A female sibling who is not an adult is a counterexample to (36). A male adult who is a sibling and a nonadult female who is a sibling are counterexamples to (37).

Let's now use the method of counterexample to test a reportive definition of the word, "courage," attempted by the Athenian general Laches in Plato's dialogue of that name:

> **38** Courage   =df.   Moving forward in a battle

To test the adequacy of (38), we try to find a real-life case that for example clearly satisfies its *definiendum* without satisfying its *definiens*. If we succeed, then that would show that (38)'s two sides are not synonymous. But suppose we can't find a real-life counterexample to (38). Shall we then declare this definition adequate? No, for the test could still proceed by thought experiment (i.e., scenarios that often exist only in thought; see Box 14). First, we describe a scenario in which someone is clearly courageous even though this person moves backward in a battle: for example, as a strategy to confuse the enemy and counteract his moves more forcefully. Then we argue that this fighter satisfies (38)'s *definiendum* but not its *definiens* and conclude that this shows Laches' attempted reportive definition to be inadequate.

On the other hand, any reportive definition that doesn't have counterexamples is adequate. When presented with a definition that seems adequate, we can test it with a thought experiment. If we try this method with (31) through (34) above, we soon discover that it's simply not possible that, for example, someone could be an attorney without being a lawyer or a sister without being a female sibling. In any possible world where someone is an attorney, that person is a lawyer, and if she is a sister, then she is also a female sibling. Since counterexamples to these definitions seem impossible, we must conclude that the definitions are adequate.

Of course, a relevant thought experiment must follow certain rules. As outlined in Box 14, one such rule requires that the described scenario be consistent, otherwise it wouldn't qualify as a *logically possible* world. Another requires that the scenario be thoroughly described in the *same language* without changing the meanings of the words. And it goes without saying that any thinker who's testing a definition by a thought experiment must be a competent user of the words involved. Since the thinkers now testing (38) are *us*, it's important that we have *no* reason to suspect that our intuitions about the meanings of the words in that definition are atypical and therefore irrelevant to the ordinary conception of them.

Ostensive and Contextual Definitions

Not all semantic definitions feature synonymous expressions, however. Among semantic definitions that don't are those that are *ostensive* or *contextual*. The *definiens* of an ostensive definition offers some examples of things paradigmatically falling under its *definiendum*—for instance,

39 To be a socialist country is to have the socioeconomic system at work in Cuba.

40 A metropolis is a city like London, São Paulo, or Tokyo.

On other hand, a *contextual definition* presents in its *definiens* another expression or context in which neither the *definiendum* nor a strict synonym of it occurs. For example, in logic, the connective "unless" is sometimes defined by equivalence with "either ... or ..." in this way:

41 "*P* unless *Q*" is logically equivalent to "either *P* or *Q*," where "either ... or ... " is neither identical to nor synonymous with "unless."

9.7 The Philosopher's Corner
Real Definitions

Not all definitions concern the meanings of linguistic expressions. Among those that don't are some that are of special interest to scientists and philosophers. This is because philosophy and the sciences aim in part at establishing what certain things and concepts *really are*. We'll now consider briefly two types of definition falling into this broad group: the real and the conceptual. A *real definition* attempts to spell out the essence or microstructure of the substance or species listed in its *definiendum*. For example,

42 Water is H_2O.

43 Lightning is an electrical discharge.

Note that the point of such definitions is not to give *meanings*. Although it might be thought that "H_2O" and "electrical discharge" are the meanings of "water" and "lightning" respectively, they are not. Suppose, for example, that the meaning of "water" was "H_2O." It would then follow that a competent user of English who did not know its chemical composition would not know what he was talking about when he used the word "water." But that's a preposterous conclusion. Surely when Shakespeare used the word "water," he knew the meaning of the word, even though no one then knew that water was H_2O! This suggests that, in a real definition, its *definiens* does not provide the *meaning* of its *definiendum* but instead its *essential nature or underlying composition*. This is neither a matter of meaning-definition nor of philosophical speculation but belongs rather to the way things are. The real definition of "lemon," for instance, would appeal to the chromosomal structure of lemons. Definitions of this sort play a central role in science, since they spell out the common essential features or mechanisms underlying the perceivable features of things. Real definitions, then, are the products of scientific investigation.

Conceptual Definitions and Philosophical Analysis

Philosophers are interested in science and of course consider real definitions. But when it comes to determining the nature of concepts, they usually focus on what might be called *conceptual definitions*. These are a crucial part of a broader method known as "philosophical analysis" or "critical philosophy," which is concerned with providing deeper insights into certain especially difficult concepts, such as "causation," "mind," "meaning," "truth," "material world," "knowledge," "free will," and many more. Philosophical definition is also a tool for clarifying the logical form of propositions, the building blocks of argument. In practicing their trade, philosophers examine definitions such as

44 Knowledge is justified true belief.

45 "*A* causes *B*" means that *B* has been observed to occur regularly after *A*.

46 The proposition "The present king of France is bald" can be analyzed as the conjunction of three propositions: "There is at least one present king of France, there is at most one present king of France, and whoever is the present king of France is bald."

(44) and (45) had a similar fate: although it was once thought that definitions along those lines correctly captured the concepts of knowledge and cause, they were later found inadequate. It then became part of the philosopher's job to propose adequate definitions to replace them. Since each turned out to be a task more difficult than might at first appear, topics of philosophical reflection developed that were devoted almost entirely to producing such definitions.

But what, exactly, is it that makes such definitions of concepts philosophical? Compare reportive definitions: given the parallel between thought and language, we may say that examples (31) through (34), discussed earlier in this chapter, are definitions of the concepts, "sister," "attorney," etc. Yet, for a number of reasons, that wouldn't make those definitions *philosophical*. First, those concepts are unproblematic, "one-criterion" concepts whose exact definition any competent speaker of the language can give. By contrast, the definition of a concept of the kind that matters to philosophy is of a sort that typically is *not* easy to give, even for the most competent speakers of the language.

The definitions of most interest to philosophers attempt philosophical *analyses* of the terms on their left-hand side. Definition (44) offers an analysis of knowledge and (45) an analysis of causation. In each case, there is a complex definiens, some of whose terms also have philosophical import, thus requiring further philosophical analysis. By contrast with a reportive definition, a philosophically interesting definition is one in which the *definiendum* and *definiens* are not obviously synonymous. Rather, the latter aims at offering an analysis of the former by a meticulous "unpacking" of its elements one by one, together with a study of its relation to other concepts or propositions. Furthermore, while a reportive definition is offered to clarify the everyday meaning of an expression, *that* meaning of the words used in a philosophical definition is already understood by philosophers, who are after something else. What could that be? A philosophical definition of a concept or proposition is an analytical elucidation, of a sort that can be useful in helping us to think more clearly. Moreover, it can help to prevent, or sometimes resolve, puzzles originating in that concept or proposition. For example, clarity about the logical form of "The present king of France is bald" once helped to resolve a puzzle about the truth value of propositions such as

47 The present king of France is not bald.

(47) seems at first odd, since it appears both true and false. But this puzzle was happily brought to an end early in the last century, when philosophical definition revealed the logical form of such propositions. It was then understood that (47) was ambiguous between these two logical forms:

47' It is false that (1) there is at least one present king of France, (2) there is at most one present king of France, and (3) whoever is the present king of France is bald.

47" (1) There is at least one present king of France, (2) there is at most one present king of France, and (3) whoever is the present king of France is not bald.

Philosophical definition thus solved this puzzle by revealing it to be one of ambiguity in logical form, which affects negative propositions of the structure "the such&such is so&so," when "the such&such" denotes something that doesn't exist.

Exercises

VII. Review Questions

1. What is a semantic definition?
2. Any definition has two parts. Name these parts and explain their roles.
3. Provide two reportive definitions and explain in each case why it counts as such.
4. What are ostensive and contextual definitions? Illustrate your answer with examples.

5. Can reportive definitions be inadequate? If so, how? If not, why not?

6. How do reportive, ostensive, and contextual definitions differ? Support your answer with examples.

VIII. **In each of the following definitions, first mark its** *definiendum* **with one line and its** *definiens* **with two lines and then reconstruct the definition in the way suggested above, making it as succinct as possible.**

1. In English, an oculist is an eye doctor.

   SAMPLE ANSWER: In English, an <u>oculist</u> is an <u>eye doctor</u>.
   oculist =df. eye doctor

2. The meaning of "He is angry" is completely identical to that of "He is inclined to exhibit anger behavior." _____

* 3. To say that an elephant is small is to say that it is an elephant that is smaller than most elephants. _____

4. One event causes another just in case if the first event had not happened, then the second event would not have happened. _____

* 5. Something is a human being if and only if it is a featherless biped. _____

6. By "glue" English speakers mean an adhesive substance used to join two surfaces. _____

* 7. A horse is a beast of burden with a flowing mane. _____

8. To name incorrectly is to misname. _____

9. What makes you timid or fearful is something that intimidates you. _____

10. An electronic apparatus for the production and control of sound is a synthetizer. _____

IX. **Determine whether the following definitions are reportive, contextual, or ostensive.**

1. Pandas are those animals that we saw in the last cage at the Washington zoo.

   SAMPLE ANSWER: Ostensive

2. "*x* is the brother of *y*" means "*x* is male and *x* and *y* have a common parent." _____

* 3. "Valor" means "courage." _____

4. To be a woman is to be a female human being. _____

5. "Bachelor" = unmarried man. _____

6. Chilis are the peppers that you ate at Garza's *Rio Grande Restaurant*. _____

* 7. "Some are philosophers" means "there are philosophers." _____

8. "Hunter" means "person who hunts." _____

* 9. Cricket is that sport which is now popular in the West Indies. _____

10. "*P* if and only if *Q*" means "If *P*, then *Q*; if *Q*, then *P*." _____

X. For each of the following reportive definitions, indicate whether it is too broad, too narrow, or both.

1. A human arm is a human limb.

SAMPLE ANSWER: Too broad

2. To be human is to be an animal. _____

* 3. "Bachelor" is meaning equivalent to "Unmarried human being who is sexually neurotic." _____

4. A paint stripper is a solvent usable for removing bright paint. _____

* 5. To say that someone is a lawyer is to say that *that* person is a litigating attorney. _____

6. Tiger =df striped animal. _____

* 7. Lemon =df. natural fruit with yellow peel and vitamin C that grows in Florida. _____

8. A woodchuck is a groundhog that lives on the prairies of Minnesota. _____

* 9. A human being is a creature with lungs. _____

10. Capitalism is a way of life in the developed world. _____

XI. **Show the inadequacy of the definitions in the above exercise by offering a counterexample to each of them.**

1. A human arm is a human limb.

   SAMPLE ANSWER: A human leg, which is a limb that is not an arm.

XII. **Redefine the expressions listed in exercise (X) in a way that avoids the objections of being too broad, too narrow or too broad and too narrow.**

1. A human arm is a human limb.

   SAMPLE ANSWER: A human arm is an upper-body limb of humans normally attached to the body at the shoulders and ending in a hand.

XIII. **Determine whether these definitions are real or conceptual:**

1. Nature is all that part of the material universe that is not mental.

   SAMPLE ANSWER: Conceptual definition

2. "p is a law of nature," is equivalent to "p is a general hypothesis which can always be relied on." _____

* 3. Heat =df. molecular motion. _____

4. Horse = perissodactyl quadruped belonging to the genus *Equus* and the family *Equidae*. _____

* 5. A proposition is true if and only if it corresponds to the facts.

   _____

6. Gold is the element with atomic number 79. _____

* 7. "Scott is the author of *Waverley*" = "There is exactly one author of *Waverley* and Scott is that person." _____

* 8. Cabbage is a leafy garden vegetable of many varieties, all belonging to the family *Cruciferi*, found in the coasts of Europe. _____

9. Goodness is what's worth having for its own sake. _____

10. Someone S means to say something beyond the literal meaning of her utterance x if and only if (i1) S intends to produce a certain response r in her audience A; and (i2) that A shall recognize S's

intention (i1), and (i3) that this recognition on the part of *A* of (i1) shall function as *A*'s reason, or part of his reason, for her response *r*. (Adapted from Peter Strawson, "Intention and Convention in Speech Acts.") _____

XIV. YOUR OWN THINKING LAB

1. Use the method of counterexample to show the inadequacy of the following definitions:

A.   Knowledge =df. Having a true belief.

B.   *A* causes *B* =df. *B* has been observed to occur regularly after *A*.

C.   Morally right action =df. Action that obeys the laws of the state.

D.   Being hungry =df. Asserting that one desires food.

E.   Guilty person =df. Someone who has been convicted of a crime.

2. Explain why thought experiments would support the adequacy of the following definitions:

A.   2 =df. Smallest even number.

B.   Mother =df. Female parent.

C.   Tennis player =df. One who plays tennis.

D.   Rectangle =df. Plane figure with four straight sides forming four right angles.

E.   Straight line =df. Line that is the shortest path between two points.

■ Writing Project

Some have argued that abortion is morally abhorrent because no clear line can be drawn to distinguish morally between the primitive organism formed at conception and the baby who is born nine months later. Write a short paper in which you present a slippery slope argument of your own to support the view that abortion is wrong, and then criticize it on the basis of what you've learned in this chapter about the slippery slope fallacy. Finally, say whether you think these criticisms of slippery slope amount to a successful defense of abortion rights or not. Perhaps the antiabortion side can still prevail and has strong arguments to offer? Who do you think is right in this dispute? Give reasons to support your conclusions.

■ Chapter Summary

1. **Unclear Language and Argument**
   Unclarity in what speakers say often results from unclarity in their inferences.

2. **Semantic Unclarity**
   Vagueness
   - When a term is vague to a significant degree, its reference is unclear.
   - When a statement is vague to a significant degree, it is neither determinately true nor determinately false.

   Ambiguity
   - When an expression is ambiguous, it has more than one meaning, and it is unclear which meaning is intended by the speaker.

3. **The Sorites Paradox**
   A seemingly valid argument with a vague term in its premises and conclusion (such as "heap") and a preposterous conclusion (such as that many grains of sand don't make a heap). The argument raises a paradox, or puzzle without obvious solution, because it appears to be valid, yet has true premises and a plainly false conclusion.

4. **The Slippery Slope Fallacy**
   An argument that moves through a continuum of cases, from a premise involving a certain (covertly vague) expression that appears determinately true, to a conclusion that seems the unavoidable result of sound reasoning. Yet it's not sound, since it fails to notice that small differences in a *series of cases* can add up to a big difference between the initial case and that described in the argument's conclusion.

5. **Equivocation**
   A fallacy committed by an argument in which some crucial expression occurs with more than one meaning.

6. **Amphiboly**
   A fallacy committed by an argument in which an awkward grammatical construction, or confusing word-order, in the premises creates ambiguity and leads one to draw the wrong conclusion from those premises.

7. **Confused Predication**

Fallacy of Composition

- An argument that concludes that a whole (class, group) itself has a certain property *on the basis of* its parts' or members' each having that property individually.

Fallacy of Division

- An argument that concludes that each part of a whole (class, group) has a certain property *on the basis of* the whole's having that property.

8. **Definition**

Reconstructing a Definition

- A definition has two sides: what is to be defined, or *definiendum*, and what provides the definition, or *definiens*.

Three Classes of Semantic Definition

- Reportive Definition: it gives the everyday meaning of a word (or some larger linguistic expression). To test its adequacy, we use the method of thought experiment and counterexample.

- Ostensive Definition: it gives the meaning of a word by pointing to some examples of things paradigmatically denoted by that word.

- Contextual Definition: it gives the meaning of a word by presenting another expression that can replace that word without being a synonym of it.

■ Key Words

Semantic unclarity	Confused predication
Vagueness	Composition
Borderline case	Paradox
Indeterminacy	Division
Sorites	Definiendum
Slippery slope fallacy	Definiens
Ambiguity	Reportive definition
Equivocation	Ostensive definition
Amphiboly	Contextual definition
Predicate	Philosophical analysis

Avoiding Irrelevant Premises

This chapter is devoted to the fallacies of relevance. You'll learn about six different ways in which premises may be irrelevant to the conclusion they're supposedly supporting. There is also a discussion of how logical thinkers can take account of emotion in reasoning. The topics to be examined include

- Appeal to pity.
- Appeal to force.
- Appeal to emotion.
- Ad hominem.
- Beside the point.
- Straw man arguments.
- Nonfallacious appeals to emotion in everyday reasoning.

10.1 Fallacies of Relevance

Another source of error in reasoning that can cause an argument to be misleading is the failure of premises to be relevant to the conclusion they are offered to support. Even if a premise is plainly true, if it is also *irrelevant* to the conclusion it is supposedly backing up, then it cannot count as a reason for it, and the argument fails. Arguments that are fallacious by virtue of having irrelevant premises often rely on distractions that draw attention away from what truly matters for the conclusions at hand and thus are sometimes employed as rhetorical tricks by artful persuaders who aim to influence us by psychologically effective but logically defective means. There are several types of informal fallacy that manifest this form of error. Often known as *fallacies of relevance*, we shall consider six of them here.

10.2 Appeal to Pity

One type of fallacy of relevance is the *appeal to pity* (or *ad misericordiam*).

> An argument commits the fallacy of appeal to pity if and only if its premises attempt to arouse feelings of sympathy as a means of supporting its conclusion.

Consider, for example, an argument that was once made on behalf of clemency for Rudolf Hess, a former associate of Hitler arrested in Britain during World War II and later sentenced to life imprisonment for war crimes. In 1982, when Hess was old and in poor health, some people argued that he should be freed from prison. The argument went this way:

1. 1. Hess has already spent more than forty years in prison.
    2. He is in his eighties now and his health is failing.
    3. This elderly man should be permitted to spend his last years with his family.
    _____
    4. Hess should be granted clemency.

But Hess's age and failing health were irrelevant to the real issue: his *guilt* as one of the founders of a regime that had terrorized

---

BOX 1 ■ HOW TO AVOID APPEAL TO PITY

1. Note that an argument whose premises attempt to provoke *feelings of sympathy* that might move an audience to accept its conclusion commits the fallacy of appeal to pity.
2. Any such argument should be rejected, since it provides no reason relevant to its conclusion—that is, it provides no *rational* support for it.

Europe. Many Russians, whose country had suffered millions of deaths at the hands of the German invaders, recognized this argument as an appeal to pity and objected vigorously. As a result, Hess died in prison (his sentence was never commuted).

It's worth noting, however, that it's not only on behalf of scoundrels and criminals that people resort to the appeal to pity. We find it in everyday life in many guises, including some uses we may (wrongly) think free of this fallacy—for example, when a student argues

> 2   You gave me a *B* in this course, but ... can't you give me an *A*? If I don't have an *A*, then it'll mean that my grade average will fall and I won't be able to get into law school! And I've been working hard all semester.

The argument in fact is:

> 2' 1. I've been working hard in this course.
>   2. Any grade below an *A* would adversely affect my chances for law school.
>   _____
>   3. I should get an A in this course.

This argument plainly commits the fallacy of appeal to pity. For one thing, how hard the student has been working is not logically relevant to its conclusion. (What *would* be relevant would be *showing that one has actually done A work* rather than *B* work.) The argument may succeed in making the professor feel sorry for the student, but it fails to make its conclusion rationally acceptable.

More generally, an appeal to pity is a fallacious argument trading on the fact that feeling sorry for someone is often psychologically motivating. Yet that is not a *good reason* for the argument's conclusion. Logical thinkers would want to be able to recognize and avoid this fallacy. For some tips on this, see Box 1.

10.3 Appeal to Force

Another informal fallacy trading on feelings, though in an entirely different way, is the appeal to force (sometimes called *ad baculum*–literally, "to the stick").

> An argument commits the fallacy of appeal to force if and only if it resorts to a threat as a means of supporting its conclusion.

In any argument that commits this fallacy, the arguer attempts to arouse feelings of fear in someone as a way of getting her to accept a conclusion (it's as if he were saying, "Agree with me *or else!*"). And, of course, such a threat need not be a *physical* threat. It might merely hint darkly of unfortunate consequences awaiting those who disagree with the arguer. To detect (and avoid) the fallacy of appeal to force in arguments, the rule is to check their premises as suggested in Box 2.

When Richard J. Daley was mayor of Chicago, from 1955 until his death in 1976, he exercised near-autocratic control over the Cook County Democratic Party organization. Public officials were well aware that they served at the pleasure of Mayor Daley and that any evidence of their disloyalty could have adverse consequences. Every time Daley would run for reelection, the word would go out to senior public officials serving in his administration:

3 We think it might be a good idea for you to get out and campaign for Mayor Daley in this election, Mr. Parks Commissioner [Street Commissioner, Fire Commissioner ... etc.], because if you don't, and Mayor Daley wins ... well ... you might be out of a job! And ... you know ... we'd *hate* to see you lose your job! So, really,

BOX 2 ■ HOW TO AVOID APPEAL TO FORCE

1. Note that an argument whose premises merely express a threat of *unpleasant consequences* for those who refuse to accept the argument's conclusion commits the fallacy of appeal to force.
2. Any such argument should be rejected, since its premises provide only a "reason" that is irrelevant to the argument's conclusion—thus falling short of *rationally* supporting it.

we're just giving you a little bit of friendly advice here ... that's all. We're looking out for you!

This may sound innocuous, but it's really a thinly veiled threat:

3' 1. If you don't campaign for Mayor Daley's reelection, you'll lose your job.
   2. You ought to campaign for Mayor Daley's reelection.

(3') qualifies as an appeal to force. After all, the *reason* it offers (what'll happen to the addressee if she or he doesn't campaign for Mayor Daley), although no doubt *psychologically* powerful as a motivator of enthusiastic campaigning, is not relevant to the conclusion that the addressee should campaign for Mayor Daley. In itself, it gives no reason why Daley *deserves to be reelected*, so that people can campaign for him with a good conscience. Notice that it would have been possible to give an entirely different argument for the same conclusion that would commit *no* fallacy: campaigners could simply have said,

4 You ought to get out and campaign for Mayor Daley in this election because of all the great things the Daley administration has done for the city of Chicago.

and then *listed* the accomplishments of the Daley administration. (In fact, there were many.) Thus completed, (4)'s premises would be relevant to the argument's conclusion, and might very well support it. By contrast, (3')'s premise is completely irrelevant to the argument's conclusion.

10.4 Appeal to Emotion

So far, we've seen two ways in which fallacies of relevance might be committed by arguments that offer premises appealing to our emotions in ways utterly irrelevant to supporting their conclusions. A third variation on this common sort of mistake is found in the *fallacy of appeal to emotion.*

> An argument commits the fallacy of appeal to emotion if and only if it attempts to support its conclusions by appealing to people's feelings rather than to their reason.

This fallacy is sometimes called *ad populum:* literally, "to the people." In any argument that commits it, emotively charged language is used to try to persuade someone to accept a certain conclusion. In some cases, the language employed for this purpose may include images that carry emotive force, as can be seen from the immense popularity of this fallacy in television commercials and other advertising media. But often appeals to emotion are made by using words carefully chosen for maximum emotional impact. To detect and avoid this fallacy, follow the rules in Box 3.

Appeal to emotion is, of course, a medium much beloved by stem-winding political orators. In 1896, populist Democrat William Jennings Bryan drew upon biblical allusions to argue that the "gold standard" in U.S. monetary policy was bad for working people:

> 5 You shall not press down upon the brow of labor this crown of thorns; you shall not crucify mankind upon a cross of gold.

And forty years later, in the depths of the Great Depression, President Franklin D. Roosevelt attempted to rally support for his reforms with emotive language of stirring intensity:

> 6 This generation of Americans has a rendezvous with destiny.

Notice that each of these examples amounts to a premise offered in support of a conclusion to the effect: "Therefore you should support *my* programs!" But both try to move their audiences through the psychological power of emotively charged phrases

> ## BOX 3 ■ HOW TO AVOID APPEAL TO EMOTION
>
> 1. Be on guard for arguments that attempt, through the use of emotively charged words or images, to elicit a strong psychological response conducive to the acceptance of its conclusion.
> 2. Any such argument commits the fallacy of appeal to emotion and should be rejected. Why? Because its premises offer only "reasons" that are irrelevant, in the way suggested in (1), to the argument's conclusion. No such argument can provide *rational* support for its conclusion.

such as "crucify mankind," "crown of thorns," "rendezvous," "cross," and "destiny." As these examples show, the fallacy of appeal to emotion is as likely to be committed by mainstream politicians as it is by demagogues and despots (such as Adolf Hitler, who used it constantly). But it is a fallacious form of argument, whoever indulges in it.

Sometimes reasoning that commits the fallacy of appeal to emotion rests on a clever use of images that provoke a strong emotional response. When President Lyndon Johnson was running for reelection in 1964, his campaign sought to capitalize on prevalent voter fears about the alleged recklessness of his opponent, Sen. Barry Goldwater. In a charged Cold War era, some feared that Goldwater might be too quick to resort to nuclear weapons, and Johnson's campaigners wanted to exploit this uneasiness. So the Democratic Party ran a television commercial that opened with a view a of sunny meadow and a little girl picking flowers, then cut to a dark screen with the fiery mushroom cloud of a nuclear explosion billowing up into the night sky. Across a black screen the message then flashed: "VOTE FOR PRESIDENT JOHNSON." One of the most notorious examples of emotively charged images in the history of political advertising, the commercial was widely denounced as tasteless and quickly withdrawn.

The Bandwagon Appeal

Some forms of emotional appeal are intended to take advantage of common feelings that seem to be part of human nature; for example, when books are marketed as "best-sellers" or a film is touted as "the Number One Hit Movie of the Summer!" This so-called *bandwagon appeal* exploits our desire to join in with the common experiences of others and not be left out.

Appeal to Vanity

On the other hand, when an expensive, imported sports car is advertised as

7   Not for everyone—this is the car that tells the world who you are!

The advertiser is making an appeal to the prospective buyer's *vanity*. Appeal to vanity is another of the varieties of *ad populum*. In much the same way, Virgin Atlantic Airways has decided to call its premium-class service, not 'first class' but 'upper class.' Can we see what is going on here?

10.5 Ad Hominem

So far we've been looking at arguments in which emotively charged language or images interfere with the legitimate purpose of premises and attempt to persuade, not by actually offering support for a conclusion but by introducing irrelevant considerations that may be psychologically effective. Another way in which arguments can fail because of irrelevant premises, however, is the very common fallacy of *ad hominem* (literally, "to the man"), which has less to do with emotion than with personal attack. It is sometimes called "argument against the person," but we shall call it by its Latin name, since that has now come to be familiar in everyday usage.

> An argument commits the fallacy of ad hominem if and only if it attempts to discredit someone's argument or point of view by means of personal attack.

That is, the fallacious ad hominem rests on some personal consideration strictly irrelevant to the matter at hand, which is intended to undermine someone's credibility as a means of indirectly

BOX 4 ■ HOW TO AVOID A FALLACIOUS AD HOMINEM ARGUMENT

1. Beware of any argument that appeals to some personal facts (or alleged facts) that are irrelevant to its conclusion.
2. Any such argument commits the fallacy of *ad hominem* and should be rejected, for its premises are irrelevant to its conclusion—that is, they are offered as a means of attempting to discredit an argument or point of view by discrediting the person who presents or defends it.

attacking the person's position or argument. The problem with such an ad hominem, of course, is that in this way the question of the real merit of that person's position is evaded. Instead, the ad hominem offers only a cheap shot aimed at the person herself. Before turning to some specific arguments of this sort, notice that they all fail to support their conclusions—yet they can be recognized easily and avoided in the way suggested in Box 4.

Suppose a Harvard graduate in the U.S. Senate, Senator Foghorn, has been caught using public funds to pay for expensive, luxury vacations for himself and his family, and imagine that another legislator, Senator Gasbag, makes a speech denouncing this impropriety. Foghorn then cannot resist pointing our that Gasbag's college days were spent at Yale. In a speech on the Senate floor, Foghorn loudly responds,

8   These charges are all false! And these unfounded accusations are coming from exactly the place we would expect. Apparently Sen. Gasbag, like all Yalies, cannot resist the temptation to besmirch the reputation of a Harvard man!

Here Senator Foghorn's argument is an ad hominem that attempts to discredit Gasbag's statements, not by speaking to their *content* (the accusations of impropriety) but by pointing to Gasbag's personal background—the fact that he is a Yale graduate. Its clear assumptions are that *all* Yalies are naturally prejudiced against Harvard graduates and that *that* is why Gasbag is saying these things! But Foghorn's argument simply engages in personal attack: it introduces an irrelevant consideration that has no power to *actually* discredit the opponent's claim (though it may appear to do so).

The thing to keep in mind is that it's not *who says it* that makes a claim good or bad but rather whether there are in fact good reasons to back it up. Those reasons should be judged on their own merits: either they provide some support for the claim or they don't. In our example, we would of course need to hear Sen. Gasbag's argument—presumably citing facts in support of the conclusion that Foghorn had behaved inappropriately—in order to determine this.

The Abusive Ad Hominem

Sometimes ad hominem arguments attack a person's character. Suppose a moviegoer announces,

> **9** I have no desire to see Woody Allen's latest movie. I'm sure it's worthless, and I wouldn't waste my money on it—not after what I know about him now! He betrayed Mia Farrow and broke her heart when he took up with Mia's adopted daughter, Soon-Yi Previn. So his movies are without artistic merit as far as I'm concerned.

Now (9) plainly commits the fallacy of ad hominem, since it seeks to discredit Woody Allen as a film director, not by invoking evidence that his movies are artistically questionable but by a personal attack that refers to his relationship to Soon-Yi Previn (whom he later married). Note that this ad hominem is of a more abusive sort, since it attacks Allen's *character*—he is denounced on moral grounds as a "betrayer," which is, of course, a term of contempt. But, whatever we may think of Allen's personal qualities, does any of that prove that his *films* are bad? Isn't all of that simply irrelevant to an assessment of his art?

Tu Quoque

Finally, there is another variety of ad hominem that must be mentioned. A fallacy of ad hominem is also committed when one tries to refute someone's point of view by calling attention to the person's hypocrisy regarding that very point of view. This is sometimes called a *tu quoque* argument (literally, "you also"), and it is simply another version of personal attack. For example, consider how Thomas Jefferson's writings must have sounded to the British in his day. Jefferson famously wrote, in the *Declaration of Independence*, "We hold these truths to be self-evident, that all men are created equal, that they are endowed by their creator with certain unalienable rights, that among these are life, liberty, and the pursuit of happiness." But one can easily imagine how this must have been received in conservative circles in Britain in 1776. Tories certainly regarded this lofty language as risible political rhetoric, since they knew very well that Jefferson was himself a prominent slave holder. In London, Dr. Samuel Johnson scoffed, "How is it that we hear the loudest yelps for 'liberty' among the drivers of Negroes?" Johnson's remark could be expanded into an extended argument that looks like this:

10 1. Jefferson claims that all men are created equal and have rights to liberty.
2. But Jefferson himself is a slave owner.
3. He preaches lofty principles for others that he does not practice himself.
4. Jefferson's claims about liberty and equality are false.

Yet if any did actually offer such an argument, it would have committed the fallacy of tu quoque, a form of ad hominem. The imagined argument, after all, tries to bring a personal matter—Jefferson's real-life hypocrisy about race and human nature—into the discussion to cast doubt on his assertions about human equality and rights. Now it is of course true that the Sage of Monticello did not permit his own black slaves to enjoy the very liberty and equality he so forcefully advocated for himself and his fellow white men. But did that *personal failure* go any way at all toward showing that Jefferson's claims about liberty and equality were false? Naturally, we all think that people should not be hypocrites. People should practice what they preach. Yet if someone fails to heed this moral maxim and we point out his hypocrisy, we have not thereby proved that what he preaches is false. In fact, we are only indulging in a form of personal attack, or ad hominem.

Nonfallacious Ad Hominem

Before we leave the discussion of ad hominem, there remains one important clarification that should be added. Some uses of argument against the person are not fallacious, for there are contexts in which such an argument may be in order. In public life, for instance, the moral character of a politician may be a highly relevant issue to raise during a campaign, since we do very reasonably expect our elected leaders to be trustworthy. In the first example given above, Sen. Gasbag's speech calling Sen. Foghorn's personal rectitude into question amounts to a kind of personal attack, but it commits no fallacy (as does Foghorn's reply), since conduct that is unethical (or illegal!) would *not* be irrelevant to an assessment of a person's fitness to serve as a senator. Gasbag's remarks, then, could justifiably be seen as an ad hominem argument but not a fallacious one, for they commit no fallacy of irrelevant premises.

Similarly, in the Anglo-American system of justice, which employs an adversarial model in court—with attorneys on opposing sides each presenting an argument for their client's case and trying to undermine their opponent's position—some of what happens in the courtroom may appear to be ad hominem. Here, after all, attorneys might try to discredit a witness by presenting evidence about his personal life.

But in fact this does not amount to a fallacious ad hominem at all, since in the courtroom, the reliability of a witness is not irrelevant. Given that the purpose of a witness just is to *give testimony*, it is highly relevant to know whether the person can be believed or not. Thus an attorney does not commit a fallacy of ad hominem when she appeals to relevant personal matters in an attempt to discredit the claims made by a witness. An attorney's job is to defend her client's interest by aggressively pressing his case, and part of that may include presenting facts about a witness's background and personal life in an effort to undermine his credibility. This is a kind of personal attack, but it commits no fallacy.

Logical thinkers must bear in mind that courtroom procedure is a specialized subject in the law and that we're not attempting here to venture into its complexities. When one is called to serve on a jury, one should follow the instructions of the judge. The important thing to notice now, however, is simply that there can be some uses of ad hominem that are not fallacious, and that it is the context that determines when this is so.

10.6 Beside the Point

An argument might commit a fallacy of relevance by offering premises that simply *have little or nothing to do with its conclusion*. Maybe they support some conclusion, but they don't support the one given by the argument. When this happens, the argument is a *beside the point* fallacy (also known as *ignoratio elenchi*).

An argument commits the fallacy of beside the point if and only if its premises fail to support its conclusion by failing to be logically related to its conclusion, though they may support some *other* conclusion.

When an argument commits this fallacy, we may at first find ourselves unable to identify the source of the confusion. For example, imagine that opponents of cruelty to animals introduce legislation to ban the mistreatment of chickens, pigs, and cows in certain "factory farms." But suppose the corporations who own the farms respond,

11 These farms are not cruel to animals. After all, the farms provide the food that most consumers want, and they do so in a manner that is cost-effective; moreover, these poultry, pork, and beef products are nourishing and contribute to the overall health of American families.

The odd thing about (11) is that nothing in its premises contributes toward providing support for the conclusion, "These farms are not cruel to animals." Perhaps the premises support some conclusion, but they don't support *that* one, since they offer no reason to think that the factory farms in question are not cruel. As a result, (11) commits the beside the point fallacy.

10.7 Straw Man

Finally, let us consider a type of informal fallacy committed by
any argument where the view of an opponent is misrepresented
so that it becomes vulnerable to certain objections. The distorted
view may consist of a statement or a group of related statements
(i.e., a position or a theory). Typically ignored in such distortions
are charity and faithfulness, the principles of argument reconstruction discussed in Chapter 4. Given the principle of charity,
interpreting someone else's view requires that we maximize the
truth of each of its parts (in the case of an argument, premises
and conclusion) and the strength of the logical relationship
between them. Given the principle of faithfulness, such interpretation requires that we strive for maximum fidelity to the
author's intentions. It is precisely the lack of charity, faithfulness,
or both, in the interpretation of the views of others with whom
the arguer disagrees that results in *straw man*.

An argument commits the fallacy of straw man if and only
if its premises attempt to undermine some view through
misrepresenting what that view actually is.

Situations where this type of informal fallacy often occurs include
deliberations such as debates and controversies. Straw man is (re-
grettably) a common tactic in public life, often heard in the rhetoric
of political campaigns. Typically, the straw-man argument ascribes
to an opponent some views that are in fact a distortion of his actual

BOX 6 ■ WHAT'S GOING ON IN A STRAW MAN ARGUMENT?

1. A straw man argument attempts to raise an objection O against a certain view, call it V.
2. But the argument misrepresents V as being in fact W, where W is vulnerable to the objection O.
3. The argument concludes by rejecting V on the basis of O.

But does O really undermine V? It seems not. After all, O is an objection only to W, a distorted rendering of V, not to V itself.

views. These misrepresentations may be extreme, irresponsible, or even silly views that are easy to defeat. The opponent's position, then, becomes a "straw figure" that can be easily blown away. But to refute *that* position is, of course, not at all to disprove the person's actual position. This can be seen in Box 6, which outlines what's going on in straw man arguments.

It is not difficult to find examples of this fallacy in political debates. Imagine two rival political candidates, one of whom is trying to undermine the credibility of the other by arguing

12 1. My opponent's international policy is: Wait for foreign permission before acting.
   2. Waiting for foreign permission before acting is inconsistent with promoting our national security and our right to act in our own self-interest.
   3. Both promoting our national security and our right to act in our own self-interest are reasonable.
   4. My opponent's international policy is unreasonable.

Suppose that there is, in fact, no evidence that the opponent actually holds the view ascribed to her in the first premise; then what? In that case, (12) is a straw man argument.

To detect (and avoid) a fallacy of this sort, the rule is to check whether an argument's reasons against a certain view can really count as reasons against *that* view. Always ask yourself whether the target view has been reconstructed according to the principles of charity and faithfulness.

BOX 7 ■ HOW TO AVOID A STRAW MAN ARGUMENT

In objecting to a view V, if the argument goes, "View V is wrong because it faces objection O," keep in mind that, whether O is an objection to V or not depends on whether V has been construed in accordance with faithfulness and charity.

Exercises

I. Review Questions

1. What does it mean to say that an argument's premises are "irrelevant" to its conclusion?
2. How is the fallacy of appeal to pity a fallacy of "irrelevant premises"?
3. What is the fallacy of appeal to force?
4. What is the fallacy of appeal to emotion?
5. What is the bandwagon appeal? How does it differ from an appeal to vanity?
6. What is an ad hominem argument?
7. Do all ad hominems involve an attack on someone's character?
8. Are all ad hominem arguments fallacious? What is a tu quoque argument?
9. What is the "beside the point" fallacy?
10. What is a straw man argument? And how does it amount to a fallacy?

II. For each of the following arguments, identify the informal fallacy it commits (sometimes an argument may commit more than one).

1. CBS News is trying to make people believe that there are unsafe working conditions in this factory. But I tell you this: anyone who plans to continue working for me should not talk to reporters.

   SAMPLE ANSWER: Appeal to force

* 2. I deserve a better grade on this exam, Professor Arroyo, because I studied hard for it. _____

3. You cannot say that divorce is immoral, because you yourself are divorced. _____

* 4. A Princeton student found guilty of plagiarism admitted that the work was not her own but argued that the university ought not to

penalize her for this infraction, since she had been "under enormous pressure at the time, having to meet a deadline for her senior thesis with only one day left to write the paper." (*New York Times*, May 7, 1982.) _____

5. If Einstein's theory is right, then everything is relative. But 9/11 really happened, and that's a fact. So not everything is relative. Therefore Einstein's theory is wrong. _____

6. We needn't take seriously what the Rev. Brimstone says when he tells us that people should always be honest in their dealings with others. Just yesterday the Billy Brimstone Evangelistic Association was found guilty of soliciting funds for missionary work and then using them to buy the Rev. Brimstone a new Cadillac. _____

* 7. Everywhere, people are increasingly getting rid of their iPods and instead listening to music on their cell phones. That's the way to listen to music on the move! So, if you're up to date and in touch with the latest things, you'll get rid of your iPod and use the phone to listen to music. _____

8. I know you're the coach of this baseball team, and you're entitled to your opinion. But I'm the owner of this ball club, and you work for me. If you really want Scooter Wilensky to play third base, you can put him there. Of course, I can always find another coach. _____

9. Everybody visits the Art Institute of Chicago. Therefore you should too. _____

*10. It's true that Knute Hamsun, the early-twentieth century Norwegian novelist, won the Nobel Prize for Literature, but as far as I am concerned his works are worthless. Anyone who collaborated with the Nazis, as Hamsun did during World War II, was not capable of producing works with literary merit. _____

11. A protestor demonstrating against the new president said "A recount of the ballots is needed in this presidential election. If not, we will blockade airports and highways, we'll take over embassies, and we'll bring traffic to a halt all over the country." _____

12. Those who refuse to accept my conclusion are just too pig-headed to admit that I'm right. _____

*13. In Britain, the president of the Royal Society has suggested that scientific research on how to protect the environment should be supported by "carbon taxes," levied on countries producing the most air and water pollution. But this is nonsense, for his own country would be near the top of the list, and he himself drives a pollution-producing car! _____

14. The governor shouldn't be blamed for his staff members' lying under oath to the grand jury. After all, he was under tremendous pressure at the time. _____

15. Humans are capable of creativity. Therefore creativity is a value. _____

*16. Many contemporary physicists accept Heisenberg's indeterminacy principle, which implies that everything is indeterminate. But this cannot possibly be correct, as shown by the fact that mathematical truths are determinate. _____

17. Professor Nathan's history of the Catholic Church is a classic. But she is a Protestant, so we cannot expect her treatment of Catholicism to be fair. _____

18. In his dialogue *Meno*, Plato describes an exchange between Socrates and Anytus, a powerful and influential Athenian politician. Socrates suggests that the reason why the sons of prominent Athenian families often turn out badly is that their parents do not know how to educate them. To this, Anytus replies, "Socrates, I think that you are too ready to speak evil of men; and, if you will take my advice, I would advise you to be careful. Perhaps there is no city in which it is not easier to do men harm than to do them good, and this is certainly the case at Athens, as I believe you know." _____

*19. Over 2 million people die in the United States every year. Therefore the United States is a dangerous place to visit, and we should take our vacation elsewhere. _____

20. Rev. Armstrong urges us not to support the war, saying that violence is barbaric in all forms and only breeds more violence in return. But his view should be rejected, since it amounts to arguing that our nation's enemies are not bad guys at all, and that we should just surrender to them. _____

21. Paul Robeson's accomplishments as an actor and singer are overrated. Really, he was not good at either. After all, he was well known to be pro-Communist and an admirer of Stalin. _____

*22. Global war is inevitable, for the cultures of East and West are radically different. _____

23. My opponent, Senator Snort, endorses the Supreme Court's view that prayer in public schools is a violation of the First Amendment.

But I say to you, what is this but an endorsement of atheism? Senator Snort clearly thinks that people of faith have no place in today's America. _____

24. I know I've failed to pay my rent for the past three months, but if you evict me I'll have no place to go. How can you throw me, an eighty-year-old grandmother, out onto the street? _____

*25. Mafioso to shopkeeper: "You got a nice business here. It'd be a shame if somethin' were to happen to it." _____

26. Advertisement: "You've always known that Mercedes-Benz was the car for you. It's not a car for everybody. But then, you're not just anybody. When you've truly achieved a place of distinction in life, you know you're ready. Mercedes-Benz." _____

27. According to contemporary biology, species evolve over time. But I have never seen any animals evolving. Have you? Has *anyone* ever seen animals evolving? Contemporary biology is false.

_____

*28. Everything that today we admire on earth—science and art, technique and innovations—is only the creative product of a few peoples and perhaps originally of *one* race. [Therefore, on the Germans] now depends also the existence of this entire culture. If they perish, then the beauty of this earth sinks into the grave with them .... The man who misjudges and disdains the laws of race actually forfeits the happiness that seems destined to be his. He prevents the victorious march of the best race and with it also the presumption for all human progress .... All that is not race in this world is trash. (Adolf Hitler, *Mein Kampf*.)

_____

29. Dear State Senator: Our organization believes that protecting the environment is an issue of paramount importance. Unless your legislature passes the Clean Air and Water Act, we will urge all business meetings, conventions, and tourists to boycott your state indefinitely. _____

*30. Darwin's theory of evolution cannot be correct. It holds that we all evolved from monkeys! But monkeys do not evolve into people. And we are too different to have evolved from them. Thus Darwin's theory of evolution has to be false. _____

31. Los Angeles has twenty or thirty downtowns. There is no conventional pattern of people commuting to work in one direction in the morning and the reverse in the evening. So it seems there is no central authority in organizing the city or its government. _____

32. French actress Brigitte Bardot insists that cruelty to animals is a serious crime, and that we should treat our dogs and cats humanely. But we cannot take this seriously. She is well known for expressions of bigotry toward ethnic and religious minority immigrants in France.

_____

*33. Although there is a greater and greater global demand for energy, we in the industrialized world would suffer as a result of a drastic decline in our quality of life if our government imposed energy-restricting policies. Thus we must have no energy-restricting in the United States. _____

34. My opponent, Representative Smith, says she favors abolishing the death penalty. But what she is really saying is that it's just fine for murderers to be housed and fed for years at taxpayer expense, and that it's OK with her if they are ultimately released to prey on our citizens again. _____

*35. In the Gospel of St. John, Nathaniel expresses doubt, on first hearing of Jesus's teachings, that there could be a truly learned rabbi from such an obscure small town: "Nazareth! Can anything good come out of Nazareth?"(_John, I: 46_). _____

III. YOUR OWN THINKING LAB

1. For each of the following claims, construct an argument that attempts to support it but fails by virtue of committing at least one of the fallacies discussed in this chapter.

A. Members of the Board, I think it's time now for me to be promoted.

B. This a case in which the Supreme Court ought to spare execution.

C. Al Gore's views on global warming are wrong.

D. Football is a great entertainment.

E. Evolutionary theory contradicts the facts.

2. What's the matter with the following arguments?

A. "Abortion is offensive to many people. Therefore abortion is wrong."

B. "Former President Bill Clinton was found to have lied about his affair with a White House intern. This suggests that his foreign policy was unacceptable."

C. "As long as I get a cut from your profits, nobody gets hurt. Understand?"

10.8 The Philosopher's Corner

Is the Appeal to Emotion Always Fallacious?

In this chapter, the appeal to emotion was identified as one of the fallacies of relevance. But, it will be objected, it simply *cannot be* that a logical thinker's *only* appropriate attitude toward emotion is a wary distrust. Given the large role of emotion in human life—indeed, if we consider that life would surely be impoverished without it—philosophers can ill afford to ignore emotion, and logical thinking ought to have a way of accommodating the many benign manifestations of it that commit no fallacies.

What, then, are some of these? First, emotions plainly have an important role in motivating our actions. Feelings, sentiments, desires, and ordinary inclinations and aversions of many sorts all move us to act in everyday life in ways that involve no fallacious inferences. We need not go so far as holding that reason "is and ought to be the slave of the passions" to recognize that our feelings and desires motivate our actions. And actions motivated by feelings may be guided by reason (e.g., "Don't do to others what you'd not like done to you").

Second, being alert to the personal emotional commitments of our loved ones, friends, and coworkers can give us reasons for action or for forbearance. If we know what others care about—especially what matters to them in deep and important ways—then we'll know how to avoid saying things that will hurt their feelings. This is a concern about emotion (theirs!) that commits no fallacy. Similarly, if we know that mentioning certain subjects will cause a certain person to become enraged, then it's not fallacious to conclude that we should take his feelings into account and try to avoid such talk in his presence unless it's necessary.

Third, emotions may appropriately move us to take action for the sake of strangers who are suffering or in peril. When reports of famine, war, epidemics, and natural disasters motivate us to contribute to relief programs, we are following our feelings of compassion for our fellow human beings and commit no fallacy. Likewise, when our instincts of fairness move us to speak out on behalf of minorities subjected to prejudice or discrimination, there is no fallacy in acting on these feelings. And when we read of outrageous acts of brutality and violence or criminal acts of an especially nefarious sort, there is no fallacy in concluding that such acts ought to be punished or prevented if possible. Finally, we may, of course, appropriately and rationally respond to emotion in our desire to aid needy individuals, as when a doctor acts to relieve her patient's suffering or when we give our pocket change to a homeless person begging on the street.

What all of the above examples have in common is this: they are appeals to emotion that are *not irrelevant* as reasons for our conclusions. That is, they represent types of situation in which one may rationally be moved by emotion. In the fallacy of appeal to emotion (ad populum), by contrast, the use of emotion always represents a *diversion* from the matter at hand, often a subtle attempt at manipulating one's feelings for the sake of some strictly irrelevant consideration that does not actually contribute to supporting the argument's conclusion (though it may appear to do so). Logical thinkers are advised to beware of such trickery, as it amounts to an abuse of reason.

But the purpose of logical thinking is not to turn people into coldly rational beings without emotions, like Star Trek's Mr. Spock. (Of course, since Spock is a Vulcan, not a human being, he may be inclined to overestimate the value of rigidly rational behavior and to underrate the value of ordinary affections). There are, after all, many occasions in life when it would be inappropriate, even *crazy*, to be too rational. Think of falling in love, for instance, or expressing affection toward one's parents or toward one's children. Sentiments and desires are essential to any life that is recognizably *human*, and logical thinkers commit no fallacy when they are moved in appropriate ways by emotion.

Exercises

IV. Some of the following arguments commit a *fallacy* of appeal to emotion and some don't. Determine which is which.

1. Cousin Ed is always getting into scrapes with the law and can't seem to stay out of jail. But Aunt Betty and Uncle Jake love him nonetheless. So I ought not to make jokes about Ed in their presence.

   SAMPLE ANSWER: Not a fallacy of appeal to emotion

* 2. As your representative in Congress, I have sworn upon the altar of God to uphold the sacred freedoms of our mighty democracy! Despite the scurrilous attacks of my yelping dog opponents, who accuse me of tax evasion, I have always defended the American way! Thus, I ought to be reelected. _____

3. News reports from Zambia describe a nation devastated by an epidemic of AIDS. When I read of people dying for lack medical care, I feel horrible about this. Therefore I'm contributing to relief efforts to send doctors to Zambia. _____

4. "I feel very bad for the couple next door," said Mary Ellen. "Jack and Harry have been told that gay couples are not welcome at their church. So I'm going to invite them to mine." _____

* 5. Jurors in the Enron case were infuriated by the lies and deceptions perpetrated by the company's executives. "We are appalled," one juror said, "and therefore we are asking for the stiffest sentences possible." _____

6. In a famous television advertisement for an after-shave lotion, a commercial aired during televised sports events and aimed at men, a woman in revealing dress purrs, "There's *something* about an Aqua Velva man." _____

7. *The Da Vinci Code* is the number-one best-selling book in America. So I really ought to read it. _____

8. I know she misses me. I miss her too. So, I'm going to email her some photos of me that were taken just yesterday. I know she'll like that.
_____

* 9. Dear Membership Committee: When I heard that the Davis family's application for membership in the Country Club was rejected because some members did not like their religion, I was shocked. I was furious. So I have decided to resign from the Country Club as of today. _____

*10. Now all the guys at school are driving pickup trucks. The bigger the better! Everybody in our school has got one, and I feel that I've got to be part of this. So I am going to buy a pickup truck. _____

▪ Writing Project

Read the "Letters to the Editor" section of your local daily newspaper every day for one week. Collect as many examples as you can find of fallacies of relevance committed by letter writers, and then write a short paper in which you report on these fallacious arguments. In each case, identify the fallacy committed and explain precisely how that fallacy is committed by that particular argument. Describe in this way *all* of the examples of fallacies you've found. (If your search also turns up examples of *other* types of fallacy besides fallacies of relevance, include your analyses of those arguments in your discussion too.)

■ Chapter Summary

1. Fallacies of Relevance:

   An argument fails if its premises turn out to be *irrelevant* to the conclusion they're intended to support, since its premises then cannot count as reasons for its conclusion. This happens in different ways in all of the fallacies of relevance.

2. Appeal to Pity:

   An argument commits the fallacy of appeal to pity if and only if its premises attempt to arouse feelings of sympathy as a means of supporting its conclusion.

3. Appeal to Force:

   An argument commits the fallacy of appeal to force if and only if it resorts to a threat in an attempt to support its conclusion.

4. Appeal to Emotion:

   An argument commits the fallacy of appeal to emotion if and only if it appeals to people's feelings rather than to their reason in its attempt to support its conclusion.

5. Ad Hominem:

   An argument commits the fallacy of ad hominem if and only if it attempts to discredit someone's argument or point of view by means of personal attack.

6. Beside the Point:

   An argument commits the fallacy of beside the point if and only if its premises have nothing at all to do with the conclusion they are offered to support, though they may support some *other* conclusion.

7. Straw Man:

An argument commits the fallacy of straw man if and only if its premises attempt to undermine some view through misrepresenting what that view actually is.

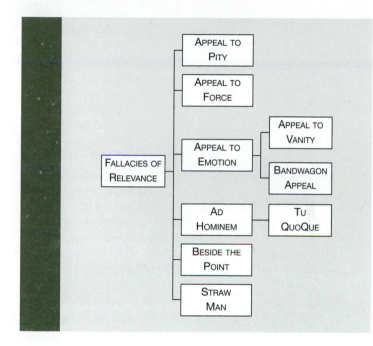

■ Key Words

Irrelevant premise
Appeal to pity
Appeal to force
Appeal to emotion
Bandwagon argument
Fallacy of relevance

Appeal to vanity
Ad hominem
Tu quoque
Beside the point
Straw man argument

More on Deductive Reasoning

Compound Propositions

This chapter examines in detail compound propositions, the building blocks of propositional arguments. Its topics include

- A closer look at propositional arguments, first introduced in Chapter 5.

- The distinction between simple and compound propositions.

- Five types of compound proposition: negation, conjunction, disjunction, material conditional, and material biconditional.

- How to translate compound propositions into symbolic notation, including conventions for punctuation and the concept of a "well formed formula."

- The use of truth tables in defining the connectives truth-functionally.

- How to identify contingencies, tautologies, and contradictions with truth tables.

- Some philosophical issues regarding tautologies and other types of necessary propositions.

11.1 Argument as a Relation Between Propositions

In this chapter we'll return to the topic of deductive reasoning. Recall that the contents of an argument's premises and conclusion are propositions. A valid argument (or inference) can then be regarded as a strong logical relation among certain propositions—namely, those that are the content of the statements or beliefs making up its premises and conclusion. In some arguments, such as syllogistic ones, that relation depends on the *terms inside those propositions*. We'll study arguments of that sort in Chapters 13 and 14. Here we'll have a look at compound propositions, the building blocks of propositional arguments. Consider

1 1. If the earth is a planet, then it moves.

2. If the earth does not move, then it is not a planet.

The propositions expressed by (1)'s premise and conclusion are *that if the earth is a planet, then it moves* and *that if the earth does not move, then it is not a planet.* Since in (1) the relation of inference depends entirely on the relation between those propositions, (1) is a propositional argument.

Note that (1)'s premise and conclusion are each *compound* propositions, which are made up of the *simple* propositions *that the earth is a planet* and *that the earth moves,* together with the logical connections expressed by "if ... then ..." and "not." Such logical connections are known as *truth-functional connectives,* and we'll look closely at five of them in the next section. Provisionally, we shall note their names and standard notation in English:

TRUTH-FUNCTIONAL CONNECTIVES	STANDARD ENGLISH EXPRESSION
negation	not P
conjunction	P and Q
disjunction	either P or Q
conditional	if P then Q
biconditional	P if and only if Q

Our symbolic notation so far consists of capital letters such as *P*, *Q*, *R*, and so on, each used as a dummy for *any* proposition. We'll introduce other capital letters from *A* to *O* to represent specific propositions, reserving *P* through *W* to represent nonspecific propositions such as those just provided for the standard English expression of the truth-functional connectives. When possible, we'll pick the first letter of a word inside the proposition that we are to represent in symbols, preferably a noun if available. For example, "If the earth is a planet, then it moves" may be represented as "If *E*, then *M*," where

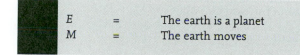

E	=	The earth is a planet
M	=	The earth moves

In any given context, we'll resort to the same chosen symbol every time the proposition it symbolizes occurs again—and if we have already used a certain letter to stand for a *different* proposition, then a letter of another word, preferably a noun in the proposition in question will serve. The argument form of example (1) above may now be represented by replacing the propositions occurring in its premise and conclusion with a propositional symbol in this way, while retaining the connective "if ... then" in English. The resulting representation is,

1' 1. If *E*, then *M*
    2. If not *M*, then not *E*

We'll eventually introduce symbols for "if ... then" and the other connectives. But first, let's consider the following arguments with an eye toward reconstructing their forms:

2 1. Ottawa is the capital of Canada.
    2. **It is not the case** that Ottawa is **not** the capital of Canada.

3 1. **Either** Fido is in the house **or** he's at the vet.
    2. Fido is **not** in the house.
    3. Fido is at the vet.

4   1. Jane works at the post office **and** Bob at the supermarket.

     2. Bob works at the supermarket.

5   1. TV is amusing **if and only if** it features good comedies.

     2. TV **does not** feature good comedies.

     3. TV is **not** amusing.

Once we have identified any occurrent connective (in boldface for emphasis) and simple propositions and replaced the latter with propositional symbols, we obtain

2' 1. O

     2. It is not the case that not O

3' 1. Either F or E

     2. not F

     3. E

4' 1. J and B

     2. B

5' 1. A if and only if C

     2. not C

     3. not A

Although these feature connectives, not all propositional argument forms do: one known as "identity" doesn't. It runs,

6   1. P

     2. P

In (6), the propositional symbol P stands for exactly the same proposition in the premise and in the conclusion. Any actual argument with this form would, of course, be valid, since if its premise were true, its conclusion could not be false. But this is not our present concern. Rather, in this section we considered the relation that makes an argument propositional and discovered that in any such argument, premises and conclusions often feature truth-functional connectives, so let's now look more closely at these.

11.2 Simple and Compound Propositions

Any proposition that has at least one connective is *compound*; otherwise it is simple. For example,

> 7 Celine Dion is a singer **and** Russell Crowe is an actor.

This is a compound proposition, while these two are simple:

> 8 Celine Dion is a singer.

> 9 Russell Crowe is an actor.

A compound proposition can be created out of any of these by means of negation, which is the only connective that may affect a single simple proposition by itself. For example,

> 10 Russell Crowe is not an actor.

And, as in the case of (7), a compound proposition can be created out of (8) and (9) by means of the appropriate connectives. But which, exactly, are the appropriate connectives? Any connective that is truth-functional, where

> A logical connective is *truth-functional* if and only if the truth value of the compound proposition it creates is determined entirely by the truth values of its component proposition(s).

Now that we have understood that the logical connectives that matter to propositional arguments are truth-functional, in most contexts we can omit this epithet and call them simply "connectives." We'll consider five such connectives, keeping in mind that any proposition affected by one or more of them is *compound*. Furthermore, recall that, since statements are the standard linguistic expressions of propositions, statements too are simple or compound, depending on whether or not they are affected by a connective.

> ## BOX 1 ■ SUMMARY: COMPOUND PROPOSITION
>
> - A proposition is *compound* if and only if it is affected by a truth-functional connective. Otherwise the proposition is simple.
> - The truth value of a compound proposition is determined entirely by the truth values of its component proposition or propositions.
> - Negation is the only connective that can affect a single proposition.

Negation

Negation is a truth-functional connective standardly expressed in English by "not," which is symbolized in logic by the so-called tilde, ~. When applied to one or more propositions, negation, in effect, creates a compound proposition, as in

11 Oxygen is **not** the lightest element.

12 **It is not the case** that Mary is at the library.

In ordinary English, negation may occur in any part of a statement (at the beginning, in the middle, and even at the end!). To represent the forms of (11) and (12) *as formulas in logic*, the negation would in each case go first, preceding each of the propositions. For negation, we'll use the tilde, and for each proposition, as before, the first letter of the first noun occurring in it when available (see previous section). Thus, in the cases of (11) and (12) we obtain these formulas

11' ~O

12' ~M

Whether in the English or in the logical notation, (11) and (12) are compound propositions because each falls within the scope of (i.e., is affected by) a negation used as a truth-functional connective.

Negation determines the truth value of any proposition under its scope in a simple way:

> 1. A negation is true if and only if the negated proposition is false.
> 2. A negation is false if and only if the negated proposition is true.

Thus, when a proposition is the logical negation of another, the two could not both have the same truth value: where P is true, $\sim P$ is false; where P is false, $\sim P$ is true. Thus, (14), below, is not the negation of (13), since both propositions are false.

13 All orthodontists are tall.

14 No orthodontists are tall.

Now consider these:

15 Some orthodontists are not tall.

16 Some orthodontists are tall.

(15) is the negation of (13), and (16) in the negation of (14), for those pairs could not have the same truth value. In any case, (11) above, which is true, is the negation of "Oxygen is the lightest element," which is false. And since any pair of negations cancel each other out, if it is true that

17 Lincoln was assassinated,

it is also true that

18 It is not the case that Lincoln was not assassinated.

Negation could also be expressed in a number of other ways (e.g., "it is not true that," "it is false that," "it never happened that"), including the prefixes "in," "un," and "non." Propositions featuring any of the latter are often represented as negations. For example, since in

19 My right to vote is inalienable,

"inalienable" means "not alienable," (19) is logically equivalent to

19' My right to vote is not alienable.

Similarly, since "unmarried" means "not married," (20) and (20') are equivalent:

20 Condoleezza Rice is unmarried.

20' It is not the case that Condoleezza Rice is married.

And since "nonvoter" means "not a voter," these are also equivalent:

21 Uncle Irving is a nonvoter.

21' Uncle Irving is not a voter.

Conjunction

Conjunction is a compound proposition created by a truth-functional connective standardly expressed in English by "and" and in logical notation by a symbol called "dot," generally represented as •. The connective for conjunction is placed between the two conjoined propositions. These may themselves be simple or compound propositions. Let's consider the conjunctions of some simple propositions:

22 Mount Everest is in Tibet and Mont Blanc is in France.

23 Tibet and France are European countries.

Their forms may be represented, respectively, as

22' $E • B$

23' $I • F$

(22) and (23) both fall within the scope of a conjunction expressed by "and" and therefore are compound propositions. Conjunction is a truth-functional connective because it determines the truth value of the compound proposition affected by it, given the values of its members. Each member of a conjunction is called "conjunct." The rule used to establish the truth value of a conjunction may be stated as follows:

> The conjunction is true if and only if its conjuncts are both true. Otherwise, the conjunction is false.

Given this rule, (22) is true, since both its conjuncts are in fact true. But if one conjunct is false and the other true or both are false, then the conjunction is false. Thus, (23) is false, since one of its conjuncts is false (namely, "Tibet is an European country"). And these are also false:

24 Mount Everest is in Tibet and Mont Blanc is in Italy.

25 Mount Everest is in Peru and Mont Blanc is in Italy.

In a conjunction, then, falsity is like an infection: if there's any at all, it corrupts the whole compound. (Logical thinkers who are contemplating a career in politics should keep this in mind.) Note also that, like (23), many conjunctions in ordinary language are abbreviated. For instance,

26 Rottweilers and Dobermans are fierce dogs.

This is just a shortened way of saying

27 Rottweilers are fierce dogs and Dobermans are fierce dogs.

Yet

28 Rottweilers and Dobermans are barking at each other,

is not short for a conjunction of two simple propositions but is rather a single proposition about a certain relation between some such dogs.

Another thing to notice is that the order of conjuncts can be reversed without affecting the truth value of the compound. Assuming that (26) is true, the facts that make it true are exactly the same as those that make "Dobermans are fierce dogs and Rottweilers are fierce dogs" true, which are also the same that make (27) true. However, we must be careful about this, for not all reversals of conjunctions are logically equivalent. When they are not, conjunction is not used as a *truth-functional* connective: something beyond the truth values of the conjuncts and their combination matters in determining the truth value of any such conjunction. For example,

29 He took off his shoes and got into bed.

The facts that make (29) true do not seem to be the same as those that make (30) true.

30 He got into bed and took off his shoes.

The *order* of events, and therefore, of the conjuncts, does matter in these nontruth-functional conjunctions, as it also does in

31 He saw her and said hello.

32 He said hello and saw her.

Finally, note that besides "and," there are a number of English expressions for conjunction, including "but," "however," "also", "moreover," "yet," "while," "nevertheless," "even though," and "although."

Disjunction

This type of compound proposition is created by the truth-functional connective standardly expressed in English by "or" and in logical notation by the so-called wedge, **v**. Either expression is placed between the two propositions in disjunction, which may themselves be simple or compound propositions. Each member of a disjunction is called "disjunct." Here are two disjunctions involving simple propositions as disjuncts—one in English:

33 Rome is in Italy or Rome is in Finland,

and the other in symbolic notation:

34 $I \vee F$

(33) and (34) are compound propositions because each is affected by a truth-functional connective. Disjunction is a truth-functional connective because it determines the truth value of the compound proposition it creates entirely on the basis of the values of its members and the following rule:

The disjunction is false if and only if its disjuncts are both false. Otherwise, the disjunction is true.

Following this rule, we may say that (33) is true. After all, one of its disjuncts is true—and, given the above rule, if one of the disjuncts is true, or if both are true, then the disjunction is true. But (35) is false, for its disjuncts are both false:

35 Either snow tires are useful in the tropics or air conditioners are popular in Iceland.

In addition to "or," disjunction can be expressed by "either ... or ...," "unless," "neither ... nor ...," and other locutions of our language. Thus this is also a disjunction:

36 She is the director of the project, unless the catalog is wrong,

which is equivalent to

36' Either she is the director of the project, or the catalog is wrong.

This disjunction,

37 Neither the CIA nor the FBI tolerates terrorists,

is a shortened way of saying

37' Neither the CIA tolerates terrorists nor the FBI tolerates terrorists.

Since "neither ... nor ..." is a common way to express the negation of a disjunction, (37) is logically the same as (or equivalent to)

38 It is false that either the CIA tolerates terrorists or the FBI tolerates terrorists.

Thus, both (37) and (38) may be symbolized as

38' ~(C v F)

Furthermore, (37) and (38) are logically equivalent to

39 The CIA doesn't tolerates terrorists and the FBI doesn't tolerate terrorists,

which may be symbolized as

39' ~C • ~F

Note, finally, that any truth-functional disjunction offers two alternatives and that this can be done in two different ways. A disjunction can be *inclusive,* in the sense that it may mean "either P or Q or both." But it can also be *exclusive,* meaning "either P or Q but not both." For the propositional arguments discussed in this book, we'll focus only on inclusive disjunction, whose truth value rule is given above.

Material Conditional

This type of compound proposition, also called "material implication" or simply "conditional," is created by a truth-functional logical connective, standardly expressed in English by "if ... then ...," and in logical notation by the so-called horseshoe, $\supset$. Consider

40 If Maria is a practicing attorney, then she has passed the bar exam.

This may be represented as

40' $M \supset E$

The simple proposition standardly preceded by "if" is called the *antecedent;* the one that follows "then," is the *consequent,* marked in (40) with ... and ..., respectively. (40) is a compound proposition because it is affected by "if ... then ...," a truth-functional connective that determines the truth value of the conditional entirely on the basis of both the values of its antecedent and consequent, together with the following rule:

> The conditional is false if and only if its antecedent is true and its consequent false. Otherwise the conditional is true.

Thus, any conditional with a true consequent is true, and any conditional with a false antecedent is true.

The two propositions in a conditional, which may themselves be either simple or compound, stand in a *hypothetical* relationship, where neither antecedent nor consequent is *asserted independently.* Does (40) assert that Maria *is* a practicing attorney? No. Does it claim that she *has* passed the bar exam?

No. Rather, in any conditional "If *P*, then *Q*," *P* and *Q* stand in a hypothetical relationship such that *P*'s being true implies that *Q* is also true. To challenge a conditional, one has to show that its antecedent is true and its consequent false at once. For example,

41 If Bob speaks loudly, then he is angry.

This could be challenged by pointing to a situation in which Bob spoke loudly but wasn't angry—that is, by pointing to a situation in which the truth of the antecedent would *not* be sufficient for the truth of the consequent.

Notice that sometimes the "then" that often introduces the consequent of a conditional sentence may be left out. Moreover, besides "if ... then ...," many other linguistic expressions can be used in English to introduce one or the other part of a conditional sentence. Such expressions may precede that sentence's consequent, its antecedent, or both—as shown in the examples below, where double or single *underlines* are used to mark, respectively, expressions introducing an antecedent or a consequent:

42 Maria's being a practicing attorney is sufficient for her having passed the bar exam.

43 Maria has passed the bar exam provided she is a practicing attorney.

44 Supposing that Maria is a practicing attorney, she has passed the bar exam.

45 On the assumption that Maria is a practicing attorney, she has passed the bar exam.

46 Maria is a practicing attorney only if she has passed the bar exam.

47 That Maria is a practicing attorney implies that she has passed the bar exam.

We'll now translate these conditional sentences into our symbolic language, using *M* to stand for "Maria is a practicing attorney" and *E* for "Maria has passed the bar exam." Any of our formulas representing (42) through (47) will have *M* as the conditional's antecedent and *E* as its consequent. Thus, the symbol *M* for the antecedent will be listed first, then the horseshoe symbol for the logical connective, and *E* for the consequent last. The formula then is,

40 $M \supset E$

This correctly represents (40) and (42) through (47), since all these conditionals are logically the same. Something to keep in mind here is

> To translate a conditional sentence into the symbolic language, we must list its antecedent first and its consequent last, whether or not these two parts occur in the English sentence in that order.

Necessary and Sufficient Conditions. In order to understand what material conditionals are, it is helpful to examine the related notions of *necessary* and *sufficient conditions*. A merely necessary condition of some proposition *P*'s being true is some state of affairs *without which P could not be true* but which is not enough all by itself to *make P* true. In (40), Maria's having passed the bar exam is a necessary condition of her being a practicing attorney (she *could not be a practicing attorney* if she had not passed it, though merely having passed doesn't guarantee that she's practicing). A sufficient condition of some proposition *P*'s being true is some state of affairs that is *enough all by itself* to make *P* true but which may not be the only way to make *P* true. In (40), Maria's being a practicing attorney is sufficient for her having passed the bar exam (in the sense that the former *guarantees* the latter).

Necessary and sufficient conditions matter to a material conditional since

- Its consequent is a necessary (but not sufficient) condition for the truth of its antecedent.
- Its antecedent is a sufficient (though not a necessary) condition for the truth of its consequent.

Material Biconditional

This type of compound proposition, also called "material equivalence" or simply "biconditional," is created by the truth-functional connective standardly expressed in English by "if and only if" and in logical notation by the so-called triple bar, $\equiv$. Consider

48 Dr. Baxter is the college's president if and only if she is the college's chief executive officer.

This may be represented as

48' $B \equiv O$

(48) is a compound proposition because its members, represented as B and O in (48'), are affected by the truth-functional connective expressed in English by "if and only if." Why is this connective a truth-functional one? Because it determines the truth value of the resulting compound proposition on the basis of both the values of its members and the following rule:

> The biconditional is true if and only if its members have the same truth value—that is, they are either *both true* or *both false*. Otherwise the biconditional is false.

Given this rule, for a biconditional to be true, the truth value of the propositions making it up must be *equivalent*. When a biconditional's members have *different* truth values, the biconditional is false. Consider these biconditionals:

49 The Himalayas are a chain of mountains if and only if the Pope is the leader of the Anglican Church.

50 Los Angeles is in California if and only if Boston is in Bosnia.

51 Parrots are mammals if and only if cats are mammals.

(49) through (51) feature propositions with different truth values, and each of these biconditionals is therefore false. But when the

truth values of a biconditional's members are both the same (both true or both false), then the compound proposition would be true. For example,

52 Lincoln was assassinated if and only if Kennedy was assassinated.

53 Bejing is the capital of France if and only if Bill Gates is poor.

54 Oaks are trees if and only if tigers are felines.

Another thing to notice here is this: in any biconditional, each member is both a necessary and a sufficient condition of the other. Thus, in (48), Baxter's being the college's CEO is both a necessary and sufficient condition for her being the college's president, and her being the college's president is both a necessary and sufficient condition for her being the college's CEO. So the biconditional can be understood as the conjunction of two conditionals. Thus even though we would standardly represent (52) as

52' $L \equiv J$

(52) may also be represented as

52" $(L \supset J) \cdot (J \supset L)$

In (52"), the two conditionals whose conjunction make up a biconditional are set inside parentheses to eliminate ambiguity: parentheses are needed to indicate that the compound proposition is a conjunction of two other compound propositions—namely, the two conditionals. As this formula shows, a biconditional can be broken down into the conjunction of two conditionals representing an antecedent and a consequent that imply each other. That is why the material equivalence relation is called a biconditional.

Finally, note that there are other ways of expressing a biconditional's truth-functional connective besides "if and only if," often abbreviated "iff" in writing. Such alternative expressions include "just in case," "is equivalent to," and "when and only when."

BOX 2 ■ SUMMARY: TRUTH-FUNCTIONAL CONNECTIVES

CONNECTIVE	IN ENGLISH	IN SYMBOLS	SYMBOL'S NAME
negation	not *P*	~*P*	tilde
conjunction	*P* and *Q*	*P* • *Q*	dot
disjunction	*P* or *Q*	*P* v *Q*	wedge
conditional	if *P* then *Q*	*P* ⊃ *Q*	horseshoe
biconditional	*P* if and only if *Q*	*P* ≡ *Q*	triple bar

11.3 A Closer Look at Compound Propositions

We can now consider some compound propositions featuring one or more of the above truth-functional connectives. First, consider a simple proposition, such as

55 Oprah Winfrey is on television.

Since there is no connective affecting this proposition, this is a simple proposition that we may symbolize by a propositional letter such as

55' *O*

But a proposition affected by negation is not simple. For example,

56 Katie Couric is not on television.

We may symbolize this as

56' ~*K*

Now consider

57 Oprah Winfrey is on television but Katie Couric is not.

This is an abbreviated version of the longer proposition,

57' Oprah Winfrey is on television but Katie Couric is not on television.

Either way, we have a compound proposition featuring two connectives: conjunction and negation. The *main connective*, however, is the conjunction, whose scope is the entire compound proposition. Here the scope of negation is only the second proposition. The principle is

The scope of negation is always the proposition represented as immediately following the tilde. That proposition may be either simple or compound. In the latter case, a correct symbolic representation would require that we use, e.g., parentheses to remove ambiguity about *which* compound proposition falls within the scope of the negation.

But (57) does not require parentheses to eliminate ambiguity, since the negation clearly affects only one proposition, which we have represented as *K*. Thus, the formula that represents (57) is

57" $O \cdot \sim K$

Now what can we tell about the truth value of this formula if we know that the propositions represented by *O* and *K* are true? Given the truth-value rule for negation, $\sim K$ is then false. And given the truth-value rule for conjunction, (57) is false too.

Let's now examine

58 If both Harry and Miguel are on the team, then Bill is not in the team.

To begin, let's try to identify the *main connective* under whose scope the compound proposition featured in (58) falls. It is a conditional whose antecedent and consequent are compound propositions themselves: one is a conjunction representable as

59 $H \cdot M$

The other a negation representable as

60 $\sim B$

Therefore (58) can be represented as

58' $(H \cdot M) \supset \sim B$

This is a compound proposition that is a conditional, with a compound antecedent (in parentheses, a conjunction) and a compound consequent (a negation). Parentheses are needed only in the case of the antecedent to indicate that the main connective is the one represented by a horseshoe. No parentheses are needed in the consequent, since it is clearly B that is affected by the negation in it. (More on this in the next section.)

Let's now assume that the simple propositions represented by H and B in this formula are true, and that M is false. Given this assumption, we can determine the truth value of (58'): that compound proposition is true, since its antecedent is false. In this case, it doesn't matter at all that its consequent, ~B, is false. Why? Because given the truth-value rule for the conditional, having a false antecedent is enough to make it true. And (58')'s antecedent is false because one of the conjuncts, M, is false. Recall that according to the truth-value rule for conjunction, having a false conjunct is sufficient to make a conjunction false. Since a conditional with a false antecedent is itself true, (58') comes out true under the present assumptions, as does the English sentence represented by it, (58) above.

Let's now try another:

61 Bats are nocturnal if and only if either goldfish are mammals or squirrels are rodents.

We can represent "Bats are nocturnal" as B, "Goldfish are mammals," as G, and "Squirrels are rodents," as A. The main connective is "if and only if," which appears flanked by a simple proposition on the left and by a disjunction on the right. The whole compound proposition may then be represented with the formula,

61' $B \equiv (G \lor A)$

Let B and A be true and G false. Since we know the value of B, to determine the truth value of the biconditional we need to know the truth value of $G \lor A$. But this comes out true, for it is a disjunction with a true disjunct, A. Now, since both sides of the biconditional have been discovered to have the same truth value (namely, *true*), therefore (61') is true.

So far, we've been considering examples of compound propositions in which the truth values of their members is determined either by the facts or by stipulation. In each case, we've worked out the truth value of the compound proposition based on this information, together with the truth-value rules for the connectives occurring in the proposition. We shall later consider another procedure for determining the truth value of a compound proposition.

Punctuation Signs

Parentheses, brackets, and braces can be used to remove ambiguity in some symbolic expressions by indicating the scope of logical connectives. When a compound proposition is joined to a simple proposition or to another compound proposition by a logical connective, parentheses are the first recourse for determining the scope of occurring connectives. When the compound proposition is more complex, brackets may be needed, and for even more complex compound propositions, braces. Thus, parentheses are introduced first, then brackets, and finally braces. Here are such punctuation signs, together with examples illustrating their correct use.

parentheses	( ) as in	$(P \bullet Q) \supset R$
brackets	[ ] as in	$[(P \bullet Q) \supset R] \vee \sim S$
braces	{ } as in	$\sim\{[(P \bullet Q) \supset R] \vee \sim S\}$

Note that the compound proposition $(P \bullet Q) \supset R$ is a conditional while $P \bullet (Q \supset R)$ is a conjunction. Without brackets, the proposition $(P \bullet Q) \supset R \vee \sim S$ is ambiguous, since it is unclear which connective is its *main* connective: it admits of two different interpretations, one as a conditional, the other as a disjunction. Finally, the main connective in $\sim\{[(P \bullet Q) \supset R] \vee \sim S\}$ is the negation in the far left of this formula, which affects the whole formula. Compare $\sim[(P \bullet Q) \supset R] \vee \sim S$. Now without braces, the scope of that negation is the conditional marked by brackets, and the whole formula is not a negation but a disjunction instead.

Well-Formed Formulas

To determine whether a formula representing a compound proposition is *well formed*—that is, acceptable within the symbolic notation that we are now using—we have to pay attention to the scope of its truth-functional connectives. Within the scope of negation falls the simple or compound proposition that follows it. Negation is the only connective that has only one formula within its scope. Each of the other connectives has within its scope the two formulas, each simple or compound, that flank the connective. Punctuation signs are used to mark the scope of connectives when needed. Thus,

> Formulas such as
> $P \sim Q$
> $P \sim$
> $P \vee Q \bullet P$
> are not WFFs (short for "well-formed formulas").

Exercises

I. Review Questions

1. What is a compound proposition?
2. What are the five logical connectives?
3. What does it mean to say that a connective is truth-functional?
4. Why is negation considered a *connective*?
5. Give the truth-functional definitions of disjunction and conjunction.
6. What words other than "and" are commonly used to express conjunction?
7. What words other than "either ... or ..." are commonly used to express disjunction?
8. What words other than "if ... then ..." are commonly used to express a conditional?
9. What words other than "if and only if" are commonly used to express a biconditional?
10. Why is the biconditional also called "equivalence"?
11. Name the parts of a conditional.
12. In a material conditional, which part is understood to present a *necessary condition* of the other? Which part is understood to present a *sufficient condition* of the other?

II. **For each of the following propositions, determine whether it is simple or compound, and, if compound, identify its main connective.**

1. Franklin D. Roosevelt was not a senator.

   SAMPLE ANSWER: Compound, negation

2. Warren G. Harding did not finish his term in office. _____

* 3. Ronald Reagan was reelected if and only if Mondale was defeated. _____

4. If Lyndon Johnson was born in Texas, then so was Eisenhower. _____

5. Either Arnold Schwarzenegger was a popular actor or Richard Nixon resigned. _____

* 6. William McKinley was assassinated. _____

7. Nixon visited China only if Nixon traveled in Asia. _____

8. Woodrow Wilson will be remembered unless the League of Nations was a folly. _____

* 9. Theodore Roosevelt was a war hero but he also built the Panama Canal. _____

10. Theodore Roosevelt was born into a wealthy family of prominent New Yorkers. _____

11. It is not the case that John F. Kennedy was from Colorado. _____

*12. John F. Kennedy was assassinated in 1963, while on a visit to Dallas. _____

13. Either Calvin Coolidge was a conservative or he was from New England. _____

14. Franklin D. Roosevelt went to Yalta in 1945 for a meeting with Stalin and Churchill. _____

*15. Neither Eisenhower nor Kennedy was a pacifist. _____

16. It is false that Harry Truman was a Communist. _____

17. If Lincoln was the tallest president, then Theodore Roosevelt was the youngest. _____

*18. Franklin Roosevelt did not like Stalin, but he admired Stalin's tenacity against Hitler. _____

19. Ronald Reagan was from Illinois just in case Gerald Ford was from Michigan. _____

20. Harry Truman was a skillful politician; moreover, he was very plain-spoken. _____

*21. Herbert Hoover had the bad luck to be president during the stock market crash of 1929. _____

22. Taft was from Ohio and was the last president with a mustache. _____

23. Both Taft and McKinley were Republicans. _____

*24. That Taft was a Republican implies that Warren G. Harding was too. _____

25. Richard Nixon and Harry Truman both played the piano. _____

26. Truman played the piano; however, his daughter, Margaret, was more serious about music. _____

*27. Gerald Ford was a football star at the University of Michigan long before he was in politics. _____

28. John F. Kennedy served in the navy in World War II, but George H. W. Bush did too. _____

29. If Bill Clinton is a moderate Democrat, then Lyndon Johnson was a liberal. _____

*30. Bill Clinton admitted to smoking marijuana, but he did not inhale. _____

31. Thomas Jefferson was not a Federalist. _____

32. Lyndon Johnson liked to entertain on his Texas ranch. _____

*33. Millard Fillmore signed the Fugitive Slave Act. _____

34. It is not the case that James Madison was from Pennsylvania. _____

35. Franklin D. Roosevelt was a New Yorker if and only if Martin Van Buren was too. _____

III. Symbolize each of the propositions in (II) above.

IV. Which of the following formulas are WFFs and which aren't?

1. ~D ~ (C • B)

SAMPLE ANSWER: Not a *WFF*

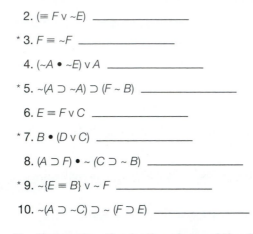

2. (≡ F v ~E) _____

* 3. F ≡ ~F _____

4. (~A • ~E) v A _____

* 5. ~(A ⊃ ~A) ⊃ (F ~ B) _____

6. E ≡ F v C _____

* 7. B • (D v C) _____

8. (A ⊃ F) • ~ (C ⊃ ~ B) _____

* 9. ~{E ≡ B} v ~ F _____

10. ~(A ⊃ ~C) ⊃ ~ (F ⊃ E) _____

V. Determine the truth values of the following formulas, assuming that *A* and *B* are true, and *C* and *D* are false.

1. ~B v ~A

SAMPLE ANSWER: False

2. A • D _____

* 3. ~B ⊃ A _____

4. ~(A ⊃ ~A) _____

5. C ⊃ B _____

* 6. B v D _____

7. C ≡ D _____

8. ~C _____

* 9. ~B v D _____

10. A ⊃ C _____

11. C v ~A _____

*12. D ⊃ ~B _____

13. ~(B ∨ C) _____

14. ~(A ∨ ~D) _____

*15. C ≡ A _____

16. ~D ∨ C _____

17. B ≡ ~A _____

*18. D • ~D _____

19. ~(A • D) _____

20. ~C ⊃ ~B _____

VI. Your Own Thinking Lab

1. For each of the formulas above, construct a statement whose truth value is as determined by the truth values assigned to it in exercise (V).

   SAMPLE ANSWER: 1. Either the Eiffel Tower is not in Paris or the Coliseum is not in Rome.
   [Tip: Find a false negation with (1)'s form in exercise (V).]

2. Describe each of the formulas in (V) above by taking into account its main connective.

   SAMPLE ANSWER: 1. A disjunction whose disjuncts are negations.

11.4 Defining Connectives with Truth Tables

We're ready now to move on to *truth tables*, a procedure that will, in the next section, allow us to determine mechanically the truth value of compound propositions of the five types discussed above. But before turning to this, let's first look closely at how each of the five truth-functional connectives can be defined by means of a truth table.

Truth Table for Negation.   The truth table here is constructed on the basis of the truth-value rule for negation given in Box 3.

BOX 3 ■ TRUTH-VALUE RULE FOR NEGATION

A negation is true if and only if the proposition denied is false. Otherwise, a negation is false.

This truth table defines negation by showing when a compound proposition ~P, the negation of a simple proposition P, is true and when it is false. To construct it, we first write down P on the top, without a negation on the left, and with a negation on the right. We then write a vertical column on the left, under P, listing *all the possible truth values of P*, which are T (true) and F (false). In the column on the right, under ~P, we apply the rule for negation to each row of the left column, and write down the truth value that we obtain on the right. The result is:

> First row: ~P is false because P is true
> Second row: ~P is true because P is false

These values, shown in the right-hand column of the truth table, are its result. An application of the rule given in Box 3 to each row in the column on the left have yielded the result in two steps. That result appears in the right-hand column, inside a box.

Truth-Tables for the Other Truth-Functional Connectives.   We'll proceed along similar lines for compound propositions under the scope of the other truth-functional connectives. First, we write columns on the left-hand side of the truth table representing all possible combinations of truth values for each simple proposition in the compound. Each column will show the values *T* (true) or *F* (false). Why only these values? Because here we follow the so-called *law of excluded middle,* according to which a proposition must have one or the other of these values. As a result, a proposition cannot be both true and false at the same time. That is,

> Each proposition is either true or false.

Once we have written down the simple propositions in the left-hand side of a truth table, to calculate the number of Ts and Fs in each column we use the formula 2^n, where 2 stands for the two truth values a proposition may have (true or false) and n for the number of propositions of different types that occur in the formula to which we'd apply the procedure. In the definition of negation, there is only one proposition, so the formula is 2^1, which produces two truth values: one T and one F. But the definition of conjunction, disjunction, conditional, or biconditional features two propositions represented by P and Q. So the formula is 2^2, which yields four places for the truth values of occurring propositions: two for T and two for F. Let's adopt the convention of assigning in the first column on the left, half Ts followed by half Fs: that is, two Ts, and two Fs (see truth tables below). In the other column on the same side of the truth table, we'll write a series of four values, distributed in this way: T, F, T, and F. On the top right-hand side of the table, we'll write the formula whose truth value we wish to determine, and below it, the truth value resulting from the application of the corresponding truth-value rule to each row of assigned values on the left. The final result is marked by putting it inside a box, and the columns are obtained by applying the truth value rule of each occurring connective to the values on the left-hand side of the truth table. Let's now construct truth tables for each of the remaining types of compound propositions.

Truth Table for Conjunction. The truth table shown below is constructed on the basis of the truth-value rule for conjunction in Box 4. It has two columns on the left, each of which assigns four truth values, two Ts and two Fs, to each of its conjuncts. Its four horizontal rows are obtained by calculating the possible

A conjunction is true if and only if its conjuncts are both true.
Otherwise a conjunction is false.

$P\,Q$	$P \cdot Q$
T T	T
T F	F
F T	F
F F	F

combinations of those values and applying the rule in Box 4. The
result, highlighted on the right, shows that a conjunction is true
just in case the two conjuncts are true.

Truth Table for Disjunction. Box 5 below provides the truth-
value rule for disjunction, on the basis of which we can construct its truth table. This has two columns on the left, each of
them assigning four truth values, two Ts and two Fs, to each
of the disjuncts. Its four horizontal rows are the result of reading the possible combinations of those values while applying
the rule in Box 5. The final result, inside the box in the right-
hand column, amounts to a definition of disjunction: it shows
that a disjunction is true just in case at least one of its disjuncts
is true. Equivalently, it defines disjunction as a compound
proposition that is false just in case both of its disjuncts
are false.

A disjunction is true if and only if at least one disjunct is true.
Otherwise a disjunction is false.

P Q	P v Q
T T	T
T F	T
F T	T
F F	F

Truth Table for the Material Conditional. This truth table is constructed on the basis of the truth-value rule provided in Box 6. As before, it has two columns on the left, each assigning four truth values, two Ts and two Fs, to its antecedent and its consequent. Its four horizontal rows are obtained by calculating the possible combinations of those values and applying the rule in Box 6. The result, inside the box on the right-hand side, amounts to a definition of the material conditional. It shows that it is true in all cases except when its antecedent is true and its consequent false.

BOX 6 ■ TRUTH-VALUE RULE FOR THE MATERIAL CONDITIONAL

A conditional is false if and only if its antecedent is true and its consequent false. Otherwise, a conditional is true.

P Q	P ⊃ Q
T T	T
T F	F
F T	T
F F	F

Truth Table for the Material Biconditional. This truth table is constructed on the basis of the truth-value rule in Box 7. Again, two columns on the left are each assigning four truth values, two Ts and two Fs, to each simple proposition in the formula. Its four horizontal rows are obtained by calculating the possible

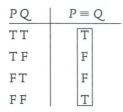

$P\,Q$	$P \equiv Q$
T T	T
T F	F
F T	F
F F	T

combinations of those values and applying the rule in Box 7. The truth table's result appears inside the box on the right and the truth table amounts to a definition of the material biconditional. It shows that it is true just in case its two members have exactly the same truth value: that is, they are either both true or both false.

The five truth tables we've now constructed provide truth-functional definitions for each of the five logical connectives. We can now use truth tables to determine the truth values of other compound propositions featuring such connectives.

11.5 Truth Tables for Compound Propositions

Important information about the truth value of any given compound proposition can be obtained with a truth table. To construct a truth table for a compound proposition, first we need to determine how many different simple propositions make up the one whose value we wish to check. We then assign all possible truth values to them in the way outlined above. For example, let's consider (57') again,

57' $O \cdot {\sim}K$

BOX 8 ■ TRUTH TABLES FOR COMPOUND PROPOSITIONS

As we've seen, in a truth table, the number of truth values assigned to each simple proposition on the left-hand side depends on how many different propositions occur in the formula at the top of the right-hand side, whose truth value we wish to determine. For any simple proposition there are only two possible truth values (true and false), therefore for a compound proposition such as ~P, only two rows are needed. But with more propositions, the number of truth values would increase according to the formula 2^n: with two, it's four lines; with three, it's eight lines; with four, it's sixteen lines; and so on. In the case of (62), then, we need four lines. And, just to make sure that we get all possible combinations of truth values, we'll adopt this convention: in the column under whatever letter symbol is farthest to the left, we put T in the top half of the rows and F in the bottom half; in the column under the other letter symbol to the right of that, we put a sequence of alternating T's and F's.

The truth table for it looks like this:

62	O K	$O \bullet {\sim}K$
	T T	F F
	T F	T T
	F T	F F
	F F	F T

The formula on the right-hand side of this truth table is a conjunction of O, whose values we read in the first column on the left, and ~K, whose values we need to determine. We do this first, by applying the truth-value rule for negation to each row in the second column on the left. Once we determine ~K's values, we enter them under the tilde on the right. We then determine the truth value of the conjunction by applying the truth-value rule for conjunction to O's values (available on the left-hand side of the truth table) and ~K's values (under the tilde). We enter the values thus obtained under the dot, marking the resulting column with a box. This column under the main connective is the most important one, because it provides information about the truth values of the compound proposition O • ~K. It tells us that this compound proposition is true only when O and ~K are true (as shown in the second horizontal row). On all other assignments of values, that proposition is false.

Now let's construct a truth table for

58' $(H • M) \supset$ ~B

The truth table for (58') is:

63 H M B	$(H • M)$	$\supset$	~B
T T T	T	F	F
T T F	T	T	T
T F T	F	T	F
T F F	F	T	T
F T T	F	T	F
F T T	F	T	T
F F T	F	T	F
F F F	F	T	T

On its left-hand side, this truth table shows all possible combinations of truth values for the three members of the compound proposition represented by the formula on its right-hand side. That formula, whose truth value we want to determine, has three different simple propositions symbolized by *H*, *M*, and *B*. As before, to calculate the number of rows needed, we use the algorithm 2^n, here 2^3, which reveals that eight rows are needed. Accordingly, we assign *T*s and *F*s to the three columns on the left—beginning with the one farthest to the left (the one under *H*), which has the top half *T*s and the bottom half *F*s—and continue to divide that pattern in half as we move across to each of the two other columns to the right (under *M* and *B*). This convention guarantees that we do get all possible combinations of truth values. On the top line, it's all *T*s, on the bottom line, it's all *F*s, and in between are all other possible arrangements.

Once we have entered these values, we look at the compound proposition formula on the top right. It is a conditional, so the main connective is $\supset$, under which we place the final result (inside the box). But we can determine the possible truth values of the conditional only *after* we first find the possible truth values of the antecedent, $H \cdot M$, and the consequent, ~B. Those truth values make up the column under $\cdot$ and the column under ~. The final step consists in applying the rule for the truth value of the conditional to those two columns.

11.6 Logically Necessary and Logically Contingent Propositions

Contingencies

What, then, have we learned about the compound propositions on the right-hand side of truth tables (62) and (63)? Just this: that each is neither necessarily true nor necessarily false but instead *sometimes true and sometimes false, depending on the truth values of its component simple propositions and its logical connectives.* Any such compound proposition is said to be a *contingency*. A compound proposition is shown to be a contingency if the truth table for it displays at least one T and at least one F in the column under the main connective. Under the $\supset$ in (63), and under the $\cdot$ in (62), there is at least one T and at least one F. In light of that result, each of these compound propositions whose truth value has thereby been checked is a contingency.

Contradictions

But now consider this compound proposition:

64   $B \equiv \text{~}B$

Since (64) contains no proposition other than B, which occurs twice, the algorithm 2^1 yields two places for truth values, one for T and the other for F. Accordingly, the truth table runs:

65

B	B	$\equiv$	~B
T		F	F
F		F	T

This truth table reveals (64) to be a *contradiction*. Contradictions are compound propositions that are always false simply by virtue of their form (and regardless of the actual truth values of their component simple propositions). In a truth table for a contradiction the column under the main connective symbol is all *F*s.

Tautologies

At the opposite extreme from contradictions are *tautologies*, propositions that are necessarily true, simply by virtue of their form (and regardless of the actual truth values of their component simple propositions). Any tautology whose truth value is tested with a truth table would have a column under the formula's main connective with all *T*s. The negation of (64) above is a tautology, which reads

66 ~(B ≡ ~B)

We construct the following truth table for this proposition:

67

B	~(B	≡	~B)
T	T	F	F
F	T	F	T

Since (67) shows all *T*s under the formula's main connective, it confirms that (66), the proposition thus tested, is a tautology.

Exercises

VII. Review Questions

1. What is a proposition's form?
2. What is a truth table?
3. How are truth tables used to define the five propositional connectives?

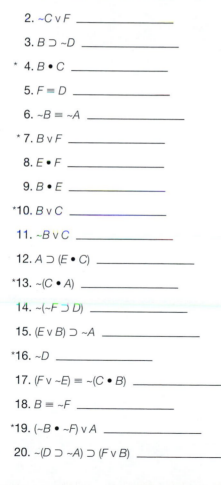

4. In a truth table for a compound proposition, how do we know how many horizontal rows are required? What is the rationale for this?
5. In a truth table for a compound proposition, which column is the most important? And what does that column tell us?
6. What is a tautology?
7. What is a contradiction?
8. What is a contingency?

VIII. For each of the following formulas, determine its truth value. Assume the following truth values: *A*, *B*, and *C* are true; *D*, *E*, and *F* are false.

1. *A* • *E*

   SAMPLE ANSWER: False

2. ~*C* v *F* _____

3. *B* ⊃ ~*D* _____

* 4. *B* • *C* _____

5. *F* ≡ *D* _____

6. ~*B* ≡ ~*A* _____

* 7. *B* v *F* _____

8. *E* • *F* _____

9. *B* • *E* _____

*10. *B* v *C* _____

11. ~*B* v *C* _____

12. *A* ⊃ (*E* • *C*) _____

*13. ~(*C* • *A*) _____

14. ~(~*F* ⊃ *D*) _____

15. (*E* v *B*) ⊃ ~*A* _____

*16. ~*D* _____

17. (*F* v ~*E*) ≡ ~(*C* • *B*) _____

18. *B* ≡ ~*F* _____

*19. (~*B* • ~*F*) v *A* _____

20. ~(*D* ⊃ ~*A*) ⊃ (*F* v *B*) _____

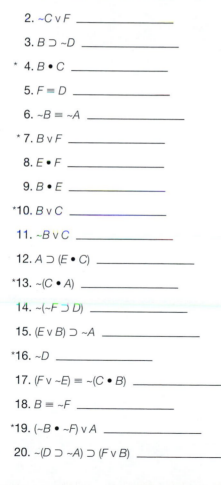

21. $E \equiv (F \vee C)$ _____

*22. $B \bullet (D \vee C)$ _____

23. $(A \supset F) \bullet \sim(C \supset \sim B)$ _____

24. $\sim(E \equiv B) \vee \sim F$ _____

*25. $\sim[(A \supset \sim C) \supset \sim(F \supset E)]$ _____

IX. **For each of the following formulas, construct a truth table to determine whether it is a contingency, tautology, or contradiction.**

1. $W \supset \sim K$

SAMPLE ANSWER: Contingency

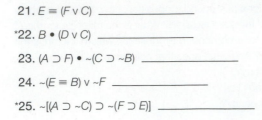

W K	$W \supset \sim K$
T T	F F
T F	T T
F T	T F
F F	T T

2. $(L \vee N) \vee A$ _____

* 3. $B \supset (M \supset B)$ _____

4. $\sim J \bullet (G \vee N)$ _____

* 5. $\sim[(A \bullet B) \supset (B \bullet A)]$ _____

6. $D \vee (\sim M \supset \sim D)$ _____

7. $\sim[\sim(A \bullet B) \equiv (\sim A \vee \sim B)]$ _____

* 8. $(\sim A \vee \sim B) \supset (B \bullet A)$ _____

9. $(F \supset \sim N) \bullet \sim(F \supset \sim N)$ _____

*10. $\sim A \equiv \sim(\sim K \vee \sim H)$ _____

11. $(D \vee M) \supset (M \vee D)$ _____

*12. $\sim[(\sim A \bullet H) \vee \sim(H \supset \sim I)]$ _____

13. $(E \bullet \sim G) \supset G$ _____

14. $A \equiv \sim\sim A$ _____

15. $\sim(A \equiv B) \equiv \sim L$ _____

*16. $\sim\{[A \cdot (B \cdot C)] \equiv [(A \cdot B) \cdot C]\}$ _____

17. $\sim\{[(A \cdot B) \vee (\sim B \supset A)] \supset B\}$ _____

*18. $(A \cdot B) \equiv (B \cdot A)$ _____

19. $(\sim B \supset A) \equiv [(B \vee \sim D) \supset C]$ _____

*20. $(A \equiv B) \equiv [(A \supset B) \cdot (B \supset A)]$ _____

X. **Symbolize each of the following propositions and determine by the truth-table procedure whether it is a contingency, tautology, or contradiction. Use the symbols in parentheses.**

1. If Earth is the center of the universe, then our planet is special. (E, O)

SAMPLE ANSWER: Contingency

$E\ O$	$E \supset O$
T T	T
T F	F
F T	T
F F	T

* 2. Earth is not the center of the universe or our planet is special. (E, O)

_____

3. Either our planet is special or it isn't. (O) _____

* 4. Earth is not the center of the universe just in case there is something special about our planet. (E, O) _____

5. There is something special about our planet; however, Earth is not the center of the universe. (O, E) _____

6. It is false that either our planet is special or it isn't. (O) _____

* 7. If Earth is the center of the universe and there is something special about our planet, then there is something special about our planet. (E, O) _____

8. It is not the case that human life has value if and only if human life has value. (H) _____

9. Human life has a purpose, but it is not the case that it has value. (L, H) _____

10. Human life has value only if it has a purpose. (H, L) _____

*11. Human life has value and a purpose if and only if it is not false that human life does have value and a purpose. (H, L) _____

*12. It is not the case that both Earth is the center of the universe and there is something special about our planet just in case it is false that human life has value and a purpose. (E, O, H, L) _____

13. Neither is Earth the center of the universe nor is there something special about our planet. (E, O) _____

*14. Neither is Earth the center of the universe nor is there something special about our planet if and only if both Earth is not the center of the universe and it is not the case that there is something special about our planet. (E, O) _____

15. Either human life has both value and a purpose or if it is false that there is something special about our planet, then Earth is the center of the universe. (H, L, O, E) _____

XI. YOUR OWN THINKING LAB

Write down ordinary English sentences for each of the formulas below following this glossary: F = Fred is at the library; M = Mary is at the library; L = The library is open; I = I have internet access; E = The essay is due on Thursday.

* 1. $M \cdot \sim L$

  2. $F \equiv (L \cdot M)$

* 3. $F \equiv (L \lor \sim M)$

  4. $(L \cdot I) \supset (F \lor M)$

* 5. $E \equiv (L \supset I)$

  6. $(E \cdot L) \supset (M \lor F)$

* 7. $\sim[\sim F \supset (\sim L \lor M)]$

  8. $(M \cdot F) \equiv (E \cdot L)$

11.7 The Philosopher's Corner

Tautologies and Other Necessary Propositions

In this chapter, we've seen that any given compound proposition must be of one or the other of three types: a tautology (which is *always true*), a contradiction (which is *always false*), or a contingency (which is *sometimes true and sometimes false*). Thus, logical tautologies and contradictions are, respectively, necessarily true and necessarily false. Yet they are not the only types of necessarily true and necessarily false propositions. Furthermore, logical contingencies are not the only type of contingent propositions. But how do we decide whether a proposition falls within one category or the other? What, exactly, makes a proposition *necessary* or *contingent*? Here the principles are,

- For any necessary proposition, there is *no* possible world where it could have a different truth value.
- For any contingent proposition, there is at least one possible world where it could have a different truth value.

Given these principles, tautologies and contradictions are necessary, since for any of them there is *no* possible world where its truth value could be different. And logical contingencies are contingent propositions, because they can have different truth values in different possible worlds. In the context of a truth table, a "possible world" is each row yielding a result in the boxed column—which, read horizontally, shows the scenario under which the proposition is true (or false) according to the truth values assigned to its propositional components on the left-hand side of the truth table.

In addition to logical tautologies, the category of necessarily true propositions also includes propositions such as

68 A straight line is the shortest path between two points.

69 $5 + 7 = 12$

70 A sister is a female sibling.

And, in addition to logical contradictions, necessarily false propositions include, for example,

71 No equiangular triangle has equal-sized angles.

72 $5 + 7 \neq 12$

73 A sister is a male sibling.

Surprisingly, it has even been argued that some propositions about the inner workings of the natural world are necessary. In the early 1970s, the American philosophers Saul Kripke (b.1940) and Hilary Putnam (b.1926) argued persuasively that propositions about the inner structure, or underlying mechanisms, of natural things, if true, are true in every possible world, and thus are necessarily true. And if false, they are false in every possible world and thus necessarily false. The list of necessarily true propositions would then include the following and others like them:

74 Heat is molecular motion.

75 Gold has the atomic number 79.

But what if we discover that some propositions that seem necessarily true are false? In that case, the propositions would then be known to be necessarily false. It's important to bear in mind, however, that the necessary/contingent distinction concerns *how things are* rather than *what we know* about them: that is, it is a metaphysical distinction rather than an epistemological one. These two should not be confused. How we come to know about things, as we saw in Chapter 5, determines two different types of propositions: those knowable a priori (i.e., just by thinking) and those knowable only empirically (i.e., by investigation of the environment). Traditionally, logical propositions are classified among the former sort, as are mathematical propositions, such as (68) and (69) above, and conceptual ones, such as (70).

Let's now add another criterion commonly used to classify the statements that express propositions. It concerns whether or not a statement is true given the meaning of its words alone. Those statements that are true in this way are said to be *analytic*; those that aren't, *synthetic*. Consider

76 Any equiangular triangle has equal-sized angles.

77 $P \equiv Q$ is equivalent to $(P \supset Q) \cdot (Q \supset P)$

(76) is true given the meaning of such expressions as "equiangular triangle" and "triangle with equal-sized angles" alone. It is therefore analytic. But (74) and (75) are synthetic. This is because in neither case is the statement true simply by virtue of the meanings of its words alone; rather, it is true only if *the way things are* in the world is as the statement's content represents them to be. For (74) to be true, it must be the case that heat *just is* molecular motion. And for (75) to be true, it must be the case that gold *is in fact* the element with the atomic number 79.

But why is (77) analytic? Because it expresses a biconditional, whose meaning is by definition the same as that of the conjunction of two conditionals, as illustrated on its right-hand side. If recast as a compound proposition in the symbolic language developed in this chapter, it reads

77' $(P \equiv Q) \equiv [(P \supset Q) \cdot (Q \supset P)]$

The truth value of (77') can be determined with a truth table, which would yield a tautology. Compound propositions that are tautologies are analytically true—that is, true by meaning alone— while all contradictions are analytically false—that is, false by meaning alone. Recall that the truth value of any proposition of either sort depends entirely on the meaning of the truth-functional connectives affecting the simple propositions that make it up. On the other hand, statements expressing contingencies are synthetic, since their truth does not depend solely on the meaning of the truth-functional connectives affecting their simple propositions but on the truth values of those simple propositions themselves. Clearly,

78 $P \cdot Q$

is not true by the meaning of the conjunction alone; rather, its truth depends on whether *things are* as represented by P and Q.

Finally, it's important to bear in mind that not all philosophers have accepted the analytic/synthetic distinction in precisely the form we've outlined here, including the notion that mathematical propositions are analytic. The German philosopher Immanuel Kant (1724–1804) famously held that some synthetic propositions were knowable a priori, and that propositions of mathematics, such as (68) and (69), were among them. On this view, it is not part of the meaning of "straight line" to be *the shortest path between two points* or that of 7+5 to be 12. Nevertheless, he argued that their truth was in some sense necessary and knowable just by thinking.

Let's now sum up these categories:

1. Necessary vs. Contingent

    Necessarily true propositions are true in every possible world (as, e.g., in tautologies). Necessarily false ones are false in every possible world (as, e.g., in contradictions). Contingent propositions are those that have different truth values in different possible worlds. On a traditional view, the truths of logic are necessary propositions, but so are mathematical and conceptual truths. Furthermore, propositions about the inner structure or mechanism of natural and scientific kinds are now commonly added to the category of necessary propositions.

2. A priori vs. Empirical

    The categories of "a priori" and "empirical" concern *how we know* a proposition. Those involving logical, mathematical, and conceptual truths are a priori, or knowable just by thinking, while those requiring investigation of the environment are empirical (i.e., knowable only by observation).

3. Analytic vs. Synthetic

    A statement is analytic if it is true by the meaning of its words alone; otherwise it is synthetic. On a traditional view, all statements expressing a priori truths are analytic and all expressing empirical truths synthetic. But on a Kantian view, the truths of math and some other a priori truths are synthetic.

Exercises

XII. Given the Kripke-Putnam view, determine whether each of the following propositions is necessary or contingent. (Tip: You don't need to *know whether any proposition is true.* For each of them, consider whether it could have a different truth value in some possible worlds).

1. Oxygen is a colorless, odorless, and tasteless gas.

   SAMPLE ANSWER: Contingent

2. The North-American mountain beaver is stout and short-limbed. _____

* 3. A rectangle is a figure with exactly four internal angles. _____

4. An electron is an elementary particle carrying a unit charge of negative electricity. _____

* 5. Benjamin Franklin invented the bifocals. _____

6. Benjamin Franklin was Benjamin Franklin. _____

* 7. $3 + 3 = 6$ _____

8. A swimmer is someone who swims. _____

* 9. Impeachment is a formal accusation issued by a legislature against a public official charged with a crime or other serious misconduct. _____

10. My car's odometer is out of order. _____

*11. $\sim\sim P$ is logically equivalent to P. _____

12. If "P and Q" is true, then P is true and Q is true. _____

*13. Oxygen is the element with the atomic number 8. _____

14. The symbol for oxygen is O. _____

*15. If an argument is valid, it is not possible that its premises are true and its conclusion false. _____

*XIII. Assuming that each proposition above is true, is it knowable a priori or empirically?

*XIV. Which statement in exercise (XII) above is analytic and which synthetic according to the *traditional view*.

*XV. Classify the statements in exercise (XII) above according to the *Kantian view* of which are analytic and which synthetic.

■ Writing Project

The truth tables for the five truth-functional connectives amount to *semantic definitions* of those connectives. Write a short paper in which you first reproduce the truth table for each of the connectives and then discuss the question of *what kind* of definition each amounts to in light of the distinction drawn in Chapter 9 between different types of semantic definition.

■ Chapter Summary

1. **Argument as a Relation Between Propositions**

   When the relation of inference hinges on the relation between whole propositions, the argument is *propositional*.

2. **Simple and Compound Propositions**

   A proposition is *compound* if and only if it is affected by a truth-functional connective. Otherwise, the proposition is simple.

3. **Truth-Functional Connectives**

   Negation

   A negation is true if and only if the proposition denied is false. Otherwise, it is false.

   Conjunction

   A conjunction is true if and only if its conjuncts are both true. Otherwise it is false.

   Disjunction

   A disjunction is true if and only if at least one disjunct is true. Otherwise it is false.

   Material Conditional

   A conditional is false if and only if its antecedent is true and its consequent false. Otherwise it is true.

   Material Biconditional

   A biconditional is true if and only if both members have the same truth value. Otherwise it is false.

4. **Truth Tables for the Five Connectives**

   Negation

P	$\sim P$
T	F
F	T

Conjunction		Disjunction		Conditional		Biconditional	
$P\,Q$	$P \cdot Q$	$P\,Q$	$P \lor Q$	$P\,Q$	$P \supset Q$	$P\,Q$	$P \equiv Q$
T T	T	T T	T	T T	T	T T	T
T F	F	T F	T	T F	F	T F	F
F T	F	F T	T	F T	T	F T	F
F F	F	F F	F	F F	T	F F	T

5. **Tautologies, Contradictions, and Contingencies**

Tautology: a compound proposition that is necessarily true, simply by virtue of its form (and regardless of the truth values of its component simple propositions). In a truth table for a tautology, the column under the formula's main connective shows all *T*s.

Contradiction: a compound proposition that is necessarily false, simply by virtue of its form (and regardless of the truth values of its component simple propositions). In a truth table to test a contradiction the column under the main connective symbol is all *F*s.

Contingency: a compound proposition that may be either true or false, depending on the truth values of its component simple propositions, and whose truth table displays in the column under the main connective at least one *T* and one *F*.

Two Distinctions for Propositions and One for Statement

1. Necessary vs. Contingent
   Necessarily true propositions are true in every possible world. Contingent propositions are those that may have a different truth value in different possible worlds. Besides the truths of logic, only mathematical and conceptual truths are necessarily true. But propositions about the inner structure or mechanism of natural and scientific kinds are now added to this category in the Kripke-Putnam view.
2. A priori vs. Empirical
   These categories concern how we *know* that a proposition is true or false. Propositions involving logical,

mathematical, and conceptual truths are a priori, or knowable just by thinking, while propositions requiring investigation of the environment are empirical.

3. Analytic vs. Synthetic

A statement is analytic if it is true by the meaning of its parts alone—otherwise, it is synthetic. On a traditional view, all and only statements expressing a priori truths are analytic, and all and only those expressing empirical truths synthetic. But on a Kantian view, the truths of math and some other a priori truths are synthetic.

■ Key Words

Simple proposition
Compound proposition
Truth-functional connective
Negation
Conjunction
Disjunction
Material conditional
Tautology
Contradiction
Contingency
Material equivalence
Material biconditional

Antecedent
Consequent
Sufficient condition
Necessary condition
Propositional logic symbols
Conjunct
Disjunct
Analytic statement
Synthetic statement
Truth table
Law of excluded middle

The Cash Value of Argument Form

In this chapter you'll learn some ways to check the validity of propositional arguments. The topics will include

- The use of truth tables in checking argument forms for validity.
- Some standard valid argument forms in propositional logic: modus ponens, modus tollens, contraposition, hypothetical syllogism, and disjunctive syllogism.
- Formal fallacies: affirming the consequent, denying the antecedent, and affirming a disjunct.
- An introduction to proofs of validity.
- The so-called *reductio ad absurdum* as a tactic for refuting a disputed claim.

12.1 Checking Validity with Truth Tables

As we have seen, truth tables provide a procedure for determining whether a compound proposition is a tautology, contradiction, or contingency. Moreover, they generate that outcome in a mechanical way, applying certain rules that yield a result in a finite number of steps. But they have another use that we'll explore at length here: they allow us to determine mechanically whether an argument is valid or not. Consider, for example, this argument

1   1. Either buffalo are prairie animals or coyotes are.

      2. Buffalo are prairie animals.

      3. Coyotes are not prairie animals.

To determine whether (1) is valid or not requires that we first obtain its argument form. We translate (1)'s premises and conclusion into our standard symbolic notation and obtain:

1'   1. $B \lor C$

      2. B

      3. $\sim C$

Our next step is to transform this vertical listing of premises and conclusion into a horizontal one, using commas to separate premises and writing the symbol $\therefore$, which reads "therefore," in front of the conclusion. This gives us

1" $B \lor C, B \therefore \sim C$

We can now test this argument form for validity with a truth table. We enter the formula at the top of the truth table on its right-hand side and each *different* simple proposition that occurs in that formula on the left-hand side. Next, we assign truth values to those simple propositions, following the algorithm 2^n, which for the formula under consideration is 2^2 (since the simple propositions occurring in it are two, B and C). Once this is done, we focus on the smaller formulas that represent the argument's premises and conclusion, calculating their truth values one at a time. These calculations are performed in the standard way described in Chapter 11. In the final step, we check (in a way we'll presently explain) to see whether the argument is valid or not. Our truth table for checking the validity of (3) above looks like this:

2	B C	B v C, B ∴ ~C
	T T	T T F ←
	T F	T T T
	F T	T F F
	F F	F F T

In (2), a value has been calculated for each formula representing the argument's premises and conclusion. How? By reasoning as follows: the first premise is a disjunction, so its truth value is calculated by applying the truth-value rule for disjunction to B and C, whose values have been assigned on the left-hand side. The first column on the right, placed under the wedge, shows the result of this calculation. Since the second premise, B, is a simple proposition, we *cannot* calculate its values by using any of the truth-value rules for connectives. So we assign to B the same values that we have assigned it in the first column on the left-hand side of the table. That is, we simply transfer those values to the second column on right-hand side of the table (this step can be omitted, since B's values are readily available in the first column on the left and could be read directly from there). We then proceed to calculate the truth value of $\sim C$ by applying the truth-value rule for negation to the values of C, which are displayed in the second column on the left. We write down the results of this calculation under the tilde, as shown by the truth table's third column on the right. We're ready now to check whether the formula on its top right-hand side is a valid argument form. To determine this, we scan horizontally each row displaying the values of premises B v C and B, and conclusion $\sim C$ *(ignoring all vertical columns)*. We are looking for a row where the premises are all true and the conclusion false. And we do find *precisely that* in the first row. This shows the argument represented by the formula to be invalid, since

> If a truth table devised to test the validity of an argument displays at least one row where premises are all true and conclusion false, that proves the invalidity of the argument tested.

BOX 1 ■ WHAT DO TRUTH TABLES HAVE TO DO WITH VALIDITY?

The relation between validity and truth tables is simply this:

■ If it is possible for an argument to have all of its premises true and its conclusion false at once—that is, if this occurs on one or more rows in its truth table—then the form is invalid (as is any argument with that form).

■ But if this is *not* possible—that is, if its truth table shows no such row—then the form is valid.

(Recall that, if an argument is such that it is possible for all of its premises to be true and its conclusion false at once, then the argument is invalid.)

The first row (indicated by an arrow) in the above truth table demonstrates the invalidity of the form being tested (see rationale in Box 1). In this way we show that (1) is invalid. Similar truth tables could be constructed to demonstrate the invalidity of any argument of the same form. For example,

> 3 Either the media lead to public awareness, or public opinion leads to public policy. Since the media lead to public awareness, it is not the case that public opinion leads to public policy.

Since this argument has the same form as (1) above, the results of any correct truth table for checking its validity would be exactly the same as those displayed in (2). (You should construct such a truth table for your own practice.)

Let's now use a truth table to check the validity of another argument:

> 4 1. If Sally voted in the presidential election, then she is a citizen.
> 2. Sally is not a citizen.
> _____
> 3. Sally did not vote in the presidential election.

This has the form,

> 4' $M \supset C, \sim C \therefore \sim M$

First, notice that there are only two *different* simple propositions in this argument form, M and C, each of which occurs twice. Thus we need only four assignments of values (two Ts and two Fs) on the left-hand side of the truth table and four horizontal rows. The next step is to calculate the truth value of (4')'s premises and conclusion. Each of these is a compound proposition, for which we'll write the truth value in the column under its connective symbol: in the first premise, under ⊃, and in the second premise and conclusion under ~. In this argument there are no simple propositions; to test for validity, therefore, we scan *only* the rows in columns under the connectives: in the premises, these are the columns under the horseshoe ⊃ and the tilde ~, and in the conclusion, it's the column under the tilde ~. We're looking for a row in which *all the premises* are true and the conclusion false, which would indicate invalidity. But the scan shows that there is no such row in this truth table.

5	M C	M ⊃ C,	~C ∴	~M
	T T	T	F	F
	T F	F	T	F
	F T	T	F	T
	F F	T	T	T

The absence of such a row means that (4'), and therefore also (4), is valid. This test proves validity because the truth table gives an exhaustive list of all possible combinations of truth values of the premises and conclusion, and no horizontal row shows that the former can be true and the latter false at once. Thus in all arguments with (4')'s form, the premises entail the conclusion. Consider,

6 If Professor Tina Hare is at the University of Liverpool, then she works in England. Professor Tina Hare doesn't work in England. Thus, Professor Tina Hare is not at the University of Liverpool.

7 If the Earth is not a planet, then Mars is not a planet. But Mars is a planet. Hence, the Earth is a planet.

For your own practice, construct a truth table for these arguments to check their validity. You'll see that their final result will be exactly like that in (5) above.

Let's try one more argument, this time more complex. For example,

> **8** Since France is not a member of the union, it follows that Britain is not. For if France is not a member, then either the Netherlands is or Britain is.

We can reconstruct (8) as

> **8'** 1. France is not a member of the union.
> 2. If France is not a member of the union, then either the Netherlands is a member of the union or Britain is a member of the union.
> _____
> 3. Britain is not a member of the union.

which has the form,

> **8"** ~F, ~F ⊃ (N v B) ∴ ~B

To test (8") for validity, we first note that since three different simple propositions occur in it, the truth table will need eight horizontal lines. Once we write down all possible combinations of truth values for these simple propositions on the left-hand side of the truth table, we then calculate the truth values of premises and conclusion and enter the results under each connective symbol on the right-hand side. Here is the truth table, with the rows showing the argument's invalidity indicated by an arrow:

9	F N B	~F,	~F ⊃ (N v B)	∴ ~B
	T T T	F	F T T	F
	T T F	F	F T T	T
	T F T	F	F T T	F
	T F F	F	F T F	T
	F T T	T	T T T	F ←
	F T F	T	T T T	T
	F F T	T	T T T	F ←
	F F F	T	T F F	T

The more complex formula in (9)'s right-hand side is the one representing the argument's second premise: it's got three connectives in it. How do we determine which is the most important?

We do this reading carefully and looking at the parentheses: they tell us that it is the horseshoe placed between ~*F* and (*N* v *B*). But in order to determine the truth values in the column under the horseshoe, we first have to know the possible truth values of its antecedent, ~*F*, and its consequent, (*N* v *B*). Once we have the value of ~*F*, which can be obtained by applying the rule for the truth value of negation to *F* on the left-hand side of the truth table, we enter those values under ~*F*, the first premise of the argument (so they don't need to be written twice if desired). The value of (*N* v *B*) can be obtained by applying to the values of *N* and *B* the rule for the truth value of the disjunction on the left-hand side of the truth table. To calculate the value of ~*B*, we proceed in a manner similar to that in which we calculated the values of ~*F*. Once this is done, then, ignoring all the other columns, we scan each horizontal row showing the truth value for each premise and conclusion on the right-hand side of the truth table. We ask ourselves: Is there any horizontal row in which both premises are true and the conclusion false? And the answer is yes! It happens twice: on rows 5 and 7. Thus the argument form (8″) has been proved invalid; and so any argument that has it, such as (8) above, is invalid.

BOX 2 ■ HOW TO CHECK VALIDITY WITH TRUTH TABLES

- When we use a truth table to check an argument's validity, we first write the formula capturing the argument's form at the top on the right.
- Each different type of proposition that occurs in that formula goes at the top on the left.
- The rows under the formula itself offer an exhaustive list of possible combinations of truth values for premises and conclusion.
- To decide whether an argument form is valid or not, we scan each row under the formula.
- Any row showing that there is one configuration of truth values in which premises are true and the conclusion false proves that the argument form is invalid.
- If there is no such row, then the argument form is valid.

Exercises

I. Review Questions

1. How do we construct a truth table to check an argument form for validity?
2. In a truth table to check the validity of an argument, how do we tell whether the argument is valid or not?
3. What does it mean for an argument to be valid?
4. Why is a truth table a mechanical procedure for checking the validity of an argument?
5. If any such truth table's rows show at least one false premise, is that relevant to determining the argument's validity? If so, how? If not, why not?

II. For each of the following argument forms, construct a truth table to determine whether it is valid or not.

1. $H \supset \sim K, \sim K \therefore H$

   SAMPLE ANSWER: Invalid

H K	$H \supset \sim K, \sim K \therefore H$
T T	F F F
T F	T T T
F T	T F F
F F	T T T ←

2. $L \vee N, \sim N \therefore L$ _____

3. $R \supset (M \supset R) \therefore M \vee R$ _____

* 4. $J, \sim J \vee \sim N \therefore \sim N$ _____

5. $\sim(B \equiv A) \supset \sim L \therefore L \supset (B \equiv A)$ _____

6. $D \vee (\sim M \supset \sim D) \therefore M \supset D$ _____

7. $\sim(G \bullet E), \sim G \therefore E \bullet \sim G$ _____

* 8. $\sim C \vee \sim B, \sim(B \bullet A) \therefore A \vee C$ _____

9. $(F \supset \sim N) \bullet \sim(F \supset \sim N) \therefore \sim N$ _____

*10. $\sim B, \sim(\sim K \equiv \sim H) \therefore K \supset \sim H$ _____

11. $(D \vee M) \supset (M \vee D) \therefore M \vee D$ _____

12. ~[(~A • H) v (H ⊃ ~B)] ∴ ~A • ~H _____

*13. K • (~E v O), ~E ⊃ ~K ∴ O _____

*14. E ⊃ A, ~~A ∴ ~E v ~A _____

15. A ⊃ B ∴ ~(~B ⊃ ~A) _____

16. ~M v O, M ∴ O _____

17. A • B ∴ ~A _____

18. C ⊃ D ∴ D ⊃ C _____

19. C ⊃ D ∴ ~C v D _____

20. C ⊃ D, ~C ∴ ~D _____

21. A ≡ B ∴ [(A ⊃ B) • (B ⊃ A)] _____

*22. H • (~I v J), J ⊃ ~H ∴ J _____

*23. ~O, A ⊃ B ∴ ~O • B _____

24. C ⊃ D, D ∴ C _____

25. C ∴ C v D _____

III. **Translate each of the following arguments into symbolic notation, then construct a truth table to determine whether it is valid or invalid.**

1. Henry's running for mayor implies that Bart will not move to Cleveland, for if Henry runs for mayor, then Jill will resign, and Jill's resigning implies that Bart will not move to Cleveland. (H, J, B)

SAMPLE ANSWER: Valid

H	J	B		H ⊃ J,	J ⊃	~B	∴	H ⊃	~B
T	T	T		T	F	F		F	F
T	T	F		T	T	T		T	T
T	F	T		F	T	F		F	F
T	F	F		F	T	T		T	T
F	T	T		T	F	F		T	F
F	T	F		T	T	T		T	T
F	F	T		T	T	F		T	F
F	F	F		T	T	T		T	T

2. If Quebec is a part of Canada, then some Canadians are voters. If Ontario is a part of Canada, then some Canadians are voters. Hence, if Quebec is a part of Canada, then Ontario is a part of Canada. (*B*, *C*, *O*) _____

* 3. Algeria will not intervene politically if and only if Britain will not send economic aid. Thus Algeria will intervene politically unless France will not veto the treaty, for Britain will not send economic aid only if France will veto the treaty. (*A*, *B*, *F*) _____

4. Neither Detroit nor Ann Arbor has cold weather in February. If Michigan sometimes has snow in winter, then either Detroit or Ann Arbor has cold weather in February. Therefore it is not the case that Michigan sometimes has snow in winter. (*D*, *A*, *M*) _____

5. Either the examinations in this course are too easy or the students are extremely bright. In fact the students are extremely bright. From this it follows that the examinations in this course are not too easy. (*E*, *B*) _____

* 6. If John is a member of the Elks lodge, then either Sam used to work in Texas or Timothy is a police officer. But it is not the case that Sam used to work in Texas and Timothy is not a police officer. Therefore John is not a member of the Elks lodge. (*J*, *A*, *I*) _____

* 7. Both antelopes and Rotarians are found in North America. But Rotarians are found in North America if and only if Frenchmen rarely drink gin. It follows that if it is not the case that Frenchmen rarely drink gin, then antelopes are not found in North America. (*A*, *O*, *F*)

_____

8. Dogs are not always loyal. For rattlesnakes are always to be avoided unless either dogs are always loyal or cats sometimes behave strangely. (*D*, *A*, *C*) _____

9. If either Romans are not fast drivers or Nigeria does have a large population, then it is not the case that both Nigeria does have a large population and Argentinians are coffee drinkers. Hence, Romans are fast drivers, for Argentinians are coffee drinkers only if Nigeria does not have a large population. (*F*, *N*, *A*) _____

*10. We may infer that mandolins are easy to play but French horns are difficult instruments. For mandolins are easy to play if and only if either didgeridoos are played only by men or French horns are difficult instruments. But if French horns being difficult instruments implies that didgeridoos are not played only by men, then it is not the case that mandolins are easy to play. (*M*, *F*, *D*) _____

11. If both Ellen is good at math and Mary is good at writing, then Cecil is a pest. It follows that Mary is good at writing. For either Cecil is not a pest unless Mary is not good at writing, or both Ellen is not good at math and Cecil is a pest. But Cecil is a pest if and only if Ellen is good at math. (*E*, *M*, *C*) _____

*12. Penguins are not commonly found in Arabia. For manatees like being under water unless penguins being commonly found in Arabia implies that alligators do not like being under water. But penguins are commonly found in Arabia if and only if neither alligators nor manatees like being under water. (*E*, *M*, *A*) _____

12.2 Reviewing Some Standard Argument Forms

Being able to recognize forms that are always valid and forms that are always invalid can be helpful in deciding whether certain arguments are valid or not. Any argument that is an instance of one or more valid forms is itself valid. At the same time, any argument having an invalid form is itself invalid. Where any such form has been identified, no truth table is needed. Once we have identified some such forms, we know that the argument is valid (or invalid). Let's first consider five basic valid argument forms that we've already encountered briefly in Chapter 5.

Modus Ponens

A common valid argument form with a conditional premise, another premise that affirms the antecedent of that conditional, and a conclusion that asserts its consequent is:

10
1. $P \supset Q$
2. P
3. Q

This form is called *modus ponens,* as is any argument that exemplifies it. Because the antecedent in a material conditional expresses a sufficient condition for the truth of the consequent and the antecedent is asserted as being true in a modus ponens, any argument with this form is valid. In other words, if it's true that P implies Q and also true that P, then Q follows necessarily.

Arguments (11) and (12), which are instances of modus ponens, are therefore valid.

11 1. If José is mayor, then he is a public official.
2. José is mayor.
3. He is a public official.

12 1. Groundhogs are rodents.
2. Groundhogs are rodents only if they are mammals.
3. Groundhogs are mammals.

Recall that "only if" is just another way of expressing "if ... then ... ," and that the simple proposition preceding "only if" is the antecedent. In (12) the conditional premise comes second and its antecedent is affirmed in the first premise, but that does not affect its status as an instance of modus ponens. Plainly, (12) is valid. Now consider this argument:

13 Since Joey's conviction implies that his defense was a failure, therefore his defense was a failure. After all, Joey was convicted.

Here there are two premise indicators, "since" and "after all," and a conclusion indicator, "therefore." We can reconstruct this argument as

14 1. Joey was convicted.
2. Joey's conviction implies that his defense was a failure.
3. Joey's defense was a failure.

Since "implies" is just another way of expressing a conditional, (14) can be recast as

15 1. Joey was convicted.
2. If Joey was convicted, then his defense was a failure.
3. Joey's defense was a failure.

Either way, the argument has the valid form,

15' 1. J
2. $J \supset D$
3. D

which is a modus ponens.

Modus Tollens

Another very common valid argument form is *modus tollens*: it has two premises, one a conditional and the other a denial of its consequent, and a conclusion that denies the conditional's antecedent:

16 1. $P \supset Q$
2. $\sim Q$
3. $\sim P$

Recall that, in a conditional, the consequent expresses a necessary condition for the truth of the antecedent; thus, denying the consequent entails the denial of the antecedent. Therefore any argument that is an instance of this form is valid. For example,

17 Harry will not graduate in May, because he'll graduate only if he passes English lit, and he will not pass English lit.

Grammatically speaking, this is of course a single sentence with three statements in it. But there is an argument here: the premise indicator, "because," tells us that the last two statements are premises; thus the first statement is the conclusion. Arranged in standard logical order, they are

17' 1. Harry will graduate in May only if he passes English lit.
2. He will not pass English lit.
3. Harry will not graduate in May.

Once we've replaced "only if" by the standard "if ... then ...," the argument reads,

18 1. If Harry will graduate in May, then he will pass English lit.
2. He will not pass English lit.
3. Harry will not graduate in May.

Thus (17) and (18) have the same valid argument form, a modus tollens, which can be represented as

18' 1. $H \supset L$
2. $\sim L$
3. $\sim H$

Finally, consider

> **19** Microorganisms can cause infections. But if germs are not to be avoided, then microorganisms cannot cause infections. Hence, germs are to be avoided.

Here the argument form is also a modus tollens:

19' 1. M
2. $\sim G \supset \sim M$
3. G

Now notice that pairs of negations cancel each other out. Thus, M in premise 1 is logically equivalent to $\sim\sim M$. But then premise 1 is the negation of premise 2's consequent, $\sim M$. And conclusion 3 negates its antecedent (since G is equivalent to $\sim\sim G$, it is the negation of $\sim G$). But that is exactly the form of a modus tollens!

Contraposition

Contraposition is an argument form consisting of a single premise that is a conditional and a conclusion that switches the premise's antecedent and consequent and denies each. Here is the form:

20 1. $P \supset Q$
2. $\sim Q \supset \sim P$

Why is this form valid? For the same reason modus tollens is: since the consequent of a material conditional expresses a necessary condition for the truth of the antecedent, it necessarily follows that the denial of the consequent implies the denial of the antecedent.

Thus we have

> **21** 1. If Anna is a revolutionary, then Anna is opposed to the established order.
> 2. If Anna is not opposed to the established order, then Anna is not a revolutionary,

which is valid, since its form is

21' 1. $A \supset O$
2. $\sim O \supset \sim A$

Thus, (21) is an instance of contraposition and is therefore valid.

Hypothetical Syllogism

Hypothetical syllogism is a valid argument form featuring three conditionals: two in the premises and one in the conclusion. A closer look at this form reveals that premise 1's consequent is premise 2's antecedent and premise 1's antecedent together with premise 2's consequent are, respectively, the antecedent and consequent of the conclusion:

22 1. $P \supset Q$
    2. $Q \supset R$
    3. $P \supset R$

Obviously, since the antecedent of a conditional expresses a sufficient condition for the truth of its consequent, when P is a sufficient condition for Q, and Q a sufficient condition for R, it follows that P is a sufficient condition for R. For example:

23 1. If Elaine is a newspaper reporter, then she is a journalist.
    2. If Elaine is a journalist, then she knows how to write.
    3. If Elaine is a newspaper reporter, then she knows how to write.

This argument is an instance of hypothetical syllogism and so is valid. Notice that the order of the premises does not matter for the argument to have the form of a hypothetical syllogism. Consider,

23' 1. Elaine is a journalist only if she knows how to write.
     2. That Elaine is a newspaper reporter implies that she is a journalist.
     3. That Elaine is a newspaper reporter implies that she knows how to write.

Both (23) and (23') have the form

23" 1. $E \supset J$
     2. $J \supset H$
     3. $E \supset H$

which is that of a hypothetical syllogism.

Disjunctive Syllogism

Finally, in our sample of valid argument forms, there is one that does not use conditionals at all: disjunctive syllogism. Here, one premise presents a disjunction and the other denies one of the two disjuncts, from which the affirmation of the other disjunct then follows as the conclusion. A disjunctive syllogism that is in the standard order (with the disjunctive premise first) may be correctly represented in one or the other of these two ways, depending on which disjunct is denied:

24

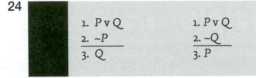

1. $P \vee Q$
2. $\sim P$
3. Q

1. $P \vee Q$
2. $\sim Q$
3. P

The principle here is: Given the truth-functional definition of inclusive disjunction, if a premise that is an inclusive disjunction is true but one of its disjuncts false, it follows that the other disjunct is true. Thus, any argument with one of (24)'s forms is valid. For example,

25 1. Either my car was towed away by the police or my car was stolen.
2. My car was not towed away by the police.
3. My car was stolen.

which plainly has the form,

25' 1. $C \vee O$
2. $\sim C$
3. O

This is an instance of disjunctive syllogism and is therefore valid. Here again, the order of the premises does not matter; so (25') may also be expressed as

25" 1. $\sim C$
2. $C \vee O$
3. O

which equally illustrates a disjunctive syllogism.

One more thing: remember that disjunction can also be expressed using "unless" instead of "or." Thus we might have

26 1. Eddy will watch *The Simpsons* tonight unless he plays football.

2. He will not play football tonight.

3. Eddy will watch *The Simpsons* tonight.

which we could symbolize as

26' 1. $E \lor F$

2. $\sim F$

3. E

And this plainly is a disjunctive syllogism. Knowing this, we already know that (26) is valid.

When we set about trying to analyze propositional arguments, it's immensely helpful to be able to recognize these five basic valid argument forms, because any time you find an argument that has one, *you thereby know that it's valid!* No other procedure is required.

Exercises

IV. Review Questions

1. Can you name the five valid argument forms of propositional arguments discussed here?
2. For each of these five valid forms, can you say precisely what the form is?
3. Given what a material conditional is, it's easy to see why the above four valid forms that employ conditionals are valid. Explain.
4. Which of the valid forms employs disjunction? And why is the form valid?
5. Suppose the order of the premises in a valid propositional argument is changed. Does that affect the validity of the argument?
6. When you have established that an argument is a modus tollens, what have you discovered about that argument? Explain.

V. For each of the following argument forms, determine which one of the above five valid forms it exemplifies.

1. $A \supset \sim B$

A

$\sim B$

SAMPLE ANSWER: Modus ponens

2. $K \lor N \lor A$
$\dfrac{\sim A}{(K \lor N)}$

*3. $L \supset \sim M$
$\dfrac{B \supset L}{B \supset \sim M}$

4. $\sim(F \cdot H)$
$\dfrac{A \supset (F \cdot H)}{\sim A}$

*5. $\sim E \supset \sim D$
$\dfrac{\sim E}{\sim D}$

*6. $(A \lor L) \supset (B \cdot C)$
$\dfrac{}{\sim(B \cdot C) \supset \sim(A \lor L)}$

7. $\sim C \lor \sim A$
$\dfrac{A}{\sim C}$

*8. $(A \cdot \sim F) \supset \sim G$
$\dfrac{G}{\sim(A \cdot \sim F)}$

9. $J \supset A$
$\dfrac{A \supset \sim C}{J \supset \sim C}$

10. $\sim H \supset \sim(E \lor A)$
$\dfrac{}{(E \lor A) \supset H}$

11. $\sim B \equiv C$
$\dfrac{(\sim B \equiv C) \supset \sim A}{\sim A}$

*12. $A \lor (G \lor F)$
$\dfrac{\sim(G \lor F)}{A}$

VI. In this section, five valid argument forms were discussed. Symbolize each of the following arguments and determine which of those five forms it exemplifies.

1. Wynton Marsalis is an authority on music, for he is a famous jazz trumpeter who is equally well known as a performer of classical

music. But if he is a famous jazz trumpeter who is equally well known as a performer of classical music, then Wynton Marsalis is an authority on music. (F, A)

SAMPLE ANSWER: $F \supset A, F \therefore A$ modus ponens

2. Ernie is a liar or Ronald is not a liar. It is not the case that Ronald is not a liar. Therefore Ernie is a liar. (E, L) _____

* 3. If Staten Islanders are not Mets fans then Manhattan's being full of fast talkers implies that Queens is not the home of sober taxpayers. Thus, if it is not the case that Manhattan's being full of fast talkers implies that Queens is not the home of sober taxpayers, then it is not the case that Staten Islanders are not Mets fans. (I, M, H)

_____

4. Penelope is not a registered Democrat. For Penelope is a registered Democrat only if she is eligible to vote in the United States. But she is not eligible to vote in the United States. (D, E) _____

* 5. If Democrats are always compassionate, then Republicans are always honest. For if Democrats are always compassionate, then they sometimes vote for candidates who are moderates. But if they sometimes vote for candidates who are moderates, then Republicans are always honest. (D, M, H) _____

* 6. If Emma is a true pacifist, then she is not a supporter of war. Emma is a true pacifist. It follows that she is not a supporter of war. (E, A)

_____

7. If this cheese was not made in Switzerland, then it's not real Emmentaler. Therefore, if it is real Emmentaler, then it was made in Switzerland. (C, E) _____

* 8. Either gulls sometimes fly inland or hyenas are not dangerous. But hyenas are dangerous. So, gulls sometimes fly inland. (G, H)

_____

9. If both Enriquez enters the race and Warshawsky resigns, then Bosworth will win the election. But if Bosworth will win the election, then Mendes will not win the election. Thus, if both Enriquez enters the race and Warshawsky resigns, then Mendes will not win the election. (E, A, B, M) _____

*10. Microbes are not creating chronic diseases such as diabetes, multiple sclerosis, and even schizophrenia. Hospitals need to improve their cleaning practices only if it is the case that microbes are creating many chronic diseases such as diabetes, multiple sclerosis, and even schizophrenia. It follows that hospitals need not improve their cleaning practices. (*M, H*) _____

11. California farmers grow either vegetables that thrive in warm weather or citrus fruits and bananas. Since they don't grow citrus fruits and bananas, they must grow vegetables that thrive in warm weather. (*A, C, B*) _____

12. Steve's attacker was not a great white shark. An attack of the sort he suffered last week must be by either a great white shark or by a shark of another type that felt threatened in the presence of a swimmer unknowingly wading into its feeding area. Therefore Steve was attacked by a shark of another type that felt threatened in the presence of a swimmer unknowingly wading into its feeding area. (*G, A*)

_____

VII. YOUR OWN THINKING LAB

1. Construct an argument of your own for each of the argument forms listed in exercise V.

12.3 Formal Fallacies

Already we have seen that arguments may have defects of various kinds that cause them to fail. Types of defects that undermine arguments constitute the so-called fallacies, which can be grouped under one or the other of these categories:

■ *Formal fallacies*: arguments that are invalid by virtue of having a form that appears to be one of the valid argument forms of propositional arguments but is not.
■ *Informal fallacies*: arguments that are defective by virtue of other common errors of reasoning that may involve either an argument's form or content.

All formal fallacies have in common that they occur in an argument that has a superficial similarity to some valid form but departs from that form in some specifiable way. They are therefore instances of failed deductive arguments. Recall that an argument is invalid if it is possible that an argument with the same form could have true premises and a false conclusion. To prove the invalidity of an argument, then, it is enough to find a single case of an argument with exactly the same logical form whose premises are true and conclusion false. Consider the following argument:

> **27** 1. If the messenger came, then the bell rang about noon.
> 2. The bell rang about noon.
> _____
> 3. The messenger came.

This argument is invalid because it is possible for its premises to be true and its conclusion false. Even if the premises and conclusion all happen to be true in a certain case, there are other scenarios in which arguments with an identical form could have true premises and a false conclusion. Suppose that the messenger didn't come but the bell did ring about noon, though it was a neighbor who rang it. In this scenario, (27)'s premises are true and its conclusion false. Thus, the scenario amounts to a counterexample that shows the invalidity of (27).

It is often possible to find real-life counterexamples that prove the invalidity of certain arguments. Yet we could do without such counterexamples, since to show that an argument is invalid, it is sufficient to describe a "possible world" (which may or may not be the actual world—it's simply a scenario involving no internal contradiction) where an argument with the same form would have true premises and a false conclusion.

Thus the invalidity of an argument can be proved in the way just shown: one tries to describe a scenario where the premises of the argument in question are true and its conclusion is false. If such a scenario is not forthcoming, we may extract the argument form—which, in the case of (27), is

> **27'** 1. $P \supset Q$
> 2. Q
> _____
> 3. P

and try to find an example of an argument with the same form that in some possible scenario would have true premises and a false conclusion. For example,

> **28** 1. If George W. Bush is a Democrat, then he is a member of a political party.
> 2. George W. Bush is a member of a political party.
> _____
> 3. George W. Bush is a Democrat.

(28) shows that, in a scenario where the possible world is the actual world, an argument with the same form as (27) has true premises and a false conclusion. By the definition of invalidity, (28) is invalid. At the same time, it amounts to a counterexample to any argument with the same form.

Affirming the Consequent

The above notoriously invalid arguments are both instances of *affirming the consequent.*

> Affirming the consequent is the fallacy committed by any argument featuring a conditional premise, another premise affirming that conditional's consequent, and a conclusion affirming its antecedent.

Affirming a proposition amounts to saying that it is true. In arguments that commit this fallacy, what is affirmed is the consequent of a material conditional. This always expresses only a *necessary but not a sufficient* condition for the truth of the conditional's antecedent. As a result, the truth of the consequent never guarantees that of the antecedent (which is the conclusion in affirming the consequent). Here are some more examples of arguments that affirm the consequent and so are invalid:

29 1. If I dieted, then I lost weight.
   2. I lost weight.
   3. I dieted.

30 1. If I got a job, then I have money.
   2. I have money.
   3. I got a job.

31 1. If I drank coffee, then there's caffeine in my bloodstream.
   2. There's caffeine in my bloodstream.
   3. I drank coffee.

In each of these arguments, it is possible that both premises could be true and the conclusion false at once. Therefore in none of them do the premises entail the conclusion.

> ### BOX 3 ■ HOW TO AVOID AFFIRMING THE CONSEQUENT
>
> In a modus ponens, a premise affirms the antecedent (not the consequent) of the other premise (while the conclusion affirms the consequent).
>
> ■ Thus, watch out for any argument that appears to be a modus ponens but is not, since *its conditional premise's consequent is affirmed by the other premise* (while its antecedent is affirmed by the argument's conclusion).

Denying the Antecedent

Another formal fallacy that may undermine propositional arguments is *denying the antecedent.*

> Denying the antecedent is the fallacy committed by any argument featuring a conditional premise, another premise denying that conditional's antecedent, and a conclusion denying its consequent.

Any argument that commits this fallacy has the invalid form

32   1. $P \supset Q$
      2. $\sim P$
      3. $\sim Q$

Suppose we run across an argument of this sort:

33   1. If Oscar is a violinist with the Boston Symphony, then he can read music.
      2. In fact, Oscar is not a violinist with the Boston Symphony.
      3. He cannot read music.

Clearly, this argument is invalid. Oscar's being a violinist with the Boston Symphony Orchestra is a sufficient condition of his being able to read music (if he's in the BSO, that *guarantees* that he can read music). But it's not a necessary condition, since lots of people can read music who are not in the Boston Symphony! Thus,

BOX 4 ■ HOW TO AVOID DENYING THE ANTECEDENT

In a modus tollens, the consequent of the conditional premise is denied by the other premise (while its antecedent is denied by the conclusion).

■ Thus, watch out for any argument that appears to be a modus tollens but is not, since *its conditional premise's antecedent is denied by the other premise* (while its consequent is denied by the argument's conclusion).

the conclusion "Oscar cannot read music" does not follow with necessity. In brief, (33) is invalid because it has (32)'s form: it commits the fallacy of denying the antecedent. More generally, any argument that instantiates this fallacy is invalid because denying the antecedent of the conditional premise amounts to saying that that antecedent is false. But the antecedent of a material conditional expresses a sufficient *though not a necessary* condition for the truth of the consequent: so the antecedent could be false and the consequent true. Thus, from a denial of the antecedent of a conditional, it does not follow that its consequent is also to be denied.

Affirming a Disjunct

Another formal fallacy is *affirming a disjunct*:

Affirming a disjunct is the fallacy committed by any argument featuring a premise that is an inclusive disjunction, another premise affirming one of the disjuncts, and a conclusion denying the other disjunct.

This fallacy is committed by any argument of one of these forms:

34
1. $P \lor Q$	or	1. $P \lor Q$
2. P		2. Q
3. $\sim Q$		3. $\sim P$

Affirming a disjunct is an invalid form because, as we saw earlier in our discussion of the truth-functional connectives, "or" is to be understood in the *inclusive* sense (i.e., either P or Q or both)—not the exclusive sense (i.e., either P or Q but not both). The inclusive disjunction is true in all cases except where both disjuncts are false. Thus, assuming that a certain inclusive disjunction is true, denying one disjunct (which amounts to saying that it is false) entails that the other disjunct must be true. But *affirming* one of its disjuncts (which amounts to saying that it is true) does *not* entail the denial of the other—that is, it does not entail that the other is false. (In the case of an *exclusive disjunction*, what we are calling "affirming a disjunct" would not be a fallacy.) Consider the following example:

35 1. Either my car was towed away by the police or my car was stolen.
2. My car was in fact towed away by the police.
3. My car was not stolen.

Is there any way this conclusion could be false if both premises were true? Yes! A possible scenario is that thieves came in the night and broke into my car, then drove it to an illegal parking space, from which the police towed it! If that were the case, then both of (35)'s premises would be true and its conclusion false at once. Thus the conclusion does not follow *necessarily* from the premises—it is not entailed by them. So the argument is invalid. But the thing to notice is that (35) instantiates the invalid form (34), affirming a disjunct: since the "either ... or ..." connective in

---

BOX 5 ■ HOW TO AVOID AFFIRMING THE CONSEQUENT

Note that in a disjunctive syllogism, a premise denies one of the disjuncts of the other premise, and the conclusion asserts the other.

■ Thus, watch out for any argument that appears to be a disjunctive syllogism but is not, since one of its premises asserts a disjunct of the other premise while its conclusion denies the other.

BOX 6 ▪ SUMMARY: SOME FORMAL FALLACIES

Affirming the Consequent	Affirming a Disjunct
$P \supset Q$	$P \lor Q$
$\underline{Q}$	$\underline{P}$
P	$\sim Q$
	$P \lor Q$
Denying the Antecedent	$\underline{Q}$
$P \supset Q$	$\sim P$
$\underline{\sim P}$	
$\sim$Not Q	

---

(35) is inclusive, to affirm one of the two alternatives does not entail a denial of the other. In any case where the "or" has this sense—that is, where it represents the truth-functional disjunction connective as defined in the last chapter—arguments with (34)'s forms commit a formal fallacy and are invalid.

We have identified, then, three types of invalid forms a propositional argument might have which constitute three types of formal fallacy. Whenever you find an argument that has one, a truth table is not required. All you need to do to prove invalidity is simply to show that the argument has one of these forms: affirming the consequent, denying the antecedent, or affirming a disjunct. If you can keep separate in your mind these three invalid forms and the five valid forms discussed earlier, you should find it much easier to distinguish valid and invalid propositional arguments.

Exercises

VIII. Review Questions

1. One method of proving invalidity is the counterexample method. What is this method?
2. What is a possible world?
3. What is a formal fallacy?
4. Can you name three invalid argument forms recognized in propositional logic?

5. How can we know that a form is invalid?
6. How does the fallacy of affirming a disjunct bear on inclusive disjunction?
7. How does affirming a disjunct differ from disjunctive syllogism?
8. How does affirming the consequent differ from modus ponens?
9. How does denying the antecedent differ from modus tollens?
10. What's the cash value of recognizing that an argument commits a formal fallacy?

IX. Some of the following are formal fallacies and some are valid arguments. Indicate which is which, identifying any fallacy and valid argument form by name.

1. If the defendant's 1999 Toyota sedan was used as the getaway car in the robbery, then it was not in the mechanic's garage with a cracked engine block on the date of the crime. But it was in the mechanic's garage with a cracked engine block on that date! From this it follows that the defendant's 1999 Toyota sedan was not used as the getaway car in the robbery.

SAMPLE ANSWER: Modus tollens; valid

2. If this car has faulty brakes, then it's dangerous to drive. But this car does not have faulty brakes. Therefore it's not dangerous to drive. _____

* 3. If our public officials take bribes, then there is corruption in our government. But if the mayor and several city council members were paid to support the appropriations bill, then our public officials take bribes. So, if the mayor and several city council members were paid to support the appropriations bill, then there is corruption in our government. _____

4. Barry is a union member, for he will not cross the picket line. And if he were a union member then he would not cross the picket line. _____

* 5. Ireland does not allow abortion. Either Ireland allows abortion or Ireland is a conservative country. Hence, Ireland is a conservative country. _____

6. Either we'll stop polluting the environment or life on earth will eventually die out. But in fact we will stop polluting the environment. Thus, life on earth will not eventually die out. _____

* 7. If Desmond is a successful film critic, then he is a good writer. But Desmond is not a successful film critic. Therefore he is not a good writer. _____

8. These sculptures are expensive only if they're rare. So it must be that they are rare, since they're very expensive. _____

* 9. If cardiac surgeons are Mercedes-Benz owners, then they have driver's licenses; so if cardiac surgeons don't have drivers licenses, then they are not Mercedes-Benz owners. _____

10. If Bob has no record of military service, then he is not a combat veteran. It follows that Bob has no record of military service, since he is not a combat veteran. _____

*11. Either Darwin's theory provides a roughly accurate account of the origin of the human species, or the method of carbon-14 dating that has been used to establish the age of hominid fossils is not reliable. But that method is reliable. Therefore Darwin's theory provides a roughly accurate account of the origin of the human species. _____

12. Atkinson will run for reelection unless Hernandez does. Accordingly, Atkinson will not run, because Hernandez will run for reelection. _____

*13. Zebras are mammals. But if zebras are mammals, then they are warm-blooded creatures. From this we may infer that zebras are warm-blooded creatures. _____

14. Since clams are not mammals, they are shellfish. For if clams are shellfish, then they are not mammals. _____

*15. If Frank Sinatra was born in Brooklyn, then he was a New Yorker. But Sinatra was not a New Yorker, so he was not born in Brooklyn. _____

16. Jack will buy either a bulldog or a Labrador retriever. But in fact Jack will buy a Labrador retriever. Therefore Jack will not buy a bulldog. _____

*17. If Tom's barbecued steaks are tender, then they weren't overcooked. Since Tom's barbecued steaks weren't overcooked, we may conclude that they are tender. _____

18. If this scarf isn't too colorful, then Anne will like it. But this scarf is too colorful. Therefore Anne will not like it. _____

*19. Barbados is sunny; however, London often has rain. But if it is not the case that both Barbados is sunny and London often has rain, then Nebraska is densely populated. Therefore Nebraska is not densely populated. _____

20. Either tortillas or tamales are tasty with salsa picante. Tortillas are tasty with salsa picante. Therefore tamales are not tasty with salsa picante. _____

X. **Each of the following arguments has either a valid or an invalid form of the sort discussed above. Represent it in symbolic notation, name its form, and say whether it's valid or invalid.**

1. Ankara is the capital of Turkey. Consequently, Turkey's capital is in Asia Minor, for if Ankara is the capital of Turkey, then Turkey's capital is in Asia Minor. (*A, C*)

   SAMPLE ANSWER: $A \supset C$, A ∴ C; modus ponens; valid

2. Either Tony Soprano will finally get whacked or *The Sopranos* will have another hit season on television. But Tony will not get whacked. So *The Sopranos* will have another hit season on television. (*D, H*)

   _____

3. Bengal tigers are not seen anywhere in the world today only if they are extinct. But Bengal tigers are not extinct; hence they are sometimes seen in the world today. (*B, E*) _____

* 4. If Eminem is a hiphop artist, then he is a musician. But Eminem is not a hiphop artist. We can infer that he is not a musician. (*E, M*)

   _____

5. If belief in evolution is not prevalent in America, then high school science education is ineffective. It follows that if high school science education is effective, then belief in evolution is prevalent in America. (*B, E*) _____

* 6. Homer Simpson will vote in the election unless he decides that all the candidates are crooks. Since he has in fact decided that all the candidates are crooks, Homer will not vote in the election. (*H, D*)

   _____

* 7. That fruit bats sleep in the daytime implies that they fly only at night; for if fruit bats sleep in the daytime, then they are nocturnal creatures, and if they are nocturnal creatures, then they fly only at night. (*B, N, F*) _____

8. Plutonium is radioactive, for either plutonium is radioactive or both argon and cobalt are too; but it is not the case that both argon and cobalt are radioactive. (*F, A, C*) _____

9. If Christina Aguilera is a big star, then her songs are featured on MTV. It follows that Christina Aguilera's songs are featured on MTV, since she is a big star. (*C, H*) _____

10. That Eric is a NASCAR fan implies that he doesn't mind loud noise. Thus if Eric does mind loud noise, then he is not a NASCAR fan. (*E, H*) _____

*11. If Boris is a member of the Communist Party, then he is not an enthusiastic supporter of big business. But Boris is an enthusiastic supporter of big business, so he is not a member of the Communist Party. (*M, E*) _____

*12. Jason would buy a house in Acapulco only if he won the lottery. Since he did win the lottery, it follows that he will buy a house in Acapulco. (*J, L*) _____

XI. YOUR OWN THINKING LAB

1. Give two examples of your own illustrating the following: affirming the consequent, denying the antecedent, and affirming a disjunct.

2. Use the method of counterexample to explain why your examples are invalid.

3. For each of the propositional arguments below, give its form and standard name (if any), decide whether it is valid or not, and propose an argument of your own with exactly the same form.

   A. If the cold front is here, then we don't go to the beach. Thus, if we go the beach, then the cold front is not here.

   B. Either the small apples or the ripe ones are on sale. The ripe apples are on sale. Therefore the small apples are not on sale.

   C. She is at Lalo's if her class is over. She is at Lalo's. Therefore her class is over.

   D. I don't see my glasses there. If I don't see them there, then they are not there. Hence they are not there.

   E. If Ptolemy was right, then the sun and planets orbit the Earth. But it is not the case that the sun and planets orbit the Earth. Therefore Ptolemy was not right.

   F. The ring is made of either gold or silver. In fact, it is not made of silver. Therefore it is made of gold.

G. If the pool doesn't have chlorine, then it is not safe to swim in it. Since it is not safe to swim in it, it follows that the pool doesn't have chlorine.

H. Irving is either a bachelor or he is married. He is not married. Therefore he is a bachelor.

I. If magnets cure rheumatism, then there is a market for them. But since it is not the case that magnets cure rheumatism, there isn't a market for them.

J. There is a storm outside. If there is a storm outside, I'd better stay indoors. So, I'd better stay indoors.

K. If Mary knows Juan, then she knows Jennifer. She knows Jennifer. Therefore she knows Juan.

L. Tokyo is the capital of either Japan or Bangladesh. Tokyo is not the capital of Japan. So Tokyo is the capital of Bangladesh.

M. Customer Service handles complaints about merchandise that is either damaged or imperfect. Customer Service handles complaints about merchandise that is damaged. Therefore, Customer Service doesn't handle complaints about merchandise that is imperfect.

N. If the Big Bang theory is not wrong, then the universe is expanding. The Big Bang theory is not wrong. So, the universe is expanding.

O. Either students who got As or those who have missed no class are eligible for the prize. Students who have missed no class are eligible for the prize. So students who got As are not eligible for the prize.

12.4 An Informal Approach to Proofs of Validity

Some valid argument forms such as those discussed above are often used as *basic rules* of inference in the so-called *proofs* of validity. This is a procedure designed to show the steps by which the conclusion of a valid propositional argument follows from its premises. In constructing a proof for an argument, we assume that it *is in fact valid*, and we try to show this. Before we can proceed to construct some such proofs, we'll add other basic valid argument forms to our list so that we can have enough *rules of inference* to prove the conclusions of a great number of valid propositional arguments. In addition, we'll introduce some *rules of replacement*, which will enable us to replace logically equivalent expressions, so that one may be substituted for the other in whatever contexts they occur.

The Basic Rules

In constructing our proofs of validity, then, we'll need some valid argument forms and some logical equivalences between compound propositions. The former will serve as rules of inference, which will permit us to draw a conclusion from a premise or premises. The latter will serve as rules of replacement, which will permit us to substitute one expression for another that is logically equivalent to it. Our list of rules includes the following:

Basic Rules of Inference

1. *Modus Ponens* (MP) $P \supset Q, P \therefore Q$
2. *Modus Tollens* (MT) $P \supset Q, \sim Q \therefore \sim P$
3. *Hypothetical Syllogism* (HS) $P \supset Q, Q \supset R \therefore P \supset R$
4. *Disjunctive Syllogism* (DS) $P \vee Q, \sim P \therefore Q$
5. *Simplification* (Simp) $P \cdot Q \therefore P$
6. *Conjunction* (Conj) $P, Q \therefore P \cdot Q$
7. *Addition* (Add) $P \therefore P \vee Q$

Basic Rules of Replacement

8. *Contraposition* (Contr) $(P \supset Q) \equiv (\sim Q \supset \sim P)$
9. *Double Negation* (DN) $P \equiv \sim\sim P$
10. *De Morgan's Theorem* (DeM) $\sim(P \cdot Q) \equiv (\sim P \vee \sim Q)$
                                 $\sim(P \vee Q) \equiv (\sim P \cdot \sim Q)$
11. *Commutation* (Com) $(P \vee Q) \equiv (Q \vee P)$
                                 $(P \cdot Q) \equiv (Q \cdot P)$
12. *Definition of Material Conditional* (Cond) $(P \supset Q) \equiv (\sim P \vee Q)$
13. *Definitions of Material Biconditional* (Bicond) $(P \equiv Q) \equiv [(P \supset Q) \cdot (Q \supset P)]$
                                 $(P \equiv Q) \equiv [(P \cdot Q) \vee (\sim P \cdot \sim Q)]$

What Is a Proof of Validity?

Proofs of validity may be formal or informal. In a formal proof, the relation of entailment is taken to obtain strictly between certain well-formed formulas of a system of logic that *need have no* interpretation in a natural language (such as English, Portuguese, Chinese, etc.). Furthermore, the basic rules of inference and replacement used in formal proofs are such that they could be used to prove the conclusion of *any* valid propositional argument from its premises. On the other hand, in the informal proofs proposed here, entailment is taken to be a relation that obtains between certain propositions that are expressible in a natural language. When a proof is offered as involving only formulas, it is assumed in the informal approach that these have an interpretation in a natural language. Moreover, the basic rules offered in our informal approach fall short of allowing proofs of validity for *any* valid propositional argument.

BOX 7 ■ HOW TO SHOW VALIDITY WITH PROOFS

Keep in mind that

- Some valid argument forms, the number of which varies from system to system, amount to rules of inference, since they can be used to deduce the conclusion of a valid argument from its premises.

- Some biconditional expressions, the number of which varies from system to system, amount to rules of replacement, since they can be used to replace an expression in the right-hand column with the logically equivalent one in the left-hand column, and vice-versa. This can be done in all contexts where one of the expressions occurs.

- Some rules of inference and rules of replacement are considered *basic* in the sense that they are *accepted without proof.*

- For any valid argument whose form differs from those of the basic rules, its validity is *in principle* demonstrable by constructing a proof. Any argument for which it is **not** possible *at least in principle* to show its validity with a proof is invalid.

We'll construct proofs to check the validity of certain arguments and assume that those arguments have an interpretation in English, even though for the sake of convenience they may be offered only in the symbolic notation. For valid arguments that are expressed in English, we'll first translate them into the symbolic notation. Then we'll proceed to prove their validity by using the rules listed above in a way that we'll explain shortly. These rules can be used to demonstrate the validity of many propositional arguments, and we shall next see just how this is done.

Whether in a formal or informal approach, all proofs of validity require that we assume that, for any valid argument, it must *in principle* be possible to show its validity by the proof procedure, which shows that a valid argument's conclusion follows from its premises once we apply to these one or more basic rules of inference and/or replacement. Such rules are "basic" in the sense of being *accepted without a proof*. (Since any proof at all within this system would *assume at least some of them*, there are basic rules that cannot be proved within the system.)

How to Construct a Proof of Validity

Let's now put our basic rules to work and demonstrate the validity of the following argument:

36 Both Alice and Caroline will graduate next year. But if Caroline will graduate next year, then Giselle will win a scholarship if and only if Alice will graduate next year. So, either Giselle will win a scholarship if and only if Alice will graduate next year, or Helen will be valedictorian.

First, we translate the argument into the symbolic notation as follows:

36' $A \cdot C, C \supset (G \equiv A) \therefore (G \equiv A) \vee H$

We can now prove that this argument's conclusion, $(G \equiv A) \vee H$, follows from its premises. How? By showing that such a conclusion can be deduced from (36')'s premises by applying to them only basic rules of inference and replacement. Our proof, whose four steps (numbered 3, 4, 5, and 6) aim at deducing the intended conclusion from (36′)'s premises, runs

36″ 1. $A \cdot C$
    2. $C \supset (G \equiv A)$ $/\therefore (G \equiv A) \vee H$
    3. $C \cdot A$ from 1 by Com
    4. C from 3 by Simp
    5. $G \equiv A$ from 2 and 4 by MP
    6. $(G \equiv A) \vee H$ from 5 by Add

In line 3, we deduce $C \cdot A$ by applying commutation (see *Com* in the rules above) to premise 1. Any time we deduce a formula, we *justify* what we've done on the right-hand side of the proof. In this example, the justification includes expressions such as "from," "and," and "by" that we'll later omit ("from") or replace by punctuation marks ("and" and "by"). Note that a proof's justification requires two things: (a) that we state the premise number to which a certain rule was applied (if more than one, we write down the premises' numbers in the order in which the rule was applied to them), and (b) that we state the name of the rule applied. After justifying how a formula was deduced from the premise/s of an argument, that formula can be counted as a new premise listed with its own line number. Since "$C \cdot A$" in line 3 has been deduced from the argument's premises, it is now a premise that can be used in further steps of the proof. In fact, it is used in line 4 to deduce C in the way indicated on the right-hand side of that line. Premises 2 and 4 allow us to deduce "$G \equiv A$" in line 5, which follows from them by modus ponens (*MP*). In line 6, addition (*Add*) allows us to deduce the formula that proves (36)'s validity: namely, the conclusion of that argument. We have thus shown that its conclusion follows from its premises, and we have done so by showing that it can be obtained by applying only basic rules of inference and replacement to those premises. Thus (36) has been proved valid.

Proofs vs. Truth Tables

As we've seen, in the case of truth tables, the truth values of an argument's premises and conclusion are assigned according to rules associated with the truth-functional connectives involved in that argument. Although here we've defined only five such connectives, their total number is in fact sixteen. This is a fixed number. By contrast, the actual number of valid argument forms and logically equivalent expressions that could be used to construct proofs of validity may vary from one deductive system to another. Furthermore, the proof procedure allows for *no* fixed number of steps to correctly deduce an argument's conclusion from its premises: it often depends on which premises and basic rules we decide to use.

Since in these respects proofs permit a certain degree of flexibility, it is sometimes possible, within a single system of basic rules, to construct more than one correct proof to demonstrate the validity of a certain argument. That is, unlike a truth table, a proof is not a mechanical procedure that always yields a result in the same way in a fixed number of steps. Moreover, it might happen that, in constructing a proof for a certain valid argument, we err in our assessment of its validity. We might simply "fail to see" at the moment that certain rules can be put at the service of deducing that argument's conclusion from its premises and mistakenly conclude that the argument is invalid. That's why we say that, for any valid argument, one could *in principle* construct a proof of its validity. It must be admitted, however, that proofs do have one big advantage over truth tables: namely, that the latter tend to be very long and unwieldy when an argument features propositions of many different types. Proofs face no such problem.

Exercises

XII. Review Questions

1. In what does the method of proof consist?
2. How do proofs compare with truth tables?
3. What is a rule of inference?
4. How are rules of inference used in a proof?
5. What are rules of replacement?
6. In this section, a distinction has been drawn between a formal and an informal approach to proofs. What is that distinction?

XIII. Justify the steps of each of the following proofs of validity using the rules of inference and replacement given in this section.

1. 1. $A \supset B$
   2. $\sim B$ $/\therefore \sim A \bullet (\sim B \vee C)$
   3. $\sim A$ 1, 2 MT   SAMPLE ANSWER
   4. $\sim B \vee C$ 2 Add
   5. $\sim A \bullet (\sim B \vee C)$ 3, 4 Conj

2. 1. $\sim D \supset \sim E$
   2. $E \vee \sim(I \supset D)$
   3. $I \supset D$ $/\therefore E \bullet D$
   4. $\sim\sim(I \supset D)$
   5. E
   6. $\sim\sim E$
   7. $\sim\sim D$
   8. D
   9. $E \bullet D$

*3. 1. $\sim D \bullet C$
   2. $F \supset \sim C$
   3. $\sim F \supset (E \vee D)$ $/\therefore D \vee E$
   4. $\sim\sim C \supset \sim F$
   5. $C \supset \sim F$
   6. $C \supset (E \vee D)$
   7. $C \bullet \sim D$
   8. C
   9. $E \vee D$
   10. $D \vee E$

4. 1. $\sim A \bullet (A \vee E)$ $/\therefore E \vee \sim E$
   2. $\sim A$
   3. $(A \vee E) \bullet \sim A$
   4. $A \vee E$
   5. E
   6. $E \vee \sim E$

*5. 1. $(G \supset D) \supset \sim F$
   2. $D \supset F$
   3. $D \bullet C$ $/\therefore \sim(G \supset D)$
   4. $\sim F \supset \sim D$
   5. $(G \supset D) \supset \sim D$
   6. D
   7. $\sim\sim D$
   8. $\sim(G \supset D)$

6. 1. $A \supset \sim(B \supset \sim D)$
  2. $\sim(B \supset \sim D) \supset \sim D$
  3. D /∴ ~A
  4. $A \supset \sim D$
  5. $\sim\sim D$
  6. $\sim A$

* 7. 1. $(D \supset C) \vee \sim(A \vee B)$
  2. A /∴ ~D ∨ C
  3. $\sim(A \vee B) \vee (D \supset C)$
  4. $A \vee B$
  5. $\sim\sim(A \vee B)$
  6. $D \supset C$
  7. $\sim D \vee C$

8. 1. $(\sim D \cdot C) \cdot H$ /∴ ~H ∨ ~D
  2. $\sim D \cdot C$
  3. $\sim D$
  4. $\sim D \vee \sim H$
  5. $\sim H \vee \sim D$

* 9. 1. $(E \vee A) \supset C$
  2. $[(E \vee A) \supset C] \supset (E \cdot G)$ /∴ C
  3. $E \cdot G$
  4. E
  5. $E \vee A$
  6. C

10. 1. $(D \supset C) \supset \sim(A \cdot B)$
  2. $\sim D \supset (A \cdot B)$ /∴ D ∨ ~(D ⊃ C)
  3. $\sim(A \cdot B) \supset \sim\sim D$
  4. $(D \supset C) \supset \sim\sim D$
  5. $(D \supset C) \supset D$
  6. $\sim(D \supset C) \vee D$
  7. $D \vee \sim(D \supset C)$

*11. 1. $(\sim H \vee L) \supset \sim(I \cdot G)$
  2. $G \cdot I$ /∴ ~L • H
  3. $I \cdot G$
  4. $\sim\sim(I \cdot G)$
  5. $\sim(\sim H \vee L)$
  6. $\sim\sim H \cdot \sim L$
  7. $H \cdot \sim L$
  8. $\sim L \cdot H$

12. 1. $(B \supset C) \lor \sim A$
2. $\sim(B \supset C) \lor A$ $/\therefore A \equiv (B \supset C)$
3. $(B \supset C) \supset A$
4. $\sim A \lor (B \supset C)$
5. $A \supset (B \supset C)$
6. $[A \supset (B \supset C)] \bullet [(B \supset C) \supset A]$
7. $A \equiv (B \supset C)$

XIV. Translate each of the following arguments into symbolic notation using the propositional symbols inside parentheses and construct a correct proof of validity for it.

1. The Bensons and the Nelsons will be at the party. But if the Nelsons are at the party, then the Finnegans will not be there. The Finnegans will be at the party only if the Bensons will not be there. It follows that the Finnegans will not be at the party. (B, N, F)

   SAMPLE ANSWER:

   1. $B \bullet N$
   2. $N \supset \sim F$
   3. $F \supset \sim B$ $/\therefore \sim F$
   4. $N \bullet B$ 1 Com
   5. N 4 Simp
   6. $\sim F$ 2, 5 MP

2. If elephants are mammals, then they are not warm-blooded creatures. It is not the case that elephants are not warm-blooded creatures. From this we may infer that either elephants are not mammals or they are not warm-blooded creatures. (E, C)

3. Either municipal bonds will not continue to be a good investment or stocks will be a wise choice for the small investor at the present time. Municipal bonds will not continue to be a good investment. Therefore, stocks will be a wise choice for the small investor at the present time. (M, C)

* 4. If Romania establishes a democracy, then Bulgaria will too. Either Mongolia will not remain independent or Romania will not establish a democracy. Bulgaria will not establish a democracy but Romania will. Thus Mongolia will not remain independent. (D, B, M)

5. Zoe will not resign next week, for Keith will serve on the committee, and either Zoe will not resign next week or Oliver will. But if Zoe

does resign next week, then Keith will not serve on the committee. (*K, E, O*)

* **6.** Honduras will support the treaty, but it is clear that either Russia will not support it or Japan will support it. Japan's supporting the treaty implies that Honduras will not support it. So, Japan will not support the treaty. (*H, I, J*)

7. If Macedonians and the Danes were polytheists, then most ancient Europeans also were. The Romans' not being polytheists implies that both the Macedonians and the Danes were polytheists. It follows that if most ancient Europeans were not polytheists, then the Romans were polytheists. (*M, D, E, O*)

* **8.** Railroads are safe investments but oil companies are not. It follows that oil companies are not safe investments but public utilities are, because railroads are safe investments only if public utilities are too. (*I, C, B*)

9. Dramatists are not opinionated or historians are not disputatious. For if dramatists are opinionated, then musicians are not good at math. But musicians are good at math. (*D, M, H*)

*** 10.** Sicily is an island. Besides, if Italy is the home of famous soccer players, then Egypt is not the birthplace of Caesar. In addition, if Italy is not the home of famous soccer players, then Norway's being full of tourists implies that Egypt is not the birthplace of Caesar. It follows that Sicily is an island, and Egypt's being the birthplace of Caesar implies that if Norway is full of tourists, then Egypt is not the birthplace of Caesar. (*I, H, E, N*)

12.5 The Philosopher's Corner

Reductio ad Absurdum Arguments

Earlier we saw that the term "argument," as used in logic, does not mean a hostile verbal exchange between two people but rather a group of statements that attempt to make a supported claim. However, we'd be leaving out something important if we didn't admit the plain fact that arguments often *are* used in the course of ordinary disputation of many kinds. In formal debates, courts of law, philosophical essays, exchanges between candidates in political campaigns, and informal discussions on popular and scientific topics of every sort, arguments play a crucial role. A well-constructed argument is a useful weapon in the hands of a skilled debater, rhetorician, attorney, or scholar. Whenever we hope to prevail in a dispute over some contested point or to convince someone else of a controversial conclusion, we need the best arguments we can get. Fortunately, there are some standard tactics that have been developed by philosophers and which have become part of the armament of logical thinkers. Here we'll discuss one of them: *reductio ad absurdum*.

> *A reductio ad absurdum* is an argument that attempts to refute (i.e., disprove) a claim by showing that if one were to accept it as true, one would be required also to accept some further claim that is manifestly absurd.

Because "absurdity," in this context, can mean at least three different things, however, we can distinguish three different types of reductio (as they're usually called). The strongest form of reductio occurs when one demonstrates that the disputed claim involves internal inconsistencies such that holding it leads to some conclusion that is self-contradictory. The next strongest form is one that shows that a commitment to the disputed claim leads to a conclusion that is false. The weakest is one that shows that a commitment to the disputed claim leads to a conclusion that, though not proven false, is wildly implausible or likely to be false. For a summary of these three types of reductio argument, see Box 8.

Any reductio could be reconstructed as broadly having the form of a modus tollens. Suppose there is some claim C that we find objectionable. Then, by reductio, we might argue that accepting C implies also accepting some absurd further claim A. But since A amounts to a claim that should be rejected, we can conclude that C should also be rejected. Thus the broad form of the argument is a modus tollens that runs

37 $C \supset A, \sim A \therefore \sim C$

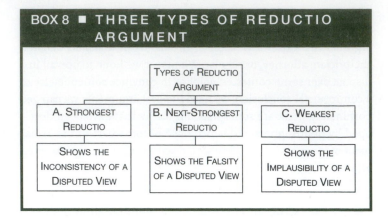

BOX 8 ■ THREE TYPES OF REDUCTIO ARGUMENT

TYPES OF REDUCTIO ARGUMENT

A. STRONGEST REDUCTIO

SHOWS THE INCONSISTENCY OF A DISPUTED VIEW

B. NEXT-STRONGEST REDUCTIO

SHOWS THE FALSITY OF A DISPUTED VIEW

C. WEAKEST REDUCTIO

SHOWS THE IMPLAUSIBILITY OF A DISPUTED VIEW

Reductio and the Divine Command Theory

All three of the different versions of reductio are commonly used by philosophers. An example of a refutation making use of what we've just called the "weak" reductio is the following. It concerns a doctrine in moral philosophy known as the divine command theory, according to which right and wrong are entirely determined by God's approval or disapproval, in the absence of which nothing at all would be either right or wrong. Thus, on this view, the "rightness" of any right action *just consists in* its being approved of by God, and the "wrongness" of any wrong action *just consists in* its being forbidden by God. Now although this doctrine undoubtedly has a certain appeal in that it appears to provide (for religious believers at any rate) an objective basis for morality, it has been thought by many to be vulnerable to a reductio: namely, that if the divine command theory is true, then *just anything* could be morally right if God approved of it! But none of us believes that just anything could be right. Can we imagine, for instance, that it could be right to capture children and torture them to death? Yet anyone who accepts the divine command theory, it seems, is committed to saying that it would be right if God approved of it. Does this not begin to sound absurd? Perhaps that is why not only philosophers but also many theologians prefer to keep their distance from the divine command theory. This is, of course, just one example of reductio ad absurdum. But it is typical of the way such arguments work.

> ## BOX 9 ■ ASSESSING REDUCTIO ARGUMENTS
>
> ■ A *reductio* broadly has the argument form of a modus tollens. It is therefore a valid argument.
> ■ Like any other valid argument, however, to succeed, it needs premises that are likely true and more acceptable than its conclusion.

Exercises

XV. Discuss each of the following *reductio* arguments and, when possible, determine whether it exemplifies a type A, B, or C *reductio*.

* 1. According to naturalism, traditional philosophy cannot justify its claims and should be replaced by science. But this is itself a philosophical claim! Thus, if true, it couldn't be justified! So, we should reject naturalism, since if it is correct, it is self-contradictory.

* 2. Since sensations are crucial to consciousness and therefore to having a mind, robots have minds if and only if they can have sensations. But it is false that they can have sensations. Therefore robots do not have minds.

* 3. According to some philosophers, there is a sharp fact/value distinction, so that no judgments could be both factual and evaluative. Given their view, only judgments that can be verified by observation can represent the facts, and no evaluative judgment can be verified in that way. But if this is correct, then historical claims, which are not verifiable by observation, would fail to be factual. Lacking truth value, claims involving history would be as fictional as those in novels and poetry! Since this is beginning to sound preposterous, the view must be rejected.

4. The principle of cultural moral relativism is that whenever there is a radical difference in the moral outlooks of two culturally diverse groups, each outlook applies to or binds only its own group. The British philosopher Bernard Williams (1929–2003) argued that this principle should be understood as saying that "the right attitude to different outlooks is to leave them and those who hold them alone.

This can be fine in some circumstances (though hardly in all), but this principle itself is manifestly not relativist, but rather an absolute principle of toleration ... [It follows that] relativism must ... offend against its own restrictions."[1]

5. Some contemporary philosophers recommend rejecting the received view of the world with its prevalent attitude of *seriousness*. They advocate replacing seriousness by laughter or by simply "being in the world." Clearly if you truly laugh at everything or relax and simply exist in the world, you don't take anything seriously. But there is room for objecting as follows: when those philosophers recommend such attitudes, aren't they being *serious* about it?

XVI. **In the passage below, American philosopher W. V. Quine (1908–2000) is concerned with *radical translation*, or the attempt to interpret expressions in a native language never encountered before. Suppose some linguists are about to translate a native's utterance as *P and not P*. How could Quine's proposal below be used in a *reductio* of that translation?**

On Quine's view, radical translation should follow the maxim of interpretative charity, which holds that, in interpreting the utterances of a native, we must choose the translation that "makes his message less absurd." Charity recommends that "assertions startlingly false on the face of them are likely to turn on hidden differences of language .... The common sense behind the maxim is that one's interlocutor's silliness, beyond a certain point, is less likely than bad translation—or, in the domestic case, linguistic divergence."[2]

■ Writing Project

Choose a disputed question of applied ethics,—which may include such topics as the morality of abortion, capital punishment, globalization, stem-cell research, etc.—and write a short essay (no more than 2 pages) where you offer a reductio argument against some view on the chosen topic that you think has at least

---

[1] *Pp. 545–582 in Ethics (A. C. Grayling ed., Philosophy: A Guide Through the Subject. Oxford, UK: Oxford University Press).*
[2] *Pp. 58–59 in W. V. Quine, Word and Object (Cambridge, MA: The MIT Press, 1960).*

implausible consequences. Organize your paper according to the following format:

1. Take the chosen view as your target piece.
2. State the thesis or argument of the target piece that will be objected to in your critical response. Support your descriptions of the target view with examples.
3. State the objection.
4. Argue that your objection has the form of a modus tollens and identify the corresponding type of reductio you have offered according to the classification proposed in this chapter.

■ Chapter Summary

> In a truth table devised to test the validity of an argument, if there is *at least one* row where premises are all true and the conclusion false, then that proves the invalidity of the argument tested. If there is no such row, then that proves it is valid.

Formal Fallacies

Affirming the Consequent

$P \supset Q$

Q
___
P

Denying the Antecedent

$P \supset Q$

$\sim P$
___
$\sim Q$

Affirming a Disjunct

$P \vee Q$ $P \vee Q$

P Q
___   ___
$\sim Q$ $\sim P$

Basic Rules of Inference

1. *Modus Ponens* (MP) $P \supset Q, P \therefore Q$
2. *Modus Tollens* (MT) $P \supset Q, {\sim}Q \therefore {\sim}P$
3. *Contraposition* (Contr) $P \supset Q \therefore {\sim}Q \supset {\sim}P$
4. *Hypothetical Syllogism* (HS) $P \supset Q, Q \supset R \therefore P \supset R$
5. *Disjunctive Syllogism* (DS) $P \mathbf{v} Q, {\sim}P \therefore Q$
   $P \mathbf{v} Q, {\sim}Q \therefore P$
6. *Simplification* (Simp) $P \cdot Q \therefore P$
   $P \cdot Q \therefore Q$
7. *Conjunction* (Conj) $P, Q \therefore P \cdot Q$
8. *Addition* (Add) $P \therefore P \mathbf{v} Q$

Basic Rules of Replacement

9. *Double Negation* (DN) $P \equiv {\sim}{\sim}P$
10. *De Morgan's Theorem*
    (DeM) ${\sim}(P \cdot Q) \equiv ({\sim}P \mathbf{v} {\sim}Q)$
    ${\sim}(P \mathbf{v} Q) \equiv ({\sim}P \cdot {\sim}Q)$
11. *Commutation* (Com) $(P \mathbf{v} Q) \equiv (Q \mathbf{v} P)$
    $(P \cdot Q) \equiv (Q \cdot P)$
12. *Definition of Material
    Conditional* (Cond) $(P \supset Q) \equiv ({\sim}P \mathbf{v} Q)$
13. *Definitions of Material
    Biconditional* (Bicond) $(P \equiv Q) \equiv [(P \supset Q) \cdot (Q \supset P)]$
    $(P \equiv Q) \equiv [(P \cdot Q) \mathbf{v} ({\sim}P \cdot {\sim}Q)]$

■ Key Words

Rule of inference
Rule of replacement
Counterexample
Formal fallacy
Modus ponens
Modus tollens
Disjunctive syllogism

Affirming the consequent
Denying the antecedent
Affirming a disjunct
Contraposition
Hypothetical syllogism
Proof of validity
Reductio ad absurdism

CHAPTER

Categorical Propositions

Chapter Objectives

In this chapter you'll read about logical relations between categorical propositions, which are the building blocks of syllogistic arguments. The topics include

- What categorical propositions are and the elements that make them up.
- The different types of categorical propositions and the kinds of class-relationship they represent.
- How to recognize nonstandard categorical propositions in everyday language and how to translate these into standard-form categorical propositions.
- How to represent categorical propositions in Venn diagrams.
- The traditional square of opposition.
- The problem of existential import.

13.1 What Is a Categorical Proposition?

Categorical Propositions

Categorical propositions are propositions that represent relations of inclusion or exclusion between classes of things—for example,

1   All philosophers are wise persons.

2   No philosophers are wise persons.

Or between partial classes—such as

3   Some philosophers are wise persons.

Or between partial classes and whole classes—such as

4   Some philosophers are not wise persons.

The relationships between classes that matter for categorical propositions are, then, these four

■ Whole inclusion of one class inside another
■ Mutual, total exclusion between two classes
■ Partial inclusion, whereby part of one class is included inside another
■ Partial exclusion, whereby part of one class is wholly excluded from another

In the above examples of categorical propositions, "philosophers" is the subject term and "wise persons" the predicate term. These terms are the logical, rather than syntactical, subject and predicate of a categorical proposition. Each of them denotes a class of entities: that made up by all and only the entities to which the term applies. Thus, "philosophers" denotes the class of philosophers and "wise persons" that of persons who are wise.

Categorical propositions (1) through (4) represent four ways in which the class of philosophers and the class of wise persons can stand in relationships of inclusion or exclusion. Each of these relationships may be represented in one of the following ways:

1' All philosophers are wise persons.

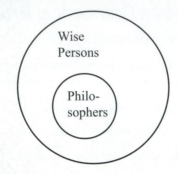

2' No philosophers are wise persons.

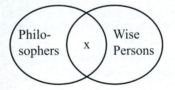

3' Some philosophers are wise persons.

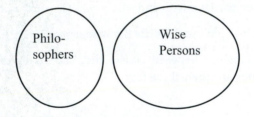

4' Some philosophers are not wise persons.

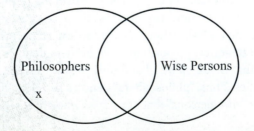

In traditional logic, the sort of logic first developed in antiquity by Aristotle (384–322 B.C.E.), the standard notation to represent the logical form of categorical propositions is to use *S* as a symbol for any subject term, and *P* for any predicate term. In that notation, then, the logical form of the above categorical propositions is, respectively,

1. All *S* are *P*
2. No *S* are *P*
3. Some *S* are *P*
4. Some *S* are not *P*

In traditional logic, only statements that can be shown to have these logical forms qualify for expressing a categorical proposition. Any such proposition always represents one of the four relationships between classes mentioned above, which can now be described by using the symbols *S* and *P*, which stand for the classes denoted by the proposition's subject and predicate. Those relationships are as in Box 1. But we can also represent them by circle diagrams, in which case we'd have

All *S* are *P*

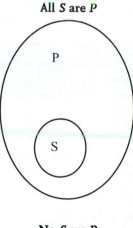

No *S* are *P*

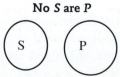

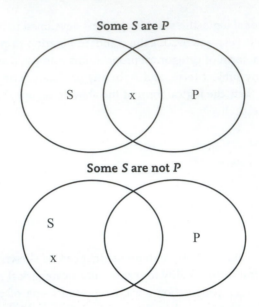

Some S are P

Some S are not P

Note that in the first two diagrams the terms S and P stand for classes, while in the other two the symbol x is introduced to stand for *at least one* member of the class denoted by S. If at least one member of that class is included in the class denoted by P, that's logically equivalent to saying that some S are P. If at least one member of the class S is *not* included in the class denoted by P, that's logically equivalent to saying that some S are not P.

> ## BOX 1 ■ THE CLASS RELATIONS INVOLVED IN CATEGORICAL PROPOSITIONS
>
> ■ In (1), the entire class of S is included inside the class of P.
> ■ In (2), the classes of S and P wholly exclude each other.
> ■ In (3), part of the class of S is included in the class of P.
> ■ In (4), part of the class of S is excluded from the class of P.

Standard Form

Statements (1) through (4) above illustrate *standard-form* categorical propositions. They are all composed of certain basic elements. Among these are, of course, the subject and predicate terms (which are *not* the *grammatical* but rather the *logical* subject and predicate of the proposition). Another basic element of standard categorical propositions is its so-called *quantity,* marked by a *quantifier*—an expression indicating whether the proposition's relation of inclusion or exclusion involves whole or partial classes. In (1) and (2), this is done by means of the *universal* quantifiers "all" and "no" (the latter combining the universal quantifier with negation), in (3) and (4) by "some," which is a *particular* (in the sense of nonuniversal) quantifier. Standard categorical propositions are also said to have *quality:* each categorical proposition is either *affirmative* or *negative,* depending on whether it lacks or contains *negation.* Statements (1) and (3) are affirmative, while (2) and (4) negative. Finally, there is the *copula* or verb of being, that may occur in singular ("is" / "is not") or plural ("are" / "are not"). These, then, are the basic elements of any categorical proposition in standard form.

> Any standard form categorical proposition has
>
> - A quantity (it is either universal or particular)
> - A quality (it is either affirmative or negative)
> - A SUBJECT term and a PREDICATE term
> - A copula connecting those terms

In any given categorical proposition, it is the combination of quantifier and the presence or absence of negation that determines its *type.* As shown in Box 2, there are four types of standard categorical propositions, each with its characteristic logical form—namely, universal affirmative, universal negative, particular affirmative, and particular negative.

BOX 2 ■ STANDARD CATEGORICAL PROPOSITIONS

NAME	TYPE	FORM
A	Universal Affirmative	All S are P
E	Universal Negative	No S are P
I	Particular Affirmative	Some S are P
O	Particular Negative	Some S are not P

In traditional logic, the capital letters *A*, *E*, *I*, and *O* are used as names of the four types of categorical propositions. Each letter is a shorthand way of referring to propositions falling under one of the four types. The use of these letters is a mnemonic device invented by traditional logicians from the Latin words *affirmo* ("I affirm") and *nego* ("I deny"). The first vowel of each word stands for the universal categorical propositions—*A* for universal affirmative and *E* for universal negative—and the second vowel for particular propositions—*I* for particular affirmative and *O* for particular negative. Hereafter we shall refer to each of the four types of categorical proposition by using these letter names. Thus consider again our previous examples:

1 All philosophers are wise persons.

2 No philosophers are wise persons.

3 Some philosophers are wise persons.

4 Some philosophers are not wise persons.

These illustrate, respectively, an *A* proposition, an *E* proposition, an *I* proposition, and an *O* proposition.

Nonstandard Categorical Propositions

Of course, very few propositions are already in the standard form—that is, only some have explicitly all the elements found in an *A*, *E*, *I*, or *O* proposition. However, it seems possible to translate many nonstandard categorical propositions into one of these forms by making some changes. For example, (5) is a categorical proposition that can be translated into the *A* proposition (5'):

5 Cobras are dangerous.

5' All cobras are dangerous.

Quantifiers such as "each," "every," "any," "everything," "everyone," and the like are universal and therefore logically equivalent to "all." Note that they are often omitted in propositions such as (5). When that happens, the quantifier must be made explicit if the proposition is to be in standard form. Furthermore, certain conditionals can also be translated into *A* propositions: to say that all cobras are dangerous is logically equivalent to saying that

5" If something is a cobra, then it is dangerous.

Therefore when you encounter conditionals such as (5″), you must translate them as *A* propositions. Keep in mind that the default quantifier for any seemingly universal affirmative proposition is "all" except when careful reading of the proposition suggests a nonuniversal quantifier. For example,

6   The dogs bark at night.

This does not translate into an *A* proposition in standard form but rather into an *I* proposition such as

6' Some dogs are nighttime barkers.

Although (6') sounds odd in English, what matters here is logical form: translating a proposition into standard categorical form, often has that linguistic side effect.

What about nonstandard universal negative propositions? Consider

7   No one in my class plays Scrabble.

Since (7) is an *E* proposition, we'll make the necessary changes to obtain one in the standard form. For example,

7' No classmates of mine are Scrabble players.

Here again, a conditional can be translated into a *E* proposition: to say "No classmates of mine are Scrabble players" is to say

7" If someone is my classmate, then that person is not a Scrabble player.

Note that a conditional that can be adequately translated into an *E* proposition must have a negation in its consequent. Now consider

8   There are classmates of mine who play Scrabble.

This translates into the *I* proposition

8' Some classmates of mine are Scrabble players,

as does

8" Classmates of mine who play Scrabble exist.

That is, any proposition about what exists or "what there is" translates into an *I* proposition, provided that it doesn't have negation. When such a proposition does have negation, as in

9 There are classmates of mine who do not play Scrabble,

it translates into *O* propositions, such as

9' Some classmates of mine are not Scrabble players.

We shall have more to say on translation under "Existential Import" below. But in the next section we'll first consider some inferences that can be drawn from categorical propositions.

Exercises

I. Review Questions

1. What is a categorical proposition?
2. What is a categorical proposition's standard form?
3. What are the four types of categorical propositions? Can you give an example of each?
4. What are the "terms" of a categorical proposition?
5. What is meant by "subject" and "predicate" as applied to categorical propositions?
6. In a standard-form categorical proposition, what part is the quantifier?
7. What are some examples of nonstandard quantifiers and the standard quantifiers into which they're translatable?
8. In a standard-form categorical proposition, what part is the copula?
9. What do *A* and *I* propositions have in common? And what about *E* and *O*?
10. What do *A* and *E* propositions have in common? And what about *I* and *O*?

II. **For each of the following, mark its subject term with a straight line and predicate term with two lines and determine the type and name of the categorical proposition it exemplifies.**

1. No poodle is a dangerous dog.

   SAMPLE ANSWER: No <u>poodle</u> is a <u>dangerous dog</u>. Universal negative, *E*.

2. Some chemicals are acids. _____

* 3. Some firefighters are not men. _____

4. No vegetarians are fond of mutton. _____

* 5. Some precious metals are not available in Africa. _____

   6. No vehicle that has no flashing light on top is an emergency vehicle. _____

* 7. Some historians are persons who are interested in the future. _____

   8. Some blizzards that produce no ice are not road hazards. _____

* 9. All spies are persons who cannot avoid taking risks. _____

  10. Some universities that are not very selective are institutions that charge high tuition. _____

III. **From exercise II above, select a proposition illustrating each of the four categorical proposition types and diagram it in the way suggested in this section.**

SAMPLE ANSWER: No poodle is a dangerous dog.

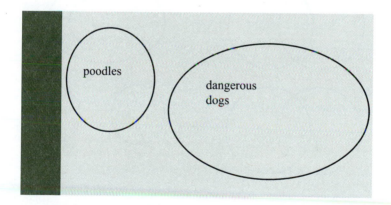

IV. **For each of the following propositions, give the name of the categorical proposition type it exemplifies and rewrite it in standard form:**

   1. There are Bostonians who are not Red Sox fans.

   SAMPLE ANSWER: *O:* Some Bostonians are not Red Sox fans.

* 2. No movie star loves being ignored by the media.

3. Every mollusk is a shellfish.

* 4. No member of Congress who's being investigated can leave the country.

5. If someone is a mayor, then she is a politician.

* 6. There are mathematical equations that do not amount to headaches.

7. A college with a high out-of-state tuition is not within my budget.

* 8. There are dogs that don't bark.

9. Precious metals are still available in many parts of Africa.

*10. Speedy vehicles that don't put their occupants at risk exist.

V. YOUR OWN THINKING LAB

For each of the following, write down two categorical propositions of the type represented by the diagram, one in the standard form and the other in some nonstandard form.

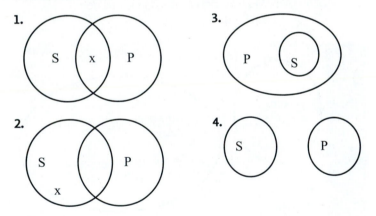

13.2 Venn Diagrams for Categorical Propositions

We may now represent the four types of categorical propositions by means of standard Venn diagrams (devised by the English logician, John Venn, 1834–1923). A Venn diagram for a categorical proposition employs two intersecting circles, the one on the left representing the class denoted by its subject term, the one on the right the class denoted by its predicate. Let's first consider a Venn diagram and some equivalent notations for a universal affirmative proposition such as

10 All U.S. citizens are voters.

Boolean notation:

$S\overline{P} = 0$

A proposition, traditional notation:

All S are P

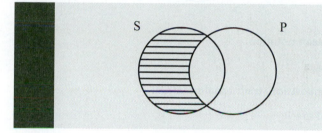

The Venn diagram representing (10) consists of two intersecting circles, one for the subject term ("U.S. citizens") and the other for the predicate ("voters"). Since, according to (10), all members of the class denoted by its subject term are members of the class denoted by its predicate term, the crescent-shaped part of S that has no members (i.e., that representing U.S. citizens who are not voters) has been shaded out in the diagram. With the Venn diagram technique, shading a space means that *that* space *is empty*. Thus, in the above diagram, S non-P is shaded out, to represent that there *is nothing* that is S that is non-P. This is consistent with reading (10) as saying that the subclass of *U.S. citizens who are not voters* is an empty subclass—or, equivalently, that *there are no U.S. citizens who are not voters*.

To the left of the diagram, (10)'s translation is provided, first, in the algebraic notation introduced by the English mathematician George Boole (1815–1864), which reads "S non-P equals 0," and then in the notation of traditional logic, reading "All S are P." What both say is captured by the Venn diagram on the right: namely, that the subclass of *S* non-*P* (represented by the shaded portion of the diagram) is empty.

Now let's look at (11), an instance of the universal negative.

11 No U.S. citizens are voters.

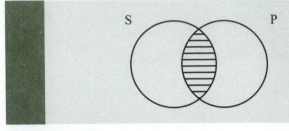

Boolean notation:

S P = 0

E **proposition, traditional notation:**

No *S* are *P*

Since (11) is a universal proposition, its Venn diagram shows an empty subclass that has been shaded out: the football-shaped center area, the intersection of "*S* and *P*," which represents the *U.S. citizens who are voters*. The diagram thus captures that (11) *denies that there are any such voters*: in other words, asserting (11) amounts to saying that the class of voting U.S. citizens has no members. To the left of the diagram, (11)'s Boolean notation "*S P* = 0" tells us that the subclass "*S P*" is empty. Immediately below, we find (11)'s notation and type in traditional logic. Keep in mind that for any universal categorical proposition (whether affirmative or negative), there will be a part of the circles shaded out, to indicate that *that* part has no members.

Next, consider the particular affirmative

12 Some U.S. citizens are voters.

Boolean notation:

S P ≠ 0

I **proposition, traditional notation:**

Some *S* are *P*

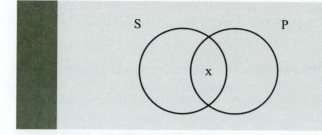

This time, no universal claim is being made but rather a *particular* one: a claim about *part* of a class. As a result, the diagram shows no shading at all, but an x instead, in the area where there are some members. Since "some" logically amounts to "at least one," (12) is equivalent to

    12′ There is at least one U.S. citizen who is a voter.

Putting an x in the football-shaped center space indicates that *that* space, *S P, is not empty*—that it has some members (at least one). To the left of the diagram, we find (12)'s Boolean translation "*S P ≠* 0," which tells us that the subclass "*S P*" (i.e., the football-shaped area in the center) is not empty—together with its type and notation in traditional logic.

    Finally, what about a particular negative? Consider

13 Some U.S. citizens are not voters.

Boolean notation:

$S \overline{P} \neq 0$

O proposition, traditional notation:

Some S are not P

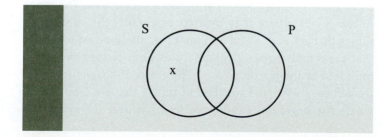

Because (13) is also a particular proposition, there's no shading in its Venn diagram. And, again, if "some" means "at least one," then (13) is logically equivalent to

13' There is at least one U.S. citizen who is not a voter.

That *the class of U.S. citizens who are not voters* (the crescent-shaped space on the left side of the diagram) is not empty—that it has at least one member—is represented in that subclass, "*S* non-*P*," with an *x*. The same is expressed both by the Boolean translation to the left of the diagram, which tells us that "*S* non-*P* is not empty," and by the notation in traditional logic that follows.

With these four diagrams, then, we can represent all of the different types of class relationship featured in the four types of categorical propositions. In the next chapter, we'll see how Venn diagrams can be used to check the validity of some syllogistic arguments. But first, let's look more closely at the spaces represented by a Venn diagram for categorical propositions. These are as follows:

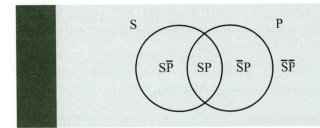

The two intersecting circles represent the two classes of things related in a categorical proposition—the one on the left, the class denoted by its subject, the one on the right, the class denoted by its predicate. The circles also determine four subclasses that we may identify with the spaces drawn. The space in the center, where they overlap, represents the subclass of things that are both *S* and *P* at once (i.e., the subclass of things that are simultaneously members of both classes), which is indicated by the notation "*S P*." The crescent-shaped space on the left represents the subclass of things that are *S* but not *P*, where the negation is indicated by a bar over the symbol *P*.

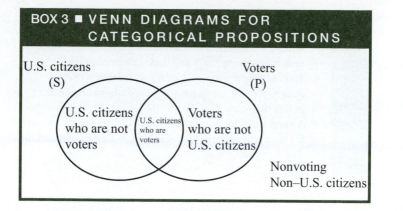

BOX 3 ■ VENN DIAGRAMS FOR CATEGORICAL PROPOSITIONS

U.S. citizens (S)

Voters (P)

U.S. citizens who are not voters

U.S. citizens who are voters

Voters who are not U.S. citizens

Nonvoting Non–U.S. citizens

The crescent-shaped space on the right represents the subclass of things that are *P* but not *S*, where the negation is indicated by a bar over the symbol *S*. The space outside the two interlocking circles represents the class of things that are neither *S* nor *P*. As we have seen, with these spaces we can use the Venn diagram technique to represent the class inclusion and exclusion relationships described in each of the four standard categorical propositions. To see how this works, let's start with a concrete example. Consider the four categorical propositions that may be constructed out of "U.S. citizens" as the subject term and "voters" as the predicate term. All four relationships of inclusion and exclusion between the class of U.S. citizens and the class of voters, as represented in those propositions, are captured in the Venn diagram in Box 3. There we may identify the following subclasses: (1) U.S. citizens who are voters, (2) U.S. citizens who are not voters, (3) voters who are not U.S. citizens (which would include, for instance, those who vote in other countries), and (4) non–U.S. citizens who are nonvoters (which would include, for instance, not only current citizens of other countries who do not vote, but Henry VIII, Julius Caesar, and even things like the Eiffel Tower, the Magna Carta, and the Grand Canyon—in fact *everything* we can think of belongs to one or the other of these four possible subclasses).

For each categorical proposition, then, there is a Venn diagram that shows the relationship of inclusion or exclusion that it involves. The bottom line is:

> - The areas displayed by a Venn diagram relevant to representing a categorical proposition are three: those inside each intersecting circle and their intersection itself.
> - A Venn diagram for an *A* or *E* proposition shows a shaded area where there are no members. No x occurs in this diagram.
> - A Venn diagram for an *I* or *O* proposition shows an x in the area where there are members. No area is shaded in this diagram.

Exercises

VI. Review Questions

1. In the previous section, Venn diagrams were used to represent categorical propositions. Explain how this technique works.
2. What do Venn diagrams for universal propositions have in common? And what about those for particular propositions?
3. What does it mean when a space is shaded out?
4. What does it mean when an *x* is placed in one of the circles?
5. What do the two circles stand for in a Venn diagram for a categorical proposition?

VII. Determine whether each Boolean notation for the diagram on the right is correct. If it isn't, provide the correct one.

* 1. $SP = 0$

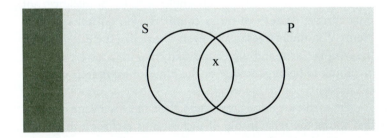

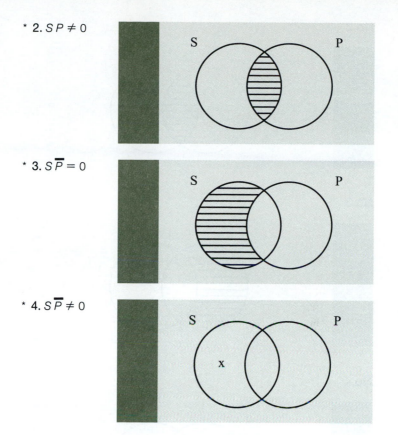

* 2. $SP \neq 0$

* 3. $S\overline{P} = 0$

* 4. $S\overline{P} \neq 0$

VIII. For each of the categorical propositions below, first write its form and name according to traditional logic, and then, match it with the correct Venn diagram and Boolean notation.

Venn diagrams

No.1

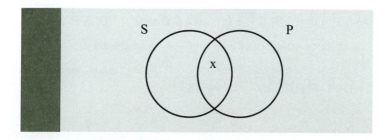

No.2

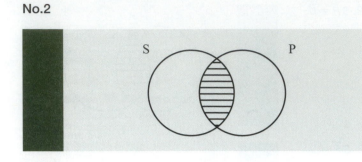

No.3

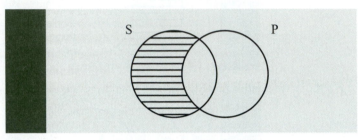

No.4

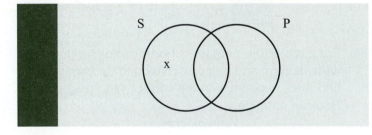

Boolean notation

(A) $SP = 0$;   (B) $S\overline{P} = 0$;   (C) $SP \neq 0$;   (D) $SP \neq 0$

1. No Sumo wrestlers are men who wear small-size shirts.

   SAMPLE ANSWER: Traditional logic: *E* proposition, No *S* are *P*. Venn diagram No.2, Boolean notation A

2. Some sports cars are very expensive machines.

* **3.** All llamas are bad-tempered animals.

4. Some grocers are not members of the Rotary Club.

5. All waterfalls are places people in kayaks should avoid.

* **6.** No spiders are insects.

7. Some advertisers are artful deceivers.

8. Some cowboys are not rodeo riders.

* **9.** No atheists are churchgoers.

10. All oranges are citrus fruits.

11. Some rivers that do not flow northward are not South American rivers.

*__12.__ If a number is even, then it is not odd.

13. There are marathon runners who eat fried chicken.

14. Some accountants who are graduates of Ohio State are not owners of bicycles.

*__15.__ Not all oils are good for you.

16. Some reference works are books that are not in the library.

17. If an architect is well known, then that architect has good taste.

*__18.__ Nothing written by superstitious people is a reliable source.

19. Chiropractors who do not have a serious degree exist.

*__20.__ Some resorts that are not in the Caribbean are popular tourist destinations.

13.3 The Square of Opposition

The Traditional Square of Opposition

Categorical propositions of the above four types were traditionally thought to bear logical relations to each other that enable us to draw certain *immediate inferences*. These are single-premise arguments, to some of which we'll turn now. We'll first look at the immediate inferences represented in the *traditional square of opposition*, a figure that looks like this:

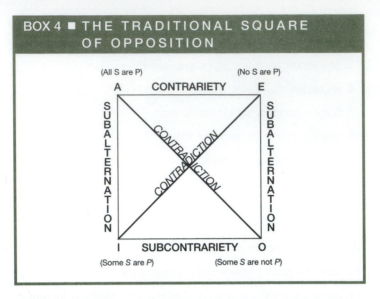

BOX 4 ■ THE TRADITIONAL SQUARE OF OPPOSITION

The relations represented in the traditional square of opposition, which involve two categorical propositions at a time, are as follows:

Relation	Established Between	Name of Related Propositions
Contradiction	A and O; E and I	Contradictories
Contrariety	A and E	Contraries
Subcontrariety	I and O	Subcontraries
Subalternation	A and I; E and O	Superalterns A and E; Subalterns I and O

Let's now take up each of these relations in turn.

Contradiction.   Propositions of the types in diagonally opposite corners of the square are *contradictories*. Propositions that stand in the relation of *contradiction* cannot have the same truth value: if one is true, then the other is false, and vice versa. Thus, A and O propositions will always have opposite truth values if their subjects and predicates are the same, as will propositions of types E and I. Thus, if it is true that

   1   All philosophers are wise persons,

then it's false that

4 Some philosophers are not wise persons.

On the other hand, if (1) is false, then that's logically the same as saying that (4) is true. Similarly, if it's true that

3 Some philosophers are wise persons,

that is, there is at least one philosopher who is a wise person, then it is false that

2 No philosophers are wise persons.

And conversely, if (3) is false, then (2) is true. When we infer the truth value of a proposition from that of its contradictory, as we've been doing here, we make a valid immediate inference, a single-premise argument whose conclusion must be true if its premise also is. But contradiction is only one sort of valid immediate inference according to traditional logicians; as we shall see next, there are others.

BOX 5 ■ CONTRADICTION

| A and O | ⇨ ⇦ | Contradictories |
| E and I | ⇨ ⇦ | Contradictories |

Contrariety, Subcontrariety, and Subalternation. The traditional square of opposition also includes the following logical relationships between propositions, which are valid given certain assumptions that we'll discuss presently:

A and E	⇨	Contrariety
I and O	⇨	Subcontrariety
A and I	⇨	Subalternation
E and O	⇨	Subalternation

Contrary propositions cannot both be true at once but can both be false. For instance, by contrariety, if it's true that

14 All bankers are cautious investors.

then we can infer that it's false that

15 No bankers are cautious investors.

That's because these categorical propositions cannot both be true. Yet they could both be false (as in fact they are).

But contrariety differs from subcontrariety, and neither of these is the same as contradiction. Subcontrary propositions *can* both be true at once but *cannot* both be false. By subcontrariety, if it's false that

16 Some students are vegetarians

then it must be true that

17 Some students are not vegetarians.

That's because these categorical propositions cannot both be false. But they could both be true (as in fact they are).

Finally, there is the relationship of subalternation, which is a little more complex, since the correct inference of truth values varies depending on whether we go from the universal proposition to the corresponding particular or the other way around. Logically speaking, to say that an *A* proposition and the corresponding *I* proposition are in the relation of subalternation is to say that if the *A* proposition is true, then the *I* proposition must be true as well, but also that if the *I* proposition is false, then the *A* must be false. And similarly for an *E* proposition and the corresponding *O*, to say that they are in the relation of subalternation means that if the *E* proposition is true, then necessarily the *O* proposition is true, but also that if the *O* is false, then the *E* must be false as well. In either case, the universal proposition is called "superaltern," and the particular of the same quality "subaltern." So

> Subalternation is a relation
> - Between *A* and *I* (*A* superaltern, *I* subaltern)
> - Between *E* and *O* (*E* superaltern, *O* subaltern)
>
> In this relation,
> - Truth transmits downward (from superaltern to subaltern)
> - Falsity transmits upward (from subaltern to superaltern

Let's reason by subalternation as traditional logicians would. Suppose it's true that

18 All trombone players are musicians.

Then it must also be true that

19 Some trombone players are musicians.

This suggests that truth transmits downward. At the same time, since it is false that some trombone players are not musicians, it follows that it is also false that no trombone players are musicians—and this suggests that falsity transmits upward. But a false superaltern such as

14 All bankers are cautious investors,

clearly fails to entail a false subaltern, since that some bankers are cautious investors is true. And a true subaltern such as

17 Some students are not vegetarians,

fails to entail a true superaltern, since that no students are vegetarians is false.

Truth-Value Rules and the Traditional Square of Opposition

Let's now summarize all relationships represented in the traditional square of opposition, together with the rules to be used for drawing immediate inferences from it. These are:

Contradiction: Contradictory propositions cannot have the same truth value (if one is true, the other must be false, and vice versa).

Contrariety: Contrary propositions cannot both be true at once but can both be false.

Subcontrariety: Subcontrary propositions cannot both be false at once but can both be true.

Subalternation

1. From the superaltern to subaltern (i.e., from the universal proposition to the particular proposition of the same quality):

   > If the superaltern is true, then the subaltern must be true.

   > If the superaltern is false, then the subaltern is undetermined.

2. From the subaltern to superaltern (i.e., from the particular proposition to the universal proposition of the same quality):

If the subaltern is true, then the superaltern is undetermined.

If the subaltern is false, then the superaltern must be false.

Given the relationships of contradiction, contrariety, subcontrariety, and subalternation represented in the traditional square of opposition, then assuming the truth values listed on the left, we can infer the values listed on the right.

If A is true ⇨ E is false, O is false, and I is true.

If A is false ⇨ E is undetermined, O is true, and I is undetermined.

If E is true ⇨ A is false, I is false, and O is true.

If E is false ⇨ A is undetermined, I is true, and O is undetermined.

If I is true ⇨ A is undetermined, E is false, and O is undetermined.

If I is false ⇨ A is false, E is true, and O is true.

If O is true ⇨ A is false, E is undetermined, and I is undetermined.

If O is false ⇨ A is true, E is false, and I is true.

Existential Import

Although inferences by contrariety, subcontrariety, and subalternation are all licensed as valid by the traditional square of opposition, our ability to draw such inferences is undermined by a significant difference between universal propositions on the one hand and particular propositions on the other: namely, that the latter (I and O) have *existential import*, while the former (A and E) do not. That is, I and O propositions implicitly assume the existence of the entities denoted by their subject terms. Since "some" is logically the same as "at least one," therefore an I proposition such as

20 Some cats are felines.

is logically equivalent to

20' There is at least one cat that is a feline.

Note that "*there is* at least one cat ... " amounts to "cats *exist*." Similarly, an *O* proposition such as

21 Some cats are not felines,

is logically the same as

21' There is at least one cat that is not a feline.

This likewise presupposes that *some cats exist*. On the other hand, *A* and *E* propositions have no existential import. That

22 All cats are felines

logically amounts to

22' If anything is a cat, then it is a feline.

Similarly, that

23 No cats are felines.

is equivalent to

23' If anything is a cat, then it is not a feline.

Understood in this way, a universal categorical proposition is equivalent to a conditional, a compound proposition that is false if and only if its antecedent is true and its consequent false. So (22') would be *false* if and only if there are cats but they are not felines, as would (23') if there are cats but they are felines. In all other cases, each of these would be true: for example, if cats did not exist, the antecedents of these conditionals would be false and those conditionals true (independent of the truth value of their consequents). Thus the inference by contrariety is undermined: given this understanding of universal propositions, contrary propositions could both be true in cases where their subjects are empty (i.e., have no referents). For example,

24 All unicorns are shy creatures.

This is equivalent to

24' If anything is a unicorn, then it is a shy creature.

But since *nothing is a unicorn,* (24')'s antecedent is false and the whole conditional therefore true. Now consider its contrary,

25 No unicorns are shy creatures.

This is equivalent to

25' If anything is a unicorn, then it is not a shy creature.

Here again, since nothing is a unicorn, (25')'s antecedent is false and the whole conditional therefore true. Clearly then, (24) and (25) could both be true! It follows that, unless we assume that the subject term of a true *universal* proposition is nonempty, we cannot infer that its contrary is false.

Now what about subcontrariety? This involves *I* and *O* propositions—which, on the modern understanding, do have existential import. Although given the traditional square of opposition, subcontraries cannot both be false, on the modern understanding they can. Consider now

26 Some unicorns are shy creatures.

This is equivalent to

26' There are unicorns and they are shy creatures.

Thus understood, (26) is false, since there are no unicorns. Compare

27 Some unicorns are not shy creatures.

This is equivalent to

27' There are unicorns and they are not shy creatures.

Since there are no unicorns, (27) turns out to be false as well. Thus (26) and (27) could both be false at once. It follows that we cannot draw valid inferences by subcontrariety.

Finally, consider subalternation. From what we have just seen, this relation also begins to look suspicious. How can one validly infer, for example, from an *A* proposition that has no existential import, an *I* proposition that does? Of course, *I*-from-*A* and *O*-from-*E* inferences might seem unproblematic at first, whenever the things denoted by their subject terms *exist*—for example trombone players, accountants, and tigers. But when we're talking about entities whose existence is questionable, inference by subalternation leads to absurdities. Consider, this *I*-from-*A* argument:

28 1. <u>All unicorns are shy creatures.</u>
  2. Some unicorns are shy creatures.

Since the conclusion in (28) is equivalent to (26') above, the argument appears to have "proved" that unicorns exist! Clearly something has gone wrong with this attempt to draw a conclusion by subalternation. It fails because it ignores a crucial distinction between the premise and conclusion here: namely, that the premise has no existential import, while the conclusion (its subaltern) does have it.

The Modern Square of Opposition

Venn diagrams are of course consistent with the modern view of the square of opposition. After all, it is only for particular propositions that we're required to use an *x* to indicate where there are members of the subject class (if they exist at all). Universal propositions never require us to indicate where there *are* members but only where there aren't any (by shading). In any case, some qualifications of the allowable valid inferences according to the square of opposition are needed to restrict the range of valid inferences involving categorical propositions. As

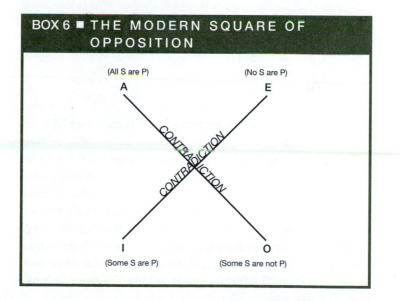

BOX 6 ■ THE MODERN SQUARE OF OPPOSITION

(All S are P)
A

(No S are P)
E

CONTRADICTION

CONTRADICTION

I
(Some S are P)

O
(Some S are not P)

shown in Box 6, the modern square modifies the traditional one so that it leaves out the relationships of subalternation, contrariety, and subcontrariety, retaining only contradiction as a relation sanctioning valid immediate inferences. Contradiction holds between *A* and *O* and between *E* and *I* propositions, which are in opposite corners of the square, marked by the two diagonals.

From this modern square we can see two things about a proposition and the negation of its contradictory:

1. **They are logically equivalent.**
   a. If the proposition in one corner is true, then the *negation* of its contradictory must be true.
   b. If the proposition in one corner is false, then the *negation* of its contradictory must be false.

2. **They entail each other.** Given (1a), any inference from a proposition to the negation of its contradictory preserves truth value and is therefore valid.

Here, then, is a complete list of the equivalences (and entailment relations) between a proposition of one of the four standard types and the negation of its contradictory sanctioned by the modern square of opposition:

$$
\begin{array}{lll}
1. & A & \equiv & \text{not } O \\
2. & E & \equiv & \text{not } I \\
3. & I & \equiv & \text{not } E \\
4. & O & \equiv & \text{not } A \\
\end{array}
$$

So, given (1), if "All oranges are citrus fruits" is true, then "It is not the case that some oranges are not citrus fruits" must be true; and vice versa. But given (4), if "Some oranges are not citrus fruits" is true, then "All oranges are citrus fruits" must be false, while "It is not the case that all oranges are citrus fruits" must be true. You should try, as an exercise, to run an example for each of these equivalences. The bottom line is that for the listed propositions, each pair have the same truth value: if one is true, the other must also be true, and if one is false, the other must likewise be false. The former yields validity, the two combined logical equivalence.

BOX 7 ■ LOGICAL EQUIVALENCE AND VALIDITY

Logical Equivalence

When two propositions are logically equivalent, if one is true, then the other is also true, and if one is false, then the other must be false as well. This is because the conditions under which they are true or false are the same. Thus, logically equivalent propositions have the same truth values: they are either both true or both false. As a result, one of them could be substituted for the other while preserving the truth value of the larger expression in which they occur, provided that neither occurs in a special context that could not allow such substitutions. For example, a proposition P is logically equivalent to "It is not the case that not P"; therefore one can be replaced by the other while preserving the truth value of the larger expression in which one of them occurs, provided that, for instance, the expression does not occur inside quotation marks. (For more on this, see "Use and Mention," Section 2.6 in Chapter 2.)

Validity

When two propositions are logically equivalent, if one is true, the other is true as well. This satisfies the definition of entailment or valid argument: logically equivalent propositions entail each other. Any argument from one to the other is valid.

Exercises

IX. Review Questions

1. What is an immediate inference?
2. What is a valid immediate inference?
3. Which propositions are contradictories? What does this mean? Support your answer with examples.
4. Which propositions are contraries? What does this mean? Support your answer with examples.
5. Which propositions are subcontraries? What does this mean? Support your answer with examples.
6. Subalternation works differently depending on whether it is an inference from superaltern to subaltern or vice versa. Explain.
7. Given the modern square of opposition, are there valid immediate inferences by contrariety? If yes, support your answer with an example. If not, why not?

8. Given the modern square of opposition, are there valid immediate inferences by subcontrariety? If yes, support your answer with an example. If not, why not?

9. Given the modern square of opposition, are there valid immediate inferences by subalternation? If yes, support your answer with an example. If not, why not?

10. What does it mean to say that certain propositions have existential import? Which categorical propositions have it, according to the modern interpretation of the square of opposition?

X. **For each of the following, first name the type of the proposition related to it by contrariety or subcontrariety and state that proposition. Then assume that the proposition given is *true* and determine the truth value of its contrary or subcontrary.**

1. All Icelanders are believers in elves.

    SAMPLE ANSWER: *E.* Contrary. No Icelanders are believers in elves. False.

2. No epidemics are dangerous. _____

* 3. Some humans are not mortal. _____

4. No river boat gamblers are honest men. _____

* 5. All labor unions are organizations dominated by politicians. _____

6. Some conservatory gardens are not places open to the public. _____

* 7. Some lions are harmless. _____

8. No used car dealers are people who can be trusted. _____

* 9. Some bats are not nocturnal creatures. _____

10. Some historians are interested in the past. _____

XI. **For each of the propositions above, assume that it is false and determine the truth value of its contrary or subcontrary.**

    SAMPLE ANSWER: 1. *E.* Contrary. Undetermined.

XII. **For each of the following, name the categorical proposition type of its contradictory and state that proposition.**

1. All bankers are fiscal conservatives.

   SAMPLE ANSWER: *O*. Some bankers are not fiscal conservatives.

* 2. No Democrats are opponents of legalized abortion. _____

   3. Some SUVs are vehicles that get good gas mileage. _____

* 4. All professional athletes are highly paid sports heroes. _____

   5. Some tropical parrots are not birds that are noisy and talkative. _____

* 6. Some chipmunks are shy rodents. _____

   7. No captains of industry are cheerful taxpayers. _____

* 8. Some cartographers are amateur musicians. _____

   9. All anarchists are opponents of civil authority. _____

*10. Some airlines are not profitable corporations. _____

XIII. Suppose each categorical proposition listed in the previous exercise is true. What could you know about the truth value of its contradictory? And suppose it is false. What could you know about the truth value of its contradictory?

XIV. For each of the following, first name the type of the proposition related to it by subalternation and state that proposition. Then, assume that the proposition given is true and determine the truth value of its superaltern or subaltern.

   1. Some westerns are not good movies.

   SAMPLE ANSWER: *E* Superaltern. No westerns are good movies. Undetermined.

   2. Some string quartets are works by modern composers.

* 3. No butterflies are vertebrates.

   4. No parakeets are philosophy majors.

* 5. Some comets are not frequent celestial events.

6. All Internal Revenue agents are hard workers.

* 7. Some porcupines are not nocturnal animals.

8. Some Rotarians are pharmacists.

* 9. No extraterrestrials are Republicans.

10. All amoebas are primitive creatures.

XV. For each of the propositions above, assume that it is *false* and determine the truth value of its superaltern or subaltern.

XVI. Suppose each proposition listed below is true. Determine the truth value of all propositions related to it according to the traditional square of opposition, specifying the names of their categorical proposition types, relationship to the given proposition, and content. (Tip for in-class correction: Move clockwise through the relations in the square.)

1. All tables are pieces of furniture.

SAMPLE ANSWER: *E* Contrary. No tables are pieces of furniture. False.
O Contradictory. Some tables are not pieces of furniture. False.
I Subaltern. Some tables are pieces of furniture. True.

2. Some griffins are mythological beasts.

3. No liars are reliable sources.

* 4. Some bassoonists are anarchists.

5. All trombone players are musicians.

* 6. No Americans are people who care about global warming.

7. All white horses are horses.

* 8. All acts of cheating are acts that are wrong.

9. Some cyclists are not welcome in the Tour de France.

*10. Some things are things that are observable with the naked eye.

XVII. Assuming that the propositions listed in the previous exercise are *false*, what is the truth value of each proposition related to them by the traditional square of opposition?

XVIII. Your Own Thinking Lab

1. Assuming that the propositions listed in XVI above are true, use the *modern square of opposition* to draw a valid inference from each of them.

   SAMPLE ANSWER: 1. All tables are pieces of furniture.
   It is false that some tables are not pieces of furniture.

2. Consider propositions such as "No centaur is a freemason," "All hobbits live underground," and "Some cyclops are nearsighted." What's the matter with them according to modern logicians? Explain.

* 3. Determine which logical relation among those represented in the traditional square of opposition holds between premise and conclusion in each of the following arguments. Is the argument valid according to the modern square of opposition? Discuss.

   A. All automobiles that are purchased from used car dealers are good investments. Therefore some automobiles that are purchased from used car dealers are good investments.

   SAMPLE ANSWER: Subalternation. Invalid by the modern square.

   B. Some residents of New York are dentists. Therefore it is not true that no resident of New York is a dentist.

   *C. No boa constrictors are animals that are easy to carry on a bicycle. Therefore, it is false that boas constrictors are animals that are easy to carry on a bicycle.

   D. Some motorcycles that are made in Europe are not vehicles that are inexpensive to repair. Therefore it is not the case that all motorcycles that are made in Europe are vehicles that are inexpensive to repair.

   *E. It is false that some restaurants located in bus stations are places where one is likely to be poisoned. Therefore some restaurants located in bus stations are not places where one is likely to be poisoned.

F. It is not the case that some politicians are not anarchists. Therefore no politicians are anarchists.

*G. No pacifists are war supporters. Therefore it is not true that some pacifists are war supporters.

13.4 Other Immediate Inferences

We'll now turn to three more types of immediate inference that can be validly drawn from categorical propositions: *conversion*, *obversion*, and *contraposition*. In some cases conversion and contraposition allow an inference from a universal to a particular proposition, but the validity of those inferences requires the assumption that the subject terms in the universal premises do not refer to empty classes such as mermaids and square circles.

Conversion

Conversion allows us to infer, from a categorical proposition called the *convertend*, another proposition called its *converse* by switching the former's subject and predicate terms while retaining its original quantity and quality. Thus, from an *E* proposition such as

29 No SUV is a sports car

we can infer by conversion

29' No sports car is an SUV.

Here the convertend's subject and predicate terms have been switched, but its quantity and quality remain the same: universal negative. The inference from (29) to (29') is valid: if (29) is true, then (29') must be true as well (and vice versa). Similarly, by conversion, an *I* proposition yields an *I* converse when the subject and predicate terms of the convertend are switched. For example, the converse of

30 Some Republicans are journalists

is

30' Some journalists are Republicans.

If (30) is true, then (30') must also be true and vice versa—so the inference is valid and the two propositions logically equivalent.

For *A* propositions, however, an inference by conversion in this straightforward way would not be valid. For, clearly, from

31 All pigs are mammals

it does not follow that

31' All mammals are pigs!

Rather, an *A* proposition can be validly converted only "by limitation"—for it does follow from (31) that

31" Some mammals are pigs.

In such a case of *conversion by limitation*, the convertend's quantity has been limited in the converse: the valid converse of an *A*

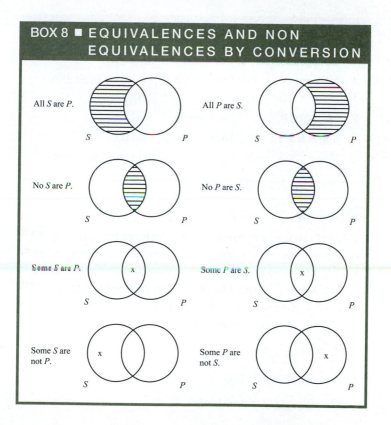

BOX 8 ■ EQUIVALENCES AND NON EQUIVALENCES BY CONVERSION

All *S* are *P*.

All *P* are *S*.

No *S* are *P*.

No *P* are *S*.

Some *S* are *P*.

Some *P* are *S*.

Some *S* are not *P*.

Some *P* are not *S*.

proposition is an *I* proposition where the subject and predicate terms have been switched and the universal quantifier "all" replaced by the nonuniversal quantifier "some."

Finally, note that in the case of O propositions, there is *no* valid conversion at all. If we tried to convert the true proposition,

32 Some precious stones are not emeralds

we'd get the false proposition,

32' Some emeralds are not precious stones.

This proves the invalidity of the inference from (32) to (32'). For any O proposition, an immediate inference by "conversion" commits the *fallacy of illicit conversion,* and the same fallacy is committed when an A proposition is inferred by "conversion" from another A proposition. To sum up, here are the rules for conversion:

> **BOX 9 ■ CONVERSION**
>
> | | Convertend | Converse | Inference |
> |---|---|---|---|
> | A | All *S* are *P* | Some *P* are *S* | (Valid by limitation only) |
> | E | No *S* are *P* | No *P* are *S* | VALID |
> | I | Some *S* are *P* | Some *P* are *S* | VALID |
> | O | Some *S* are not *P* | | (No valid conversion) |

Obversion

A categorical proposition's obverse is inferred by changing the proposition's *quality* (i.e., from affirmative to negative, or negative to affirmative) and adding to its predicate the prefix "non." The proposition deduced by obversion is called the "obverse" and that from which it was deduced, the "obvertend." The inference is valid across the board. Thus, from A proposition,

33 All eagles are birds

it follows by obversion that

33' No eagles are non-birds.

And from the E proposition,

34 No cell phones are elephants.

obversion yields

34' All cell phones are non-elephants.

The obverse of an I proposition such as (35) is (35'),

35 Some Californians are surfers.

35' Some Californians are not non-surfers.

While that of an O proposition such as (36) is (36'):

36 Some epidemics are not catastrophes.

36' Some epidemics are non-catastrophes.

In each of these, the obvertend's predicate has been replaced in the obverse proposition by the predicate for its *class complement*,

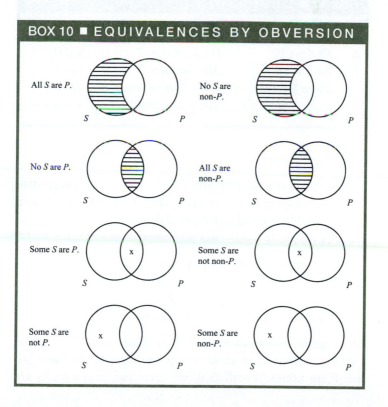

BOX 10 ■ EQUIVALENCES BY OBVERSION

All S are P.

No S are non-P.

No S are P.

All S are non-P.

Some S are P.

Some S are not non-P.

Some S are not P.

Some S are non-P.

which is the class made up of everything *outside of* the class in question. For instance, for the class of *senators* the class complement is the class of *non-senators,* which includes mayors, doctors, brick-layers, airplanes, butterflies, planets, postage stamps, inert gases, etc. ... in fact, *everything that is not a senator.* The class complement of the class of *horses* is *non-horses,* a similarly vast and diverse class of things. For the class of *diseases* the class complement is *non-diseases.* And so on. The expression that denotes any such complement is a *term complement.*

Unlike conversion, obversion is a valid immediate inference for all four types of categorical proposition. For each of the four pairs of categorical propositions listed above, an immediate inference from obvertend to obverse would be valid: if the obvertend is true, the obverse would be true too. The following table summarizes how to draw such inferences correctly:

BOX 11 ■ OBVERSION

	Obvertend	Obverse	Inference
A	All *S* are *P*	No *S* are non-*P*	VALID
E	No *S* are *P*	All *S* are non-*P*	VALID
I	Some *S* are *P*	Some *S* are not non-*P*	VALID
O	Some *S* are not *P*	Some *S* are non-*P*	VALID

Contraposition

Contraposition allows us to infer a conclusion, the *contrapositive,* from another proposition by preserving the latter's quality and quantity while switching its subject and predicate terms, each preceded by the prefix "non." Thus the contrapositive of

37 All croissants are pastries.

is

37' All non-pastries are non-croissants.

Given contraposition, an *A* proposition of the form "All *S* are *P*" is logically equivalent to another *A* proposition of the form "All non-*P* are non-*S.*" Recall that whenever two propositions are

BOX 12 ■ *A*'S EQUIVALENT AND *E*'S NON EQUIVALENT CONTRAPOSITIVES

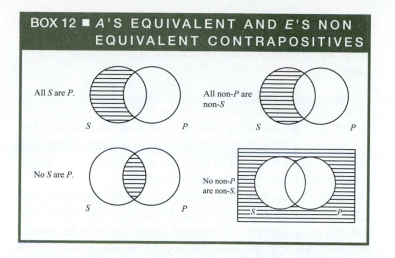

All *S* are *P*.

All non-*P* are non-*S*

No *S* are *P*.

No non-*P* are non-*S*.

logically equivalent, they have exactly the same truth value: if (37) is true, (37') is also true, and if (37) is false, (37') must be false. And, as explained in Box 7 above, whenever two propositions are logically equivalent, we may infer the one from the other: any such inference would be valid. To visualize this relationship between (37) and (37'), you may want to have a look at the corresponding Venn diagrams in Box 12 (think of *S* in the diagram as standing for croissants and *P* for pastries).

Now consider an *I* proposition such as

38 Some croissants are pastries.

BOX 13 ■ *I*'S NONEQUIVALENT AND *O*'S EQUIVALENT CONTRAPOSITIVES

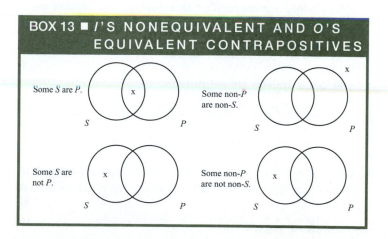

Some *S* are *P*.

Some non-*P* are non-*S*.

Some *S* are not *P*.

Some non-*P* are not non-*S*.

Proposition (38)'s contrapositive would be another proposition of exactly the same quality and quantity where the subject and predicate terms have been switched and prefixed by "non"—namely,

38' Some non-pastries are non-croissants.

But (38) and (38') are *not* logically equivalent, as can be seen in the corresponding Venn diagram (Box 13). Thus any such immediate inference drawn from one to the other would be invalid—an instance of the *fallacy of illicit contraposition*.

With *E* propositions there is also a danger of committing the fallacy of illicit contraposition. But the fallacy can be avoided by limiting the quantity of the original *E* proposition in its contrapositive. That is, an *E* proposition's valid contrapositive is an *O* proposition in which subject and predicate have been switched and prefixed by "non." Thus the contrapositive of

39 No leopards are reptiles

which is clearly true, is

39' Some non-reptiles are not non-leopards

which is logically equivalent and follows from (39). But, without limiting proposition (39)'s quantity, contraposition would be an invalid inference—namely,

40 No leopards are reptiles; therefore, no non-reptiles are non-leopards.

Finally, from an *O* proposition such as

41 Some athletes are not runners.

we can validly infer by contraposition this other *O* proposition,

42 Some non-runners are not non-athletes.

Contraposition of an *O* proposition yields a logically equivalent *O* proposition; thus, inferences from one to the other are always valid.

BOX 14 ■ CONVERSION, OBVERSION, AND CONTRAPOSITION

CONVERSION: Switch S and P, keep the same quality and quantity (exceptions: A and O)

	Convertend	Converse	Inference
A	All S are P	Some P are S	(Valid by limitation only)
E	No S are P	No P are S	VALID
I	Some S are P	Some P are S	VALID
O	Some S are not P		Not valid

OBVERSION: Change quality and add prefix "non" to P

	Obvertend	Converse	Inference
A	All S are P	No S are non-P	VALID
E	No S are P	All S are non-P	VALID
I	Some S are P	Some S are not non-P	VALID
O	Some S are not P	Some S are non-P	VALID

CONTRAPOSITION: Switch S and P and add prefix "non" to each (exceptions: E and I)

	Premise	Contrapositive	Inference
A	All S are P	All non-P are non-S	VALID
E	No S are P	Some non-P are not non-S	(Valid by limitation only)
I	Some S are P		Not valid
O	Some S are not P	Some non-P are not non-S	VALID

Exercises

XIX. Use each of the following categorical propositions as a premise in an inference by conversion, indicating when any such inference is not valid or has restrictions.

1. No accountants are spendthrifts.

SAMPLE ANSWER:
No accountants are spendthrifts.
No spendthrifts are accountants.

2. All beagles are dogs.

* 3. Some candidates are not incumbents.

4. Some trees are conifers.

* 5. All amateurs are non-professionals.

6. Some contrabassoons are antiques.

* 7. No quarks are molecules.

8. Some union workers are not clerks.

* 9. All owls are nocturnal creatures.

10. No podiatrists are assassins.

XX. Use each of the following categorical propositions as a premise in an inference by obversion.

1. Some octogenarians are regular voters.

SAMPLE ANSWER:
Some octogenarians are regular voters.
Some octogenarians are not non-regular voters.

2. All streetcars are public conveyances.

* 3. Some popular songs are hits.

4. All alloys are metals.

* 5. Some psychotherapists are not Democrats.

6. Some robberies are violent crimes.

* 7. All hexagons are plane figures.

8. No provosts are alligator-wrestlers.

* 9. Some Labrador retrievers are affectionate pets.

10. No office buildings are abstract objects.

XXI. Use each of the following categorical propositions as a premise in an inference by contraposition,

indicating when any such inference is not valid or has restrictions.

1. All infectious diseases are illnesses.

   SAMPLE ANSWER:
   All infectious diseases are illnesses.
   All non-illnesses are non-infectious diseases.

* 2. Some used car salesmen are not fast talkers.

3. No non-assassins are violent persons.

* 4. Some citizens are non-voters.

5. Some ethicists are not non-vegetarians.

* 6. No musicians are non-concert goers.

7. Some non-aligned nations are not non-signers of the recent U.N. agreement.

* 8. Some police officers are cigar smokers.

9. All turkeys are native American wildfowls.

*10. Some pickup trucks are not non-expensive vehicles.

XXII. Your Own Thinking Lab

1. Explain the notions of conversion and contraposition by limitation by appealing to *logical equivalence* and *valid inference*. Support your explanation with examples.

* 2. The following inferences are drawn by conversion, obversion, or contraposition. First, determine which is drawn by which, and whether each inference is valid. If not, could the inference be made valid? Explain.

   *A. Some students of the social sciences are not psychology majors. Therefore some psychology majors are not students of the social sciences.

   *B. No movies starring Jennifer Lopez are non-suitable films for viewing by adults. Therefore all movies starring Jennifer Lopez are suitable films for viewing by adults.

   C. All dolphins are whales. Therefore all non-whales are non-dolphins.

   *D. Some tigers are non-Bengali felines. Therefore some Bengali felines are non-tigers.

E. Some government officials are not persons who have taken bribes. Therefore some persons who have taken bribes are not government officials.

F. All news reports are pieces of writing done with word processors. Therefore some pieces of writing done with word processors are news reports.

*G. No warmongers are pacifists. Therefore, no non-pacifists are non-warmongers.

* 3. The following immediate inferences are drawn by one of the relations in the traditional square of opposition, or by conversion, obversion, or contraposition. Determine which is drawn by which, and whether the inference is valid.

A. Some non-pacifists are not non-conscientious objectors. Therefore, some conscientious objectors are not pacifists.

SAMPLE ANSWER: Contraposition, valid.

B. No animals that are avoided by letter carriers are lap dogs. Therefore, it is not the case that some animals that are avoided by letter carriers are lap dogs. _____

*C. Some candidates for public office are not persons who are well known. Therefore no candidates for public office are persons who are well known. _____

D. All carpenters are non–union members. Therefore no carpenters are union members. _____

*E. Some hallucinations are not mirages. Therefore some mirages are not hallucinations. _____

F. No non-dangerous animals are creatures that are kept in zoos. Therefore no non-creatures that are kept in zoos are dangerous animals. _____

*G. All astronauts are motorcycle riders. Therefore it is not the case that no astronauts are motorcycle riders. _____

H. Some naval ships are submarines. Therefore some naval ships are not submarines. _____

*I. All fanatics are political zealots. Therefore no fanatics are non-political zealots. _____

J. All generals are non-amateurs. Therefore all amateurs are non-generals. _____

13.5 The Philosopher's Corner

Generalization and the Appeal to Counterexample

For logical thinkers, one important insight from the modern square of opposition is that universal claims can be refuted by the particular claims that represent their contradictories—where a claim is *refuted* when *proved false*. Given the relationship of contradiction, an *A* proposition is false when its contradictory *O* is true and an *E* false when its contradictory *I* is true. In this connection, it's important to keep in mind that "some" means "at least one"; thus for example,

43 Some politicians are honest.

is logically the same as

43' There is at least one politician who is honest.

Suppose now that someone is trying to convince us that

44 No politicians are honest.

All we have to do to refute this claim is to present *one example* of a politician of unimpeachable probity. Let's assume that the following proposition is true:

45 Barbara Smith is an honest politician.

From (45), it follows that

46 There is at least one politician who is honest.

This is the same as saying

46' Some politicians are honest.

But if either of these is true, then (44) is false. After all, by contradiction, if an *I* proposition is true, an *E* proposition with the same subject and predicate must be false. The same may be inferred when an *O* proposition is true: an *A* proposition with the same subject and predicate must be false.

This logical point illustrates a tactic that is not only useful in debate but very common in philosophical argumentation: the *appeal to counterexample* as a way of refuting a generalization. Let's try another example. Suppose someone (whose acquaintance with the habits of journalists is derived largely from stereotypes in Hollywood movies) claims that

47 All newspaper reporters are heavy drinkers.

As before, all we have to do to prove (47) false is to produce *one example* of a newspaper reporter who does not drink to excess. Suppose we know that Harry Owens, a reporter for the *Daily News*, is a teetotaler—he never drinks alcohol at all. So we cite him. From the truth of this proposition,

48 Harry Owens does not drink to excess

the truth of the next follows:

49 There is at least one newspaper reporter who is not a heavy drinker.

And (49) is logically the same as saying

49' Some newspaper reporters are not heavy drinkers.

Assuming this O proposition to be true, we must conclude that its contradictory A is false. Again, we've refuted a generalization by appealing to a counterexample.

In philosophical argumentation, the appeal to counterexample is very common. A much discussed argument by counterexample concerns the branch of philosophy called *epistemology*, or theory of knowledge. From antiquity until the 1960s, the consensus among epistemologists was that

50 All cases of a person's having a justified true belief are cases of that person's having knowledge.

Given (50), for someone S to *know* a certain proposition P, it is sufficient that (1) P be true, (2) S believe that P; and (3) S be justified in (i.e., have good reasons for) believing that P. However, epistemologists have now pointed out a number of cases in which all three conditions are satisfied but the person doesn't have knowledge. Here is a version of a famous case to that effect: Smith justifiably believes that Jones owns a Ford (suppose he has known Jones from childhood, has always heard Jones say he wouldn't like to own a car of any other make, etc.). From this, Smith validly infers, and thus justifiably believes, that either Jones owns a Ford or Brown is in Barcelona—even though he doesn't really know where Brown is. As a matter of fact, Jones presently does not own a Ford but Brown is in Barcelona. But Smith's belief that Jones owns a Ford or Brown is in Barcelona is true, since Brown *is* in Barcelona. And Smith is justified in believing that disjunction: after all, he validly inferred it. Yet would we say that this is a case of knowledge? It seems not. The case then amounts to a counter-example that appears to refute (50) above. The argument runs,

> **51** 1. There is at least one case (Smith's) of a person's having a justified true belief without having knowledge.
> 2. (50) above is false.

If this argument holds up (as most philosophers now think), then the power of the appeal to counterexample is evident in an especially dramatic way, for here it has been used to undermine one of the central doctrines of epistemology.

Exercises

XXIII. What would it take to refute the following generalizations? Refute each of them by offering counterexamples and then explain the role of these in supporting the relevant *I* or *O* propositions.

1. All cases of knowledge are cases in which a person has the correct answer. _____

2. No mental state can cause a bodily state. _____

3. Knowledge and truth are one and the same. _____

4. Seeing something provides conclusive evidence for believing what one sees. _____

5. Wars are always evil. _____

6. Beliefs that are completely justified (or supported by good reasons) constitute knowledge. _____

7. Scientific theories always begin with observation. _____

8. To be in love is to exhibit love behavior. _____

■ Writing Project

Select five generalizations of pop culture that you find questionable and write a short paper in which you raise objections to them by offering support for their contradictories.

■ Chapter Summary

Categorical propositions represent relations of inclusion or exclusion between classes of things, or between partial classes, or between partial classes and whole classes.

In a Venn diagram representing a categorical proposition, the area shaded out signifies an empty set, while "x" signifies that the set has at least one member. Thus, universal propositions are represented with shaded areas, particular with an "x."

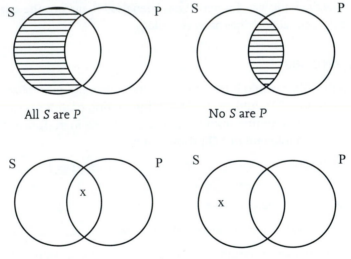

All *S* are *P*   No *S* are *P*

Some *S* are *P*   Some *S* are not *P*

Given the TRADITIONAL SQUARE OF OPPOSITION, the following relationships hold among the specified categorical propositions:

■ *A* and *O*; *E* and *I*: CONTRADICTION
Contradictory propositions cannot have the same truth value (if one is true, then the other must be false, and vice versa).

- *A* and *E*: CONTRARIETY
  Contrary propositions cannot both be true at once but can both be false.
- *I* and *O*: SUBCONTRARIETY
  Subcontrary propositions cannot both be false at once but can both be true.
- *A* and *I*; *E* and *O*: SUBALTERNATION
  If the superaltern is true, then its subaltern is true. If the superaltern is false, then its subaltern is undetermined.
- *I* and *A*; *O* and *E*: SUBALTERNATION
  If the subaltern is true, then its superaltern is undetermined. If the subaltern is false, then its superaltern is false.

Given the THE MODERN SQUARE OF OPPOSITION, the only relationship that holds between two categorical propositions is contradiction. Once we realize that only particular propositions have existential import, the rules for contrariety, subcontrariety, and subalternation cannot be applied across the board.

An immediate inference is a deductive argument with a single premise. The square can be used to draw some such inferences. Other immediate inferences are as given in the following table:

CONVERSION: *S* and *P* switch. Valid for *E* and *I*, but not *A* and *O* propositions

	Convertend	Converse	Inference
A	All *S* are *P*	Some *P* are *S*	(Valid by limitation only)
E	No *S* are *P*	No *P* are *S*	VALID
I	Some *S* are *P*	Some *P* are *S*	VALID
O	Some *S* are not *P*		Not valid

OBVERSION: Quality changes, *P* takes prefix "non." Valid for *A*, *E*, *O*, and *I* propositions

	Obvertend	Obverse	Inference
A	All *S* are *P*	No *S* are non-*P*	VALID
E	No *S* are *P*	All *S* are non-*P*	VALID
I	Some *S* are *P*	Some *S* are not non-*P*	VALID
O	Some *S* are not *P*	Some *S* are non-*P*	VALID

CONTRAPOSITION: *S* and *P* switch, each taking prefix "non."
Valid for *A* and *O* but not *E* and *I* propositions

	Premise	*Contrapositive*	*Inference*
A	All *S* are *P*	All non-*P* are non-*S*	VALID
E	No *S* are *P*	Some non-*P* are not non-*S*	(Valid by limitation only)
I	Some *S* are *P*		Not valid
O	Some *S* are not *P*	Some non-*P* are not non-*S*	VALID

■ Key Words

Categorical proposition
Subject term
Predicate term
Copula
Quantifier
Immediate inference
Existential import
Subaltern
Superaltern
Obversion
Obverse
Obvertend
Conversion
Converse
Square of opposition

Illicit contraposition
Illicit conversion
Universal affirmative
Universal negative
Particular affirmative
Particular negative
Convertend
Contraposition
Contrapositive
Appeal to counterexample
Subcontrariety
Subalternation
Venn diagram for categorical propositions
Contradiction
Contrariety

Categorical Syllogisms

Here you'll read more about traditional logic. This chapter is entirely devoted to syllogistic arguments. It first explains what categorical syllogisms are and then examines two methods of checking them for validity. The topics include

- Recognizing categorical syllogisms and the parts that make them up.
- How to put categorical syllogisms into standard order.
- How to determine the form of a syllogism on the basis of its mood and figure.
- Testing syllogism forms for validity using Venn diagrams.
- The concept of distribution of terms.
- Testing syllogism forms for validity using traditional logic's rules of validity.

- Fallacies committed when the rules of validity are broken.
- A controversy about whether reasoning involving singular terms can be cast as categorical syllogisms.

14.1 What Is a Categorical Syllogism?

Beginning in antiquity with traditional (Aristotelian) logic and continuing for many centuries in other schools of logic, a number of methods have been proposed for analyzing deductive arguments of the sort we have broadly called "syllogistic." A *syllogism* is a deductive argument with two premises. A *categorical syllogism* is a syllogism made up entirely of categorical propositions. Thus there are several different kinds of syllogistic arguments, some of which were considered in Chapters 5 and 12. In this chapter, we'll look closely at *categorical syllogisms*, which, for our purposes here, we'll refer to simply as "syllogisms." For example,

> 1. 1. All rectangles are polygons.
>   2. All squares are rectangles.
>   3. All squares are polygons.

Argument (1) is a syllogism, since it has two premises and a conclusion, all of which are categorical propositions. A closer look at (1)'s premises and conclusion reveals that it has exactly three terms in the position of subject or predicate: "rectangle," "polygon," and "square." Each of these denotes a *category* (or class) of things, and these categories are related in such a way that the argument's conclusion follows validly from its premises. According to that conclusion, the class of squares is wholly included in the class of polygons, which must be true provided that (1)'s premises are true. This is a case of a valid deductive argument: its conclusion is entailed by its premises. But other syllogisms might be invalid. When a syllogism meets the deductive standard of validity, entailment hinges on relations among the *terms* of three different types that occur as subject or predicate of the categorical propositions that make up the syllogism. Since the *validity* of an argument depends on its having a valid form, several methods have been proposed for determining when syllogisms have such forms. But before turning to these, more needs to be said about the structure of standard syllogisms.

The Terms of a Syllogism

A standard syllogism consists of three categorical propositions, two of which function as premises and one as a conclusion. Each of these has a subject term and a predicate term denoting two classes of things, with the proposition as a whole representing a certain relation of exclusion or inclusion among the classes denoted by its subject and predicate terms. Our inspection of each of the categorical propositions making up (1) above showed that its component propositions feature subject and predicate terms of *three different types*: namely, "polygon," "square," and "rectangle." In fact, this is something all standard syllogisms have in common, since they all feature terms of three different types: the so-called *major, minor,* and *middle* terms. The major term is the predicate of the conclusion, the minor term is the subject of the conclusion, and the middle term is the term that occurs only in the premises. Consider (1) again,

1   1. All rectangles are polygons.
     2. All squares are rectangles.
     3. All squares are polygons.

By looking at the predicate and subject of (1)'s conclusion, we can identify this syllogism's major and minor terms respectively: "polygons" (the conclusion's predicate) and "squares" (its subject). Notice that each of these terms occurs also in the premises, but that does not bear on their status as major and minor terms, which is determined solely by their functions as predicate and subject of the conclusion. But in (1), there is also the term "rectangles," that occurs in the subject and predicate positions in the premises. It is the middle term, so called because its function is to mediate between the two premises—to connect them, so that they're both talking about the same thing. In any syllogism, the middle term occurs in both premises but not in the conclusion. Another thing to notice is this: that although each of the three terms of argument (1) is a single word, this is not so in all syllogisms, since sometimes *phrases* can function as subject and predicate of a categorical proposition.

Let's now identify the major, minor, and middle terms in

2 1. No military officers are pacifists.
2. All lieutenant colonels are military officers.
3. No lieutenant colonels are pacifists.

By using the rule just suggested, we can determine that the major term here is "pacifists," the minor term "lieutenant colonels," and middle term "military officers."

> ## BOX 1 ■ THE TERMS OF A SYLLOGISM
>
> The important thing to keep in mind is that in order to identify the three words or phrases that are to count as the *terms* of a syllogism, *we look first to the syllogism's conclusion.* The major term is *whatever* word or phrase turns up in the predicate place (i.e., after the copula) in the conclusion. The minor term is *whatever* word or phrase turns up in the subject place (i.e., between the quantifier and the copula) in the conclusion. And the middle term is the term that does not occur in the conclusion at all but occurs in both premises—whether it be a single word, as in (1) or a more complex expression as in (2).

The Premises of a Syllogism

The conclusion of (1) above is the proposition

> 3. All squares are polygons.

In the notation of traditional logic, this is symbolized as

> 3. All S are P.

It is common practice to represent the minor and major terms of a syllogism as S and P respectively and its middle term as M. We'll adopt that practice and represent any syllogism by replacing its three terms by those symbols, keeping logical words such as quantifiers and negation. In the case of (1) above, we thus obtain

1' 1. All M are P.
2. All S are M.
3. All S are P.

In a standard syllogism, the minor and the major terms occur in *different* premises. That containing the major term is the *major premise*. Since (1)'s major term is "polygons," its major premise is

> ### 1. All rectangles are polygons.

In symbols, this becomes

> ### 1. All *M* are *P*.

The premise that contains the minor term is the *minor premise*. Since (1)'s minor term is "squares," its minor premise is

> ### 2. All squares are rectangles.

In symbols, this becomes

> ### 2. All *S* are *M*.

You may have noticed that in both examples of syllogism considered thus far, each has been arranged with its major premise first, its minor premise second, and its conclusion last. This is the *standard order* for a reconstructed syllogism. Although in ordinary speech and writing a syllogism's premises and conclusion might be jumbled in any order whatsoever, when we reconstruct it, its premises must be put into standard order (this will become especially important later). We can now determine which premise is which in (1) above:

1' 1. All *M* are *P*.   ⇦   MAJOR PREMISE
    2. All *S* are *M*.   ⇦   MINOR PREMISE
    3. All *S* are *P*.

Recognizing Syllogisms

However jumbled they may be in their real-life occurrences, syllogisms can be recognized by first identifying their conclusions.

Once we've identified the conclusion of a putative syllogism, we can check whether it is indeed a syllogism: the conclusion's predicate gives us the major term, its subject the minor term. Once we've identified these terms, we can then look at the argument's premises and ask: Which premise contains the major term? (That's the major premise.) Which contains the minor term? (That's the minor premise.) After listing these in the standard order, as premises 1 and 2 respectively and replacing its relevant terms with symbols, we are in a position to determine whether the argument is a syllogism. How? By applying to it the rule in Box 2.

BOX 2 ■ WHICH ARGUMENTS ARE SYLLOGISMS?

To qualify as a syllogism, an argument must have exactly three categorical propositions and three terms in the positions of subject or predicate, each occurring exactly twice.

Consider the following argument:

3 All governors are public officials. Therefore, some public officials are governors.

(3) is not a syllogism, for it lacks the number of terms and premises needed to qualify. Compare,

4 Since no salamanders are nocturnal animals, no salamanders are bats. For all bats are nocturnal animals.

Is (4) a syllogism? (4) consists of two sentences, and to qualify as a syllogism it must have, among other things, two premises and a conclusion. But a careful look at those two sentences reveals that they do actually express three categorical propositions. We must now determine which of them is the conclusion. Although there is no conclusion indicator here, some premise indicators such as "since" and "for," preceding the first and third propositions respectively, will help us to identify the argument's premises and thereby also its conclusion—which is

> No salamanders are bats.

From this conclusion, we can see immediately that "bats" (its predicate) is *P*, the major term, and salamanders (its subject) is *S*, the minor term. This in turn enables us to identify the major premise,

> All bats are nocturnal animals.

which contains the major term "bats" and the minor premise

> No salamanders are nocturnal animals.

which contains the minor term "salamanders." Clearly, then, the middle term is "nocturnal animals" since it is the only term of the relevant kind that occurs in both premises. We can then reconstruct the argument in standard order:

4' 1. All bats are nocturnal animals.
2. No salamanders are nocturnal animals.
3. No salamanders are bats.

When the *minor term*, *major term*, and *middle term* are replaced by *S*, *P*, and *M*, as before, we find this pattern:

4" 1. All *P* are *M*.
2. No *S* are *M*.
3. No *S* are *P*.

which is one among the many possible patterns of syllogisms. Some such patterns are valid while others are invalid. Before we turn to some methods for determining which is which, let's have a closer look at argument patterns of this syllogistic sort.

A *categorical syllogism* (or, simply, *syllogism*)

■ Is made up of three categorical propositions.
■ Has *three terms*, each of which occurs exactly twice in the
  argument.

The three terms of a syllogism are

NAME		LOGICAL FUNCTION	SYMBOL
Major term	⇨	Predicate of the conclusion	P
Minor term	⇨	Subject of the conclusion	S
Middle term	⇨	Occurs *only* in the premises	M

The occurrence of the major and minor terms in the premises
determine their names and order:

The two premises of a syllogism are

Major premise	⇨	Listed first
Minor premise	⇨	Listed second

14.2 Syllogistic Argument Forms

Traditionally, syllogisms are said to have *forms*, which are determined by their *figures* and *moods*. We'll consider these one at a
time, beginning with figure.

Figure

Since a syllogism has three terms (major, minor, and middle),
each of which occurs twice in either subject or predicate position,
there are the four possible "figures" or configurations of these
terms for any such argument:

First Figure	Second Figure	Third Figure	Fourth Figure
M P	P M	M P	P M
S M	S M	M S	M S
S P	S P	S P	S P

Each of these represents a syllogism's premises and conclusion in standard order without quantifiers and copulas. The only feature that differs substantially among them is the arrangement of the two occurrences of the middle term in the premises. Since it's only the configuration of the middle term in the premises that determines for any syllogism what its figure is, we can emphasize that by representing the position of this term alone in each figure:

First Figure	Second Figure	Third Figure	Fourth Figure
M		M	
	M	M	M
	M	M	
			M

Thus it will be a simple matter to identify the figure of any syllogism: once we have identified its middle term, we note whether it occurs in the subject or predicate place accordingly and then check which figure that amounts to. In this way, we can determine that arguments (1) and (2) are in the first figure and that (4) is in the second figure. In a similar way we can determine the figure of any proposed syllogism.

Consider this one:

5 Because some sharks are saltwater fish and no animals that can survive in a river are saltwater fish, some sharks are not animals that can survive in a river.

First, we identify the conclusion of the argument, namely,

> Some sharks are not animals that can survive in a river.

Since we now know that "sharks" is the minor term and "animals that can survive in a river" the major, we can proceed to identify this syllogism's minor and major premises and reconstruct it as follows:

5' 1. No animals that can survive in a river are saltwater fish.
2. Some sharks are saltwater fish.
3. Some sharks are not animals that can survive in a river.

By replacing the relevant terms with the symbols used above, (5')'s argument form is revealed as

5" 1. No *P* are *M*.
 2. Some *S* are *M*.
 ⎯⎯⎯⎯⎯⎯⎯⎯⎯
 3. Some *S* are not *P*.

Disregarding the quantifiers and copulas, we identify the occurrences of the middle term in the argument and can easily determine that this syllogism is in the second figure.

BOX 4 ■ HOW TO DETERMINE A SYLLOGISM'S FIGURE

- Focus only on the occurrences of the middle term in the premises, as either a subject or a predicate.
- The conclusion always has the minor term as its subject and the major term as its predicate. The predicate and subject of the conclusion determine *what are to count as the major and minor terms* in any syllogism.
- *P* stands for the major term and occurs in premise 1, which is the major premise (i.e., the premise containing the major term).
- *S* stands for the minor term and occurs in premise 2, which is the minor premise (i.e., the premise containing the minor term).

Mood

What about *mood*? As we've seen, a syllogism is made up of three categorical propositions: two make up its premises and one its conclusion. And any categorical proposition must be one or the other of four types: universal affirmative, universal negative, particular affirmative, or particular negative—whose names are, respectively, *A*, *E*, *I*, and *O*.

> The mood of a syllogism consists in a list of the names of its three component propositions.

In (5") above, the major premise is type *E*, the minor premise is *I*, and the conclusion is *O*; thus its mood is *EIO*. In the other examples above, the mood is (1) *AAA*, (2) *EAE*, and (4) *AEE*. Now consider this argument form:

6 1. Some *P* are *M*.
    2. Some *M* are *S*.
    3. Some *S* are not *P*.

In (6), both premises are type *I* and the conclusion is type *O*. Hence, (6)'s mood is *IIO* and its figure, the fourth. How about this one?

7 1. No *P* are *M*.
    2. No *S* are *M*.
    3. Some *S* are *P*.

Since (7)'s premises are both type *E* and its conclusion type *I*, its mood is *EEI*. At the same time, given the position of (7)'s middle term, the argument form exemplifies the second figure.

Determining a Syllogism's Form

So (7)'s mood and figure together are *EEI-2*. Since the mood and figure of a syllogism constitute its *form*, we may equivalently say that (7)'s form is *EEI-2*, as (6)'s form is *IIO-4*, and so on. The *form* of a syllogism, then, is given by the combination of its mood and figure.

In traditional logic, determining the forms of syllogisms was crucial to establishing their validity, for it is the form that can reveal whether a syllogism follows or flouts certain rules of validity that we'll consider later. Before we do that, however, let's review the steps described so far. Let's try the whole process of finding a syllogism's form, starting at the beginning. Consider this argument:

8 No campus residence halls without computer hookups are good places to live. After all, some campus residence halls without computer hookups are old buildings, but some old buildings are not good places to live.

BOX 5 ■ A SYLLOGISM'S FORM

Mood + *figure* = *form*

Argument (8)'s conclusion is

> No campus residence halls without computer hookups
> are good places to live.

How do we know? Because we have read the argument carefully and asked ourselves: What claim is being made? (In addition, the premises are introduced by an indicator, "after all".) Having found the conclusion, we then look for its predicate and subject, which are the major and minor terms, respectively:

> $P =$ good places to live.
> $S =$ campus residence halls without computer hookups.

We can now identify the syllogism's major and minor premises. Since the major premise must contain the major term, it must be

> 1. Some old buildings are not good places to live.

We can therefore put this as the first premise. Similarly, the minor premise must contain the minor term, so it must be

> 2. Some campus residence halls without computer hookups are old buildings.

That is the second premise. Thus the reconstructed syllogism is

9 1. Some old buildings are not good places to live.
   2. Some campus residence halls without computer hookups are old buildings.
   3. No campus residence halls without computer hookups are good places to live.

Argument (9) illustrates a pattern that may be represented as

9' 1. Some M are not P.
   2. Some S are M.
   3. No S are P.

Any syllogism illustrating this pattern would be of the form *OIE*-1. For example,

> **10** 1. Some CIA operatives are not FBI agents.
> 2. Some women are CIA operatives.
> ___
> 3. No women are FBI agents.

Now something has gone wrong with (10) and any other syllogism along the same pattern—that of (9) above. Clearly, any such syllogism may have true premises and a false conclusion. Next we'll consider which syllogistic patterns are valid and which are not.

Exercises

I. Review Questions

1. What is generally understood by "syllogism" and "categorical syllogism"?
2. How do we identify the major term, minor term, and middle term of a syllogism?
3. What is meant by "major premise"?
4. What is meant by "minor premise"?
5. When is a syllogism in standard order?
6. How do we identify the mood of a syllogism?
7. How do we identify the figure of a syllogism?
8. How do we determine the form of a syllogism?

II. For each of the following arguments, determine whether it is a syllogism. If it isn't, indicate why, and move on to the next argument. If it is, put the syllogism into standard order, and replace its major, minor, and middle terms with the appropriate symbols *P*, *S*, or *M*.

1. Some dinosaurs are not members of the reptile family. For no members of the reptile family are mammals and some dinosaurs are mammals.

   SAMPLE ANSWER:

1. No members of the reptile family are mammals.	No *P* are *M*.
2. Some dinosaurs are mammals.	Some *S* are *M*.
3. Some dinosaurs are not members of the reptile family.	Some *S* are not *P*.

2. Some Japanese car manufacturers make fuel-efficient cars, but no fuel-efficient cars are pickup trucks. Since all pickup trucks are expensive vehicles, therefore no Japanese car manufacturers make expensive vehicles.

* 3. All North American rivers are navigable. It follows that no North American rivers are non-navigable.

4. Some summer tourists are mountain climbers, for some risk takers are summer tourists and all mountain climbers are risk takers.

* 5. No Sinatra songs are popular with first-graders, since all Sinatra songs are romantic songs and no romantic songs are popular with first-graders.

* 6. Some men are Oscar winners but no Oscar winners are talk-show hosts. Thus, some men are not talk–show hosts.

7. Some persons knowledgeable about heart disease are not members of the American Heart Association. For one thing, although some cardiologists are members of the American Heart Association, some aren't. In addition, all cardiologists are persons knowledgeable about heart disease.

8. No eye doctors are optometrists but some eye doctors are professionals with M.D. degrees. It follows that some professionals with M.D. degrees are not optometrists.

* 9. All metals are substances that expand under heat. Therefore, it is not the case that some metals are not substances that expand under heat.

10. No conservatives are supporters of gay marriage. Hence, some supporters of gay marriage are persons who favor abortion rights, since no conservatives are persons who favor abortion rights.

*11. All computer scientists are programmers, and some programmers are pool players. It follows that some computer scientists are pool players.

12. No movie reviewers are mathematicians. Since all mathematicians are experts in geometry and some mathematicians are experts in geometry, it follows that no movie reviewers are experts in geometry.

III. For each of the following syllogistic patterns, identify its mood and figure.

1. 1. Some *M* are *P*.
   2. Some *M* are *S*.
   3. Some *S* are not *P*.

   SAMPLE ANSWER: IIO-3

2. 1. No *M* are *P*.
   2. No *S* are *M*.
   3. No *S* are *P*.

3. 1. Some *P* are not *M*.
   2. Some *S* are not *M*.
   3. All *S* are *P*.

* 4. 1. All *M* are *P*.
   2. Some *S* are *M*.
   3. All *S* are *P*.

5. 1. Some *P* are *M*.
   2. Some *S* are *M*.
   3. Some *S* are *P*.

* 6. 1. No *P* are *M*.
   2. All *M* are *S*.
   3. All *S* are *P*.

7. 1. Some *M* are *P*.
   2. All *M* are *S*.
   3. No *S* are *P*.

* 8. 1. Some *M* are not *P*.
   2. Some *S* are not *M*.
   3. No *S* are *P*.

9. 1. Some *P* are *M*.
   2. All *S* are *M*.
   3. All *S* are *P*.

*10. 1. Some *M* are not *P*.
   2. Some *S* are *M*.
   3. Some *S* are *P*.

11. 1. Some *P* are not *M*.
    2. Some *M* are not *S*.
    3. Some *S* are *P*.

*12. 1. No *M* are *P*.
     2. No *M* are *S*.
     3. All *S* are *P*.

IV. **Reconstruct each of the following syllogisms and give its form:**

1. Since all Italian sports cars are fast cars, it follows that no fast cars are inexpensive machines, because no inexpensive machines are Italian sports cars.

   SAMPLE ANSWER: *EAE*-4

1. No inexpensive machines are Italian sports cars.	1. No *P* are *M*
2. All Italian sports cars are fast cars.	2. All *M* are *S*.
3. No fast cars are inexpensive machines.	3. No *S* are *P*

2. Because no airlines that fly to Uzbekistan are airlines that offer discount fares, some airlines that offer discount fares are carriers that are not known for their safety records. For some carriers that are not known for their safety records are airlines that fly to Uzbekistan.

* 3. Since some residents of California are people who are not Lawrence Welk fans, and all people who listen to reggae music are people who are not Lawrence Welk fans, we may infer that some residents of California are people who listen to reggae music.

4. No members of the Committee for Freedom are people who admire dictators. For all members of the Committee for Freedom are libertarians, and no libertarians are people who admire dictators.

* 5. All loyal Americans are people who are willing taxpayers. Hence, all people who are willing taxpayers are supporters of the president in his desire to trim the federal budget, for all loyal Americans are supporters of the president in his desire to trim the federal budget.

6. All Rottweilers that are easily annoyed are animals that are avoided by letter carriers; for some lap dogs are not Rottweilers that are easily annoyed, but no animals that are avoided by letter carriers are lap dogs.

* 7. No reptiles weighing over 80 pounds are animals that are convenient house pets. After all, all animals that are convenient house pets are creatures your Aunt Sophie would like, but no creatures your Aunt Sophie would like are reptiles weighing over 80 pounds.

8. Since some senators are people who will not take bribes, and all people who will not take bribes are honest people, it follows that some senators are honest people.

* 9. No explosives are safe things to carry in the trunk of your car, for some explosives are devices that contain dynamite and some devices that contain dynamite are not safe things to carry in the trunk of your car.

10. No sturgeons are surgeons. Hence some sturgeons are not beings who are licensed to perform a coronary bypass, since some beings who are licensed to perform a coronary bypass are surgeons.

*11. No pacifists are persons who favor the use of military force. Hence some persons who favor the use of military force are not conscientious objectors, for some pacifists are not conscientious objectors.

12. Some rhinos are not dangerous animals, because all dangerous animals are creatures that are kept in zoos, and some rhinos are not creatures that are kept in zoos.

V. YOUR OWN THINKING LAB

1. For each of the following syllogistic forms, provide a syllogism that is an instance of it:

   1. *AAA*-1
   2. *AEE*-2
   3. *OAO*-3
   4. *EIO*-4
   5. *AII*-3
   6. *EAE*-1
   7. *EAE*-2
   8. *AEE*-4
   9. *IAI*-3
   10. *IAI*-4

2. All of the above syllogistic forms are valid. What do you now know about the conclusion of a syllogism that exemplifies any of them?

And what would you know about any such syllogism if its premises were in fact true?

14.3 Testing for Validity with Venn Diagrams

Syllogisms can have configurations that make up 256 different forms. Since some of these are valid and some are not, it is essential that there be some dependable way of determining, for any given syllogistic form, whether it is valid. In fact there are several different ways of doing this, but we shall focus here on one very widely accepted technique based on Venn diagrams, the rudiments of which we examined in Chapter 13.

How to Diagram a Standard Syllogism

In using Venn diagrams to check the validity of syllogisms, we adapt that system of two-circle diagrams for categorical propositions to a larger diagram with three interlocking circles.

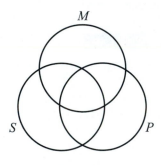

Figure 1

Here the circles represent the three distinct classes of things denoted by the three terms of a syllogism. The two bottom circles, labeled *S* and *P*, represent the classes denoted by the syllogism's minor and major terms. The top circle, labeled M, represents the class denoted by the syllogism's middle term. Now notice another thing about this diagram: we can find within it subclass spaces of two important shapes that will be crucial to our diagrams. We've already encountered these in the two-circle diagrams discussed in

BOX 6 ■ VENN DIAGRAMS AND SYLLOGISTIC FORMS

Starting from this basic diagram, we can represent any of the possible forms of syllogism. Once a complete Venn diagram is drawn for any syllogism, it shows whether the argument is valid or invalid.

the last chapter. They are the American football shape (Figure 2) and the crescent (Figure 3):

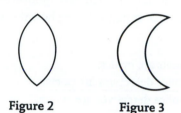

Figure 2   **Figure 3**

On the three-circle Venn diagram, the football shape can be found in three places. Can you see where? The crescent can be found in six places. Can you locate these? For the purpose of putting shading or *x*'s on the three-circle Venn diagram, *the only subclass spaces we'll be concerned with are those in the shape of either a football or a crescent.* If you try to shade, or put an *x* in, any other shape, you'll not be using the Venn system.

Finally, notice that, on the three-circle diagram, there are three different ways of grouping the circles together into pairs.

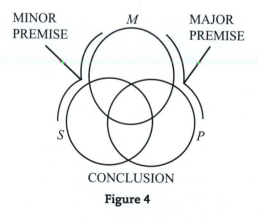

Figure 4

These three groupings mark the areas where each of a syllogism's three propositions are represented: M and P are used to diagram its *major premise*, M and S its *minor premise*, and S and P its *conclusion*. Again, the purpose of drawing this sort of three-circle Venn diagram is to test the validity of a syllogism. But the test requires that we diagram propositions across two circles at a time, using what we have learned in Chapter 13 about Venn diagrams for each of the four types of categorical proposition. To do this, we take into account, one at a time, pairs of circles representing the major premise, minor premise, and the conclusion, in each case ignoring the circle that is irrelevant to the task at hand. To see how this works, let's test a syllogism.

11   1. No poets are cynics.
       2. All police detectives are poets.
       3. No police detectives are cynics.

A quick look reveals that this syllogism is already in standard order, so the first step in argument analysis has been done. We can then see that the major term is "cynics," the minor term "police detectives," and the middle term "poets," so that the argument is an instance of the form *EAE*-1, which we could spell out in this standard way:

11'   1. No M are P.
       2. All S are M.
       3. No S are P.

BOX 7 ■ STARTING OUT A VENN DIAGRAM'S VALIDITY TEST

Diagram only the syllogism's premises. Do not try to diagram the conclusion.

Now, are syllogisms of this form valid or invalid? A Venn diagram can test this. Box 7 gives us the first rule to follow in implementing this test. So we are concerned at this stage only with the two pairs of circles representing the major and minor premises, which in the diagram are:

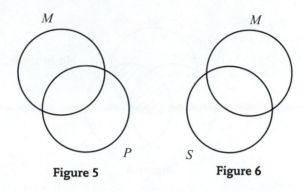

Figure 5   **Figure 6**

Now, which premise shall we diagram first? Here the rule, whose rationale will become apparent later, is in Box 8. In (11')'s case, both premises are universal, so it's a matter of indifference which one we choose to diagram first. Let's arbitrarily choose the major premise, which in (11') is "No *M* are *P*". This is an *E* proposition, and recall that the Venn diagram for such propositions is

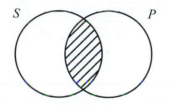

No *S* are *P*

Figure 7

BOX 8 ■ HOW TO DIAGRAM A SYLLOGISM'S PREMISES

If one premise is universal and the other particular, you must diagram the universal premise first, whichever it is. But if both premises are universal or both particular, it doesn't matter which is diagrammed first.

When drawn directly on the pair of circles in the larger diagram, the diagram in Figure 7 looks like this:

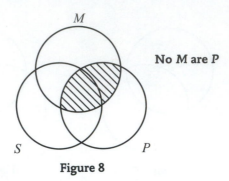

No *M* are *P*

Figure 8

So much for the major premise. Now what about the minor? In (11') the minor premise is "All *S* are *M*," which is clearly an *A* proposition. And the two-circle Venn diagram for that, you'll recall, is

All *S* are *P*

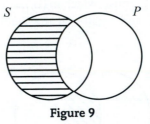

Figure 9

If we represent the minor premise in this way, the larger diagram will then look like this:

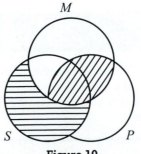

Figure 10

Here we have both premises in the diagram: at this point, the diagram is complete. We'll put no more marks on it. Now for the final step: We simply ignore the circle for the middle term altogether and *look at* the circles representing the syllogism's conclusion, asking ourselves, do we have there a two-circle Venn diagram symbolizing the type of categorical proposition exemplified by the argument's conclusion? If *yes*, then the diagram shows its form to be *valid*. If *no*, then the diagram shows it to be *invalid*. Since the conclusion in (11') is "No *S* are *P*," and that is an *E* proposition, whose diagram is the same as in Figure 7 above; and since a glance at Figure 10 reveals that the football-shaped space where *S* and *P* overlap has indeed gotten shaded out, the diagram proves (11')'s form, *EAE*-1, to be valid. This means, then, that *any syllogism whatsoever* having that form will also be valid. The principle here is simple:

> If in diagramming both premises of a syllogism, we've *automatically* diagrammed its conclusion, the argument is valid. Any time this fails to happens, the syllogism is invalid.

Now let's test another syllogism with a Venn diagram:

12   1. Some conservatives are public figures.
     2. All politicians are public figures.
     3. Some politicians are conservatives.

Here again we find a syllogism that is already in standard order, so that the first step in the analysis has been done. With the argument arranged in this order, it's then clear that its major

BOX 9 ■ HOW TO READ A VENN DIAGRAM'S RESULT

In using a Venn diagram as a test of validity, we diagram a syllogism's premises first and then check whether we can read off its conclusion unambiguously from what's already in the diagram. If we can, then the syllogism is valid. If not, then it's invalid.

term is "conservatives," its minor term "politicians," and its middle term "public figures." Argument (12)'s pattern is

12' 1. Some *P* are *M*.
2. All *S* are *M*.

3. Some *S* are *P*.

which is *IAI*-2. To check the validity of a syllogism with this pattern, we'll construct a Venn diagram. Recall that *only the premises* are diagrammed (not the conclusion) and notice that, in this argument, the order in which the premises are diagrammed *does* matter. That's because here, one premise is universal and the other particular, and, given the rule in Box 8, in any such case the universal premise must be diagrammed first and the particular second. For this syllogism, then, we have no choice but to diagram the minor premise first and the major premise second. The minor premise is an *A* proposition represented in the Venn diagram in this way:

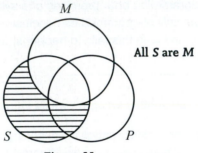

Figure 11

Next, we add to the diagram the syllogism's major premise, an *I* proposition that, once incorporated in the diagram, makes it look like this:

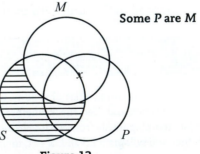

Figure 12

Since the Venn diagram for any *I* proposition is

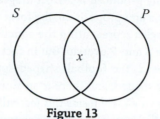

Figure 13

therefore in the case of the syllogistic form we are representing now, the diagram of its major premise is

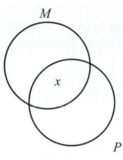

Figure 14

But why does the *x* in Figure 12 fall on the line within the football-shaped space where *M* and *P* intersect? Clearly, if we're going to put an *x* inside this football to indicate that at least some *M* are *P*, we have to decide which side of the line in that space the *x* goes on. Had one or the other half of the football been shaded, the *x* would have gone in the unshaded part. But here there's no shading, so we have no justification for choosing one side of the line over the other—all we know is that the *x* goes *somewhere* inside the football, and we express this noncommittal position by putting the *x* *on the line* dividing the football-shaped space (*x*'s don't always go on lines like this, but here it does).

Now let's look at Figure 12 and see what it tells us about the validity or invalidity of the form *IAI-2*, which is that of syllogisms such as (12) above. Because the conclusion of this argument is "Some *S* are *P*," the form will be shown valid only if the process of diagramming the two premises as we've described has automatically produced a correct diagram for that conclusion. Since that is an *I* proposition, the form would be valid only if the pair of circles representing the conclusion shows an x in the space where *S* and *P* overlap. But in fact we do *not* find that at all. In Figure 12, the football-shaped space where *S* and *P* overlap is partly shaded, and there is an x on its outer edge. Because there is no x clearly *inside this football*, however, we must conclude that the Venn diagram has shown *IAI*-2 to be an invalid form. Here the process of diagramming the two premises *failed to produce automatically* a diagram for the conclusion in the bottom pair of circles. Thus *IAI*-2 is invalid, and argument (12), which has this form, is an invalid syllogism. We've proved that, whatever the truth values of its component propositions (in this case, they're *all true*), its conclusion does not follow validly from its premises.

Finally, let's use a Venn diagram to test the validity of syllogisms of the form *OIE*-1. For example, (9) above, whose form we spelled out as

9' 1. Some *M* are not *P*.
  2. Some *S* are *M*.
  ———————————
  3. No *S* are *P*.

Because both premises are particular, it doesn't matter which one is diagrammed first. We choose to diagram the minor premise first, which we represent in this way:

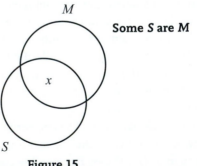

Figure 15

On the larger diagram, the diagram for that premise looks like this:

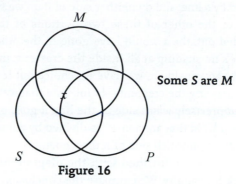

Some *S* are *M*

Figure 16

The diagram for the major premise shows an *x* in the part of *M* that is outside of *P*.

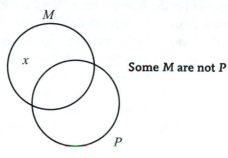

Some *M* are not *P*

Figure 17

When we represent that premise in the three-circle diagram, we get this:

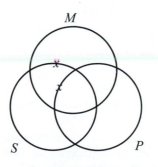

Figure 18

Why? Because, in Figure 18, the crescent-shaped space where the x goes in representing "Some M are not P"; is itself divided by a line, and on neither side of it do we find shading. Had one or the other of these two portions of the crescent been shaded out, the x would have gone in the *other* part. But here, there's no shading at all inside the crescent; therefore if we are to put an x inside it, we have no choice but to put the x on the line dividing the crescent—to indicate that we're noncommittal about precisely *which* side of the line it goes on. Given that the crescent, "M that are *non-P*" is divided by a line, it is simply not decidable on which side of it the x goes.

Now we're finished with the diagramming and ready to check for validity. We compare the conclusion of the argument with the part of the diagram that represents it. Do they match up? Clearly, in this case they do not. For the conclusion of the argument is the E proposition "No S are P". A correct Venn diagram for any such proposition shows the intersection between S and P shaded out (see Figure 7 above). But that is not what Figure 18 represents. So here's an instance where the process of diagramming the premises *did not* automatically produce in the bottom pair of circles a diagram that represents the conclusion as given. Thus the Venn diagram proves the form OIE-1 to be invalid. We conclude that argument (9) is invalid.

BOX 10 ■ SUMMARY

How to test the validity of a syllogism with a Venn diagram:

- Draw three intersecting circles.
- Diagram only the premises.
- If one premise is universal and the other particular, you must diagram the universal premise first, whichever it is.
- But if both premises are universal or both particular, it doesn't matter which is diagrammed first.
- Once you have diagrammed the premises, if the conclusion is already unequivocally diagrammed too, then the argument is valid. Otherwise, the argument is invalid.

Exercises

VI. Review Questions

1. In using a Venn diagram to represent an argument form, what are the only two shapes in which shading or an *x* can go?
2. In a three-circle Venn diagram, what is represented by each of the circles?
3. Which part of a Venn diagram represents the major premise of a syllogism?
4. Which part of a Venn diagram represents the minor premise of a syllogism?
5. In diagramming a syllogism with a Venn diagram, which premise is diagrammed first?
6. How do we tell, using a Venn diagram, whether a syllogism is valid or not?

VII. Reconstruct each of the following syllogisms, identify its form and test it for validity with a Venn diagram.

1. Since all logicians are philosophers and some philosophers are not vegetarians, it follows that some logicians are not vegetarians.

   SAMPLE ANSWER: 1. Some philosophers are not vegetarians.
   2. All logicians are philosophers.
   3. Some logicians are not vegetarians.

   1. Some *M* are not *P*.   OAO-1
   2. All *S* are *M*.
   3. Some *S* are not *P*.   INVALID

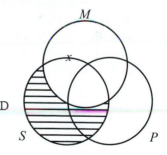

2. No dictators are humanitarians, because no tyrants are humanitarians, and some dictators are tyrants.

3. Some medical conditions that are not treatable by conventional means are causes of death. Hence, some causes of death are not

things related to eating pizza, for no medical conditions that are not treatable by conventional means are things related to eating pizza.

* 4. Some taxi drivers are people who never run red lights, because all taxi drivers are people who are not elitists, and some people who never run red lights are people who are not elitists.

5. Some economists who are members of the faculty at the University of Chicago are not monetarists; so, no monetarists are White Sox fans, for all economists who are members of the faculty at the University of Chicago are White Sox fans.

6. Since all readers of poetry are benevolent people, it follows that no fanatics are benevolent people, for no fanatics are readers of poetry.

* 7. No armadillos are intelligent creatures, for all intelligent creatures are things that will stay out of the middle of the highway; but no armadillos are things that will stay out of the middle of the highway.

8. No newspaper columnists are motorcycle racers; however, some motorcycle racers are attorneys. Therefore some attorneys are not newspaper columnists.

9. Some candidates for public office are not persons who are well known. After all, some citizens who are listed on the ballot are not persons who are well known, and all citizens who are listed on the ballot are candidates for public office.

10. Because some axolotls are creatures that are not often seen in the city, we may infer that some mud lizards that are found in the jungles of southern Mexico are creatures that are not often seen in the city, since all axolotls are mud lizards that are found in the jungles of southern Mexico.

11. Since some members of Congress are not senators, it follows that some members of Congress are not experienced politicians, for all senators are experienced politicians.

12. Some historical developments are not entirely explainable. After all, all historical developments are contingent things, and no contingent things are entirely explainable.

*13. All orthodontists are dentists who have done extensive postdoctoral study, but no impoverished persons are dentists who have done extensive postdoctoral study. Thus no orthodontists are impoverished persons.

14. All people who ride bicycles in rush hour traffic are courageous people, for some courageous people are professors who are not tenured members of the faculty, and no professors who are not tenured members of the faculty are people who ride bicycles in rush hour traffic.

15. Some investment brokers are not Harvard graduates. So, some financiers are not investment brokers, since some financiers are not Harvard graduates.

*16. All philosophy majors are rational beings, but no parakeets are rational beings. Therefore no parakeets are philosophy majors.

17. Since some wars are inevitable occurrences, and no inevitable occurrences are things that can be prevented, it follows that some wars are not things that can be prevented.

18. All factory workers are union members, for some union members are not persons who are easy to convince and some factory workers are not persons who are easy to convince.

*19. Since no hallucinations are optical illusions, we may infer that some misunderstandings that are not avoidable are optical illusions, for some misunderstandings that are not avoidable are hallucinations.

20. Some senators who are not opponents of foreign aid are friends of the president. But all friends of the president are influential people who are well informed about world events; hence some senators who are not opponents of foreign aid are influential people who are well informed about world events.

21. Some fantastic creatures that are not found anywhere in nature are not dogfish. So we may infer that no dogfish are fish that bark, since some fantastic creatures that are not found anywhere in nature are fish that bark.

*22. Some college presidents are not benevolent despots, for no benevolent despots are defenders of faculty autonomy, and no defenders of faculty autonomy are college presidents.

23. Since some elderly professors who are not bald are respected scholars, it follows that some classical philologists are respected

scholars, for no elderly professors who are not bald are classical philologists.

24. Some people who have quit smoking are people who are not enthusiastic sports fans, but no soccer players are people who are not enthusiastic sports fans. So some people who have quit smoking are soccer players.

*25. All philanderers are habitual prevaricators. Therefore no preachers who are well-known television personalities are philanderers, because no habitual prevaricators are preachers who are well-known television personalities.

26. Some pinchpennies are not alumni who are immensely wealthy, for no pinchpennies are generous contributors to their alma mater, and some alumni who are immensely wealthy are generous contributors to their alma mater.

27. All persons employed by the state government are civil servants, for no persons employed by the state government are persons who are eligible to participate in the state lottery, and no civil servants are persons who are eligible to participate in the state lottery.

*28. Since all great music is uplifting, it follows that some jazz is great music, for some jazz is uplifting.

29. No Muscovites are country bumpkins, but some Russians who are veterans of World War II are not Muscovites. Hence, some country bumpkins are not Russians who are veterans of World War II.

*30. Some interest-bearing bank accounts are not an effective means of increasing one's wealth. After all, some investments that are insured by the federal government are not an effective means of increasing one's wealth, and all investments that are insured by the federal government are interest-bearing bank accounts.

VIII. YOUR OWN THINKING LAB

1. It is sometimes said that the conclusion of a valid syllogism is already contained in its premises. How could this be explained in connection with Venn diagrams for testing the validity of syllogisms?

2. For each form represented below, give two syllogisms of your own:

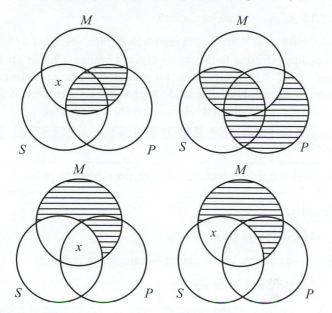

14.4 Distribution of Terms

Although Venn diagrams provide a reliable way of checking syllogistic forms for validity, they are not the only way of doing so. Another method relies on a short list of rules of validity that any indisputably valid syllogism must follow and a list of fallacies that any such syllogism necessarily avoids. We'll devote the remainder of this chapter to a look at some details of this technique, which is based on one of the traditional parts of Aristotelian logic.

To use this method, it's first necessary to understand the notion of *distribution of terms*.

Earlier, we saw that one use of the word "term" is to refer to the substantive parts of a categorical proposition: its *subject* and *predicate* are its *terms*. To describe a term as "distributed" is to say that it's referring to an entire class. In a proposition that is universal affirmative, the pattern of distribution is:

> *A* proposition: subject *distributed*, predicate *undistributed*.

Thus, in

> **13** All oranges are citrus fruits,

the subject term, "oranges," is distributed since, preceded by "all," it's plainly referring to the whole class of oranges. But its predicate term, "citrus fruits," is *not* distributed, since no universal claim of any kind is being made here about all members of the class of things to which it refers—namely citrus fruits.

In a proposition that is universal negative the pattern of distribution is:

> *E* proposition: subject *distributed*, predicate *distributed*.

Consider,

> **14** No apples are citrus fruits.

This is—as we saw in Chapter 13—logically equivalent to

> **14'** No citrus fruits are apples.

Either way, these propositions deny, of the whole class of apples, that it includes citrus fruits, and of the whole class of citrus fruits, that it includes apples. Put a different way, (14) is asserting that there is total, mutual exclusion between the whole classes of apples and citrus fruits. So it's clear that in (14) *both* the subject term and the predicate term are distributed. Here something is being said about *entire classes* (namely, that they exclude each other).

Let's now turn to the patterns of distribution for particular propositions, which include particular affirmatives such as

> **15** Some oranges are edible fruits,

and particular negatives such as

> **16** Some oranges are not edible fruits.

The pattern of distribution for any particular affirmative proposition is

> *I* proposition: subject *undistributed*, predicate *undistributed*.

and for any particular negative proposition, it is

> *O* proposition: subject *undistributed*, predicate *distributed*.

(15) amounts to the proposition that there is at least one orange that is an edible fruit. This proposition's subject is undistributed because this term doesn't refer to the whole class of oranges. Similarly, its predicate term, "edible fruits," is equally undistributed, since this term doesn't refer to the whole class of edible fruits but only to those edible fruits that are oranges.

Finally, although the subject of (16) is not distributed, for the same reason just provided for the subject of (15), its predicate term *is*. Why? Because it refers to the class of edible fruits as a whole, which becomes plain when (15) is recast as the proposition that there is at least one orange that is *not* in the *class* (taken as a whole) of edible fruits.

To sum up, the four patterns of distribution are as follows:

A (universal affirmative)	All *S* are *P*	Subject distributed, predicate not
E (universal negative)	No *S* are *P*	Both terms distributed
I (particular affirmative)	Some *S* are *P*	Neither term distributed
O (particular negative)	Some *S* are not *P*	Predicate distributed, subject not

Keeping in mind the patterns of distribution outlined in Box 11 will make it easier for you to use the rules of validity to determine whether syllogistic argument forms are valid or invalid.

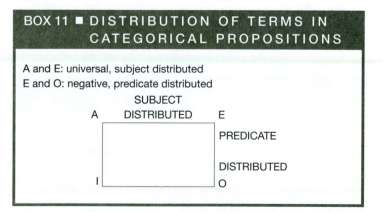

BOX 11 ■ DISTRIBUTION OF TERMS IN CATEGORICAL PROPOSITIONS

A and E: universal, subject distributed
E and O: negative, predicate distributed

SUBJECT

A   DISTRIBUTED   E

PREDICATE

DISTRIBUTED

I   O

14.5 Rules of Validity and Fallacies

Here we'll consider six rules that can be used to test whether any given syllogism is valid. We'll also look at the fallacies that are committed when these rules are broken. First proposed in Aristotelian logic, rules along the lines we'll discuss here represent an alternative to Venn diagrams as a procedure for determining the validity of syllogisms. Let's consider each of these rules one at a time, together with its rationale.

RULE 1: *A syllogism must have exactly three terms.*

The conclusion of a syllogism is a categorical proposition where two terms are related in a certain way. But they could be so related only if there is a third term to which the subject and predicate of the conclusion are each independently related. That is, for a syllogism's conclusion to follow validly from its two premises, there must be precisely three terms, no more and no fewer, each occurring twice: the major term as the predicate of the conclusion and as either the subject or predicate of the major premise; the minor term as the subject of the conclusion and as either the subject or predicate of the minor premise; and the middle term once in each of the premises, where it may appear as either subject or predicate.

Syllogisms sometimes flout this rule of validity by having some term used *with two different meanings* in its two occurrences, so that the argument equivocates (see Chapter 9). Any such argument is said to commit the *fallacy of four terms* (or *quaternio terminorum*). For example, consider

> **17** 1. All the members of that committee are snakes.
> 2. All snakes are reptiles.
> _____
> 3. All members of that committee are reptiles.

BOX 12 ■ DETERMINING VALIDITY WITH THE SIX RULES

- ■ Any syllogism that *obeys all six rules* is *valid.*
- ■ Any syllogism that *breaks even one rule* is *invalid,* though some syllogisms may break more than one.

Here the term "snakes" is plainly used with two different meanings. As a result, the syllogism commits the fallacy of four terms and is therefore invalid.

> RULE 2: *The middle term must be distributed at least once.*

A syllogism's middle term, you'll recall, is the term that occurs in both premises (and *only* in the premises). It functions to connect the minor and major terms, so that the relation among these could be as presented in the syllogism's conclusion. But the middle term can do that only if it's referring to a whole class in at least one of the premises, for if it refers to one class or part of a class in the major premise and another in the minor, then the minor and major terms would be connected to things that have nothing in common. As a result, the relation among these terms would not be as presented in the syllogism's conclusion. Any such syllogism commits the fallacy of *undistributed middle* and is invalid—as, for example, is this argument:

18 1. All feral pigeons are birds with feathers.
     2. Some birds with feathers are animals that distract attackers.
     —————————————————————
     3. Some animals that distract attackers are feral pigeons.

> RULE 3: *If any term is distributed in the conclusion, it must be distributed also in the premise in which it occurs.*

Recall that the mark of validity for an argument is that its conclusion must follow necessarily from its premises. But no argument can be valid if its conclusion says more than what is already said in the premises. Syllogisms, which are deductive arguments, fail to be valid when their conclusions go beyond what is supported by their premises. That is the case of a syllogism whose minor or major term is distributed in the conclusion (thus referring there to a whole class) but not in the premise in which it also occurs (thus referring there to only part of a class). Any such syllogism commits the *fallacy of illicit process*, which may involve either the minor or major term. Thus, the fallacy has the following two versions:

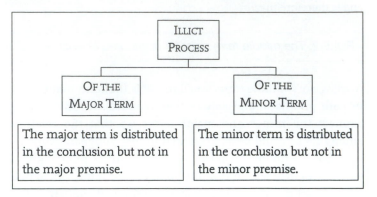

Consider,

19 1. All tigers are felines.
2. No lions are tigers.
3. No lions are felines.

The term "felines" in (19)'s conclusion involves the whole class of felines, which is said to be excluded from the whole class of lions. But premise 1 is not about the whole class of felines, since there the term "felines" is not distributed. The fallacy committed by this argument is illicit process of the major term (for short, "illicit major"). Now consider,

20 1. All suicide bombers are terrorists.
2. All suicide bombers are opponents of the status quo.
3. All opponents of the status quo are terrorists.

The term "opponents of the status quo" in (20)'s conclusion involves a whole class of people with a certain view, which is said to be included in the class denoted by the major term. But premise 2 is not about that whole class of people, since there the term "opponents of the status quo" is the predicate of an *A* proposition and therefore not distributed. The fallacy committed by this argument is illicit process of the minor term (for short, "illicit minor").

Finally, notice that it is also possible for an argument to commit *both* of these fallacies at once. One more thing: since there's no distribution in a type-*I* proposition, any syllogism with a type *I* conclusion obeys rule 3 by default. But if the conclusion is an *A*, *E*, or *O* proposition, then it'll have some distributed term in it, and the logical thinker will want to make sure that any term distributed in the conclusion is also distributed in the appropriate premise.

> RULE 4: *A valid syllogism cannot have two negative premises.*

If a syllogism's major premise is negative, the classes denoted by its middle and major terms either wholly or partially exclude each other. And if its minor premise is also negative, the classes denoted by its middle and minor term also either wholly or partially exclude each other. From such premises no conclusion about the relation between the classes denoted by the minor and major terms validly follows. When this happens, the argument is said to commit the *fallacy of exclusive premises*—for example,

21 1. No ferns are trees.
    2. <u>Some elms are not ferns.</u>
    3. Some elms are not trees.

The upshot of rule 4 is that certain combinations in the premises will always render a syllogism invalid: *EE*, *EO*, *OE*, and *OO*. To avoid this fallacy, if one of the syllogism's premises is negative, the other must be affirmative.

> RULE 5: *If there is a negative premise, the conclusion must be negative; and if there is a negative conclusion, there must be one negative premise.*

Recall that affirmative categorical propositions represent *class inclusion*, either whole inclusion of one class in another (*A* proposition) or inclusion of part of a class within another class (*I* proposition). Thus, the class inclusion represented in a syllogism's affirmative conclusion could be validly inferred only when *both* premises also represent class inclusion. On the other hand, a syllogism's negative conclusion, which would represent a relation of *class exclusion*, cannot follow validly from two affirmative premises (which assert only relations of inclusion).

When rule 5 is violated, a syllogism commits either the fallacy of *drawing an affirmative conclusion from a negative premise* or that of *drawing a negative conclusion from two affirmative premises*. Either way, the syllogism is invalid. For example,

22 1. All humans are mammals.
2. Some lizards are not humans.
3. Some lizards are mammals.

This commits the fallacy of drawing an affirmative conclusion from a negative premise; while

23 1. All poets are creative writers.
2. All creative writers are authors.
3. No authors are poets.

commits the fallacy of drawing a negative conclusion from two affirmative premises. Syllogisms flouting rule 5 are so obviously invalid that it is rare to encounter them. Finally, note that any syllogism containing only affirmative propositions obeys rule 5 by default.

> **RULE 6:** *If both premises are universal, the conclusion must be universal.*

As we saw in the previous chapter, of the four types of standard categorical propositions, only *I* and *O* carry *existential import*; that is, only these presuppose the existence of the entities denoted by their subject terms. Thus there is no valid syllogism with two universal premises and a particular conclusion. Any such syllogism draws a conclusion with existential import on the basis of premises having no such import. Syllogisms of this sort violate rule 6, committing the so-called *existential fallacy*. For example,

24 1. All beings that breathe are mortal.
2. All mermaids are beings that breathe.
3. Some mermaids are mortal.

Finally, note that any syllogism in which one or more of its premises is particular (i.e., type *I* or *O*) obeys rule 6 by default.

The Rules of Validity vs. Venn Diagrams

Each of the six rules of validity stipulates a *necessary condition* of validity in syllogisms. Thus a syllogism that obeys any one of these rules meets a necessary condition of being valid. But that is of course not yet to meet a *sufficient condition* of validity. Only *obeying all six rules together* is a sufficient condition for the validity of a syllogism. This technique thus provides a method of checking for validity that is every bit as reliable as that of Venn diagrams. The rules could, then, be used together with the Venn diagrams, so that if we make a mistake in one method, the other method will catch it. Any syllogistic form that commits one or more of the above fallacies will show up as invalid on a Venn diagram, and any time the diagram shows a form to be invalid, it will be found to commit one or more fallacies. Likewise, any syllogistic form that obeys all six rules will be shown valid by a Venn diagram.

In order to use the method of rules and fallacies to check syllogism forms for validity, you'll want to do two things: (1) keep clearly in mind which rules and fallacies go together, and (2) remember that the rules and fallacies are *not* two different ways of saying the same thing. The rules are prescriptions about what should be kept in mind in assessing the validity of a syllogism. The fallacies are *errors* in the reasoning underlying certain syllogisms that break the rules. Each fallacy can be associated with the flouting of one or more rules.

Again, the six rules collectively stipulate the necessary and sufficient conditions of *validity* for syllogisms, but committing *even one* of the fallacies makes a syllogism *invalid*. Since it's valid syllogisms that preserve truth, the rules are to be obeyed and the fallacies to be avoided.

Let's now summarize the eight fallacies and the six rules of validity that they violate.

Fallacy	Rule Violated	
Four terms	1	A syllogism must have exactly three terms.
Undistributed middle	2	The middle term must be distributed at least once.
Illicit process of the major/minor term	3	If any term is distributed in the conclusion, it must also be distributed in one of the premises.
Exclusive premises	4	A valid syllogism cannot have two negative premises.
Affirmative from a negative/Negative from two affirmatives	5	If there is a negative premise, the conclusion must be negative; and if there is a negative conclusion, one premise must be negative.
Existential fallacy	6	If both premises are universal, the conclusion must be universal.

Exercises

IX. Review Questions

1. What are the "terms" of a categorical proposition?
2. What does it mean to speak of a term as "distributed"?
3. What are the four distinguishing patterns of distribution found in the four different types of categorical proposition?
4. What are the six rules that give the necessary and sufficient conditions of validity in syllogisms?
5. Can you name, for each of the six rules of validity, the fallacy (or fallacies) committed when the rule is broken?
6. Can you explain what has gone wrong in each of the eight fallacies that amount to violations of the rules of validity?
7. If you've drawn a Venn diagram that appears to show a certain syllogistic form valid but you've also discovered that the form appears to commit a fallacy in violation of one of the rules of validity, what should you conclude?

X. **For each of the following, determine whether it is an *A*, *E*, *I*, or *O* proposition and whether its subject and predicate are distributed.**

1. All wombats are marsupials.

   SAMPLE ANSWER: A. Subject distributed; predicate
                        undistributed.

2. Some alligator wrestlers are not emergency room patients.
   _____

* 3. Some rare coins are expensive things to insure. _____

4. No vampires are members of the Rotary Club. _____

5. Some citrus fruits are not things grown in Rhode Island.
   _____

* 6. All chess players are patient strategists. _____

7. No interstate highways are good places to travel by bicycle.
   _____

8. Some politicians are not persons who have been indicted by the
   courts. _____

* 9. Some motorcycles are collectors' items. _____

10. All movies starring Tom Hanks are films worth seeing.
    _____

*11. Some paintings by Rubens are not in museums. _____

12. No Yorkshire terriers are guard dogs. _____

13. Some airlines are not transatlantic carriers. _____

*14. All professional astrologers are charlatans. _____

15. Some Texans are stockbrokers. _____

XI. **Reconstruct each of the following syllogisms, identify
its form, and determine whether it is valid or not by applying the rules of validity. For any syllogism that is
invalid, name the fallacy (or fallacies) it commits.**

1. Some astronauts are not musicians trained in classical music. So,
   no members of the New York Philharmonic are astronauts, for all

members of the New York Philharmonic are musicians trained in classical music.

SAMPLE ANSWER:

1. Some astronauts are not musicians trained in classical music.

2. All members of the New York Philharmonic are musicians trained in classical music.

3. No members of the New York Philharmonic are astronauts.

> 1. Some P are not M.   OAE-2   INVALID
>
> 2. <u>All S are M.</u>   illicit process of the major term
>
> 3. No S are P.

2. Since all generals who are veterans of the Vietnam War are experienced soldiers and all experienced soldiers are persons who are practiced in the art of planning battle strategies, it follows that some persons who are practiced in the art of planning battle strategies are generals who are veterans of the Vietnam War.

* **3.** Since no people who are truly objective are people who are likely to be mistaken, it follows that no people who ignore the facts are people who are truly objective, for all people who ignore the facts are people who are likely to be mistaken.

4. All submarines are warships, but some naval ships are not submarines. Hence some naval ships are not warships.

* **5.** Some people who bet on horse races are people who can afford to lose, since some people who bet on horse races are people who expect to win, and no people who expect to win are people who can afford to lose.

6. All persons with utopian ideals are fanatics, because some fanatics are political zealots, even though some political zealots are not persons with utopian ideals.

* **7.** Some metals are copper alloys, but all copper alloys are good conductors of electricity. It follows that some good conductors of electricity are not metals.

8. Some Connecticut firms are corporations. After all, some Connecticut firms are insurance companies and all insurance companies are corporations.

* 9. No egalitarians are sympathetic dissidents; thus no sympathetic dissidents are rabble rousers, for some rabble rousers are egalitarians.

10. All passenger pigeons are birds. For some passenger pigeons are not intelligent creatures, but all birds are intelligent creatures.

*11. Since some coaches are not talent scouts, we may infer that no athletes are talent scouts. After all, some athletes are not coaches.

12. Some gangsters are criminals, and all gangsters are pedestrians, so no criminals are pedestrians.

*13. Some living things are pigs, for all college men are living things, and some college men are pigs.

14. Some fast vehicles are helicopters, because some fast vehicles are warplanes, but some helicopters are not warplanes.

*15. All postmodernists are admirers of Heidegger. No admirers of Heidegger are utilitarians. Hence no postmodernists are utilitarians.

16. Since all good investments are smart purchases, no smart purchases are municipal bonds. After all, some municipal bonds are good investments.

*17. All paramecia are single-celled organisms, and all single-celled organisms are invertebrates; therefore all paramecia are invertebrates.

18. Whereas some flash drives are handy devices, some handy devices are not DVDs, for no DVDs are flash drives.

*19. Because all good neighbors are well-intended zealots, no well-intended zealots are respectful people, for all good neighbors are respectful people.

20. No Scandinavian nations are tax havens. After all, some Scandinavian nations are countries in Europe, but some countries in Europe are tax havens.

*21. Since some traitors are not benefactors, it follows that all embezzlers are traitors, for no embezzlers are benefactors.

22. Some board games are not contests of strategy, but all contests of strategy are chess matches. Thus all chess matches are board games.

*23. No angora goats are hamsters. No angora goats are great white sharks. Therefore no great white sharks are hamsters.

24. Some large natural disasters are tropical storms, for some hurricanes are large natural disasters, and all hurricanes are tropical storms.

*25. Some average people are not photogenic. Accordingly, some average people are not television news anchors, since all television news anchors are photogenic.

XII. YOUR OWN THINKING LAB

1. The six rules discussed in this section can be used to test the validity of syllogistic arguments such as those in (XI). For any argument with the same form, what would these rules show?

2. Provide syllogisms of your own whose forms illustrate each of the four figures and use Venn diagrams to check those forms for validity.

3. For each of the arguments in (2), check for validity using the rules of validity. If any argument is invalid, name the fallacy (or fallacies) it commits.

14.6 The Philosopher's Corner

Standard Syllogisms and Singular Propositions

Categorical propositions are the building blocks from which standard syllogisms are constructed. The traditional theory of the syllogism, introduced by Aristotle in the fourth century B.C.E., was long held by logicians to capture comprehensively the most fundamental valid argument forms. Yet there are a vast number of such forms that do not fit easily, or at all, into the standard forms of propositions that can serve as premises or conclusions of syllogisms. According to traditional logicians, however, propositions of those forms can be transformed or translated into one or other of the four standard categorical propositions that constitute syllogisms. For example,

25 1. Television news anchors are inquisitive.
   2. Soledad O'Brien is a television news anchor.
   3. Soledad O'Brien is inquisitive.

By translating this argument into standard form, we obtain

25' 1. All television news anchors are inquisitive.
   2. Anyone identical to Soledad O'Brien is a television news anchor.
   3. Anyone identical to Soledad O'Brien is inquisitive.

In (25'), the term "Soledad O'Brien" is taken to refer to a class of things that has exactly one member: Soledad O'Brien. As a result, the validity of (25) can be accounted for by showing that it does after all have a syllogistic form that is recognizably valid—namely,

25" 1. All M are P.
   2. All S are M.
   3. All S are P.

Argument (25)'s validity, then, is beyond question; but how plausible is the recast of its premise 2 and conclusion 3 in (25')? In connection with this, questions arise as to whether it makes sense to classify all possible propositions into "universal" or "particular." Note that a proposition of either sort is a quantified one, since it falls under the scope of a quantifier that is either universal (for A and E propositions) or existential (for I and O propositions). We may call the former "universal generalizations" and the latter "existential generalizations." Now consider

26 1. Bicycles are fun to ride.
   2. That's a bicycle.
   3. That's fun to ride.

As in the case of argument (25), it is not at all obvious that this argument's premise 2 and conclusion 3 are generalizations (i.e., quantified propositions). But for traditional logicians they would be. To make (26) fit into the syllogistic valid forms, they would translate them, for example, as follows:

26' 1. All bicycles are vehicles that are fun to ride.

2. All members of the class of *that* are bicycles.

3. All members of the class of *that* are vehicles that are fun to ride.

Here "members of the class of *that*" denotes a class with exactly one member: that bicycle.

Yet it seems most unlikely that ordinary speakers offering arguments such as (26) intend to say something as complicated as what we have here! The speakers' intuitions seem incompatible with the traditional logician's account, and if those intuitions are correct, then valid arguments such as (25) and (26) have a logical form that does not fit into any of the standard valid syllogistic patterns. On an alternative view, the second premise and the conclusion of these arguments do not express generalizations of any sort, but rather *singular propositions*—that is, propositions that directly invoke specific things (objects or individuals), presenting them as having a certain property or being related to other thing/s. What makes a proposition singular is that it features a singular term. For example,

27 Aristotle was fond of syllogisms.

28 That *tree* is an oak.

29 CNN features more commercials than Fox.

On the alternative view we are considering, each underlined term here is singular. Prime cases of singular terms are ordinary proper names ("Aristotle," "Fido," "CNN," etc.). But the category also includes demonstratives ("this," "that," etc.), indexicals ("I," "you," etc.), and more complex terms containing some of these ("those shoes," "we the people," etc.). A consequence of this view is that, when a speaker says something intended to be a singular proposition but the entity thereby invoked doesn't exist, no proposition has been expressed. Suppose someone says,

30 Santa Claus is a Christmas visitor.

Since Santa Claus doesn't exist, (30) not only fails to express a singular proposition but fails to express any proposition at all! To explain such an outcome, we may notice that since "Santa Claus" lacks a referent, therefore (30) lacks a truth value, and so is not capable of expressing a proposition.

In any case, by contrast with a singular proposition, a generalization never invokes specific individuals: its so-called subject and predicate terms denote properties or attributes—in the examples above, the properties of *being a television news anchor*, *being inquisitive*, etc. Properties determine sets of things. As we saw in Chapter 13, *A*, *E*, *I*, and *O* propositions are about sets standing in relations of total or partial inclusion or exclusion, as the case may be, for each proposition type. On the traditional logician's view, (27) above really says

27' Anything that satisfies being Aristotle also satisfies being fond of syllogisms,

which amounts to saying that anything that has the property of being Aristotle also has the property of being fond of syllogisms. But then the statement is not about a certain specific individual who is said to be fond of syllogisms but about whoever satisfies the property "being Aristotle," who is also said to satisfy "being fond of syllogisms." When translated into the notation for categorical propositions in standard form, (27) becomes

27" All *S* are *P*

But this runs into the objection that it misconceives the role of proper names (and other singular terms) in the propositions in which they occur. A pioneer in making this point about names was J. S. Mill, who, in his *System of Logic* (1843), held that although an ordinary proper name is often associated with certain properties in the speakers' minds, especially when it is first introduced, such properties do not enter into the proposition expressed by a statement containing the name. According to Mill, a name is like a tag or label for the designated object or individual. Thus, a town may be called "Dartmouth," observes Mill, if it lies at the mouth of the River Dart. Yet it would ordinarily keep the name even after the river had changed its course. In the early 1970s, Saul Kripke and others vindicated Mill's account of proper names, further developing it into a view of names that is currently one of the contending theories in the literature of philosophy of language.

An adequate treatment of that theory is, of course, far beyond the scope of our discussion here. For present purposes, it's enough to bear in mind that, on this alternative view, any singular proposition such as (27) contains the referred individual or entity, which we may symbolize with a lowercase letter. Thus, (27)'s form is

27″ *a* has property *F*

where F is the property of being fond of syllogisms.

Here is the upshot of this controversy: although the singular proposition view might face problems of its own, when it comes to propositions involving putative candidates for singular terms, the traditional logician's recasting of those propositions to make them fit into standard syllogistic arguments seems at odds with the ordinary intuitions of speakers. Furthermore, although traditional syllogistic logic accounts for the validity of many syllogisms, it never comes close to offering a complete account of validity for other types of deductive argument—among which those discussed in Chapter 12 are but a small sample.

Exercises

XIII. Which of the following qualifies as a singular term? For any term that doesn't, rewrite the term as a predicate expressing a property.

   1. Einstein SAMPLE ANSWER: Singular term

   2. Yellow _____

* 3. Pencil _____

   4. That tiger _____

   5. I _____

* 6. Pluto _____

   7. BBC _____

* 8. Classroom _____

   9. Bakery _____

*10. Those rabbits _____

 11. Poet _____

*12. Fountain of Youth _____

XIV. Which of the following qualify as singular propositions and which as generalizations? In the latter case,
distinguish between universal and existential generalizations.

1. Honda is a Japanese company SAMPLE ANSWER: Singular
proposition.

2. This is a sample of water. _____

* 3. Each item in this box is yellow. _____

4. Canadian ducks are on the lake. _____

* 5. Dogs bark. _____

6. Nothing that barks is an animal. _____

* 7. Dogs are in Riverside Park. _____

8. Some animals are not cats. _____

* 9. Fido barks. _____

10. She sings operas. _____

XV. How would traditional logicians understand the form of
any proposition above that qualifies as singular? And
what about the Millians?

XVI. For each of the following, reconstruct the argument first
according to the traditional logician's view and then indicate which casting of premises and conclusion would
be rejected within the Millian view.

1. Newspapers lead to public awareness. The *St. Louis Post-Dispatch*
is a newspaper. Thus, The *St. Louis Post-Dispatch* leads to public
awareness.

SAMPLE ANSWER:

1. All newspapers are things that lead to public awareness.

2. Anything identical to The *St. Louis Post-Dispatch* is a
newspaper.

3. Anything identical to The *St. Louis Post-Dispatch* is a thing
that leads to public awareness.

Rejected: 2 and 3.

> Reason: replacing "The *St. Louis Post-Dispatch*" with "Anything identical to... " is at odds with common intuitions about what the arguer intends to say.

2. No taxi driver gets bored. Carol is a taxi driver. Therefore Carol doesn't get bored.

* 3. Mexico is a neighboring country. Neighboring countries are friends of ours. Therefore Mexico is a friend of ours.

4. Industrial countries produce significant greenhouse gas emissions. The United States is an industrial country. Therefore the United States produces significant greenhouse gas emissions.

* 5. Hippos don't do well in cold weather. That animal recently brought to San Antonio's zoo is a hippo. Therefore that animal recently brought to San Antonio's zoo doesn't do well in cold weather.

6. Horses defeat mules in local derbies. Mr. Ed is a horse. Therefore Mr. Ed defeats mules in local derbies.

* 7. Americans have consumer expectations. Since he is an American, he has consumer expectations.

8. Jessica is a space traveler. Space travelers live stressful lives. It follows that Jessica lives a stressful life.

XVII. Use your answers to the previous exercise to either support or undermine the traditional logician's view of propositions containing singular terms.

XVIII. Explain what, if anything, traditional logicians could say to account for the form of a proposition such as "Gertrude visits the library if she is in town." And what, if anything, would Millians say about "Oliver Twist is an orphan"?

XIX. What's at issue in the following passage? Which of the two rival views of propositions containing proper names would it support?

1. If, like the robber in the Arabian Nights, we leave a mark with chalk on a house to enable us to know it again, the mark has a purpose, but it has not properly any meaning. The chalk declares anything about the house.... The object of making the mark is merely a

distinction. I say to myself, All these houses are so nearly alike that if I lose sight of them I shall not again be able to distinguish that which I am now looking at, from any of the others.... When we impose a proper name, we perform an operation in some degree analogous to what the robber intended in chalking the house. We put a mark, not indeed upon the object itself, but, so to speak, upon the idea of the object. A proper name is but an unmeaning mark which we connect in our minds with the idea of the object, in order that whenever the mark meets our eyes or occurs to our thoughts, we may think of that individual object. (J. S. Mill, *A System of Logic*, 1843.)

■ Writing Project

1. Write an essay of about three pages contrasting the traditional logician's view and the Millian view. The following format is recommended: Start out with the traditional logician's view of standard syllogisms and the propositions that make them up. That's your target piece. Appeal to the Millian view as a critical response to the traditional logician. Support the criticism with examples (here you may quote the above passage by Mill). Once you have contrasted the two views, provide your own brief critical assessment of the dispute.

2. In the writing project at the end of Chapter 1, you were asked to write a short essay defending some claim about which you felt strongly. Go back to this essay now and write a second paper in which you offer a critical assessment of your original argument, appealing to the methods of argument analysis you've learned in this course.

■ Chapter Summary

A *categorical syllogism* is a deductive argument made up of three categorical propositions. It has *three terms*, each of which occurs exactly twice in the argument, with one of these pairs of terms occurring only in the premises.

The *three terms* of a categorical syllogism are

NAME	LOGICAL FUNCTION	SYMBOL
Major term	Predicate of conclusion	P
Minor term	Subject of conclusion	S
Middle term	Occurs *only* in both premises	M

The "major premise" is the premise in which the major term appears; the "minor premise" that in which the minor term appears:

NAME	ORDER IN ARGUMENT RECONSTRUCTION
Major premise	Listed first
Minor premise	Listed second

How to test the validity of a syllogism with a Venn diagram:

- Draw three intersecting circles.
- Diagram only the premises.
- If one premise is universal and the other particular, you must diagram the universal premise first, whichever it is.
- But if both premises are universal or both particular, it doesn't matter which is diagrammed first.
- Once you have diagrammed the premises, if the conclusion is already unequivocally diagrammed too, the argument is valid. Otherwise, the argument is invalid.

Syllogisms that violate any of the following rules are invalid:

- RULE 1: *A syllogism must have exactly three terms.* An argument that violates this rule commits the FALLACY OF FOUR TERMS.
- RULE 2: *The middle term must be distributed at least once.* An argument that violates this rule commits the FALLACY OF UNDISTRIBUTED MIDDLE.
- RULE 3: *If any term is distributed in the conclusion, it must be distributed also in one of the premises.* An argument that violates this rule commits either the FALLACY OF ILLICIT PROCESS OF THE MAJOR TERM (where the major term is distributed in the conclusion but not in the major premise) or that of ILLICIT PROCESS OF THE MINOR TERM (where the minor term is distributed in the conclusion but not in the minor premise) It is also possible for an argument to commit *both* of these fallacies at once.
- RULE 4: *A valid syllogism cannot have two negative premises.* An argument that violates this rule commits the FALLACY OF EXCLUSIVE PREMISES.
- RULE 5: *If there is a negative premise, the conclusion must be negative; and if there is a negative conclusion, there must be one*

negative premise. An argument that violates this rule commits either the FALLACY OF AFFIRMATIVE FROM A NEGATIVE or that of NEGATIVE FROM TWO AFFIRMATIVES.

- RULE 6: *If both premises are universal, the conclusion must be universal.* An argument that violates this rule commits the EXISTENTIAL FALLACY.

■ Key Words

Categorical syllogism
Syllogism
Terms
Major term
Minor term
Middle term
Major premise
Minor premise
Mood
Figure
Illicit process of the minor term
Singular term
Singular proposition

Syllogism form
Rules of validity
Venn diagram
Fallacy of four terms
Undistributed middle
Illicit process of the major term
Exclusive premises
Affirmative from a negative
Negative from two affirmatives
Existential fallacy
Proper name
General proposition

Appendix: Summary of Informal Fallacies

Fallacies of Failed Induction

Hasty generalization
Drawing a conclusion about an entire class of things on the basis of an observed sample that is either too small or atypical, or both.

Weak analogy
Claiming that two compared cases are relevantly alike when in fact they are not.

False cause
Claiming that there is a significant causal connection between two events when in fact there is either minimal causal connection or none at all.

Post hoc ergo propter hoc   Holding that some earlier event is the cause of some later event when the two are in fact not causally related.

Non causa pro causa   Misidentifying some event contemporaneous with another as its cause when in reality it's not.

Oversimplified cause   Overstating the causal connection between two events, so that what is in fact only a contributory cause is taken as a sufficient cause.

Appeal to ignorance
Taking some conclusion as true because it's not been proved false or as false because it's not been proved true.

Appeal to unqualified authority
Taking some claim to be true on the basis of the testimony of some alleged "authority" who in reality lacks expertise of the relevant sort or holds a view that is not representative of the consensus of expert opinion.

Fallacies of Presumption

Begging the question
An argument that is circular, in that at least one of its premises assumes the very conclusion it's offered to support.

Begging the question against
An argument in which at least one premise is itself controversial and therefore not better established than the conclusion it is offered to support.

Complex question
A question that is unfair to some individuals or things because it is phrased in a way that presupposes something not yet proved about them.

False alternatives
Of two alternatives offered in a disjunction, the mistake of treating them as exclusive or as exhaustive when in fact they are not.

Accident
Applying a general rule or principle inappropriately so that it is invoked in a case that is rightly an exception

Fallacies of Unclear Language

Slippery slope
The mistake of assuming that what holds for some case A holds also for the apparently very different case Z, on the basis of there being a series of cases $B, C, ...Y$ between A and Z where each successive pair in the series differ only minimally from each other.

Equivocation
An argument in which some word or phrase occurs with different meanings that bear on the argument's conclusion

Amphiboly
A sentence, ambiguous by virtue of its awkward construction, that, if treated as a premise, invites a mistaken conclusion to be drawn from it.

Confused predication

Composition   Arguing that because the parts of some complex whole or the members of a class have a certain attribute, the whole or class itself must have it.

Division   Arguing that because some complex whole or class has a certain attribute, each part of that whole or member of the class must have it.

Fallacies of Relevance

Appeal to pity
Attempting to arouse feelings of sympathy as a means of trying to get someone to accept a conclusion.

Appeal to force
Resorting to threats as a way of trying to persuade someone to accept a conclusion.

Appeal to emotion
Resorting to emotively charged language or images in an effort to persuade someone or some group to accept a conclusion.

Ad hominem
Attempting to discredit a person's or a group's argument, belief, point of view, or achievement by means of an irrelevant personal attack.

Beside the point
Offering premises that are entirely irrelevant to the conclusion in need of support.

Straw man
Misrepresenting a position to make it appear weaker than it is, so that objections then offered to that distorted version will appear to undermine the original.

Answers to Selected Exercises

CHAPTER 1

IV.

4. No argument **10.** Argument **13.** No argument **16.** Argument **18.** No argument **20.** Argument

VI.

3. Badgers are native to southern Wisconsin. <After all, > (they are always spotted there). **6.** (In the past, every person who ever lived did eventually die.) [This suggests that] all human beings are mortal. **9.** Online education is a great option for working adults in general, regardless of their ethnic background. <For one thing,> (there is a large population of working adults who simply are not in a position to attend a traditional university.) **12.** (There is evidence that galaxies are flying outwards and apart from each other.) [So] the cosmos will grow darker and colder.

VIII.

3. Incompatible **5.** Compatible **8.** Compatible

CHAPTER 2

II.

3. Rhetorical power **5.** Evidential support **8.** Logical connectedness **10.** Linguistic merit and rhetorical power **12.** Logical connectedness **15.** Linguistic merit

III.

2. Rhetorical power **4.** Evidential support **6.** Logical connectedness **8.** Evidential support **10.** Logical connectedness **12.** Rhetorical power

IV.

3. Weak logical connectedness **6.** Strong logical connectedness **9.** Failed logical connectedness

V.

3. Impossible. This scenario is ruled out by the definition of rational acceptability. **6.** Possible **8.** Impossible. This scenario is ruled out by the definition of linguistic merit. **10.** Impossible. This scenario is ruled out by the definition of rhetorical power. **13.** Possible **15.** Possible

VIII.

3. Expressive use **5.** Directive use **7.** Informative use **10.** Expressive use **12.** Directive use **15.** Expressive use

IX.

4. Imperative sentence **7.** Declarative sentence **10.** Interrogative sentence **13.** Declarative sentence **16.** Exclamatory sentence **19.** Declarative sentence

X.

3. Interrogative sentence. Possible indirect use: directive, whereby the speaker implores the addressee to stop making fun of Harry. **5.** Exclamatory sentence. Possible indirect use: informative, whereby the speaker tells the addressee that the King has died. **7.** Interrogative sentence. Possible indirect use: informative, whereby the speaker tells the addressee that she thinks the person is pretending to be sleepy. **10.** Declarative sentence. Possible indirect use: expressive, whereby the speaker expresses hope that things will go better in the future.

XI.

3. (A) Those players are automata resembling humans. (B) Those players act mechanically. **6.** (A) We are coming near to a mountain that is a volcano. (B) We are about to have a crisis. **9.** (A) Jim wears two different hats. (B) Jim plays two different roles, or has two different official responsibilities. **12.** (A) That city is populated by insects. (B) That city is crowded, with many people in the street. **15.** (A) He is a piece of burnt bread. (B) He's finished.

XIII.

1. Beth refers to the "same costume" type, while Bob, the "same costume" token. **3.** What May says is true if Moe and Brian are reading different tokens of the same book type—e.g., they're both reading *The Grapes of Wrath* but different *copies* of that novel.

XIV.

2. "Water" is mentioned in premise 1 and used in premise 2. "H_2O" is used in premise 2, but mentioned in the conclusion. **4.** "Jack the Ripper" is used in premise 1 but mentioned in the other.

XV.

1. For some philosophers, the expressions "mercy killing" and "voluntary active euthanasia" mean the same. But others argue that there is no such thing as voluntary active euthanasia. If they are right, then "voluntary active euthanasia" is a misleading expression, and the practice sometimes called "euthanasia" cannot be the same as what's called "mercy killing." **4.** Suppose that the term "knowledge" is equivalent in meaning to the expression, "justified true belief." In addition, suppose that we have a clear idea of what "true" and "belief" each means. Even so, to know what "knowledge" means we would need to know what "justification" means.

CHAPTER 3

II.

3. Nonbelief **5.** Belief **7.** Nonbelief **9.** Belief

III.

4. The nonbelief about whether the sun will rise tomorrow. **6.** The disbelief that the earth is not a planet. The belief that the earth is a planet. **8.** The nonbelief about whether galaxies are flying outward. **10.** The belief that I am thinking. **12.** The nonbelief about whether there is life after death. **14.** The nonbelief about whether humans have evolved or were created by God.

IV.

1. Because under special circumstances (e.g., a threat) a person's behavior may not express his actual beliefs. The same could happen if he is insincere—i.e., he intends to misrepresent his beliefs. **6.** The options are belief, disbelief, and nonbelief about whether *there is life after death.*

VI.

3. Inaccurate: the statement is false. **5.** Neither: "tallness" doesn't clearly apply or fail to apply to George W. Bush. **7.** Neither: the statement contains an evaluative expression ("better than"). **10.** Accurate: the statement is true. **13.** Accurate: the statement is true. **15.** Neither: it is an imperative sentence.

IX.

3. INCONSISTENT. The beliefs are logically contradictory. **5.** CONSISTENT. In a possible world, both beliefs could be true. **7.** INCONSISTENT. The beliefs are logically contradictory. **9.** INCONSISTENT. The beliefs are conceptually contradictory. **11.** CONSISTENT. These beliefs are true in all possible worlds. **13.** INCONSISTENT. The beliefs are logically contradictory. **15.** INCONSISTENT. These beliefs are false in all possible worlds.

X.

3. Conceptual **5.** Conceptual **7.** Other. The content features "inhumane" and is therefore evaluative. **8.** Empirical **11.** Other. This content features "delicious" and is therefore evaluative. **13.** Empirical **15.** Empirical

XI.

3. Nonconservative **5.** Conservative **7.** Nonconservative **9.** Conservative **11.** Conservative **13.** Nonconservative **15.** Nonconservative

XII.

3. Irrational **5.** Irrational **7.** Rational **9.** Irrational

CHAPTER 4

II.

3. Anyone born in Germany is a European. **6.** The Federal Reserve Board's predictions are reliable regarding what banks will do. **9.** She is not telling the truth. **12.** Canadians are used to cold weather. **15.** Jane is a cell phone user. **17.** Religious theories should not be taught in biology courses in public schools. **20.** Pelicans are birds.

III.

3. No real vegetarian eats meat. Mary is a real vegetarian. Thus, she doesn't eat meat. Hence, there is no point in taking her to the Steak House. **Extended argument. 5.** If the ocean is rough here, then there will be no swimming. If there is no swimming, tourists will go to another beach. Thus, if the ocean is rough here, then tourists will go to another beach. **Simple argument. 7.** No Democrat votes for Republicans. Since Pam voted for Republicans, she is not a Democrat. Thus she won't be invited to Tom's party, for only Democrats are invited to his party. **Extended argument. 9.** To understand most web pages you have to read them. To read them requires a good amount of time. Thus, to understand web pages requires a good amount of time. Since I don't have any time, I keep away from the web and as a result, I miss some news. **Extended argument.**

VI.

3. Inductive **6.** Inductive **8.** Deductive **10.** Deductive **12.** Inductive **15.** Inductive **18.** Inductive **20.** Deductive

VII.

3. Whatever is designed by Sir Norman Foster is beautiful. **6.** Whatever takes you where you want to go faster is better. **9.** Married people deal better with financial problems. **12.** Hit songs are the best songs. **15.** Soldiers ought to do whatever their commanding officer orders them to do. **18.** Whatever deters criminals from committing murder is ethically justified. **20.** You ought to obey the law.

VIII.

4. Esthetic and moral **6.** Prudential and moral **9.** Legal **10.** Prudential **13.** Moral and prudential **15.** Esthetic and prudential

IX.

3. Nonevaluative **5.** Nonevaluative **7.** Evaluative **9.** Nonevaluative **11.** Evaluative **13.** Nonevaluative **15.** Nonevaluative

XI.

4. *Is*–sentence **7.** *Is*–sentence **8.** *Ought*–sentence **10.** *Is*–sentence **12.** *Ought*–sentence **15.** *Is*–sentence

XII.

2. No *Is/Ought* problem **4.** *Is/Ought* problem **6.** *Is/Ought* problem **9.** No *Is/Ought* problem **11.** *Is/Ought* problem **14.** *Is/Ought* problem

CHAPTER 5

II.

3. Logically possible **5.** Logically possible **8.** Logically impossible

III.

4. Valid **7.** Valid **10.** Valid **13.** Valid **16.** Invalid **19.** Valid **22.** Invalid

VII.

3. Syllogistic argument **5.** Propositional argument **7.** Syllogistic argument **9.** Propositional argument **11.** Propositional argument **13.** Syllogistic argument **15.** Syllogistic argument

VIII.

4. All *C*s are *D*s
No *H*s are *D*s
No *C*s are *H*s

6. If not *M*, then *L*
Not *L*
M

9. If *F*, then *C*
If not *C*, then not *F*

11. All *B*s are *I*s
Some *B*s are *C*s
Some *I*s are *C*s

13. No *C*s are *G*s
All *G*s are *D*s
No *C*s are *D*s

15. Either *E* or not *C*
Not *E*
Not *C*

18. If *O*, then *H*
Not *H*
Not *O*

20. Either *M* or not *J*
Not *M*
Not *J*

IX.

4. Syllogistic argument **6.** Propositional argument, modus tollens
9. Propositional argument, contraposition **11.** Syllogistic argument
13. Syllogistic argument **15.** Propositional argument, disjunctive syllogism
18. Propositional argument, modus tollens **20.** Propositional argument, disjunctive syllogism

X.

3. True **5.** False **7.** False **9.** True

XI.

3. Most *C*s are *E*s
<u>*m* is not *E*</u>
m is not *C*

        Counterexample: *C* = American citizen, *E* = people permitted to vote in the United States, and *m* = a 2-year old American citizen.

5. No *A*s are *E*s
<u>Some *A*s are *H*s</u>
No *H*s are *E*s

        Counterexample: *A* = fish, *E* = mammal, and *H* = aggressive animals

7. *f* is *D*
<u>Some *D*s are *B*s</u>
f is *B*

        Counterexample: *f* = a certain mute dog, *D* = dog, and *B* = barking animal

XIV.

2. Impossible **4.** Impossible **6.** Impossible **8.** Possible

XV.

2. Entailment does matter since an argument can't be sound unless it has it.
4. There *is* a relationship between validity and truth: in a valid argument, if the premises are true, the conclusion *must* be true.

XVI.

4. Logically impossible **6.** Logically possible **8.** Logically possible **10.** Logically impossible **12.** Logically possible

XVIII.

3. True **5.** False **7.** True **9.** False

XIX.

2. Empirical **4.** Empirical **6.** A priori

XX.

2. A priori, for it attempts to prove God's existence by mere reflection on the concept of God. **4.** Empirical, for the premise that many apparently innocent people suffer rests on observation.

CHAPTER 6

II.

3. Deductive **6.** Inductive **9.** Deductive **12.** Deductive **15.** Inductive

IV.

2. Causal argument **5.** Analogy **8.** Analogy **9.** Statistical syllogism **11.** Causal argument **14.** Enumerative induction

VII.

3. Statistical syllogism, reliable **6.** Enumerative induction, not reliable **9.** Causal argument, reliable **12.** Statistical syllogism, reliable **15.** Enumerative induction, not reliable **18.** Analogy, not reliable **21.** Analogy, reliable **23.** Causal argument, undeterminable (the reliability of the argument depends on that of the cited source) **25.** Causal argument, reliable

CHAPTER 7

II.

5. Weak analogy **8.** Appeal to ignorance **11.** Appeal to unqualified authority **15.** False cause **18.** Appeal to ignorance **21.** Hasty generalization/false cause **24.** Appeal to unqualified authority **27.** Hasty generalization **31.** False cause **34.** Appeal to ignorance

IV.

3. Not a fallacy **5.** Fallacy **7.** Fallacy **9.** Not a fallacy

VI.

1. Example (1)'s weakness is in its claiming that there *are no* objects external to mind, on the grounds that one is not really certain about the existence of such objects. But all that actually follows from that premise is that *we don't know* whether such mind-independent external objects exist or not. **4.** Example (4)'s weakness is in its arguing that God *does exist* from the premise that no experts have been able to prove that He doesn't. But all that really follows is that we finally *don't know* for sure whether or not God exists. **6.** Example (6)'s weakness is in its arguing that moral judgments aren't objective, on the basis of their not having been proved objective. But here the conclusion is claiming much more than the premise supports.

CHAPTER 8

II.

3. Both **5.** Both **7.** Conceptual **9.** Both **11.** Formal

III.

3. Begs the question **5.** Begs the question **7.** Both **10.** Both **13.** Begs the question against **16.** Begs the question against **19.** Begging the question

IV.

4. Impossible **6.** Impossible **8.** Possible **10.** Impossible

V.

4. C **6.** K **8.** I

VII.

1. The argument begs the question, because in order to accept its premises you have to accept its conclusion. And it begs the question against those who argue that marriage is a union between two persons independent of their genders. **5.** To be deductively cogent, the argument must (1) be valid, and (2) have premises that are not only acceptable but more clearly acceptable than its conclusion. **6.** Such an argument could not be cogent, since it wouldn't be truth preserving—and, as a result, its conclusion could be false (even with all premises being true). But the argument need not be rejected on that ground, since it could be a inductively strong (thus making its conclusion reasonable to believe). **10.** The burden is on you. It means: it's your turn. You must offer an argument or accept defeat in the debate.

IX.

3. Accident **6.** False alternatives **9.** Complex question

X.

4. Complex question **6.** False alternatives **9.** Accident **12.** Begging the question against **15.** Complex question **20.** Accident **22.** Begging the question **25.** Complex question/accident

XII.

1. A's premise assumes the truth of a universal statement (that "death is always ..."), which is vulnerable to R's counterexample. **4.** A ignores the possibility that, unbeknownst to the dreamer, her dream may represent people acting in "ordinary" ways. For example, she might "hear" a phone ringing nearby and a roommate announcing, after taking the call, that classes are canceled for the day. Convinced that the dream sequence is an event in real time, the dreamer remains in bed, having mistaken the ringing alarm clock for the phone!

CHAPTER 9

II.

3. Not clearly vague **5.** Not clearly vague **7.** Clearly vague **9.** Not clearly vague **12.** Clearly vague

V.

3. Composition **7.** Division **10.** Slippery slope **13.** Amphiboly **17.** Slippery slope **20.** Composition **24.** Division **27.** Division **30.** Amphiboly

VIII.

3. To say that an elephant is small is to say that it is an elephant that is smaller than most elephants.

small elephant = df. elephant that is smaller than most elephants
5. Someone is a human being if and only if it is a featherless biped.

human being = df. featherless biped
7. A horse is a beast of burden with a flowing mane.

horse = df. beast of burden with a flowing mane

IX.

3. Reportive **5.** Reportive **7.** Contextual **9.** Ostensive

X.

3. Too broad and too narrow **5.** Too narrow **7.** Too broad and too narrow **9.** Too broad

XIII.

3. Real definition **5.** Conceptual definition **7.** Conceptual definition **8.** Real definition

CHAPTER 10

II.

2. Beside the point [NOT appeal to pity] **4.** Appeal to pity **7.** Appeal to emotion (bandwagon) **10.** Ad hominem **13.** Ad hominem (tu quoque) **16.** Straw man [also equivocation] **19.** Beside the point **22.** Beside the point **25.** Appeal to force **28.** Appeal to emotion **30.** Straw man **33.** Appeal to pity **35.** Ad hominem

IV.

2. Fallacy of appeal to emotion **5.** Not a fallacy of appeal to emotion **9.** Not a fallacy of appeal to emotion **10.** Fallacy of appeal to emotion (bandwagon appeal)

CHAPTER 11

II.

3. Compound. Biconditional. **6.** Simple. **9.** Compound. Conjunction. **12.** Simple. **15.** Compound. Negation of conjunction/disjunction of negations. **18.** Compound. Conjunction. **21.** Simple. **24.** Compound. Conditional. **27.** Simple. **30.** Compound. Conjunction. **33.** Simple.

IV.

3. WFF **5.** not a WFF **7.** WFF **9.** Not a WFF

V.

3. True **6.** True **9.** False **12.** True **15.** False **18.** False

VIII.

4. True **7.** True **10.** True **13.** False **16.** True **19.** True **22.** True **25.** False

IX.

3. Tautology

$B\,M$	$B \supset (M \supset B)$	
T T	T	T
T F	T	T
F T	T	F
F F	T	T

5. Contradiction

$A\,B$	$\sim [(A \cdot B) \supset (B \cdot A)]$			
T T	F	T	T	T
T F	F	F	T	F
F T	F	F	T	F
F F	F	F	T	F

8. Contingency

$A\,B$	$(\sim A \vee \sim B) \supset (B \cdot A)$			
T T	F	F F	T	T
T F	F	T T	F	F
F T	T	T F	F	F
F F	T	T T	F	F

10. Contingency

A K H	~ A ≡ ~ (~ K v ~ H)
T T T	F F T F F F
T T F	F T F F T T
T F T	F T F T T F
T F F	F T F T T T
F T T	T T T F F F
F T F	T F F F T T
F F T	T F F T T F
F F F	T F F T T T

12. Contingency

A H I	~ [(~ A • H) v ~ (H ⊃ ~ I)]
T T T	F F F T T F F
T T F	T F F F F T T
T F T	T F F F F T F
T F F	T F F F F T T
F T T	F T T T T F F
F T F	F T T T F T T
F F T	T T F F F T F
F F F	T T F F F T T

16. Contradiction

A B C	~ {[A • (B • C)] ≡ [(A • B) • C]}
T T T	F T T T T T
T T F	F F F T T F
T F T	F F F T F F
T F F	F F F T F F
F T T	F F T T F F
F T F	F F F T F F
F F T	F F F T F F
F F F	F F F T F F

18. Tautology

A B	(A • B) ≡ (B • A)
T T	T T T
T F	F T F
F T	F T F
F F	F T F

20. Tautology

A B	(A ≡ B)	≡	[(A ⊃ B)	•	(B ⊃ A)]
T T	T	**T**	T	T	T
T F	F	**T**	F	F	T
F T	F	**T**	T	F	F
F F	T	**T**	T	T	T

X.

2. Contingency

E O	~E v O
T T	F **T**
T F	F **F**
F T	T **T**
F F	T **T**

4. Contingency

E O	~E ≡ O
T T	F **F**
T F	F **T**
F T	T **T**
F F	T **F**

7. Tautology

E O	(E • O) ⊃ O
T T	T **T**
T F	F **T**
F T	F **T**
F F	F **T**

11. Tautology

H L	(H • L)	≡	~ ~(H • L)
T T	T	**T**	T F T
T F	F	**T**	F T F
F T	F	**T**	F T F
F F	F	**T**	F T F

12. Contingency

E O H L	~ (E • O) ≡ ~ (H • L)
T T T T	F T **T** F T
T T T F	F T F T F
T T F T	F T F T F
T T F F	F T F T F
T F T T	T F F F T
T F T F	T F T T F
T F F T	T F T T F
T F F F	T F T T F
F T T T	T F F F T
F T T F	T F T T F
F T F T	T F T T F
F T F F	T F T T F
F F T T	T F F F T
F F T F	T F T T F
F F F T	T F T T F
F F F F	T F **T** T F

14. Tautology

E O	~ (E v O) ≡ (~ E • ~ O)
T T	F T **T** F F F
T F	F T **T** F F T
F T	F T **T** T F F
F F	T F **T** T T T

XI.

1. Mary is at the library but the library is not open. **3.** Fred is at the library if and only if either the library is open or Mary is not at the library. **5.** The essay is due on Thursday just in case the library's being open implies that I have Internet access. **7.** It is not the case that if Fred is not at the library then either the library is not open or Mary is at the library.

XII.

3. Necessary **5.** Contingent **7.** Necessary **9.** Necessary **11.** Necessary **13.** Necessary **15.** Necessary

XIII.

3. Knowable a priori **5.** Knowable empirically **7.** Knowable a priori **9.** Knowable a priori **11.** Knowable a priori **13.** Knowable empirically **15.** Knowable a priori

XIV.

3. Analytic 5. Synthetic 7. Analytic 9. Analytic 11. Analytic 13. Synthetic
15. Analytic

XV.

3. Synthetic 5. Synthetic 7. Synthetic 9. Analytic 11. Analytic 13. Synthetic

CHAPTER 12

II.

4. Valid

J N	J,	~J	v	~N	∴	~N
T T	F	F	F			F
T F	F	T	T			T
F T	T	T	F			F
F F	T	T	T			T

8. Invalid

C B A	~C	v	~B,	~	(B • A)	∴	A v C	
T T T	F	F	F	F	T		T	
T T F	F	F	F	T	F		T	
T F T	F	T	T	T	F		T	
T F F	F	T	T	T	F		T	
F T T	T	T	F	F	T		T	
F T F	T	T	F	T	F		F	←
F F T	T	T	T	T	F		T	
F F F	T	T	T	T	F		F	←

10. Valid

B K H	~B,	~	(~ K ≡ ~ H)	∴	K ⊃ ~H
T T T	F	F	F T F		F F
T T F	F	T	F F T		T T
T F T	F	T	T F F		T F
T F F	F	F	T T T		T T
F T T	T	F	F T F		F F
F T F	T	T	F F T		T T
F F T	T	T	T F F		T F
F F F	T	F	T T T		T T

13. Valid

K E O	K • (~ E v O), ~ E ⊃ ~ K ∴ O
T T T	T F T F T F
T T F	F F F F T F
T F T	T T T T F F
T F F	T T T T F F
F T T	F F T F T T
F T F	F F F F T T
F F T	F T T T T T
F F F	F T T T T T

14. Invalid E ⊃ A, ~ ~ A ∴ ~ E v ~ A

E A	E ⊃ A, ~ ~A ∴ ~E v ~A
T T	T T F F F F ←
T F	F F T F T T
F T	T T F T T F
F F	T F T T T T

22. Invalid H • (~ I v J), J ⊃ ~ H ∴ J

H I J	H • (~I v J), J ⊃ ~ H ∴ J
T T T	T F T F F
T T F	F F F T F
T F T	T T T F F
T F F	T T T T F ←
F T T	F F T T T
F T F	F F F T T
F F T	F T T T T
F F F	F T T T T

23. Invalid ~ O, A ⊃ B ∴ ~ O • B

O A B	~ O, A ⊃ B ∴ ~ O • B
T T T	F T F F
T T F	F F F F
T F T	F T F F
T F F	F T F F
F T T	T T T T
F T F	T F T F
F F T	T T T T
F F F	T T T F ←

III.

3. Invalid

A B F	~A ≡ ~B, ~B ⊃ F ∴ A v ~F
T T T	F T F F T · T F
T T F	F T F F T · T T
T F T	F F T T T · T F
T F F	F F T T F · T T
F T T	T F F F T · F F
F T F	T F F F T · T T
F F T	T T T T T · F F ←
F F F	T T T T F · T T

6. Valid

J A I	J ⊃ (A v I), ~A • ~I ∴ ~J
T T T	T T F F F · F
T T F	T T F F T · F
T F T	T T T F F · F
T F F	F F T T T · F
F T T	T T F F F · T
F T F	T T F F T · T
F F T	T T T F F · T
F F F	T F T T T · T

7. Valid

A O F	A • O, O ≡ F ∴ ~F ⊃ ~A
T T T	T · T · F · T F
T T F	T · F · T · F F
T F T	F · F · F · T F
T F F	F · T · T · F F
F T T	F · T · F · T T
F T F	F · F · T · T T
F F T	F · F · F · T T
F F F	F · T · T · T T

10. Invalid

M F D		M ≡ (D v F), (F ⊃ ~ D) ⊃ ~ M ∴ M • F					
T T T	T	T	F	F	T	F	T
T T F	T	T	T	T	F	F	T
T F T	T	T	T	F	F	F	F
T F F	F	F	T	T	F	F	F
F T T	F	T	F	F	T	T	F
F T F	F	T	T	T	T	T	F
F F T	F	T	T	F	T	T	F
F F F	T	F	T	T	T	T	F ←

12. Invalid

E M A		M v (E ⊃ ~ A), E ≡ ~ (A v M) ∴ ~ E					
T T T	T	F	F	F	F	T	F
T T F	T	T	T	F	F	T	F
T F T	F	F	F	F	F	T	F
T F F	T	T	T	T	T	F	F ←
F T T	T	T	F	T	F	T	T
F T F	T	T	T	T	F	T	T
F F T	T	T	F	T	F	T	T
F F F	T	T	T	F	T	F	T

V.

3. Hypothetical syllogism **5.** Modus ponens **6.** Contraposition **8.** Modus tollens **12.** Disjunctive syllogism

VI.

3. ~ I ⊃ (M ⊃ ~ H) ∴ ~ (M ⊃ ~ H) ⊃ ~ ~ I Contraposition **5.** D ⊃ M; M ⊃ H ∴ D ⊃ H Hypothetical syllogism **6.** E ⊃ ~ A, E ∴ ~ A Modus ponens **8.** G v ~ H, H ∴ G Disjunctive syllogism **10.** ~ M, H ⊃ M ∴ ~ H Modus tollens

IX.

3. Hypothetical syllogism. Valid **5.** Disjunctive syllogism. Valid **7.** Denying the antecedent. Invalid **9.** Contraposition. Valid **11.** Disjunctive syllogism. Valid **13.** Modus ponens. Valid **15.** Modus tollens. Valid **17.** Affirming the consequent. Invalid **19.** Denying the antecedent. Invalid

X.

4. E ⊃ M, ~ E ∴ ~ M Denying the antecedent Invalid **6.** H v D, D ∴ ~ H Affirming a disjunct Invalid **7.** B ⊃ N, N ⊃ F ∴ B ⊃ F Hypothetical syllogism Valid **11.** M ⊃ ~ E, E ∴ ~ M Modus tollens Valid **12.** J ⊃ L, L ∴ J Affirming the consequent Invalid

XIII.

3. 1. $\sim D \cdot C$
   2. $F \supset \sim C$
   3. $\sim F \supset (E \vee D)$ $/ \therefore D \vee E$
   4. $\sim\sim C \supset \sim F$ 2 Contr
   5. $C \supset \sim F$ 4 DN
   6. $C \supset (E \vee D)$ 5, 3 HS
   7. $C \cdot \sim D$ 1 Com
   8. C 7 Simp
   9. $E \vee D$ 6, 8 MP
   10. $D \vee E$ 9 Com

5. 1. $(G \supset D) \supset \sim F$
   2. $D \supset F$
   3. $D \cdot C$ $/ \therefore \sim (G \supset D)$
   4. $\sim F \supset \sim D$ 2 Contr
   5. $(G \supset D) \supset \sim D$ 1, 4 HS
   6. D 3 Simp
   7. $\sim\sim D$ 6 DN
   8. $\sim (G \supset D)$ 5, 7 MT

7. 1. $(D \supset C) \vee \sim (A \vee B)$
   2. A $/ \therefore \sim D \vee C$
   3. $\sim (A \vee B) \vee (D \supset C)$ 1 Com
   4. $A \vee B$ 2 Add
   5. $\sim\sim (A \vee B)$ 4 DN
   6. $D \supset C$ 3, 5 DS
   7. $\sim D \vee C$ 6 Cond

9. 1. $(E \vee A) \supset C$
   2. $[(E \vee A) \supset C] \supset (E \cdot G)$ $/ \therefore C$
   3. $E \cdot G$ 1, 2 MP
   4. E 3 Simp
   5. $E \vee A$ 4 Add
   6. C 1, 5 MP

11. 1. $(\sim H \vee L) \supset \sim (I \cdot G)$
   2. $G \cdot I$ $/ \therefore \sim L \cdot H$
   3. $I \cdot G$ 2 Com
   4. $\sim\sim (I \cdot G)$ 3 DN
   5. $\sim (\sim H \vee L)$ 1, 4 MT
   6. $\sim\sim H \cdot \sim L$ 5 DeM
   7. $H \cdot \sim L$ 6 DN
   8. $\sim L \cdot H$ 7 Com

XIV.

4. 1. $D \supset B$
   2. $\sim M \vee \sim D$
   3. $\sim B \cdot D$ $/ \therefore \sim M$
   4. $D \cdot \sim B$ 3 Com
   5. D 4 Simp
   6. $\sim\sim D$ 5 DN
   7. $\sim M$ 2, 6 DS

6. 1. $H \cdot (\sim I \vee J)$
   2. $J \supset \sim H$ $/ \therefore \sim J$

   3. *H*   1 Simp
   4. ~ ~ *H*   3 DN
   5. ~*J*   2, 4 MT

8. 1. *I* • ~ *C*
   2. *I* ⊃ *B*   /∴ ~ *C* • *B*
   3. *I*   1 Simp
   4. *B*   2, 3 MP
   5. ~ *C* • *I*   1 Com
   6. ~*C*   5 Simp
   7. ~ *C* • *B*   6, 4 Conj

10. 1. *I*
   2. *H* ⊃ ~ *E*
   3. ~ *H* ⊃ (*N* ⊃ ~ *E*)   /∴ *I* • [*E* ⊃ (*N* ⊃ ~ *E*)]
   4. ~ ~ *E* ⊃ ~ *H*   2 Contr
   5. ~ ~ *E* ⊃ (*N* ⊃ ~ *E*)   4, 3 HS
   6. *E* ⊃ (*N* ⊃ ~ *E*)   5 DN
   7. *I* • [*E* ⊃ (*N* ⊃ ~ *E*)]   1, 6 Conj

XV.
1. Type A **2.** Type B **3.** Type C

Chapter 13

II.
3. Some <u>firefighters</u> are not <u>men</u>. Particular negative, *O*. **5.** Some <u>precious metals</u> were not <u>available in Africa</u>. Particular negative, *O*. **7.** Some <u>historians</u> are <u>persons who are interested in the future</u>. Particular affirmative, *I*. **9.** All <u>spies</u> are <u>persons who cannot avoid taking risks</u>. Universal affirmative, *A*.

IV.
2. *E*: No movie stars are persons who love being ignored by the media.
4. *E*: No member of Congress who's being investigated is a person who can leave the country. **6.** *O*: Some mathematical equations are not equations that amount to headaches. **8.** *I*: Some dogs are dogs that don't bark. **10.** *I*: Some speedy vehicles are vehicles that don't put their occupants at risk.

VII.
1. Incorrect. It should be: *S P* ≠ 0 **2.** Incorrect. It should be *S P* = 0 **3.** Correct
4. Correct

VIII.
3. Traditional logic: *A* proposition, All *S* are *P*. Venn diagram No.3, Boolean notation B **6.** Traditional logic: *E* proposition, No *S* are *P*. Venn diagram No.2, Boolean notation A **9.** Traditional logic: *E* proposition, No *S* are *P*. Venn diagram No.2, Boolean notation A **12.** Traditional logic: *E* proposition, No *S* are *P*. Venn diagram No.2, Boolean notation A **15.** Traditional logic: *O* proposition, Some *S* are not *P*. Venn diagram No.4, Boolean notation B **18.** Traditional logic: *E* proposition, No *S* are *P*. Venn diagram No.2, Boolean notation A **20.** Traditional logic: *I* proposition, Some *S* are *P*. Venn diagram No.1, Boolean notation *D*

X.
3. *I*. Subcontrary. Some humans are mortal. Undetermined. **5.** *E*. Contrary. No labor unions are organizations dominated by politicians. False.

7. *O* Subcontrary. Some lions are not harmless. Undetermined. **9.** *I* Subcontrary. Some bats are nocturnal creatures. Undetermined.

XII.

2. *I*. Some Democrats are opponents of legalized abortion. **4.** *O*. Some professional athletes are not highly paid sports heroes. **6.** *E*. No chipmunks are shy rodents. **8.** *E*. No cartographers are amateur musicians. **10.** *A*. All airlines are profitable corporations.

XIV.

3. *O* Subaltern. Some butterflies are not vertebrates. True. **5.** *E* Superaltern. No comets are frequent celestial events. Undetermined. **7.** *E* Superaltern. No porcupines are nocturnal animals. Undetermined. **9.** *O* Subaltern. Some extraterrestrials are not Republicans. True.

XVI.

4. *A* Superaltern. All bassoonists are anarchists. Undetermined
   E Contradictory. No bassoonists are anarchists. False
   O Subcontrary. Some bassoonists are not anarchists. Undetermined
6. *O* Subaltern. Some Americans are not people who care about global warming. True
   I Contradictory. Some Americans are people who care about global warming. False
   A Contrary. All Americans are people who care about global warming. False
8. *E* Contrary. No acts of cheating are acts that are wrong. False
   O Contradictory. Some acts of cheating are not acts that are wrong. False
   I Subaltern. Some acts of cheating are acts that are wrong. True
10. *A* Superaltern. All things are things that are observable with the naked eye. Undetermined
   E Contradictory. No things are things that are observable with the naked eye. False
   O Subcontrary. Some things are not things that are observable with the naked eye. Undetermined

XVIII.

3. C. Contrariety, invalid according to the modern square.
   E. Subcontrariety, invalid according to the modern square.
   G. Contradiction, valid according to the modern square.

XIX.

3. Some candidates are not incumbents.
   Some incumbents are not candidates. NOT VALID
5. All amateurs are nonprofessionals.
   Some nonprofessionals are amateurs. BY LIMITATION
7. No quarks are molecules.
   No molecules are quarks.
9. All owls are nocturnal creatures.
   Some nocturnal creatures are owls. BY LIMITATION

XX.

3. Some popular songs are hits.
   Some popular songs are not non-hits.

5. Some psychotherapists are not Democrats.
   Some psychotherapists are non-Democrats.

7. All hexagons are plane figures.

No hexagons are non-plane figures.

9. Some Labrador retrievers are affectionate pets.

Some Labrador retrievers are not nonaffectionate pets.

XXI.

2. Some used car salesmen are not fast talkers.

Some non-fast talkers are not non-used car salesmen.

4. Some citizens are non-voters.

Some voters are non-citizens. NOT VALID

6. No musicians are non-concert goers.

Some concert goers are not non-musicians. BY LIMITATION

8. Some police officers are cigar smokers.

Some non-cigar smokers are non-police officers. NOT VALID

10. Some pickup trucks are not non-expensive vehicles.

Some expensive vehicles are not non-pickup trucks.

XXII.

2. A. Conversion, not valid. The converse of an *O* premise is always invalid.
   B. Obversion, valid.
   D. Contraposition, not valid. The contrapositive of an *I* premise is always invalid.
   G. Contraposition, not valid. The argument could be made valid by limitation–i.e., by making its conclusion particular negative.

3. C. Subalternation, invalid.
   E. Conversion, not valid.
   G. Contrariety, valid by the traditional square only.
   I. Obversion, valid.

CHAPTER 14

II.

3. Not a syllogism: the argument has one premise.

5. No romantic songs are popular with first-graders. | 1. No *M* are *P*
   All Sinatra songs are romantic songs. | 2. All *S* are *M*
   No Sinatra songs are popular with first-graders. | 3. No *S* are *P*

6. No Oscar winners are talk show hosts. | 1. No *M* are *P*
   Some men are Oscar winners. | 2. Some *S* are *M*
   Some men are not talk show hosts. | 3. Some *S* are not *P*

9. Not a syllogism: the argument has one premise.

11. Some programmers are pool players. | 1. Some *M* are *P*
   All computer scientists are programmers. | 2. All S are M
   Some computer scientists are pool players. | 3. Some S are P

III.

4. *AIA*-1 **6.** *EAA*-4 **8.** *OOE*-1 **10.** *OII*-1 **12.** *EEA*-3

IV.

3. 1. All people who listen to reggae music are people who are not Lawrence Welk fans.
   2. Some residents of California are people who are not Lawrence Welk fans.
   3. Some residents of California are people who listen to reggae music.

   1. All P are M AII-2
   2. Some S are M
   3. Some S are P

5. 1. All loyal Americans are supporters of the President in his desire to trim the Federal budget.
   2. All loyal Americans are people who are willing taxpayers.
   3. All people who are willing taxpayers are supporters of the President in his desire to trim the Federal budget.

   1. All M are P AAA-3
   2. All M are S
   3. All S are P

7. 1. All animals that are convenient house pets are creatures your Aunt Sophie would like.
   2. No creatures your Aunt Sophie would like are reptiles weighing over eighty pounds.
   3. No reptiles weighing over eighty pounds are animals that are convenient house pets.

   1. All P are M AEE-4
   2. No M are S
   3. No S are P

9. 1. Some devices that contain dynamite are not safe things to carry in the trunk of your car.
   2. Some explosives are devices that contain dynamite.
   3. No explosives are safe things to carry in the trunk of your car.

   1. Some M are not P OIE-1
   2. Some S are M
   3. No S are P

11. 1. Some pacifists are not conscientious objectors.
    2. No pacifists are persons who favor the use of military force.
    3. Some persons who favor the use of military force are not conscientious objectors.

   1. Some M are not P OEO-3
   2. No M are S
   3. Some S are not P

VII.

4. 1. Some persons who never run red lights are people who are not elitists.
   2. All taxi drivers are people who are not elitists.
   3. Some taxi drivers are persons who never run red lights.

   1. Some P are M IAI-2
   2. All S are M
   3. Some S are P INVALID

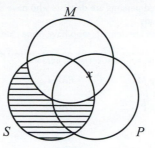

7. 1. All intelligent creatures are things that will stay out of the middle of the highway.
2. No armadillos are things that will stay out of the middle of the highway.
3. No armadillos are intelligent creatures.

1. All P are M	AEE-2
2. No S are M	
3. No S are P	VALID

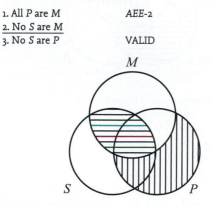

10. 1. Some axolotls are creatures that are not often seen in the city.
2. All axolotls are mud lizards that are found in the jungles of southern Mexico.
3. Some mud lizards that are found in the jungles of southern Mexico are creatures that are not often seen in the city.

1. Some M are P	IAI-3
2. All M are S	
3. Some S are P	VALID

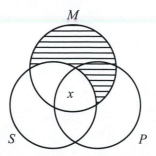

13. 1. No impoverished persons are dentists who have done extensive postdoctoral study.
   2. All orthodontists are dentists who have done extensive postdoctoral study.
   3. No orthodontists are impoverished persons.

   1. No P are M EAE-2
   2. All S are M
   3. No S are P VALID

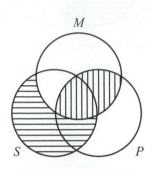

16. 1. All philosophy majors are rational beings.
   2. No parakeets are rational beings.
   3. No parakeets are philosophy majors.

   1. All P are M AEE-2
   2. No S are M
   3. No S are P VALID

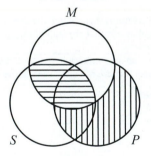

19. 1. No hallucinations are optical illusions.
   2. Some misunderstandings that are not avoidable are hallucinations.
   3. Some misunderstandings that are not avoidable are optical illusions.

   1. No M are P EII-1
   2. Some S are M
   3. Some S are P INVALID

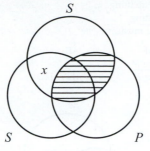

22. 1. No benevolent despots are defenders of faculty autonomy.
2. No defenders of faculty autonomy are college presidents.
3. Some college presidents are not benevolent despots.

1. No *P* are *M*	EEO-4
2. No *M* are *S*	
3. Some *S* are not *P*	INVALID

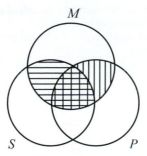

25. 1. All philanderers are habitual prevaricators.
2. No habitual prevaricators are preachers who are well-known television personalities.
3. No preachers who are well-known television personalities are philanderers.

1. All *P* are *M*	AEE-4
2. No *M* are *S*	
3. No *S* are *P*	VALID

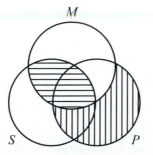

28. 1. All great music is uplifting.
   2. Some jazz is uplifting.
   3. Some jazz is great music.

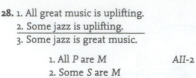

1. All *P* are *M*	AII-2
2. Some *S* are *M*	
3. Some *S* are *P*	INVALID

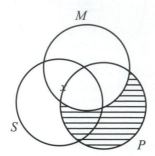

30. 1. Some investments that are insured by the federal government are not an effective means of increasing one's wealth.
   2. All investments that are insured by the federal government are interest-bearing bank accounts.
   3. Some interest-bearing bank accounts are not an effective means of increasing one's wealth.

1. Some *M* are not *P*	OAO-3
2. All *M* are *S*	
3. Some *S* are not *P*	VALID

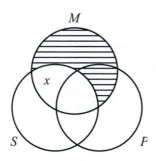

X.

3. I. Subject undistributed; predicate undistributed. **6.** A. Subject distributed; predicate undistributed. **9.** I. Subject undistributed; predicate undistributed. **11.** O. Subject undistributed; predicate distributed. **14.** A. Subject distributed; predicate undistributed.

XI.

3. 1. No people who are truly objective are people who are likely to be mistaken.
   2. All people who ignore the facts are people who are likely to be mistaken.
   3. No people who ignore the facts are people who are truly objective.

1. No P are M EAE-2   VALID
2. All S are M
3. No S are P

5.
1. No people who expect to win are people who can afford to lose.
2. Some people who bet on horseraces are people who expect to win.
3. Some people who bet on horseraces are people who can afford to lose.

     1. No M are P
     2. Some S are M
     3. Some S are P

     EII-1   INVALID   Affirmative from a negative

7.
1. Some metals are copper alloys.	1. Some P are M
2. All copper alloys are good conductors of electricity.	2. All M are S
3. Some good conductors of electricity are not metals.	3. Some S are not P

     IAO-4   INVALID   Illicit process of the major term and negative from two affirmatives

9.
1. Some rabble rousers are egalitarians.	1. Some P are M
2. No egalitarians are sympathetic dissidents.	2. No M are S
3. No sympathetic dissidents are rabble rousers.	3. No S are P

     IEE-4   INVALID   Illicit Process of the Major Term

11.
1. Some coaches are not talent scouts.	1. Some M are not P
2. Some athletes are not coaches.	2. Some S are not M
3. No athletes are talent scouts.	3. No S are P

     OOE-1   INVALID   Illicit process of the minor term and exclusive premises

13.
1. Some college men are pigs (i.e., dirty).	1. Some M are P
2. All college men are living things.	2. All M are S
3. Some living things are pigs (i.e., animals).	3. Some S are P'

     IAI-3   INVALID   Fallacy of four terms

15.
1. No admirers of Heidegger are utilitarians.	1. No M are P
2. All postmodernists are admirers of Heidegger.	2. All S are M
3. No postmodernists are utilitarians.	3. No S are P

     EAE-1   VALID

17.
1. All single-celled organisms are invertebrates.	1. All M are P
2. All paramecia are single-celled organisms.	2. All S are M
3. All paramecia are invertebrates.	3. All S are P

     AAA-1   VALID

19.
1. All good neighbors are respectful people.	1. All M are P
2. All good neighbors are well-intended zealots.	2. All M are S
3. No well-intended zealots are respectful people.	3. No S are P

     AAE-3   INVALID   Illicit process of the major term, illicit process of the minor term, and negative from two affirmatives

21.

1. Some traitors are not benefactors.	1. Some *P* are not *M*
2. No embezzlers are benefactors.	2. No *S* are *M*
3. All embezzlers are traitors.	3. All *S* are *P*

OEA-2   INVALID   Exclusive premises and affirmative from a negative

23.

1. No angora goats are hamsters.	1. No *M* are *P*
2. No angora goats are great white sharks.	2. No *M* are *S*
3. No great white sharks are hamsters.	3. No *S* are *P*

EEE-3   INVALID   Exclusive premises

25.

1. All television news anchors are photogenic.	1. All *P* are *M*
2. Some average people are not photogenic.	2. Some *S* are not *M*
3. Some average people are not television news anchors.	3. Some *S* are not *P*

AOC-2   VALID

XIII.

3. Being a pencil **6.** Singular term **8.** Being a classroom
10. Singular term **12.** Being a fountain of youth

XIV.

3. Universal generalization **5.** Universal generalization **7.** Existential generalization **9.** Singular proposition

XVI.

3. 1. All neighboring countries are friends of ours.
2. Anything identical to Mexico is a neighboring country.
3. Anything identical to Mexico is a friend of ours.
Rejected: 2 and 3.
Reason: replacing "Mexico" with "Anything identical to ..." is at odds with common intuitions.

5. 1. No hippo is an animal that does well in cold weather.
2. Any animal identical to that animal recently brought to San Antonio's zoo is a hippo.
3. No animal identical to that animal recently brought to San Antonio's zoo does well in cold weather.
Rejected: 2 and 3.
Reason: replacing "that hippo ..." with "Any/no animal identical to ..." is at odds with common intuitions.

7. 1. All Americans are beings that have consumer expectations.
2. Anyone identical to him is an American.
3. Anyone identical to him is a being that has consumer expectations.
Rejected: 2 and 3.
Reason: replacing "he" with "Anyone identical to him" is at odds with common intuitions.

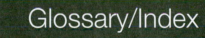

Index of Names

Glossary/Index

COMMONSENSE CLAIM A claim that expresses a belief of COMMON SENSE.

COMMUTATION *See* RULE OF REPLACEMENT.

COMPATIBLE BELIEFS Beliefs that could all be true at once. *See* also CONSISTENCY.

COMPLEX QUESTION An INFORMAL FALLACY consisting of a question that is unfair to some individuals or things because it is phrased in such a way that it presupposes something not yet proved about them. 201, 242–243, 527.

COMPOSITION The INFORMAL FALLACY committed in arguing that because the parts of some complex whole, or the members of a class, have a certain attribute, it follows that the whole or class itself has that attribute. 276–277, 528.

COMPOUND PROPOSITION A PROPOSITION that is affected by a TRUTH-FUNCTIONAL CONNECTIVE. 331 ff., 343–347, 356–359.

CONCEPT The smallest meaningful unit within a PROPOSITION that contributes to the proposition's truth value although it does not itself have a truth value. 41–42, 275.

CONCEPTUAL BELIEF A belief whose truth value is plain to anyone who understands its content. 68–70.

CONCEPTUAL CIRCULARITY A condition in which, because of a conceptual connection between an argument's conclusion and

its premises, the former may be said to be contained in the latter. 230–231. *See* also CIRCULARITY and BEGGING THE QUESTION.

CONCLUSION In an ARGUMENT, the claim for which other BELIEFS or STATEMENTS are offered in support. 13–18.

CONCLUSION INDICATOR A word or phrase appearing in an ARGUMENT that typically indicates the occurrence of the CONCLUSION directly after it. 14–18.

CONCLUSIVE REASONS Premises from which some conclusion follows with certainty. 1, 115. *See* also DEDUCTION.

CONDITIONAL A belief or statement of the form "if ... then... ." 338–340. *See* also ANTECEDENT, CONSEQUENT, and MATERIAL CONDITIONAL.

CONFUSED PREDICATION 201, 261, 275 ff., 528. *See* COMPOSITION and DIVISION.

CONJUNCT A PROPOSITION related to another by the relation of CONJUNCTION. 334.

CONJUNCTION (1) TRUTH-FUNCTIONAL CONNECTIVE expressed by "and," "but," "however," "moreover," "also," "though," "although," "furthermore,""as well as," etc. (2) COMPOUND PROPOSITION that is true only if both of its CONJUNCTS are true. 334–336, 343, 353–354, 404. *See* also RULE OF INFERENCE.

CONSEQUENT The *then*-clause of a CONDITIONAL. 338–340.

CONSERVATISM A virtue that BELIEFS have insofar as they are consistent with beliefs one already holds. 74–75.

CONSISTENCY A virtue that two or more beliefs have insofar as they are compatible, i.e., they can all be true at once. 70–74.

CONTENT NATURALISM The view that value predicates such as "good" are synonymous with purely descriptive predicates such as "well being maximizing," "produces pleasure," and "what we desire to desire." 252–256.

CONTINGENCY Compound proposition that may be either true or false, depending on the truth values of its component simple propositions. 359. *See* also TAUTOLOGY and CONTRADICTION.

CONTRADICTION (1) A relation between two propositions such that they must have opposite truth values: they cannot be both true or both false. 72–74, 440 ff. (2) A COMPOUND PROPOSITION that is necessarily false, simply by virtue of its form. 359–360.

CONTRADICTORIES Propositions that stand in the relation of CONTRADICTION. 125, 163 ff., 440 ff.

CONTRAPOSITION (1) In PROPOSITIONAL LOGIC, a valid argument form consisting of a single premise that is a CONDITIONAL and a conclusion where the premise's antecedent and consequent have been negated

and their places reversed in a new conditional. 132 ff., 386. *See* also RULE OF REPLACEMENT. (2) In SYLLOGISTIC LOGIC, an IMMEDIATE INFERENCE from a categorical proposition, wherein its subject and predicate are switched, each adding the prefix "non," while quantity and quality remain the same. 458–461.

CONTRAPOSITIVE In SYLLOGISTIC LOGIC, the proposition inferred by CONTRAPOSITION. 458–461.

CONTRARIES CATEGORICAL PROPOSITIONS that cannot both be true at once, although they can both be false. 440 ff. *See* also SQUARE OF OPPOSITION.

CONTRARIETY The relation obtaining between CONTRARIES. 440 ff.

CONTRIBUTORY CAUSE A phenomenon that is part of the reason for some condition's coming into being, though by itself neither necessary nor sufficient to bring it about. 207, 211.

CONVERSE In SYLLOGISTIC LOGIC, the proposition inferred by CONVERSION. 454 ff.

CONVERSION An IMMEDIATE INFERENCE from a CATEGORICAL PROPOSITION, wherein its subject and predicate are switched while quantity and quality remain the same. 454–456, 461.

CONVERTEND In syllogistic logic, the proposition from

which the CONVERSE is inferred. 454 ff.

COPULA In a CATEGORICAL PROPOSITION, the verb of being that connects the SUBJECT and PREDICATE terms. 425.

COUNTEREXAMPLE An example that refutes a claim or an argument—the former by showing it false, the latter by proving it invalid. 136, 159, 170–171, 393–394, 465–467.

CRITICAL THINKING See INFORMAL LOGIC.

CUTOFF Point of sharp distinction between cases to which a term determinately applies and those to which it determinately does not apply. 267. See also VAGUENESS.

DECLARATIVE SENTENCE A sentence type used to assert or deny a PROPOSITION. 42 ff.

DEFINITION A procedure to spell out the MEANING or REFERENCE of an expression. It has two parts, DEFINIEDUM and DEFINIENS. 285 ff. See also SEMANTIC DEFINITION.

DEFINIENDUM In a definition, the expression to be defined. 285 ff.

DEFINIENS In a definition, the expression that defines the DEFINIEDUM. 285 ff.

DEDUCTIVE ARGUMENT An argument whose premises are presented as guaranteeing—i.e., necessitating—the truth of the conclusion. 102–104. See also VALID ARGUMENT FORM.

DEDUCTIVE COGENCY A feature of any VALID ARGUMENT with acceptable premises whereby critical thinkers are compelled to accept its conclusion. 150–152, 227 ff.

DEDUCTIVISM The doctrine that science proceeds by DEDUCTION rather than by INDUCTION. 190–192.

DE MORGAN'S THEOREM See RULE OF REPLACEMENT.

DENYING THE ANTECEDENT The FORMAL FALLACY of attempting to deduce the negation of the consequent of a conditional by applying negation to its antecedent, invariably an invalid inference. 395–396, 398.

DIMENSIONS OF LANGUAGE Some fundamental aspects of a language that include its SYNTAX, SEMANTICS, and PRAGMATICS. 51 ff.

DIMENSIONS OF LOGICAL THINKING The descriptive, evaluative and normative aspects of reasoning. 2–3.

DIRECTIVE USE OF LANGUAGE The use of language to try to get an addressee to do something—as, e.g., in issuing a command or making a request by means of an IMPERATIVE SENTENCE or in asking a question by means of an INTERROGATIVE SENTENCE. 42–44.

DISBELIEF The psychological attitude of rejecting a PROPOSITION. 61 ff.

EVALUATIVE SENTENCE A sentence to the effect that something is good or bad, right or wrong, beautiful or ugly, just or unjust, etc. 83–85, 105–107.

EVALUATIVE PRINCIPLE An EVALUATIVE SENTENCE that expresses a general rule. 85, 105–107.

EVIDENCE Any reason based on observation, whether this be the thinker's own sense experience or someone else's (as in testimony). 29, 31–33, 166.

EVIDENTIAL SUPPORT See EVIDENCE.

EXCLAMATORY SENTENCE A sentence that serves to express the speaker's feelings usually punctuated with an exclamation point. 42 ff.

EXCLUDED MIDDLE The law that each PROPOSITION must be either true or false. 353.

EXCLUSIVE DISJUNCTION A COMPOUND PROPOSITION of the form, "either P or Q, but not both P and Q." 244–246. See also DISJUNCTION.

EXCLUSIVE PREMISES The FALLACY committed by a CATEGORICAL SYLLOGISM with two negative premises. 509.

EXISTENTIAL FALLACY In a CATEGORICAL SYLLOGISM, the mistake of inferring a particular conclusion from premises, both of which are universal. 510–511.

EXISTENTIAL GENERALIZATION See NON-UNIVERSAL GENERALIZATION.

EXISTENTIAL IMPORT In a particular affirmative or particular negative categorical proposition, the presupposition that the entity named by its subject term exists. 444–447, 510.

EXPRESSIVE USE OF LANGUAGE When language is used to express the speaker's or writer's feelings. 42–44.

EXTENDED ARGUMENT A complex ARGUMENT that consists of at least two arguments, often with the conclusion of one serving as a premise of the other. 98–99.

FACT-VALUE GAP See IS-OUGHT PROBLEM. 116–120.

FAITHFULNESS, PRINCIPLE OF Principle prescribing that arguments be reconstructed in a way consistent with the arguers' intentions. 94 ff, 139. See also CHARITY.

FALLACY A type of specious ARGUMENT whose premises fail to support its conclusion by virtue of flouting either (1) deductive standards or (2) inductive standards. 200–202. It can be FORMAL or INFORMAL.

FALLACY OF PRESUMPTION An ARGUMENT that takes for granted some background belief that is in fact debatable, so that its conclusion is not supported by its premises. One of the general categories of informal fallacy. 201, 227 ff., 527.

FALLACY OF RELEVANCE An ARGUMENT in which the premises are irrelevant to the

consequent of one is the ANTECEDENT of the other, and another conditional in the conclusion whose antecedent is the antecedent of one of those premises and whose CONSEQUENT is the consequent of the other. 132 ff., 387, 404. *See* also RULE OF INFERENCE.

IGNORATIO ELENCHI *See* BESIDE THE POINT.

ILLICIT CONTRAPOSITION In SYLLOGISTIC LOGIC, the FALLACY of inferring the CONTRAPOSITIVE of an *I* proposition, or of inferring the contrapositive of an *E* proposition without limitation. 460.

ILLICIT CONVERSION In SYLLOGISTIC LOGIC, the FALLACY of inferring the CONVERSE of an *O* proposition, or of inferring the converse of an *A* proposition without limitation. 456.

ILLICIT PROCESS OF THE MAJOR TERM In a CATEGORICAL SYLLOGISM, failure to distribute in the MAJOR PREMISE a major term distributed in the conclusion. *See* also DISTRIBUTION OF TERMS. 507–508.

ILLICIT PROCESS OF THE MINOR TERM In a CATEGORICAL SYLLOGISM, failure to distribute in the MINOR PREMISE a minor term distributed in the conclusion. *See* also DISTRIBUTION OF TERMS. 507–508.

IMMEDIATE INFERENCE A single-premise DEDUCTIVE ARGUMENT. 439 ff. *See* also SQUARE OF OPPOSITION.

IMPERATIVE SENTENCE A type of sentence commonly used to issue orders or commands. 42 ff.

INCLUSIVE DISJUNCTION A DISJUNCTION that is true just in case one, the other, or both DISJUNCTS are true. 244., 388.

INCONSISTENCY A vice that two or more beliefs have insofar as they are incompatible, i.e., they could not all be true at once. *See* also CONSISTENCY. 70–74.

INDETERMINACY *See* VAGUENESS.

INDIRECT LANGUAGE A use of language whereby a sentence is uttered with a function different from that standardly associated with sentences of the same type. 44–47, 56.

INDUCTION *See* INDUCTIVE ARGUMENT.

INDUCTIVE ARGUMENT An ARGUMENT which, if successful, provides some reason for its conclusion but falls short of guaranteeing it. 102–104, 125, 163 ff.

INDUCTIVE GENERALIZATION The conclusion of an argument by ENUMERATIVE INDUCTION. 167, 202 ff.

INDUCTIVE RELIABILITY A virtue of any inductive argumen whose form is such that, if its premises were true, it would be reasonable to accept its conclusion. 181–182, 184, 202 ff. *See* also INDUCTIVE STRENGTH.

PARADOX A problem without apparent solution, involving claims that seem equally true (or well supported) yet appear inconsistent. 267–269.

PARADOXICAL CONFRONTATION In a debate or unresolved controversy, a situation involving a standoff between two equally supported but rival claims. No progress can be made until new reasons are offered to resolve the conflict. 233 ff.

PARTICULAR PROPOSITION CATEGORICAL PROPOSITION whose STANDARD FORM is either "Some S are P" or "Some S are not P." 424 ff. See also QUANTITY.

PETITIO PRINCIPII See BEGGING THE QUESTION.

PHILOSOPHICAL ANALYSIS The method of defining a concept or proposition in terms of other concepts or propositions that are better understood. 290–292.

POST HOC ERGO PROPTER HOC A variation of the informal fallacy of FALSE CAUSE which holds that some earlier event is the cause of some later event, when the two are in fact not causally related. 201, 208–209, 526.

POSSIBLE WORLD A scenario that involves no CONTRADICTION. 71–73, 126, 288–289.

PRAGMATICS One of the DIMENSIONS OF LANGUAGE concerning aspects of an expression that arise from its use. 51, 57.

PREDICATE An expression that assigns a property to some subject in a proposition. 275.

PREDICATE TERM In a CATEGORICAL PROPOSITION, the word or phrase coming after the COPULA. 421 ff., ff. 473 ff.

PREMISE Reason offered for a certain conclusion. 13–18. See also EVIDENCE.

PREMISE INDICATOR An expression that marks the occurrence of a PREMISE. 14–18.

PRESUMPTION A strong assumption or background belief often taken for granted. 227.

PROBLEM OF INDUCTION The problem that the method of inductive reasoning cannot be itself adequately justified either *a priori* (i.e., just by philosophical thinking) or, without CIRCULARITY, by empirical means, since that would itself require INDUCTION. 190–192

PROOF A procedure for deducing a VALID ARGUMENT's conclusion by means of basic rules of inference and/or replacement that are themselves accepted without a proof within a formal system. 403 ff.

PROPER NAME A word or phrase uniquely designating one person, thing or group of things. 518.

PROPERTY An attribute, feature, or quality of a thing or individual. 575–520.

PROPOSITION The content of a BELIEF or STATEMENT that represents a state of affairs and

SELF-CONTRADICTION *See* CONTRADICTION.

SEMANTIC DEFINITION A family of procedures used to give the meaning or reference of an expression. A reportive definition gives the meaning of a word. An ostensive definition offers examples of things paradigmatically falling under its DEFINIEDUM. A contextual definition presents in its DEFINIENS another expression or context in which neither the DEFINIENDUM nor a strict synonym of it occurs. 285 ff.

SEMANTICS One of the DIMENSIONS OF LANGUAGE that concerns the MEANING and REFERENCE of linguistic expressions. 52, 57, 261 ff.

SEMANTIC UNCLARITY A problem in the use of a linguistic expression that often undermines argument. 261 ff. *See* also VAGUENESS, AMBIGUITY, and CONFUSED PREDICATION.

SIMPLE PROPOSITION A PROPOSITION that contains no TRUTH-FUNCTIONAL CONNECTIVE. 330.

SIMPLIFICATION *See* RULE OF INFERENCE.

SINGULAR PROPOSITION A PROPOSITION that directly invokes a specific thing (object or individual), presenting it as having a certain property or being related to other thing/s. 169, 518–518.

SINGULAR TERM Word or phrase, such as a PROPER NAME, demonstrative, or indexical, that points out or uniquely designates a single person, thing, or group of things. 518–520.

SKEPTIC One who doubts the possibility of knowledge. 221–222.

SLIPPERY SLOPE An ARGUMENT that assumes that what holds for some case *A* holds also for the apparently very different case *Z*, on the basis of there being a continuous series of cases *B*, *C*, ... *Y* between *A* and *Z* where the members of each successive pair in the series differ only minimally from each other. 201, 269–271, 527.

SORITES An ARGUMENT that trades on the vagueness of some term, so that although it appears a valid inference, from premises that are seemingly true it draws a conclusion that is plainly false. 267–268. *See* also VAGUENESS and PARADOX.

SOUNDNESS The good-making feature of a VALID ARGUMENT with true premises. In any such argument, the conclusion is true. 149–152, 186.

SQUARE OF OPPOSITION (1) TRADITIONAL: A diagram representing relations of CONTRADICTION, CONTRARIETY, SUBCONTRARIETY, and SUBALTERNATION among the four types of categorical proposition. 439 ff. (2) MODERN: the Boolean

among the TERMS within the PREMISES and CONCLUSION. 123, 136 ff.

SYLLOGISTIC LOGIC The study of arguments whose validity or invalidity hinges on relations among the TERMS of categorical propositions. 156.

SYNTAX One of the DIMENSIONS OF LANGUAGE that concerns the relation among expressions of a language, and which is captured by rules of grammar prescribing how to form and transform the expressions of that language. 51.

SYNTHETIC STATEMENT See ANALYTIC.

TAUTOLOGY A COMPOUND PROPOSITION that is necessarily true simply in virtue of its form. 360, 365–368.

TERMS (1) Of a categorical proposition, its SUBJECT and PREDICATE. 421 ff. (2) Of a categorical syllogism, its MAJOR TERM, MINOR TERM, and MIDDLE TERM. 473 ff.

TESTIMONY Vicarious observation commonly adduced in support of OBSERVATIONAL BELIEFS, as provided by, e.g., first-hand reports, written documents, books, the internet, road signs, and maps. 79.

TRADITIONAL LOGIC See SYLLOGISTIC LOGIC.

TRUTH A virtue of a STATEMENT or BELIEF—and thus of the PROPOSITION that is its content—often taken to consist in correspondence to the facts. See also TRUTH CONDITIONS. 32, 40–41, 65 ff., 76.

TRUTH CONDITIONS For any statement or belief that expresses a proposition, the conditions under which it would be true. 50.

TRUTH-FUNCTIONAL CONNECTIVE Expression used in such a way that the TRUTH VALUE of the COMPOUND PROPOSITION created by it is a function of the truth values of its parts. 328, 343, 351 ff. 351 ff.

TRUTH-PRESERVING ARGUMENT See VALID ARGUMENT FORM.

TRUTH TABLE A chart listing all possible truth values a proposition could have, used for (1) defining the TRUTH-FUNCTIONAL CONNECTIVES, (2) determining the truth value of COMPOUND PROPOSITIONS, 351 ff. or (3) testing propositional argument forms for validity., 374ff., 407–408.

TRUTH VALUE The status of being either true or false. It applies primarily to PROPOSITIONS, and derivatively to BELIEFS and STATEMENTS. 41.

TU QUOQUE A form of fallacious AD HOMINEM that attempts to reject a view by pointing to the holder's personal hypocrisy with regard to it. 308–309.

TYPE *vs.* TOKEN *Tokens* are instances or occurrences of a certain *type*. 52–53, 57.